Foreword

United States President Barack Obama has launched one of the world's most ambitious education reform agendas. Entitled "Race to the Top", the agenda encourages US states to adopt internationally benchmarked standards and assessments as a framework within which they can prepare students for success in college and the workplace; recruit, develop, reward, and retain effective teachers and principals; build data systems that measure student success and inform teachers and principals how they can improve their practices; and turn around their lowest-performing schools.

But what does the "top" look like internationally? How have the countries at the top managed to achieve sustained high performance or to significantly improve their performance? The OECD Programme for International Student Assessment (PISA) provides the world's most extensive and rigorous set of international surveys of the knowledge and skills of secondary school students. It allows one to compare countries on measures such as their average learning outcomes, their share of low-performing schools, the extent to which socio-economic background shapes learning outcomes and how consistently their schools deliver high quality outcomes.

When OECD Secretary-General Angel Gurría and United States Secretary of Education Arne Duncan met in April 2010, both felt that much was to be gained from a more detailed analysis of the policies and practices of those education systems that are close to the "top" or advancing rapidly. This volume takes up the challenge, and is a first step towards a deeper understanding of education systems and policy trajectories through international comparisons.

This volume is the result of a collaborative effort between the OECD, the National Center on Education and the Economy (NCEE) in Washington, government officials of the case study countries discussed, as well as international experts with extensive expertise in analysing the performance of education systems internationally. The report was prepared under the responsibility of the Indicators and Analysis Division of the OECD Directorate for Education, principally Andreas Schleicher and Richard Hopper, as part of OECD's new programme Leveraging Knowledge for Better Education Policies. The underlying studies were carried out by the NCEE in consultation with the OECD, principally by Marc Tucker, Susan Sclafani, Betsy Brown Ruzzi and Jackie Kraemer. The principal authors of the chapters in this volume are: Introduction: Marc Tucker and Andreas Schleicher, NCEE and OECD; Current performance of the United States: Andreas Schleicher; Japan: Marc Tucker and Betsy Brown Ruzzi, NCEE; China: Kai-ming Cheng, University of Hong Kong, Hong Kong, China; Canada: Robert Schwartz and Jal Mehta, Harvard University, United States; Finland: Robert Schwartz and Jal Mehta, Harvard University, United States; Germany: Marc Tucker and Betsy Brown Ruzzi, NCEE; Singapore: Vivien Stewart, Asia Society, United States; Brazil: Susan Sclafani, NCEE; Poland: Susan Sclafani, NCEE; Sweden: Betsy Brown Ruzzi, NCEE; United Kingdom: Michael Day, Training and Development Agency for Schools, United Kingdom; Lessons for the United States: Marc Tucker and Andreas Schleicher, NCEE and OECD. Richard Hopper and Susan Sclafani established and maintained the contacts with the country experts and interview partners and co-ordinated the work. Vanessa Shadoian-Gersing, Niccolina Clements, and Pedro Lenin García de León of the OECD compiled relevant quantitative data and background information on each education system. The OECD PISA team provided information and diagrams to support PISA analysis contained in this volume. Elisabeth Villoutreix of the OECD co-ordinated the steps for publication. The officials and experts whom we interviewed for this study are listed at the end of each chapter. A group of experts oversaw the development of the conceptual framework, reviewed draft chapters, discussed preliminary findings and provided guidance to the authors. These experts were Kai-ming Cheng: University of Hong Kong, Hong Kong; Michael Day: Department for Education, England; David Hopkins: University of London, England; Richard Hopper: OECD; Jackie Kraemer: NCEE; Barry McGaw: Melbourne Graduate School of Education, Australia; Elizabeth Pang: Ministry of Education, Singapore; Betsy Brown Ruzzi: NCEE; Pasi Sahlberg: CIMO Finland; Andreas Schleicher: OECD; Robert Schwartz: Harvard University, United States; Susan Sclafani: NCEE; Vivien Stewart: Asia Society, United States; Suzie Sullivan: NCEE; Marc Tucker: NCEE; Siew Hoong Wong: Ministry of Education, Singapore. The country chapter for Germany was reviewed by Eckhard Klieme from the German Institute of International Educational Research. The other country chapters were reviewed and validated by the respective national authorities.

Table of Contents

This book has...

StatLinkS ▊▊▊SL

**A service that delivers Excel® files
from the printed page!**

Look for the *StatLinks* at the bottom left-hand corner of the tables or graphs in this book.
To download the matching Excel® spreadsheet, just type the link into your Internet browser,
starting with the **http://dx.doi.org** prefix.
If you're reading the PDF e-book edition, and your PC is connected to the Internet, simply
click on the link. You'll find *StatLinks* appearing in more OECD books.

BOXES

FIGURES

TABLES

1

Introduction

A CHANGING YARDSTICK FOR EDUCATIONAL SUCCESS

Globalisation and modernisation are rapidly posing new and demanding challenges to individuals and societies alike. Increasingly diverse and interconnected populations, rapid technological change in the workplace and in everyday life, and the instantaneous availability of vast amounts of information are just a few of the factors contributing to these new demands. In this globalised world, people compete for jobs not just locally but internationally. The integrated worldwide labour market means that highly-paid workers in wealthier countries are competing directly with people with much the same skills but who demand less compensation in lower-wage countries. The same is true for people with low skills. The competition among countries now revolves around human capital and the comparative advantage in knowledge.

The effect of these developments is to raise wages in less developed countries and depress wages in the most industrialised countries. But these developments do not affect all workers equally. Job automation is proceeding even faster than the integration of the job market. If the work is routine, it is increasingly likely to be automated, although some jobs will always be done by human beings. The effect of automation, and more generally of the progress of technological change, is to reduce the demand for people who are only capable of doing routine work, and to increase the demand for people who are capable of doing knowledge work. This means that a greater proportion of people will need to be educated as professionals to do such knowledge-based work. High-wage countries will find that they can only maintain their relative wage levels if they can develop a high proportion of such knowledge workers and keep them in their work force. Increasingly, such work will require very high skill levels and will demand increasing levels of creativity and innovation.

This is not a description of one possible future, but of the economic dynamics that are currently in play. In the high-wage countries of the OECD, demand for highly-skilled people is increasing faster than supply (which the OECD indicators mirror in rising wage premiums for highly-skilled individuals) and demand for low-skilled workers is decreasing faster than supply (which the OECD indicators mirror in growing unemployment or declining wages for low-skilled individuals). Jobs are moving rapidly to countries that can provide the skills needed for any particular operation at the best rates. And the rate of automation of jobs is steadily increasing in both high-wage and low-wage countries.

These dynamics are increasing the pressure on governments to educate their citizens to earn a decent living in this environment and to offer their children an education that will ensure their life is at least as rewarding as their own. Governments need to create education systems that are accessible to everyone, not just a favoured few; that are globally competitive on quality; that provide people from all classes a fair chance to get the right kind of education to succeed; and to achieve all this at a price that the nation can afford. The aim is no longer just to provide a basic education for all, but to provide an education that will make it possible for everyone to become "knowledge workers". Such education will need to build the very high skill levels required to solve complex problems never seen before, to be creative, to synthesise material from a wide variety of sources and to see the patterns in the information that computers cannot see, to work with others in productive ways, to lead when necessary and to be a good team member when necessary. This is what is required in today's "flat" world where all work that cannot be digitised, automated and outsourced can be done by the most effective and competitive individuals, enterprises or countries, regardless of where they may be. The implication is that the yardstick for educational success is no longer simply improvement by national standards, but the best performing education systems internationally (Box 1.1).

OVERVIEW

This volume draws lessons from the education systems of a selection of top-scoring and rapidly improving countries as measured by the OECD Programme for International Student Assessment (PISA – described below). While this volume relates these lessons to the education reform agenda in the United States, they may have resonance for a wide range of countries and different types of education systems aspiring for excellence in educating their young people. This volume defines countries as high-performing if: almost all of their students are in high school at the appropriate age, average performance is high and the top quarter of performers place among the countries whose top quarter are among the best performers in the world (with respect to their mastery of the kinds of complex knowledge and skills needed in advanced economies as well their ability to apply that knowledge and those skills to problems with which they are not familiar); student performance is only weakly related to their socio-economic background; and spending per pupil is not at the top of the league tables. Put another way, this volume defines superior performance as high participation, high quality, high equity and high efficiency.

Box 1.1 **The pace of change in educational improvement**

Few countries have been able to capitalise more on the opportunities the 'flat' world provides than the United States, a country which can draw on one of the most highly educated labour forces of the industrialised nations (when measured in terms of formal qualifications).[1] However, this advantage is largely a result of the "first-mover advantage" which the United States gained after World War II by massively increasing enrolments. This advantage is eroding quickly as more and more countries have reached and surpassed the US's qualification levels among its younger age cohorts. The OECD baseline qualification for reasonable earnings and employment prospects is a high school diploma. Among OECD countries, the average proportion of young adults with at least a high school diploma has now risen to 80%; in Germany and Japan, two of the benchmark countries chosen for this volume, this figure exceeds 95%. Over time, this will translate into better workforce qualifications in OECD countries. In contrast, changes in the graduation rates have been modest in the United States and, as a result, only 8 of the 34 OECD countries now have a lower high school graduation rate than the United States. Two generations ago, South Korea had the economic output equivalent to that of Afghanistan today and was 23rd in terms of educational output among current OECD countries. Today South Korea is one of the top performers in terms of the proportion of successful school leavers, with 94% obtaining a high school diploma. Similarly, Chile moved up by 9 rank order positions, Ireland by 8 and Belgium and Finland by 4 rank order positions.

Similar trends are visible in college education. Here the United States slipped from rank 2 to rank 13 between 1995 and 2008, not because its college graduation rates declined, but because they rose so much faster in many other OECD countries. These developments will be amplified over the coming decades as countries such as China and India raise their educational output at an ever-increasing pace.

Changes are not just observed in the quantitative output of education systems, but many countries have also shown impressive improvements in the quality of learning outcomes. Korea's average performance was already high in 2000, but Korean policy makers were concerned that only a narrow elite achieved levels of excellence in PISA. Within less than a decade, Korea was able to virtually double the share of students demonstrating excellence in reading literacy. A major overhaul of Poland's school system helped to dramatically reduce performance variability among schools, reduce the share of poorly performing students and raise overall performance by the equivalent of more than half a school year. Germany was jolted into action when PISA 2000 revealed below-average performance and large social disparities in results, and has been able to make progress on both fronts. Last but not least, countries such as Brazil, Chile, Indonesia and Peru have seen impressive gains catching up from very low levels of performance.

The remainder of Chapter 1 describes the framework of analysis for this volume, the PISA measures used in this volume, and the methodology for developing the country chapters and lessons.

Chapter 2 sets the stage by analysing in-depth the performance of the United States on PISA, contrasting its relative strengths and weaknesses with those of other countries.

The subsequent chapters of this volume present detailed analyses of education systems which are either high-performing or have seen rapid improvements in their performance. For each country, desk reviews and interviews with a range of experts in the field of education were conducted. Each chapter first reviews the country's history and culture as context for understanding its education system. The chapters then go on to outline the main elements of the country's education system and how these relate to the observed outcomes. These elements vary across the education systems described, but generally include standards, examination systems, instructional systems, school finance, teacher quality, accountability, student motivation, and so on. Recent policy developments are highlighted in the context of past reforms. Each chapter concludes by drawing wider lessons.

The last chapter draws together the threads of the preceding chapters to present some of the policy lessons that can be drawn.

[Part 1/1]
Table 1.1 Basic data on the countries studied in this volume

	Quality														Equity	Coherence	Efficiency	Income	Equality
	PISA 2009 Results,[1] Table V.2.1		PISA 2009 Results,[1] Table V.2.1		PISA 2009 Results,[1] Table V.2.1		PISA 2009 Results,[1] Table V.3.1		PISA 2009 Results,[1] Table V.3.3		PISA 2009 Results,[1] Figure II.1.4b	PISA 2009 Results,[1] Table II.5.1	EAG,[2] Table B1.2	EAG,[2] Table X2.1	PISA 2009 Results,[1] Table II.1.2
	Mean PISA score on the reading scale 2009		Mean PISA score on the reading scale 2000		PISA score difference in reading between 2000 and 2009		Mean PISA score on the mathematics scale 2009		Mean PISA score on the science scale 2009		Percentage of the variance in student performance explained by student socio-economic background	Total variance between schools expressed as a percentage of the total variance within the country	Annual expenditure per student on educational core services (below tertiary) 2007	GDP per capita	Gini Index
	Score	S.E.	Score	S.E.	Score	S.E.	Score	S.E.	Score	S.E.	%	%	USD PPP	Value	Value
Brazil	412	2.7	396	3.1	16[3]	4.9	386	2.4	405	2.4	13.0	48	1 796[4]	10 770	0.57
Canada	524	1.5	534	1.6	-10	3.4	527	1.6	529	1.6	8.6	22	7 609	36 397	0.30
Shanghai-China	556	2.4	m	m	m	m	600	2.8	575	2.3	12.3	38	42 064[5]	5 340	0.42
Hong Kong-China	533	2.1	m	m	m	m	555	2.7	549	2.8	4.5	42	32 896[6]	42 178	0.43
Finland	536	2.3	546	2.6	-11	4.3	541	2.2	554	2.3	7.8	9	6 430	35 322	0.26
Germany	497	2.7	484	2.5	13[3]	4.5	513	2.9	520	2.8	17.9	60	7 072	34 683	0.27
Japan	520	3.5	522	5.2	-2	6.8	529	3.4	539	3.4	8.6	49	8 012[4]	33 635	0.34
Singapore	526	1.1	m	m	m	m	562	1.4	542	1.4	15.3	35	23 699[7]	51 462	0.42
Poland	500	2.6	479	4.5	21[3]	5.8	495	2.8	508	2.4	14.8	19	3 784	16 312	0.32
United States	500	3.7	504	7.0	-5	8.3	487	3.6	502	3.6	16.8	36	9 932	46 434	0.36
Sweden	497	2.9	516	2.2	-19[3]	6.1	494	2.9	495	2.7	13.4	19	7 878	36 785	0.23
United Kingdom	494	2.3	m	m	m	m	492	2.4	514	2.5	13.7	29	7 032	34 957	0.34
OECD average	494	0.5	497	0.6	-2	2.7	497	0.5	501	0.5	14	39	6 675	32 962	0.31

1. OECD (2010a), *PISA 2009 Results, Volumes I-V*, OECD Publishing.
2. OECD (2010b), *Education at a Glance 2010: OECD Indicators*, OECD Publishing.
3. Statistically significant.
4. Value for core and ancillary services.
5. Cumulative expenditure per student over the theoretical duration of primary studies (*PISA 2009 Results*).
6. Recurrent government expenditure on education, including primary, secondary and special education and departmental support (Hong Kong Annual Digest of Statistics 2010).
7. Cumulative expenditure per student for 6 to 15-year-olds (*PISA 2009 Results*).
Source: OECD, *PISA 2009 Database*.
StatLink http://dx.doi.org/10.1787/888932366617

The high-performing education systems included in this volume are: Canada (Ontario), China (Hong Kong and Shanghai), Finland, Japan, and Singapore. The examples of rapidly improving systems that were chosen are Brazil and Germany. Table 1.1 compares these countries on relevant measures relating to learning outcomes, equity in the distribution of learning opportunities, spending on education and the economic context of the country. These countries were chosen to provide a variety of relevant policies and practices as well as a range of education structures and models:

- Canada has been among the top performers in PISA over the last decade. Given that Canada has a decentralised education system and shares a border with the United States, Canada's experiences raise questions about why the United States has so far not equalled the performance of its northern neighbour. Ontario, the most populous province, provides a window onto some key reforms.

- China is a country newly covered in PISA. This country report focuses on the performance of Hong Kong and Shanghai, two cities each with a population as large or larger than some OECD countries. Hong Kong has long been a top performer on the PISA league tables; Shanghai was only assessed for the first time for PISA 2009, yet its first assessment already places it among the star performers. These two cities, despite being in the same country, have markedly different histories and school systems with very different governance arrangements. Contrasted they provide valuable insights on the impressive education accomplishments of a country now taking a prominent position on the world stage.

- Finland was the highest performing country on the first PISA assessment in 2000 and has performed consistently well on subsequent assessments.

- Japan, like Finland, is another country that ranked high on the initial PISA assessment and has maintained its standing on subsequent assessments.

- Singapore in its first PISA assessment in 2009 already scored near the top, having improved its education system in dramatic ways since its independence in 1965.

- Brazil is an example of a country that has managed to make considerable progress in recent years against substantial economic and social odds.

- Germany's early performance in PISA was far lower than Germans had expected. After recent reforms, Germany's performance on PISA 2009 shows how it has been able to recover a lot of the ground between its aspirations and its actual performance.

- Brief vignettes illustrate particular developments within three other countries. Poland shows how modification in its school structure appears to have made possible a significant change both in the level and distribution of student performance. Sweden shows the apparent success of a programme that provides language assistance to the children of immigrants. England describes how a concerted effort to change teacher recruitment may have played a role in improving student learning.

FRAMEWORK FOR ANALYSIS

The analysis in this volume follows a framework of analysis which suggests a continuum of approaches to education reform linked, in part, to a country's economic advancement. Developing countries with few resources to invest in education are likely to have lower levels of literacy among both students and teachers. Governments of countries with such characteristics may therefore invest more heavily into educating well a small elite to lead the country's industries and government operations while allocating remaining resources for teachers with little training. When teacher quality is so low, governments may also prescribe to teachers very precise job requirements, instructing teachers what to do and how to do it. Such systems tend to rely on "Tayloristic" methods[2] of administrative control and accountability in an effort to achieve desired results.

As developing and transition economies become more industrialised, citizens and policy makers tend to converge on different philosophy: the best way to compete in the global economy is to provide all citizens with the type and quality of education formerly provided only to the elite. To provide high-quality education to the broader population, education systems must recruit their teachers from the top of the higher education pool. But top graduates tend to find Tayloristic workplaces such as school systems using bureaucratic command-and-control systems to be unappealing options. To attract the best graduates to the teaching profession, these systems need to transform the work organisation in their schools to an environment in which professional norms of control replace bureaucratic and administrative forms of control. Equally important, more professional discretion accorded to teachers allows them greater latitude in developing student creativity and critical thinking skills that are important to knowledge-based economies; such skills are harder to develop in highly prescriptive learning environments.

All countries lie somewhere along this economic continuum. As a country's goals move from the delivery of basic skills and rote learning to the delivery of advanced, complex skills, they increasingly need: more educated teachers, more professional forms of work organisation and accountability, and more developed forms of professional practice (Figure 1.1). These fundamental differences in education system design have important ramifications for every aspect of the education system.

■ Figure 1.1 ■
Framework of analysis

Economic development

Impoverished, preindustrial low-wage	← →	High value-added, high wage

Teacher quality

Few years more than lower secondary	← →	High level professional knowledge workers

Curriculum, instruction and assessment

Basic literacy, rote learning	← →	Complex skills, creativity

Work organisation

Hierarchical, authoritarian	← →	Flat, collegial

Accountability

Primary accountability to authorities	← →	Primary accountability to peers and stakeholders

Student inclusion

The best students must learn at high levels	← →	All students must learn at high levels

Progress along each of these dimensions can be made, at least to some degree, independently of the others – but not without some penalties. For example, nations attempting to promote complex learning and creativity without improving teacher quality will likely run into difficulties. Nations that try to improve teacher quality without professionalizing their work organisation are also likely face challenges. In this framework, there is nothing inevitable about the movement from left to right, nor is it necessarily the case that policy makers will see the need for coherence in the policies in play at any one time, but there is a price to be paid for lack of coherence. Adjusting only one or two dimensions at a time without concern for a more co-ordinated adaptation of the system as a whole risks tampering with the equilibrium that pervades successful systems.

The description of successful education systems offered in this volume attempts to situate each system and its reform trajectory within this framework.

WHAT IS PISA AND WHAT CAN WE LEARN FROM IT?

Parents, students, teachers and those who run education systems are looking for sound information on how well their education systems prepare students for life. Most countries monitor their own students' learning outcomes in order to provide answers to this question. Comparative international assessments can extend and enrich the national picture by providing a larger context within which to interpret national performance. Countries inevitably want to know how they are doing relative to others, and, if other countries are outperforming them they want to know how they do it. Such assessments have gained prominence in recent years partly due to pressures from an increasingly competitive global economy that is evermore driven by human capital. As a result, the yardstick for judging public policy in education is no longer improvement against national educational standards, but also improvement against the most successful education systems worldwide.

■ Figure 1.2 ■
A map of PISA countries and economies

OECD countries

Australia	Japan
Austria	Korea
Belgium	Luxembourg
Canada	Mexico
Chile	Netherlands
Czech Republic	New Zealand
Denmark	Norway
Estonia	Poland
Finland	Portugal
France	Slovak Republic
Germany	Slovenia
Greece	Spain
Hungary	Sweden
Iceland	Switzerland
Ireland	Turkey
Israel	United Kingdom
Italy	United States

Partner countries and economies in PISA 2009

Albania	Mauritius*
Argentina	Miranda-Venezuela*
Azerbaijan	Montenegro
Brazil	Netherlands-Antilles*
Bulgaria	Panama
Colombia	Peru
Costa Rica*	Qatar
Croatia	Romania
Georgia*	Russian Federation
Himachal Pradesh-India*	Serbia
Hong Kong-China	Shanghai-China
Indonesia	Singapore
Jordan	Tamil Nadu-India*
Kazakhstan	Chinese Taipei
Kyrgyzstan	Thailand
Latvia	Trinidad and Tobago
Liechtenstein	Tunisia
Lithuania	Uruguay
Macao-China	United Arab Emirates*
Malaysia*	Viet Nam*
Malta*	

Partners countries in previous PISA surveys

Dominican Republic
Macedonia
Moldova

* These partner countries and economies carried out the assessment in 2010 instead of 2009.

PISA involves extensive and rigorous international surveys to assess the knowledge and skills of 15-year-old students. PISA is the result of collaboration of more than 70 countries interested in comparing their own student achievement with the student achievement in other countries (Figure 1.2). Every three years, PISA compares outcomes for 15-year-old students on measures of reading literacy, mathematics and science (Box 1.2 for a summary of PISA 2009). PISA's assessments are designed not only to find out whether students have mastered a particular curriculum, but also whether they can apply the knowledge they have gained and the skills they have acquired to the new challenges of an increasingly modern and industrialised world. Thus, the purpose of the assessments is to inform countries on the degree to which their students are prepared for life. Decisions about the scope and nature of the PISA assessments and the background information to be collected are made by leading experts in participating countries. Governments guide these decisions based on shared, policy-driven interests. Considerable efforts and resources are devoted to achieving cultural and linguistic breadth and balance in the assessment materials. Stringent quality-assurance mechanisms are applied in designing the test, in translation, sampling and data collection. As a result, PISA findings have a high degree of validity and reliability.

Box 1.2 **Key features of PISA 2009**

Content
- The main focus of PISA 2009 was reading. The survey also updated performance assessments in mathematics and science. PISA considers students' knowledge in these areas not in isolation, but in relation to their ability to reflect on their knowledge and experience and to apply them to real-world issues. The emphasis is on mastering processes, understanding concepts and functioning in various contexts within each assessment area.
- For the first time, the PISA 2009 survey also assessed 15-year-old students' ability to read, understand and apply digital texts.

Methods
- Around 470 000 students completed the assessment in 2009, representing about 26 million 15-year-olds in the schools of the 65 participating countries and economies. Some 50 000 students took part in a second round of this assessment in 2010, representing about 2 million 15-year-olds from 10 additional partner countries and economies.
- Each participating student spent two hours carrying out pencil-and-paper tasks in reading, mathematics and science. In 20 countries, students were given additional questions via computer to assess their capacity to read digital texts.
- The assessment included tasks requiring students to construct their own answers as well as multiple-choice questions. The latter were typically organised in units based on a written passage or graphic, much like the kind of texts or figures that students might encounter in real life.
- Students also answered a questionnaire that took about 30 minutes to complete. This questionnaire focused on their background, learning habits, attitudes towards reading, and their involvement and motivation.
- School principals completed a questionnaire about their school that included demographic characteristics and an assessment of the quality of the learning environment at school.

Outcomes
PISA 2009 results provide:
- a profile of knowledge and skills among 15-year-olds in 2009, consisting of a detailed profile for reading and an update for mathematics and science;
- contextual indicators relating performance results to student and school characteristics;
- an assessment of students' engagement in reading activities, and their knowledge and use of different learning strategies;
- a knowledge base for policy research and analysis; and
- trend data on changes in student knowledge and skills in reading, mathematics, science, changes in student attitudes and socio-economic indicators, and in the impact of some indicators on performance results.

Future assessments
- The PISA 2012 survey will return to mathematics as the major assessment area, PISA 2015 will focus on science. Thereafter, PISA will turn to another cycle beginning with reading again.
- Future tests will place greater emphasis on assessing students' capacity to read and understand digital texts and solve problems presented in a digital format, reflecting the importance of information and computer technologies in modern societies.

Inevitably, because PISA reports on the achievements of many countries against a common set of benchmarks, it stimulates discussion within participating countries about their education policies, with citizens recognising that their countries' educational performance will not simply need to match average performance, but that they will need to do better if their children want to ensure above-average wages and competitive standards of living. PISA assists this discussion by collecting a wide range of background information about each country's education system and about the perspectives of various stakeholders. This makes it possible to relate aspects of performance with important features of those systems.

Box 1.3 **Reporting results from PISA 2009**

The results of PISA 2009 are presented in six volumes:

- Volume I, *What Students Know and can Do: Student Performance in Reading, Mathematics and Science*, summarises the performance of students in PISA 2009. It provides the results in the context of how performance is defined, measured and reported, and then examines what students are able to do in reading. After a summary of reading performance, it examines the ways in which this performance varies on subscales representing three aspects of reading. It then breaks down results by different formats of reading texts and considers gender differences in reading, both generally and for different reading aspects and text formats. Any comparison of the outcomes of education systems needs to take into consideration countries' social and economic circumstances, and the resources they devote to education. To address this, the volume also interprets the results within countries' economic and social contexts. The volume concludes with a description of student results in mathematics and science.

- Volume II, *Overcoming Social Background: Equity in Learning Opportunities and Outcomes*, starts by closely examining the performance variation shown in Volume I, particularly the extent to which the overall variation in student performance relates to differences in results achieved by different schools. The volume then looks at how factors such as socio-economic background and immigrant status affect student and school performance, and the role that education policy can play in moderating the impact of these factors.

- Volume III, *Learning to Learn: Student Engagement, Strategies and Practices*, explores the information gathered on students' levels of engagement in reading activities and attitudes towards reading and learning. It describes 15-year-olds' motivation, engagement and strategies to learn.

- Volume IV, *What Makes a School Successful? Resources, Policies and Practices*, explores the relationships between student-, school- and system-level characteristics, and educational quality and equity. It explores what schools and school policies can do to raise overall student performance and, at the same time, moderate the impact of socio-economic background on student performance, with the aim of promoting a more equitable distribution of learning opportunities.

- Volume V, *Learning Trends: Changes in student Performance since 2000*, provides an overview of trends in student performance in reading, mathematics and science from PISA 2000 to PISA 2009. It shows educational outcomes over time and tracks changes in factors related to student and school performance, such as student background and school characteristics and practices.

- Volume VI, *Students On Line: Reading and Using Digital Information*, explains how PISA measures and reports student performance in digital reading, and analyses what students in the 20 countries participating in this assessment are able to do.

HOW CAN PISA BE USED TO HELP IMPROVE EDUCATION SYSTEMS?

On their own, cross-sectional international comparisons such as PISA cannot identify cause-and-effect relationships between certain factors and educational outcomes, especially in relation to the classroom and the processes of teaching and learning that take place there. However, they are an important tool to assess and drive educational change in several ways:

- PISA shows **what achievements are possible in education**. For example, PISA shows that Canadian 15-year-olds, on average, are over one school year ahead of 15-year-olds in the United States in mathematics and more than half a school year ahead in reading and science.[3] They also show that socio-economically disadvantaged Canadians are much less at risk of poor educational performance than their counterparts in the United States.

More generally, whether in Asia (*e.g.* Japan or Korea), Europe (*e.g.* Finland) or North America (*e.g.* Canada), many OECD countries display strong overall performance in international assessments and, equally important, some of these countries also show that poor performance in school does not automatically follow from a disadvantaged socio-economic background. Some countries also show a consistent and predictable educational outcome for their children regardless of where they send their children to school. In Finland, for example, which has some of the strongest overall PISA results, there is hardly any variation in average performance between schools.

- PISA is also used to **set policy targets in terms of measurable goals achieved by other systems and to establish trajectories for educational reform**. For example, the 2010 Growth Strategy for Japan sets the goal for Japan to achieve by 2020 a reduction in the proportion of low achievers and an increase of that of high achievers to the level of the highest performing PISA country and to increase the proportion of students with an interest in reading, mathematics and science to a level above the OECD average. Similarly, the Prime Minister of the United Kingdom set in 2010 the goal of raising the country's average student performance to Rank 3 on the PISA mathematics assessment and to Rank 6 on the PISA science assessment. This announcement was accompanied by a range of policies to achieve these targets. The Mexican President established a "PISA performance target" in 2006, to be achieved by 2012, which highlights the gap between national performance and international standards and allows to monitor how educational strategies succeed in closing this gap. The reform trajectory includes a delivery chain of support systems, incentive structures as well as improved access to professional development to assist school leaders and teachers in meeting the target.

- Some countries have systematically **related national performance to international assessments**, for example, by embedding components of the PISA assessments into their national assessments. For example, by linking its national assessment with PISA, Brazil is providing each secondary school with information on the progress it needs to make to match the average PISA performance level by 2021. Germany, Japan and the state of Oregon have embedded PISA items in their national/state assessments.

- PISA can help countries **gauge the pace of their educational progress**. Educators are often faced with a dilemma: if, at the national level, the percentage of students obtaining high score increases, some will claim that the school system has improved. Others will claim that standards must have been lowered, and behind the suspicion that better results reflect lowered standards is often a belief that overall performance in education cannot be raised. International assessments allow improvements to be validated internationally. Poland raised the performance of its 15-year-olds in PISA reading by the equivalent of well over half a school year's progress within six years, catching up with United States performance in 2009 from levels well below United States performance in 2000. It also reduced the proportion of students performing below the baseline level of reading performance from 23% in 2000 to 15% in 2009 (the proportion of bottom performers remained unchanged at 18% in the US during this time). Last but not least, Poland succeeded in halving performance differences between schools.

- PISA can help governments to optimise existing policies or consider more fundamental alternatives, when researchers combine **advanced forms of educational assessment with sophisticated survey research methods**. PISA collects reliable data on students' ability to apply high levels of knowledge and highly complex thinking to real-world problems. PISA's survey research also gathers a wide range of background data surrounding the education of the students being assessed. By relating these two bodies of data, and assuming that characteristic of students and principals about their educational contexts are predictive of students' long-term education experiences, one can associate certain patterns of students performance with a multitude of background data such as the qualifications of their teachers, how much those teachers are paid, the degree to which decisions are devolved from higher authorities to the school faculty, the socio-economic or minority status of the students, the nature of the assessments that students must take, the nature of the qualifications they might earn and so on, in great detail. In this way, while the causal nature of such relationships might not be established, an extensive web of correlations can be drawn between certain dimensions of student performance and a large range of factors that could conceivably affect that performance.

RESEARCH METHODS EMPLOYED FOR THE COUNTRY CHAPTERS

This volume complements the uses of PISA just described with a form of industrial benchmarking (Box 1.4). The aim of the research presented in this volume is to relate differences in student achievement between one country and another to certain features of those countries' education systems. Education is highly value-laden. Systems develop for historical reasons that reflect the values and preferences of parents, students, administrators, politicians and many others. Yet such values and preferences evolve and education systems must change to accommodate them. Decision-makers in the education arena can benefit from benchmarking research in the same way as heads of firms, learning about the range of factors that lead to success, taking inspiration from the lessons of others, and then adapting the operational elements to the local context while adding unique elements that make their own education system one of a kind.

Box 1.4 **The approach of industrial benchmarking**

Industrial benchmarking gained currency at the close of the 1970s and the early 1980s when Japanese firms began to challenge large multi-national American firms globally. Many American firms did not survive that challenge. But many that did survive did so because of their use of the benchmarking techniques they employed.

The aim of the American firms was to learn enough from their competitors to beat them at their own game. To do this, they identified their most successful competitors. But they also identified the companies that led the league tables in each of their major business process areas (e.g. accounting, sales, inventory). They collected all the information they could possibly find concerning their direct competitors and the companies that led the league tables in the relevant business processes. Some of this information appeared in the business press, some in major academic studies usually conducted and published by business school faculty, some through papers presented by staff members of their competitors in industry journals. After they had learned everything they could possibly learn in this way, they did their best to visit their competitors' work sites, sending their own leading experts to examine product designs, manufacturing techniques, forms of work organisation, training methods, anything they thought might contribute to their competitor's success.

When this research was complete, they would analyse all the information and research they had gathered. Their aim was not to replicate anything they had seen, but to build a better mousetrap than any they had seen anywhere by combining the best they had seen in one place with the best they had seen in another, along with their own ideas, to make something that would be superior to anything they had seen anywhere.com

What they discovered, of course, was that the methods, protocols, techniques and strategies they had seen were all, in one way or another built to address a particular set of circumstances. The firm doing the research rarely faced the same set of circumstances. So the firm doing the research had no need to incorporate in their design some of the workarounds that another firm had had to invent to get around some particular challenge in their own environment that no one else faced. Of course, it was equally true that the firm doing the research might have to build their own workarounds to deal with problems that other firms did not face. The important point here is that firms doing the research were not interested in replicating anything both because they were trying to build something superior to anything they had seen, but also because they did not want to incorporate unnecessary workarounds in their own designs.

The dominant research methodology in education is not built on the industrial benchmarking model but rather on the clinical research model used in medical research. In that arena, the aim is to identify the most successful drug or procedure available for any particular presenting disease. The method typically used to do this research is experimental designs in which subjects are randomly assigned to treatments. This method is preferred in order to ensure that there are no systematic differences between the groups assigned to different treatments. That being so, the observer can attribute differences in results for the individuals to the different treatments they received. Treatment A can be said to have "caused" result B.

The intent of this volume is not to specify a formula for success. This volume does not contain policy prescriptions. Rather the objective is to describe the experience of countries whose education systems have proven exceptionally successful to help identify policy options for consideration. It is intended as a resource for decision making.

While quantitative analysis can be used to apportion the relative influence of a variety of factors in determining variations in student performance in PISA, the data collected by PISA alone leave many questions unanswered. For instance, it is not possible to determine from PISA results whether teachers in the schools of a particular country are using a very powerful instructional system that would be equally effective in another country with very different class sizes. PISA data do not reveal whether new political leadership reframed the issues in education policy in such a way that facilitated the introduction of new reforms. PISA data do not show how awareness of weak education performance can mobilise a country's education establishment to reform and radically improve its education outcomes. Nor do PISA data reveal how a country's industrial and educational institutions are able to work together to leverage a qualifications structure that produces incentives for high-level student performance.

This volume provides complementary qualitative analysis of high-performing and rapidly-improving education systems to reveal possible contextual influences on education performance. The research undertaken for this volume entailed an enquiry of historians, policymakers, economists, education experts, ordinary citizens, journalists, industrialists, and educators that have allowed for an alternative benchmarking. The research began with a document review and was enriched by interviews with current and former leading policy makers and other education stakeholders in the countries and education systems concerned. The PISA data provided the basis for country selection as well as important clues for the points of investigation. The country studies have not only suggested some possible answers to interesting questions, but have also uncovered some new questions for consideration in future PISA assessments. The lessons suggested in this report emerge from instances in which PISA data and country analysis tend to converge.

Notes

1. The United States ranks third of OECD countries in terms of the proportion of adults aged between 25 and 64 with both high school education and college level/other tertiary qualifications (Tables A1.2a and A1.3a in the 2010 edition of OECD's *Education at a Glance*).

2. In the early 20th century an American mechanical engineer, Frederick Winslow Taylor, developed a scientific theory of management now known as Taylorism that was based on precise procedures and a high level of managerial control over employee work practices.

3. The progress students typically achieve over a school year was estimated as follows: Data on the grade in which students are enrolled were obtained both from the Student Questionnaire and from the Student Tracking Forms. The relationship between the grade and student performance was estimated through a multilevel model accounting for the following background variables: *i)* the *PISA index of economic, social and cultural status; ii)* the *PISA index of economic, social and cultural status* squared; *iii)* the school mean of the *PISA index of economic, social and cultural status; iv)* an indicator as to whether students were foreign born (first-generation students); *v)* the percentage of first-generation students in the school; and *vi)* students' gender. Table A2.1 in the PISA 2009 report presents the results of the multilevel model, which are fairly consistent across countries. Column 1 in Table A2.1 estimates the score point difference that is associated with one grade level (or school year). This difference can be estimated for the 28 OECD countries in which a sizeable number of 15-year-olds in the PISA samples were enrolled in at least two different grades. Since 15-year-olds cannot be assumed to be distributed at random across the grade levels, adjustments had to be made for the above-mentioned contextual factors that may relate to the assignment of students to the different grade levels. These adjustments are documented in columns 2 to 7 of the table. While it is possible to estimate the typical performance difference among students in two adjacent grades net of the effects of selection and contextual factors, this difference cannot automatically be equated with the progress that students have made over the last school year but should be interpreted as a lower boundary of the progress achieved. This is not only because different students were assessed but also because the content of the PISA assessment was not expressly designed to match what students had learned in the preceding school year but more broadly to assess the cumulative outcome of learning in school up to age 15.

Viewing Education
in the United States
Through the Prism of PISA

This chapter examines the United States' performance in PISA compared with high-performing and rapidly improving education systems and other international benchmarks. This serves as the backdrop for the examination of other education systems in Chapters 3 through 9, which look at the trajectories of education policies and practices in the benchmark systems. The concluding chapter of this report then draws some possible lessons for the United States from both the comparative data and the education policies of the countries portrayed in this report.

Since the focus of the PISA 2009 assessment was on reading, results on reading are examined in greater detail than results in mathematics and science. Unless noted otherwise, references to tables and figures refer to OECD's *PISA 2009 Results*.

LEARNING OUTCOMES

Mean performance of United States' 15-year-olds in the middle of the rankings

On the 2009 PISA assessment of 15-year-olds, the United States performs around the average in reading (rank 14[1]) and science (rank 17[2]) and below the average in mathematics (rank 25[3]) among the 34 OECD countries (Table 2.1). Figures 2.16, 2.17 and 2.18 at the end of this chapter show the relative standing of the United States compared to the benchmark countries examined in the subsequent chapters and other OECD countries.

Table 2.1 **United States' mean scores on reading, mathematics and science scales in PISA**

	PISA 2000	PISA 2003	PISA 2006	PISA 2009
	Mean score	Mean score	Mean score	Mean score
Reading	504	495		500
Mathematics		483	474	487
Science			489	502

Source: OECD (2010), *PISA 2009 Results: What Students Know and Can Do: Student Performance in Reading, Mathematics and Science (Volume I)*, OECD Publishing.
StatLink http://dx.doi.org/10.1787/888932366636

There is, of course, significant performance variability within the United States, including between individual states. Unlike other federal nations, the United States did not measure the performance of states individually on PISA. However, it is possible to compare the performance of public schools among groups of states. Such a comparison suggests that in reading, public schools in the northeast of the United States would perform at 510 PISA score points – 17 score points above the OECD average (comparable with the performance of the Netherlands) but still well below the high-performing education systems examined in this volume – followed by the midwest with 500 score points (comparable with the performance of Poland), the west with 486 score points (comparable with the performance of Italy) and the south with 483 score points (comparable with the performance of Greece). Note, however, that because of the way in which the sample was drawn, the performance estimates for the groups of states are associated with considerable error.

Performance varies even more between schools and social contexts. For example, despite the fact that the relationship between socio-economic background and learning outcomes is stronger in the United States than in the high-performing systems examined in this volume, over 20% of American 15-year-olds enrolled in socio-economically disadvantaged schools reach the average performance standards of Finland, one of the best-performing education systems.[4]

The United States has seen significant performance gains in science since 2006, which were mainly driven by improvements at the bottom of the performance distribution (visible in higher performance at the 10th and 25th percentiles) while performance remained unchanged at the top end of the performance distribution. Student performance in reading and mathematics has remained broadly unchanged since 2000 and 2003, respectively, when PISA began to measure these trends.

Average performance needs to be seen against a range of socio-economic background indicators, most of which give the United States a significant advantage compared with other industrialised countries (Box 2.1 and Table I.2.20 in *PISA 2009 Results Volume I*).

Box 2.1 **A context for interpreting the performance of countries**

The wealth of the United States means it can spend more on education. As shown in Volume II of *PISA 2009 Results, Overcoming Social Background*, the wealth of families influences the educational performance of their children. Similarly, the relative prosperity of some countries allows them to spend more on education, while other countries find themselves constrained by a lower national income. In fact, the relationship suggests that 6% of the variation between OECD countries' mean scores can be predicted on the basis of their GDP per capita. The United States, which ranks 3rd after Luxembourg and Norway in terms of GDP per capita, has a substantial economic advantage over other OECD countries because of the amount of money it has available to spend on education (Table I.1.20 in *PISA 2009 Results Volume I*).

Only Luxembourg spends more per student. While GDP per capita reflects the potential resources available for education in each country, it does not directly measure the financial resources actually invested in education. However, a comparison of countries' actual spending per student, from the age of 6 up to 15, on average, puts the United States at an even greater advantage, since only Luxembourg spends more than the United States on school education per student, on average. Across OECD countries, expenditure per student explains 9% of the variation in PISA mean performance between countries. Deviations from the trend line suggest that moderate spending per student cannot automatically be equated with poor performance by education systems. For example, Estonia and Poland, which spend around USD 40 000 per student, perform at the same level as Norway and the United States, which spend over USD 100 000 per student.[5] Similarly, New Zealand, one of the highest-performing countries in reading, spends well below the average per student (Table I.1.20 in *PISA 2009 Results Volume I*).

It is not just the volume of resources that matters but also how countries invest these, and how well they succeed in ***directing the money where it can make the most difference***. The United States is one of only three OECD countries in which, for example, socio-economically disadvantaged schools have to cope with less favourable student-teacher ratios than socio-economically advantaged schools, which implies that students from disadvantaged backgrounds may end up with considerably lower spending per student than what the above figures on average spending would suggest. With respect to spending on instruction, the United States spends a far lower proportion than the average OECD country on the salaries of high-school teachers.

At the same time, high school teachers in the United States teach far more hours, which reduces costs, but smaller class sizes are driving costs upwards (Table B7.3 in the 2010 edition of OECD's *Education at a Glance*). By contrast, Japan or Korea pay their teachers comparatively well and provide them with ample time for other work than teaching, which drives costs upwards, while paying for this with comparatively large class sizes. Finland puts emphasis on non-salary aspects of the working conditions of high-school teachers and also pays for the costs with comparatively large class sizes. Finally, the OECD indicators also show that the United States spends 11.6% of its resources for schools on capital outlays, a figure that is higher only in the Netherlands, Norway and Luxembourg (OECD average 7.6%) (Table B6.2b in the 2010 edition of OECD's *Education at a Glance*).

Parents in the United States are better educated than in most other countries. Given the close interrelationship between a student's performance and his or her parents' level of education observed in Volume II of *PISA 2009 Results*, it is also important to bear in mind the educational attainment of adult populations when comparing the performance of OECD countries, since countries with more highly educated adults are at an advantage over countries in which parents have less education. A comparison of the percentage of 35-to-44-year-olds that have attained upper secondary or tertiary levels of education, which roughly corresponds to the age group of parents of the 15-year-olds assessed in PISA, ranks the United States 8th among the 34 OECD countries (Table A1.2 in the in the 2010 edition of OECD's *Education at a Glance*).

The share of students from disadvantaged backgrounds in the United States is about average. Socio-economic disadvantage and heterogeneity in student populations pose other challenges for teachers and education systems. As shown in Volume II of *PISA 2009 Results*, teachers instructing socio-economically disadvantaged children are likely to face greater challenges than teachers with students from more privileged socio-economic backgrounds.

....

■ Figure 2.1a ■
Reading performance and GDP

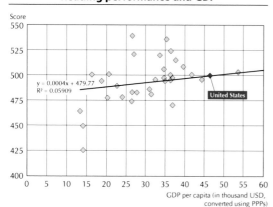

Source: OECD (2010), *PISA 2009 Results, Volume I*, Table I.2.20.
StatLink http://dx.doi.org/10.1787/888932366636

■ Figure 2.1b ■
Reading performance and spending on education

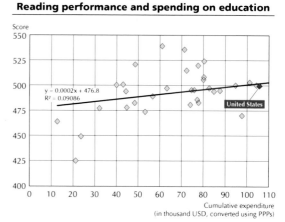

Source: OECD (2010), *PISA 2009 Results, Volume I*, Table I.2.20.
StatLink http://dx.doi.org/10.1787/888932366636

■ Figure 2.1c ■
Reading performance and parents' education

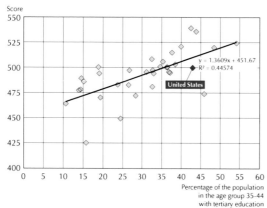

Source: OECD (2010), *PISA 2009 Results, Volume I*, Table I.2.20.
StatLink http://dx.doi.org/10.1787/888932366636

■ Figure 2.1d ■
Reading performance and share of socio-economically disadvantaged students

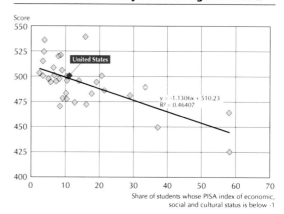

Source: OECD (2010), *PISA 2009 Results, Volume I*, Table I.2.20.
StatLink http://dx.doi.org/10.1787/888932366636

■ Figure 2.1e ■
Reading performance and proportion of students from an immigrant background

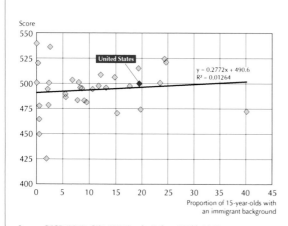

Source: OECD (2010), *PISA 2009 Results, Volume I*, Table I.2.20.
StatLink http://dx.doi.org/10.1787/888932366636

■ Figure 2.1f ■
Equivalence of the PISA test across cultures and languages

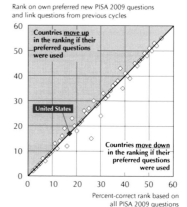

Source: OECD (2010), *PISA 2009 Results, Volume I*, Table I.2.21.
StatLink http://dx.doi.org/10.1787/888932366636

....

A comparison of the socio-economic background of the most disadvantaged quarter of students puts the United States around the OECD average while the socio-economic background of the student population as a whole ranks clearly above the OECD average.[6] In other words, while the overall socio-economic context of students in the United States is above that of a typical OECD country, the proportion of students from disadvantaged backgrounds is similar in the United States to that of OECD countries in general. The greater socio-economic variability in the United States thus does not result from a disproportional share of students from poor families, but rather from an above-average share of students from socio-economically advantaged backgrounds.

Among OECD countries the United States has the 6th largest proportion of students with an immigrant background. Integrating students with an immigrant background is part of the socio-economic challenge, and the performance levels of students who immigrated to the country in which they were assessed in PISA can only be partially attributed to the education system of their host country. With 19.5%, the United States has the 6th highest share of students with an immigrant background among OECD countries. However, the share of students with an immigrant background explains just 3% of the performance variation between countries. Among the 8 OECD countries that have between 15% and 30% of students with an immigrant background, which includes the United States, four show a smaller performance gap for immigrants on PISA while three show a larger performance gap for immigrants than the United States (Figure II.4.3 in *PISA 2009 Results, Volume II*).

The data in Figure 2.1 show that countries vary in their demographic, social and economic contexts. These differences need to be taken into account when interpreting differences in student performance. At the same time, the future economic and social prospects of both individuals and countries depends on the results they actually achieve, not on the performance they might have achieved under different social and economic conditions. That is why the results that are actually achieved by students, schools and countries are the focus of the subsequent analysis in this chapter.

Even after accounting for the demographic, economic and social contexts of education systems, the question remains: to what extent is an international test meaningful when differences in languages and cultures lead to very different ways in which subjects such as language, mathematics or science are taught and learned across countries? It is inevitable that not all tasks on the PISA assessments are equally appropriate in different cultural contexts and equally relevant in different curricular and instructional contexts. To gauge this, PISA asked every country to identify those tasks from the PISA tests that it considered most appropriate for an international test. Countries were advised to give an on-balance rating for each task with regard to its relevance to "preparedness for life", authenticity and interest for 15-year-olds. Tasks given a high rating by each country are referred to as that country's most preferred questions for PISA. PISA then scored every country on its own most preferred questions and compared the resulting performance with the performance on the entire set of PISA tasks. For the United States, its relative standing remains the same, irrespective of whether all PISA items or the items "preferred" by the United States are used as a basis for comparisons.

Relative shares of students "at risk"

Eighteen per cent of 15-year-olds in the United States do not reach the PISA baseline Level 2 of reading proficiency, a percentage that is around the OECD average and that has remained unchanged since 2000. Excluding students with an immigrant background reduces the percentage of poorly performing students slightly to 16%. By contrast, in Shanghai-China, Hong Kong-China, Canada, Finland and Korea, the proportion of poor performers is 10% or less (Figure I.2.14 in *PISA 2009 Results Volume I*).

Level 2 on the PISA reading scale can be considered a baseline level of proficiency, at which students begin to demonstrate the reading competencies that will enable them to participate effectively and productively in life. Students proficient at Level 2 are capable of very basic tasks, such as locating information that meets several conditions, making comparisons or contrasts around a single feature, working out what a well-defined part of a text means even when the information is not prominent, and making connections between the text and personal experience. Some tasks at this level require students to locate one or more pieces of information, which may need to be inferred and may need to meet several conditions. Others require recognising the main idea in a text, understanding relationships, or construing meaning within a limited part of the text when the information is not prominent and the reader must make low-level inferences. Tasks at this level may involve comparisons or contrasts based on a single feature in the text. Typical reflective tasks at this level require students to make a comparison or several connections between the text and outside knowledge, by drawing on personal experience and attitudes.

■ Figure 2.2 ■

Summary descriptions for the seven levels of proficiency in reading

Level	Lower score limit	Percentage of students able to perform tasks at each level or above (OECD average)	Characteristics of tasks
6	698	0.8% of students across the OECD can perform tasks at Level 6 on the reading scale	Tasks at this level typically require the reader to make multiple inferences, comparisons and contrasts that are both detailed and precise. They require demonstration of a full and detailed understanding of one or more texts and may involve integrating information from more than one text. Tasks may require the reader to deal with unfamiliar ideas, in the presence of prominent competing information, and to generate abstract categories for interpretations. *Reflect and evaluate* tasks may require the reader to hypothesise about or critically evaluate a complex text on an unfamiliar topic, taking into account multiple criteria or perspectives, and applying sophisticated understandings from beyond the text. A salient condition for *access and retrieve* tasks at this level is precision of analysis and fine attention to detail that is inconspicuous in the texts.
5	626	7.6% of students across the OECD can perform tasks at least at Level 5 on the reading scale	Tasks at this level that involve retrieving information require the reader to locate and organise several pieces of deeply embedded information, inferring which information in the text is relevant. Reflective tasks require critical evaluation or hypothesis, drawing on specialised knowledge. Both interpretative and reflective tasks require a full and detailed understanding of a text whose content or form is unfamiliar. For all aspects of reading, tasks at this level typically involve dealing with concepts that are contrary to expectations.
4	553	28.3% of students across the OECD can perform tasks at least at Level 4 on the reading scale	Tasks at this level that involve retrieving information require the reader to locate and organise several pieces of embedded information. Some tasks at this level require interpreting the meaning of nuances of language in a section of text by taking into account the text as a whole. Other interpretative tasks require understanding and applying categories in an unfamiliar context. Reflective tasks at this level require readers to use formal or public knowledge to hypothesise about or critically evaluate a text. Readers must demonstrate an accurate understanding of long or complex texts whose content or form may be unfamiliar.
3	480	57.2% of students across the OECD can perform tasks at least at Level 3 on the reading scale	Tasks at this level require the reader to locate, and in some cases recognise the relationship between, several pieces of information that must meet multiple conditions. Interpretative tasks at this level require the reader to integrate several parts of a text in order to identify a main idea, understand a relationship or construe the meaning of a word or phrase. They need to take into account many features in comparing, contrasting or categorising. Often the required information is not prominent or there is much competing information; or there are other obstacles in the text, such as ideas that are contrary to expectation or negatively worded. Reflective tasks at this level may require connections, comparisons, and explanations, or they may require the reader to evaluate a feature of the text. Some reflective tasks require readers to demonstrate a fine understanding of the text in relation to familiar, everyday knowledge. Other tasks do not require detailed text comprehension but require the reader to draw on less common knowledge.
2	407	81.2% of students across the OECD can perform tasks at least at Level 2 on the reading scale	Some tasks at this level require the reader to locate one or more pieces of information, which may need to be inferred and may need to meet several conditions. Others require recognising the main idea in a text, understanding relationships, or construing meaning within a limited part of the text when the information is not prominent and the reader must make low level inferences. Tasks at this level may involve comparisons or contrasts based on a single feature in the text. Typical reflective tasks at this level require readers to make a comparison or several connections between the text and outside knowledge, by drawing on personal experience and attitudes.
1a	335	94.3% of students across the OECD can perform tasks at least at Level 1a on the reading scale	Tasks at this level require the reader: to locate one or more independent pieces of explicitly stated information; to recognise the main theme or author's purpose in a text about a familiar topic; or to make a simple connection between information in the text and common, everyday knowledge. Typically the required information in the text is prominent and there is little, if any, competing information. The reader is explicitly directed to consider relevant factors in the task and in the text.
1b	262	98.9% of students across the OECD can perform tasks at least at Level 1b on the reading scale	Tasks at this level require the reader to locate a single piece of explicitly stated information in a prominent position in a short, syntactically simple text with a familiar context and text type, such as a narrative or a simple list. The text typically provides support to the reader, such as repetition of information, pictures or familiar symbols. There is minimal competing information. In tasks requiring interpretation the reader may need to make simple connections between adjacent pieces of information.

A follow-up of students who were assessed by PISA in 2000 as part of the Canadian Youth in Transitions Survey shows that students scoring below Level 2 face a disproportionately higher risk of poor post-secondary participation or low labour-market outcomes at age 19, and even more so at age 21, the latest age for which data are currently available. For example, the odds of Canadian students who had reached PISA Level 5 in reading at age 15 to achieve a successful transition to post-secondary education by age 21 were 20 times higher than for those who had not achieved the baseline Level 2, even after adjustments for socio-economic differences are made (OECD, 2010e).[7] Similarly, of the Canadian students who performed below Level 2 in 2000, over 60% had not gone on to any post-school education by the age of 21; by contrast, more than half of the students (55%) who had performed at Level 2 as their highest level were at college or university.

In mathematics, the proportion of students below Level 2 on the PISA mathematics scale is 23.4% (OECD average of 20.8%) and remained similar to the percentage in 2003 (25.7%) (Table V.3.2 in *PISA 2009 Results Volume V*). Students proficient at Level 2 in mathematics can employ basic algorithms, formulae, procedures or conventions. They can interpret and recognise mathematical situations in contexts that require no more than direct inference and extract relevant information from a single source and make use of a single representational mode. They are capable of direct reasoning and making literal interpretations of the results.

In science, the proportion of students below Level 2 on the PISA science scale is, at 18.1%, around the OECD average but has declined from 24.4% in 2006 (Table V.3.4 in *PISA 2009 Results Volume V*). To reach Level 2 requires competencies such as identifying key features of a scientific investigation, recalling single scientific concepts and information relating to a situation, and using results of a scientific experiment represented in a data table as they support a personal decision. In contrast, students who do not reach Level 2 in science often confuse key features of an investigation, apply incorrect scientific information, and mix personal beliefs with scientific facts in support of a decision.

Relative shares of top-performing students

At the other end of the performance scale, students in the United States do comparatively well at the very highest levels of reading proficiency (Levels 5 and 6), have an average share of top performers in science, but a below-average share of top performers in mathematics (Figures I.2.14, I.3.9 and I.3.20 in *PISA 2009 Results Volume I*).

Students proficient at Level 6 on the PISA reading scale are capable of conducting fine-grained analysis of texts, which requires detailed comprehension of both explicit information and unstated implications; and capable of reflecting on and evaluating what they read at a more general level. They can overcome preconceptions in the face of new information, even when that information is contrary to expectations. They are capable of recognising what is provided in a text, both conspicuously and more subtly, while at the same time being able to apply a critical perspective to it, drawing on sophisticated understandings from beyond the text. This combination of a capacity to absorb the new and to evaluate it is greatly valued in knowledge economies, which depend on innovation and nuanced decision-making that draw on all the available evidence. At 1.5%, the United States has a significantly higher share of the highest-performing readers than the average (0.8%). However, in Australia, Canada, Finland, Japan, New Zealand, Singapore or Shanghai-China, the corresponding percentages are even higher, ranging from 1.8 to 2.9%.

At the next highest level, Level 5 on the PISA reading literacy scale, students can still handle texts that are unfamiliar in either form or content. They can find information in such texts, demonstrate detailed understanding, and infer which information is relevant to the task. Using such texts, they are also able to evaluate critically and build hypotheses, draw on specialised knowledge and accommodate concepts that may be contrary to expectations. The United States has, at 10%, an above-average share of students who perform at Level 5 or above (average 8%). However, in Shanghai-China (19.5%), New Zealand and Singapore (15.7%), Finland (14.5%) and Japan (13.4%) the corresponding percentages are higher.

Only 2% of students in the United States reach the highest level of performance in mathematics, compared with an OECD average of 3%, and figures ranging up to 27% in Shanghai-China (Table I.3.1 in *PISA 2009 Results Volume I*). Students proficient at Level 6 on the mathematics scale are capable of advanced mathematical thinking and reasoning. These students can apply insight and understanding, along with a mastery of symbolic and formal mathematical operations and relationships, to develop new approaches and strategies for addressing novel situations. They can formulate and accurately communicate their actions and reflections regarding their findings, interpretations, arguments and the appropriateness of these to the given situations. At the next highest level, Level 5 on the PISA mathematics scale, students can still develop and work with models in complex situations, identifying constraints and specifying assumptions.

They can select, compare and evaluate appropriate problem-solving strategies for dealing with complex problems related to these models. Students at this level can work strategically using broad, well-developed thinking and reasoning skills, appropriate linked representations, symbolic and formal characterisations, and insight pertaining to these situations. Ten per cent of students in the United States reach the PISA mathematics Level 5, compared with 13% on average across OECD countries. In Shanghai-China, half of the students reach Level 5, in Singapore and Hong Kong-China over 30% do, and in Chinese Taipei, Korea, Switzerland, Finland, Japan and Belgium over 20% do.

Students proficient at Level 6 in science can consistently identify, explain and apply scientific knowledge and knowledge about science in a variety of complex life situations. They can link different information sources and explanations and use evidence from those sources to justify decisions. They clearly and consistently demonstrate advanced scientific thinking and reasoning, and they use their scientific understanding to solve unfamiliar scientific and technological situations. Students at this level can use scientific knowledge and develop arguments in support of recommendations and decisions that centre on personal, social or global situations. One per cent of students in the United States reach Level 6 in science, which corresponds to the OECD average. In Singapore, the percentage is 4.6%, in Shanghai-China 3.9%, in New Zealand 3.6%, in Finland 3.3% and in Australia 3%.

Students proficient at the PISA science Level 5 can identify the scientific components of many complex life situations, apply both scientific concepts and knowledge about science to these situations, and can compare, select and evaluate appropriate scientific evidence for responding to life situations. Students at this level can use well-developed inquiry abilities, link knowledge appropriately and bring critical insights to situations. They can construct explanations based on evidence and arguments that emerge from their critical analysis. Nine per cent of students in the United States reach this level, which again corresponds to the OECD average. In Shanghai-China, 24.3% of students do, in Singapore 19.9%, in Finland 18.7%, in New Zealand 17.6% and in Japan, Hong Kong-China, Australia, Germany, the Netherlands and Canada, between 12.1% and 16.6% of students reach this level.

EQUITY IN THE DISTRIBUTION OF LEARNING OPPORTUNITIES

PISA explores equity in education from three perspectives: first, it examines differences in the distribution of learning outcomes of students and schools; second, it studies the extent to which students and schools of different socio-economic backgrounds have access to similar educational resources, both in terms of quantity and quality; and third, it looks at the impact of students' family background and school location on learning outcomes. The first perspective was discussed in the preceding section; the last two are discussed below.

Equity in access to resources

A first potential source of inequities in learning opportunities lies in the distribution of resources across students and schools. In a school system characterised by an equitable distribution of educational resources, the quality or quantity of school resources would not be related to a school's average socio-economic background, as all schools would enjoy similar resources. Therefore, if there is a positive relationship between the socio-economic background of students and schools and the quantity or quality of resources, this signals that more advantaged schools enjoy more or better resources. A negative relationship implies that more or better resources are devoted to disadvantaged schools. No relationship implies that resources are distributed similarly among schools attended by socio-economically advantaged and disadvantaged students.

In around half of OECD countries, the student-teacher ratio relates positively to the socio-economic background of schools – in other words, disadvantaged schools tend to have more teachers per student. This positive relationship is particularly pronounced in Belgium, Denmark, Estonia, Germany, Iceland, Ireland, Italy, Japan, Korea, Luxembourg, the Netherlands, Portugal and Spain. This important measure of resource allocation indicates that these countries use the student-teacher ratio to moderate disadvantage. Among OECD countries, only Israel, Slovenia, Turkey and the United States favour socio-economically advantaged schools with access to more teachers (Figure 2.3). The financing of schools in the United States, which is dependent on local taxation and thus closely related to housing costs, may contribute to concentrations of disadvantaged pupils in poorly resourced schools.

In the majority of OECD countries, including the United States, more advantaged students also enjoy a higher proportion of better-qualified full-time teachers. The picture is similar when examining schools whose principals report that the lack of qualified teachers hinders learning. All of this suggests that ensuring an equitable distribution of resources is still a major challenge for the United States, but also for other countries, if not in terms of the quantity of resources, then in terms of their quality. Figure 2.3 compares the Unites States with the benchmark countries examined in subsequent chapters as well as with other OECD countries.

■ Figure 2.3 ■
Relationship between school average socio-economic background and school resources

Disadvantaged schools are more likely to have more or better resources, in **bold** if relationship is statistically different from the OECD average

Advantaged schools are more likely to have more or better resources, in **bold** if relationship is statistically different from the OECD average

Within country correlation is not statistically significant

	Simple correlation between the school mean socio-economic background and:					
	Percentage of full-time teachers	Percentage of certified teachers among all full-time teachers	Percentage of teachers with university-level (ISCED 5A) among all full-time teachers	Index of quality of school's educational resources	Computer/student ratio	Student/teacher ratio[1]
OECD						
Australia	-0.21	-0.05	0.02	0.31	0.01	-0.07
Austria	-0.13	0.21	0.64	0.03	-0.05	-0.07
Belgium	-0.18	0.05	0.58	0.02	-0.23	0.66
Canada	0.01	0.14	0.03	0.18	-0.05	0.09
Chile	-0.04	-0.01	0.25	0.35	0.32	-0.05
Czech Republic	-0.32	0.29	0.37	0.00	0.15	0.08
Denmark	0.01	-0.17	0.16	0.04	-0.08	0.27
Estonia	0.14	0.00	0.00	0.10	-0.09	0.43
Finland	0.17	-0.01	-0.01	0.13	-0.01	0.08
France	c	c	c	c	c	c
Germany	-0.15	-0.02	-0.02	0.06	-0.18	0.28
Greece	-0.11	0.06	0.24	0.16	-0.12	0.25
Hungary	-0.33	0.07	0.07	0.11	-0.20	0.02
Iceland	0.20	0.39	0.30	0.06	-0.41	0.40
Ireland	0.12	-0.10	-0.08	0.16	-0.03	0.49
Israel	-0.08	-0.06	0.20	0.25	0.08	-0.20
Italy	-0.06	0.16	0.13	0.15	-0.19	0.50
Japan	-0.14	0.04	0.20	0.17	-0.34	0.38
Korea	-0.14	0.00	-0.03	-0.04	-0.53	0.30
Luxembourg	-0.16	-0.01	0.39	0.13	-0.13	0.28
Mexico	-0.09	-0.13	-0.04	0.59	0.14	0.03
Netherlands	-0.34	-0.12	0.62	0.06	-0.16	0.38
New Zealand	-0.04	0.08	0.07	0.16	-0.02	0.11
Norway	-0.05	0.04	0.15	0.14	-0.02	0.19
Poland	-0.02	0.03	-0.05	0.06	-0.16	0.01
Portugal	0.14	-0.05	0.04	0.24	-0.02	0.39
Slovak Republic	-0.09	0.28	-0.21	-0.05	-0.06	0.00
Slovenia	0.46	0.32	0.55	0.13	-0.21	-0.25
Spain	-0.29	c	c	0.10	-0.16	0.45
Sweden	0.05	0.01	-0.04	0.26	0.13	0.12
Switzerland	-0.11	-0.07	0.24	0.10	0.03	0.06
Turkey	0.12	-0.04	0.04	0.04	-0.06	-0.26
United Kingdom	-0.36	0.05	-0.03	0.00	0.01	-0.10
United States	-0.42	-0.24	0.10	0.22	0.06	-0.17
OECD average	-0.07	0.04	0.15	0.13	-0.08	0.15
Partners						
Albania	-0.25	0.00	0.38	0.44	0.24	0.15
Argentina	0.13	0.13	0.22	0.51	0.21	-0.02
Azerbaijan	0.05	-0.06	0.44	0.19	0.17	0.23
Brazil	-0.03	0.10	0.03	0.52	0.25	-0.20
Bulgaria	-0.08	0.17	0.17	0.09	-0.17	0.21
Colombia	-0.24	-0.16	-0.08	0.53	0.19	-0.14
Croatia	0.09	0.02	0.28	0.09	0.17	0.32
Dubai (UAE)	0.32	0.61	-0.01	0.34	0.47	-0.27
Hong Kong-China	-0.19	-0.06	0.12	0.06	0.04	0.02
Indonesia	0.24	0.27	0.16	0.44	0.14	-0.16
Jordan	-0.04	0.00	-0.02	0.26	0.05	0.06
Kazakhstan	0.23	0.04	0.34	0.21	-0.12	0.44
Kyrgyzstan	0.17	0.08	0.35	0.27	0.13	0.27
Latvia	0.19	-0.03	0.19	0.14	0.00	0.38
Liechtenstein	-0.15	0.02	0.57	-0.91	0.79	0.70
Lithuania	0.21	0.09	0.19	-0.02	-0.49	0.21
Macao-China	0.11	0.05	-0.18	0.26	0.22	0.17
Montenegro	0.07	0.32	0.38	-0.11	-0.19	0.33
Panama	-0.51	-0.47	-0.13	0.68	0.38	0.03
Peru	-0.21	0.08	0.48	0.53	0.46	-0.02
Qatar	0.03	-0.04	-0.07	0.23	0.19	0.11
Romania	0.05	0.10	0.11	0.20	-0.07	-0.02
Russian Federation	0.18	0.08	0.31	0.26	0.02	0.29
Serbia	0.10	0.06	0.06	-0.01	0.00	0.11
Shanghai-China	0.14	0.13	0.32	0.16	-0.10	-0.13
Singapore	-0.13	0.00	0.22	0.10	-0.18	-0.14
Chinese Taipei	0.12	0.34	0.29	0.19	-0.04	-0.07
Thailand	0.07	0.06	0.16	0.39	0.00	-0.02
Trinidad and Tobago	-0.19	0.09	0.56	0.12	0.08	0.38
Tunisia	-0.06	0.00	0.20	0.13	0.15	-0.02
Uruguay	-0.01	0.27	0.08	0.33	0.30	0.13

1. In contrast to the other columns, negative correlations indicate more favourable characteristics for advantaged students.
Source: OECD, *PISA 2009 Database*, Table II.2.2.
StatLink ▄▄▋▋ http://dx.doi.org/10.1787/888932366636

Moderating the impact of socio-economic background on learning outcomes

Students who did not surpass the most basic performance level on PISA were not a random group and the results show that socio-economic disadvantage has a particularly strong impact on student performance in the United States: 17% of the variation in student performance in the United States is explained by students' socio-economic background. This contrasts with just 9% in Canada or Japan, two of the benchmark countries described later in this volume. In other words, in the United States, two students from a different socio-economic background vary much more in their learning outcomes than is normally the case in OECD countries. Among OECD countries, only Hungary, Belgium, Turkey, Luxembourg, Chile and Germany show a larger impact of socio-economic background on reading performance than the United States. It is important to emphasise that these countries, including the United States, do not necessarily have a more disadvantaged socio-economic student intake than other countries; but socio-economic differences among students translate into a particularly strong impact on student learning outcomes (Figure 2.4).

Similarly, among the 25 countries participating in PISA that show a more unequal distribution of income in their populations than the United States (among OECD countries, these include only Chile, Israel, Mexico, Portugal and Turkey) only Panama, Chile, Peru, Argentina, Uruguay and Turkey show a larger impact of socio-economic background on learning outcomes at school (Figure 2.4). The comparatively close relationship between the learning outcomes of students in the United States and socio-economic background is therefore not simply explained by a more socio-economically heterogeneous student population or society but, as noted before, mainly because socio-economic disadvantage translates more directly into poor educational performance in the United States than is the case in many other countries.

■ Figure 2.4 ■
Income inequality in the population and strength of the relationship between socio-economic background and performance

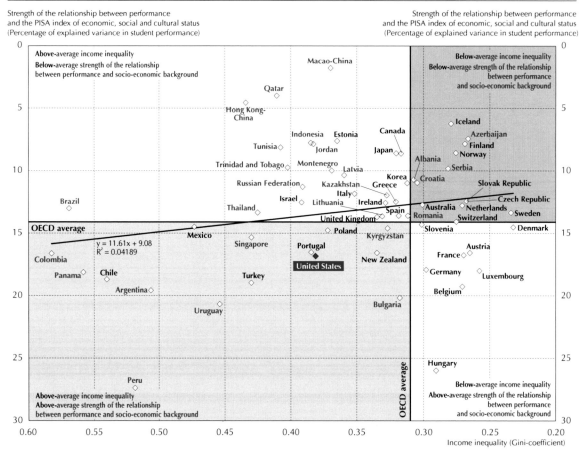

Note: The Gini coefficient measures the extent to which the distribution of income among individuals or households within an economy deviates from a perfectly equal distribution. The Gini index measures the area between the Lorenz curve and the hypothetical line of absolute equality, expressed as a proportion of the maximum area under the line. A Gini index of zero represents perfect equality and 1, perfect inequality.
Source: OECD, *PISA 2009 Database*, Table II.1.1.
StatLink ⧉ http://dx.doi.org/10.1787/888932366636

If social inequities in societies were always closely linked to the impact of social disadvantage on learning outcomes, the role for public policy to improve equity in the distribution of learning opportunities would be limited, at least in the short term. However, there is almost no relationship between income inequalities in countries and the impact of socio-economic background on learning outcomes (Figure 2.4), that is, some countries succeed, even under difficult conditions, to moderate the impact of socio-economic background on educational success.

Also in the United States, the relationship between socio-economic background and learning outcomes is far from deterministic (Figure 2.5). For example, some of the most socio-economically disadvantaged schools match the performance of schools in Finland.[8] Furthermore, as noted before, a quarter of American 15-year-olds enrolled in socio-economically disadvantaged schools reach the average performance standards of Finland, one of the best-performing education systems.[9]

It is useful to examine four of the aspects of socio-economic background and their relationship to student performance in greater detail.

Community size: While students in the United States in large cities (students attending schools located in cities with over one million inhabitants) perform at 485 score points on the PISA reading scale, below the OECD average of 493 score points, suburban schools perform, on average, just slightly higher than the OECD average. The performance challenges for the United States therefore do not just relate to poor students in poor neighbourhoods, but to many students in many neighbourhoods.[10]

Family composition: While results from PISA show that single-parent families are more prevalent in the United States than on average across OECD countries (24% of 15-year-olds in the United States come from a single-parent family compared with an average of 17%), they also show that 15-year-olds in the United States from single-parent families face a much higher risk of low performance than is the case across OECD countries (Table II.2.5 in *PISA 2009 Results Volume II*).

Immigrant students: Thirty per cent of schools in the United States have more than a quarter of students with an immigrant background. Among OECD countries, only Luxembourg, Switzerland, Australia, New Zealand, Canada and Israel show a higher concentration of students with an immigrant background in schools (the OECD average is 14%). Twelve per cent of students in the United States are enrolled in schools in which the share of immigrant students even exceeds 50%, a percentage that only Luxembourg, Canada and New Zealand exceed (Table II.4.6 in *PISA 2009 Results Volume II*). What PISA data also show is that students in the United States with an immigrant background tend to attend schools with a socio-economically more disadvantaged background, that have a lower quality of educational resources, a more disadvantageous student/staff ratio, and greater teacher shortage as reported by school principals (Table II.4.9 in *PISA 2009 Results Volume II*). Such challenges are, however, not uncommon across OECD countries.

■ Figure 2.5 ■
Relationship between school performance and schools' socio-economic background in United States

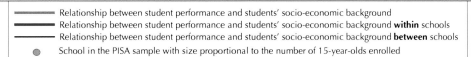

Relationship between student performance and students' socio-economic background
Relationship between student performance and students' socio-economic background **within** schools
Relationship between student performance and students' socio-economic background **between** schools
● School in the PISA sample with size proportional to the number of 15-year-olds enrolled

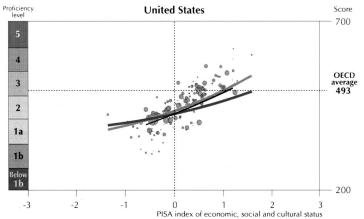

Source: OECD, *PISA 2009 Database*.
StatLink ⟨⟨⟩⟩ http://dx.doi.org/10.1787/888932366636

While it might be tempting to attribute a performance lag of countries to the challenges that immigrant inflows pose to the education system, the reading performance of students in the United States without an immigrant background is, at 506 score points, only marginally higher than the performance of all students. In fact, the reading performance gap between students with and without an immigrant background is smaller in the United States than the average gap across OECD countries (Table II.4.1 in *PISA 2009 Results Volume II*), and particularly after the socio-economic background of students is accounted for (Table II.4.1 in *PISA 2009 Results Volume II*). The same holds if the language spoken at home, instead of the immigrant background of the student, is used for comparing student groups. Among the countries that took part in the latest PISA assessment, Switzerland, Canada and New Zealand have larger immigrant intakes than the United States, but score significantly better (Figure 2.6).

■ Figure 2.6 ■

Students' reading performance, by percentage of students with an immigrant background

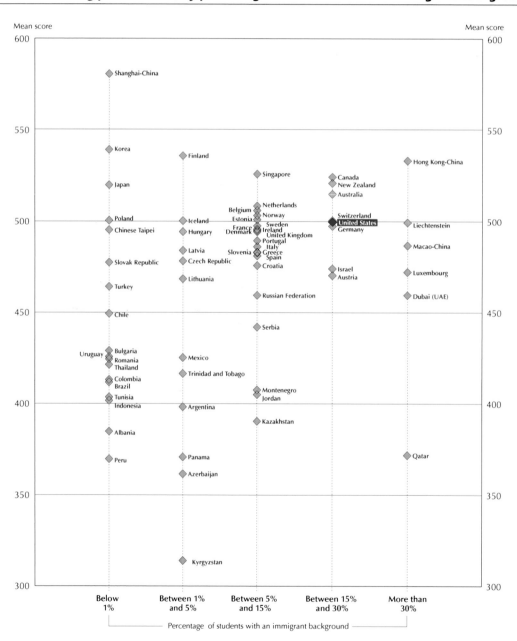

Source: OECD, *PISA 2009 Database*, Table II.4.1.
StatLink ᵐˢᵖ http://dx.doi.org/10.1787/888932366636

■ Figure 2.7 ■
Percentage of resilient students among disadvantaged students

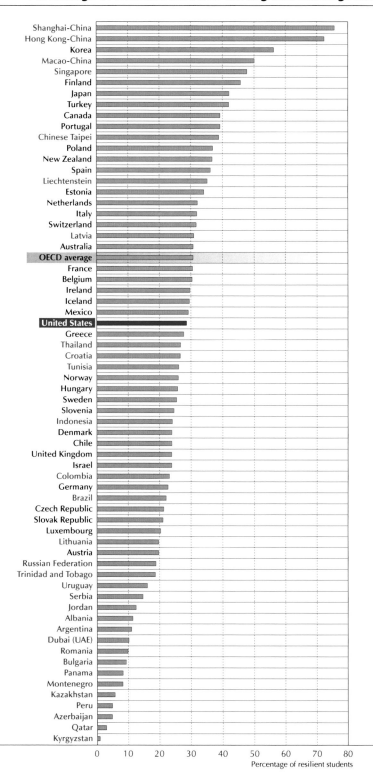

Percentage of resilient students

Note: A student is classified as resilient if he or she is in the bottom quarter of the PISA index of economic, social and cultural status (ESCS) in the country of assessment and performs in the top quarter across students from all countries after accounting for socio-economic background. The share of resilient students among all students has been multiplied by 4 so that the percentage values presented here reflect the proportion of resilient students among disadvantaged students (those in the bottom quarter of the PISA index of social, economic and cultural status).

Source: OECD, *PISA 2009 Database*, Table II.3.3.

StatLink ⟡ᵐ🇸🇱 http://dx.doi.org/10.1787/888932366636

Concentration of socio-economic disadvantaged students in schools: In the United States, there are 32% of students in schools with a socio-economically disadvantaged intake, of which 61% are students who are socio-economically disadvantaged themselves (*i.e.* they are grossly over-represented), while 30% of students are in socio-economically privileged schools of which only 6% are socio-economically disadvantaged themselves. Disadvantaged students tend to do as expected in disadvantaged schools and advantaged students tend to do worse than expected, but by about the same margin as in many other OECD countries. In schools with a mixed socio-economic intake, disadvantaged students tend to do better than expected, again by the same margin as in the OECD in general, and advantaged students tend to do as expected. In schools with a privileged socio-economic intake, disadvantaged students tend to do better than expected (but by a smaller margin compared to other OECD countries) and advantaged students tend to do better than expected (within a similar margin of other OECD countries) (Table II.5.11 in *PISA 2009 Results, Volume II*).

In general, the accuracy with which socio-economic background predicts student performance varies considerably across countries. Most of the students who perform poorly in PISA share a challenging socio-economic background and yet some of their socio-economically disadvantaged peers excel in PISA and beat the odds working against them. These students show that overcoming socio-economic barriers to achievement is possible. While the prevalence of resilience is not the same across educational systems, it is possible to identify substantial numbers of resilient students in practically all OECD countries.[11] In the United States, 7% of students can be considered resilient, in the sense that they come from the 25% of the most socio-economically disadvantaged students but nevertheless perform much better than would be predicted based on their socio-economic background (7% is also the average in the OECD) (Figure 2.7). However, in Korea, Hong Kong-China and Shanghai-China, the share of disadvantaged students who excel at school despite their disadvantaged background is about twice as high.

The cost of the achievement gap

The international achievement gap is imposing on the United States economy an invisible yet recurring economic loss that is greater than the output shortfall in what has been called the worst economic crisis since the Great Depression. Using economic modelling to relate cognitive skills – as measured by PISA and other international instruments – to economic growth shows (with some caveats) that even small improvements in the skills of a nation's labour force can have large impacts on that country's future well-being. A recent study carried out by the OECD, in collaboration with the Hoover Institute at Stanford University, suggests that a modest goal of having the United States boost its average PISA scores by 25 points over the next 20 years – which corresponds to the performance gains that some countries achieved between 2000 and 2009 alone – could imply a gain of USD 41 trillion for the United States economy over the lifetime of the generation born in 2010 (as evaluated at the start of reform in terms of the real present value of future improvements in GDP). Bringing the United States up to the average performance of Finland, the best-performing education system among OECD countries, could result in gains in the order of USD 103 trillion. Narrowing the achievement gap by bringing all students to a baseline level of proficiency for the OECD (a PISA score of about 400) could imply GDP increases for the United States of USD 72 trillion, according to historical growth relationships (OECD, 2010b). Longitudinal studies have also demonstrated that student performance at school is a good indicator of subsequent successful education and labour-market pathways (OECD, 2010a).

Although there are uncertainties associated with these estimates, the gains from improved learning outcomes, put in terms of current GDP, exceed today's value of the short-run business-cycle management. This is not to say that efforts should not be directed towards mitigating the short-term effects of the economic recession, but it is to say that long-term issues should not be neglected.

THE LEARNING ENVIRONMENT IN THE CLASSROOM AND AT SCHOOL

The effects of educational policies and practices on student achievement depend heavily on how they translate into increased learning in the classroom. Results from PISA suggest that, across OECD countries, schools and countries where students work in a climate characterised by expectations of high performance and the readiness to invest effort, good teacher-student relations and high teacher morale tend to achieve better results, on average across countries and particularly in some countries. Even after accounting for socio-economic background and other aspects of the learning environment measured by PISA, the results show that reading performance is positively related to higher values on the *PISA index of teacher-student relationship* in 10 OECD countries, including the United States; on the *index of disciplinary climate* in 16 OECD countries, including the United States; and on the *index of teacher-related factors affecting school climate* in 14 OECD countries, including the United States (Table IV.2.13c in *PISA 2009 Results Volume IV*). It is noteworthy that in no country is there a negative relationship between any of these factors and learning outcomes.

The learning environment is also shaped by parents and school principals. Parents who are interested in their children's education are more likely to support their school's efforts and participate in school activities, thus adding to available resources. These parents also tend to have an advantaged socio-economic background. In addition, school principals can define their schools' educational objectives and guide their schools towards them. PISA shows that school principals' perceptions of parents' constant pressure to adopt high academic standards and to raise student achievement tend to be positively related to higher school performance in 19 OECD countries, although that relationship is not apparent in the United States. In some other countries, much of this relationship is mediated by socio-economic factors (Tables IV.2.13b and IV.2.13c in *PISA 2009 Results Volume IV*).

PISA also shows that the socio-economic background of students and schools and key features of the learning environment are closely interrelated. Both link to performance in important ways, perhaps because students from socio-economically advantaged backgrounds bring with them a higher level of discipline and more positive perceptions of school values, or perhaps because parental expectations of good classroom discipline are higher, and teacher commitment is stronger, in schools with advantaged socio-economic intake. Conversely, disadvantaged schools may be under less parental pressure to reinforce effective disciplinary practices or ensure that absent or unmotivated teachers are replaced. In summary, students perform better in schools with a more positive school climate, partly because such schools tend to have more students from advantaged backgrounds who generally perform well, partly because the favourable socio-economic characteristics of students reinforce the favourable climate, and partly for reasons unrelated to socio-economic variables. In many countries, the effect of parental pressure is particularly closely related to socio-economic background, with little independent effect, whereas factors related to the climate within the school, such as discipline and teacher-student relations, are also related to performance independently of socio-economic and demographic variables.

Some of the factors underlying these analyses are examined in greater detail in the following sections, which also position the United States along the various dimensions.

Teacher-student relations

Positive teacher-student relations can help to establish an environment that is conducive to learning. Research finds that students, particularly disadvantaged students, tend to learn more and have fewer disciplinary problems when they feel that their teachers take them seriously. One explanation is that positive teacher-student relations help foster social relationships, create communal learning environments and promote and strengthen adherence to norms conducive to learning. PISA asked students to agree or disagree with several statements regarding their relationships with their teachers in school. These statements include whether students get along with the teachers and whether teachers are interested in their personal well-being, whether teachers take the student seriously, whether teachers are a source of support if students need extra help, and whether teachers treat the student fairly. Students in the United States reported one of the best teacher-student relations among OECD countries (Figure IV.4.1 in *PISA 2009 Results Volume IV*). For example, over 80% of students in the United States agree or strongly agree that their teachers are interested in their well-being, whereas only 28% of students in Japan do so. As in the majority of countries, there is a positive relationship between teacher-student relations and student performance in both the United States and Japan. For example, the quarter of students in the United States who reported the poorest relationships with their teachers are 1.6 times more likely to be also among the quarter of the poorest performing students (for Japan the odds are 2.0).[12] Differences in student-reported teacher interest in their well-being may reflect either different student expectations of the level of involvement of their teachers, or different roles that teachers assume with respect to their students. A low percentage of agreement with these statements suggests a possible mismatch between student expectations and what teachers are actually doing.

Disciplinary climate

The disciplinary climate in the classroom and school can also affect learning. Classrooms and schools with more disciplinary problems are less conducive to learning, since teachers have to spend more time creating an orderly environment before instruction can begin. More interruptions within the classroom disrupt students' engagement and their ability to follow the lessons. PISA asked students to describe the frequency with which interruptions occur in reading lessons. The disciplinary climate is indicated in PISA by how often student do not listen to the teacher during lessons on the language of instruction; there is noise and disorder; the teacher has to wait a long time for students to quiet down; students cannot work well; and students do not start working for a long time after the lesson begins. The majority of students in OECD countries enjoy orderly classrooms in their language classes. Some 75% of students report that they never or only in some lessons feel that students do not start working for a long time after the lesson begins; 71% of students report that they never or only in some lessons feel that students do not listen; 68% report that noise never or only in some lessons affects learning; 72% say that their teacher never or only in some lessons has to wait a long time before students settle down; and 81% of the students attend classrooms where they feel they can work well practically most of the time (Figure IV.4.2 in *PISA 2009 Results Volume IV*).

■ Figure 2.8 ■

School principals' views of how teacher behaviour affects students' learning

Index of teacher-related factors affecting school climate based on school principals' reports

A — Teachers' low expectations of students
B — Poor student-teacher relations
C — Teachers not meeting individual students' needs
D — Teacher absenteeism
E — Staff resisting change
F — Teachers being too strict with students
G — Students not being encouraged to achieve their full potential

Range between top and bottom quarter
♦ Average index

	Percentage of students in schools whose principals reported that the following phenomena hindered learning "not at all" or "very little"							Variability in the index (S.D.)
	A	B	C	D	E	F	G	
OECD								
Australia	68	85	58	86	61	96	78	0.91
Austria	86	94	78	78	76	97	87	0.84
Belgium	87	96	76	75	71	96	84	0.86
Canada	86	89	75	88	62	94	86	0.82
Chile	51	92	62	69	60	86	57	1.00
Czech Republic	83	83	94	96	86	90	75	0.72
Denmark	95	97	88	89	91	98	93	0.82
Estonia	82	87	68	89	87	82	77	0.83
Finland	94	88	67	80	84	97	86	0.69
France	w	w	w	w	w	w	w	w
Germany	82	93	77	78	70	96	89	0.75
Greece	64	82	70	86	76	89	76	1.05
Hungary	94	96	94	94	90	89	69	0.86
Iceland	90	88	71	83	84	97	92	0.85
Ireland	78	92	76	88	82	89	84	0.87
Israel	73	86	67	71	80	90	80	0.86
Italy	74	73	73	91	48	85	67	0.84
Japan	76	85	71	97	63	81	61	0.87
Korea	66	90	67	99	66	84	83	0.79
Luxembourg	95	88	64	82	84	89	71	0.71
Mexico	65	81	69	78	59	80	60	1.01
Netherlands	66	90	44	62	61	86	45	0.67
New Zealand	63	83	57	95	73	95	82	0.79
Norway	80	90	52	75	79	98	77	0.71
Poland	90	98	89	77	85	98	91	0.86
Portugal	74	96	77	98	67	100	79	0.90
Slovak Republic	87	94	88	80	79	75	78	0.79
Slovenia	83	90	78	85	68	87	81	0.84
Spain	75	91	85	91	67	92	74	0.92
Sweden	77	93	64	87	67	99	75	0.83
Switzerland	94	91	81	96	74	97	89	0.73
Turkey	28	25	39	30	25	32	27	1.29
United Kingdom	79	97	77	87	83	98	92	0.80
United States	77	90	72	91	68	96	84	0.79
OECD average	78	88	72	83	72	90	77	0.84
Partners								
Albania	86	91	91	96	93	97	81	0.84
Argentina	70	88	73	51	62	87	55	1.09
Azerbaijan	67	67	80	82	81	91	76	1.09
Brazil	56	89	58	70	64	92	65	0.95
Bulgaria	73	84	70	73	87	88	72	1.13
Colombia	66	93	66	79	49	81	63	1.09
Croatia	79	90	75	94	58	90	72	0.82
Dubai (UAE)	86	89	80	86	77	87	92	1.23
Hong Kong-China	58	93	52	87	77	94	69	0.81
Indonesia	86	96	90	97	90	92	69	0.87
Jordan	60	62	64	58	61	86	69	1.08
Kazakhstan	43	60	55	60	66	60	58	1.38
Kyrgyzstan	54	71	69	66	64	65	59	1.37
Latvia	90	93	81	91	93	89	77	0.83
Liechtenstein	94	100	80	100	83	100	100	0.49
Lithuania	94	99	93	98	96	99	96	0.68
Macao-China	73	73	44	66	66	83	57	1.38
Montenegro	85	95	73	88	88	93	58	0.71
Panama	62	89	69	75	57	81	61	1.03
Peru	64	91	72	85	69	83	63	0.95
Qatar	77	80	82	88	84	88	85	1.07
Romania	84	90	89	99	69	91	83	0.80
Russian Federation	60	79	68	78	65	56	58	1.07
Serbia	71	94	70	93	59	84	61	0.78
Shanghai-China	58	59	45	71	60	73	47	1.33
Singapore	64	83	59	84	83	90	90	0.92
Chinese Taipei	52	57	54	70	56	67	52	1.42
Thailand	67	82	72	90	90	68	87	0.86
Trinidad and Tobago	45	66	34	41	54	91	71	0.94
Tunisia	33	83	69	40	73	83	74	0.86
Uruguay	53	92	68	35	57	94	33	1.03

-3.5   -2.5   -1.5   -0.5 0 0.5   1.5   2.5 Index points

Note: Higher values on the index indicate a positive teacher behaviour.
Source: OECD, *PISA 2009 Database*, Table IV.4.5.
StatLink ⌯⌲⌳ http://dx.doi.org/10.1787/888932366636

■ Figure 2.9 ■

School principals' views of their involvement in school matters
Index of school principal's leadership based on school principals' reports

A — I make sure that the professional development activities of teachers are in accordance with the teaching goals of the school.
B — I ensure that teachers work according to the school's educational goals.
C — I observe instruction in classrooms.
D — I use student performance results to develop the school's educational goals.
E — I give teachers suggestions as to how they can improve their teaching.
F — I monitor students' work.
G — When a teacher has problems in his/her classroom, I take the initiative to discuss matters.
H — I inform teachers about possibilities for updating their knowledge and skills.
I — I check to see whether classroom activities are in keeping with our educational goals.
J — I take exam results into account in decisions regarding curriculum development.
K — I ensure that there is clarity concerning the responsibility for co-ordinating the curriculum.
L — When a teacher brings up a classroom problem, we solve the problem together.
M — I pay attention to disruptive behaviour in classrooms.
N — I take over lessons from teachers who are unexpectedly absent.

Percentage of students in schools whose principals reported that the following activities and behaviours occurred "quite often" or "very often" during the last school year

— Range between top and bottom quarter
◆ Average index

	A	B	C	D	E	F	G	H	I	J	K	L	M	N	Variability in the index (S.D.)
OECD															
Australia	98	99	64	93	76	58	89	95	81	81	97	93	94	32	1.0
Austria	89	92	41	60	67	86	84	79	67	22	75	92	87	53	0.8
Belgium	95	97	43	42	68	33	89	90	82	46	74	98	96	4	0.8
Canada	98	98	77	91	86	60	95	95	86	63	87	99	98	19	1.0
Chile	97	98	55	93	95	73	90	96	82	84	94	97	97	62	1.1
Czech Republic	95	98	57	81	79	93	86	98	83	59	93	96	75	23	0.8
Denmark	86	89	25	44	53	39	94	91	76	25	76	99	95	29	0.6
Estonia	92	94	59	84	58	75	72	93	57	62	87	83	79	24	0.9
Finland	64	75	9	46	40	61	77	95	59	13	77	98	94	39	0.7
France	w	w	w	w	w	w	w	w	w	w	w	w	w	w	w
Germany	82	94	40	57	53	82	80	85	57	33	73	95	84	42	0.7
Greece	40	78	12	61	53	46	97	96	67	34	69	98	96	63	1.0
Hungary	93	99	54	84	62	84	89	91	65	73	86	94	91	41	0.8
Iceland	88	89	39	78	77	69	87	96	54	58	87	100	75	26	0.7
Ireland	88	88	14	64	41	50	88	92	62	78	88	97	97	39	0.9
Israel	94	99	46	87	85	81	94	89	86	90	94	97	98	26	0.9
Italy	97	99	39	86	75	87	96	98	88	77	92	98	98	18	0.9
Japan	43	51	37	30	38	40	29	50	31	37	29	61	60	17	0.9
Korea	80	85	42	64	68	56	75	69	60	46	63	79	68	7	1.2
Luxembourg	87	98	32	65	52	64	96	67	74	32	47	98	98	23	1.0
Mexico	95	97	68	94	89	90	95	91	92	62	90	97	96	43	1.0
Netherlands	95	97	52	66	73	50	76	82	79	75	80	86	71	16	0.7
New Zealand	99	98	68	98	73	42	78	84	74	87	97	83	94	12	1.0
Norway	81	88	24	70	49	55	90	91	48	47	81	98	95	28	0.6
Poland	94	97	93	95	89	96	91	99	92	71	80	97	93	37	0.8
Portugal	93	97	9	94	65	49	91	89	48	82	97	99	97	7	0.7
Slovak Republic	97	99	86	87	86	90	86	98	91	76	96	91	91	15	0.7
Slovenia	99	100	77	78	85	90	90	95	85	65	93	98	94	23	0.8
Spain	86	97	28	85	55	45	86	86	66	71	92	99	99	63	0.9
Sweden	90	96	38	83	63	29	89	90	52	68	93	98	87	13	0.8
Switzerland	72	82	64	34	60	61	85	80	59	17	54	92	83	31	0.8
Turkey	85	95	70	93	85	90	75	90	87	78	93	97	99	36	0.9
United Kingdom	100	100	93	100	92	88	90	96	95	97	99	96	97	29	0.9
United States	98	98	95	96	94	72	95	97	94	88	90	97	96	16	1.1
OECD average	88	93	50	75	69	66	86	89	72	61	82	94	90	29	0.9
Partners															
Albania	97	100	98	99	94	94	90	88	93	87	93	96	96	47	0.8
Argentina	95	98	63	90	96	84	94	91	86	66	87	98	96	43	0.9
Azerbaijan	95	96	97	89	97	99	86	96	99	86	90	90	99	77	1.0
Brazil	99	99	60	94	94	91	97	97	91	94	94	99	99	44	1.1
Bulgaria	100	100	92	95	79	93	87	98	94	71	98	91	96	29	0.8
Colombia	98	99	45	85	92	88	90	96	82	87	92	96	96	31	1.2
Croatia	94	98	70	80	92	96	96	95	98	76	95	99	100	19	0.8
Dubai (UAE)	100	100	95	97	98	93	98	99	98	90	93	98	97	39	1.2
Hong Kong-China	99	99	99	97	100	93	96	98	95	92	97	96	96	45	0.9
Indonesia	94	99	88	91	99	77	89	96	96	95	96	81	93	47	1.0
Jordan	99	100	100	99	100	98	99	99	99	81	81	100	99	90	1.1
Kazakhstan	96	98	98	95	97	85	98	99	60	87	86	89	89	17	0.8
Kyrgyzstan	90	92	98	90	94	98	89	96	95	82	87	86	81	29	0.9
Latvia	96	97	80	97	83	86	85	94	85	75	83	76	85	30	0.8
Liechtenstein	53	21	3	15	14	46	82	16	10	0	13	96	58	44	0.7
Lithuania	97	98	47	92	75	60	74	89	55	65	89	95	83	7	0.8
Macao-China	100	100	88	74	82	86	93	76	86	52	88	90	90	45	0.9
Montenegro	95	100	88	97	97	100	92	100	99	84	100	100	96	23	0.7
Panama	91	95	86	88	95	84	90	92	95	85	88	97	94	43	1.1
Peru	94	98	86	88	93	80	80	94	92	84	91	91	95	45	1.1
Qatar	96	100	100	98	97	94	95	95	98	84	87	96	96	28	1.1
Romania	98	100	87	98	90	90	96	98	99	91	99	100	99	40	0.8
Russian Federation	99	99	92	89	87	95	80	99	92	55	97	96	86	31	0.9
Serbia	97	100	67	90	91	82	97	99	87	93	91	97	97	44	0.8
Shanghai-China	98	98	94	57	99	69	91	93	96	70	98	99	89	14	0.8
Singapore	100	100	99	94	94	93	93	93	98	97	96	97	96	8	0.9
Chinese Taipei	98	98	92	84	86	94	86	98	88	90	95	97	95	20	0.9
Thailand	94	99	88	98	95	97	94	98	94	95	96	97	97	45	0.9
Trinidad and Tobago	97	98	60	86	88	71	94	95	84	92	95	97	98	26	1.0
Tunisia	84	97	92	92	97	60	97	82	84	40	59	99	99	45	1.1
Uruguay	85	98	89	90	90	81	92	94	84	45	73	98	100	25	1.0

-3 -2 -1 0 1 2 3 4 Index points

Note: Higher values on the index indicate greater involvement of school principals in school matters.
Source: OECD, *PISA 2009 Database*, Table IV.4.8.

StatLink ⟐⟐⟐ http://dx.doi.org/10.1787/888932366636

The United States does reasonably well on this measure, but the benchmark countries Japan, Korea or Germany show a significantly better disciplinary climate. What is also noteworthy is that there is considerable variation on this measure among students in the United States, and the quarter of students who reported the poorest disciplinary climate are twice as likely to be poor performers. This odds ratio is the second highest among all countries participating in PISA (OECD average odds 1.4) (Table IV.4.2 in *PISA 2009 Results Volume IV*).

It is noteworthy that the judgment of school principals on the disciplinary climate in the United States is less positive than what students report, and the mismatch between these perspectives may indicate differences in what students and school principals perceive to be problems (Table IV.4.4 in *PISA 2009 Results Volume IV*).[13]

Teacher-related factors affecting the school climate

To determine the extent to which teacher behaviour influences student learning, school principals in PISA were asked to report the extent to which they perceived learning in their schools to be hindered by such factors as teachers' low expectations of students, poor student-teacher relations, absenteeism among teachers, staff resistance to change, teachers not meeting individual students' needs, teachers being too strict with students, and students not being encouraged to achieve their full potential. The United States performed around the OECD average on these measures, but the reports from school principals highlight a number of challenges: 23% of students in the United States are enrolled in schools whose principals reported that teachers' low expectations of students hinder learning to some extent or a lot (in contrast, in the benchmark country Finland, that percentage is just 6%), 28% that this is the case because teachers do not meet individual students' needs, and 32% because staff resist change (Figure 2.8). In contrast, only 4% of school principals see teachers being too strict with students as a problem, and 10% or less see poor student-teacher relationships or teacher absenteeism as a problem that hinders learning.

HOW SCHOOLING IS ORGANISED

Governance of school systems

Many countries have pursued a shift in public and governmental concern away from mere control over the resources and content of education towards a focus on outcomes. This becomes evident when the distribution of decision-making responsibilities in education is reviewed across successive PISA assessments. In addition, school systems have made efforts to devolve responsibility to the frontline, encouraging responsiveness to local needs, and strengthening accountability (Figures 2.10 and 2.11). PISA shows a clear relationship between learning outcomes and the relative autonomy of schools in managing instructional policies and practices across systems when autonomy is coupled with accountability. Of course, the United States is a decentralised education system too, but while many systems have decentralised decisions concerning the delivery of educational services while keeping tight control over the definition of outcomes, the design of curricula, standards and testing, the United States is different in that it has decentralised both inputs and control over outcomes. That has only just begun to change with the recent introduction and progressive adoption, by individual states, of common core educational standards. Moreover, while the United States has devolved responsibilities to local authorities or districts, their schools often have less discretion in decision-making than is the case in many OECD countries. In this sense, the question for the United States is not just how many charter schools it establishes but how to build the capacity for all schools to exercise responsible autonomy, as happens in most of the benchmark systems.

Important organisational features of school systems are the degree to which students and parents can choose schools, and the degree to which schools are considered autonomous entities that make organisational decisions independently of district, regional or national entities. Results from PISA suggest that school autonomy in defining curricula and assessments relates positively to the systems' overall performance (Figure 2.11, Figures IV.3.3 and IV.2.4a in *PISA 2009 Results Volume IV*). For example, school systems that provide schools with greater discretion in making decisions regarding student assessment policies, the courses offered, the course content and the textbooks used, tend to be school systems that perform at higher levels.

Data from PISA also show that in school systems where most schools post achievement data publicly, schools with greater discretion in managing their resources tend to show higher levels of performance. In school systems where schools do not post achievement data publicly, a student who attends a school with greater autonomy in resource management than the average OECD school tends to perform 3.2 score points lower in reading than a student attending a school with an average level of autonomy. In contrast, in school systems where schools do post achievement data publicly, a student who attends a school with above-average autonomy scores 2.6 points *higher* in reading than a student attending a school with an average level of autonomy (Table IV.2.5 in *PISA 2009 Results Volume IV*).

■ Figure 2.10 ■

How much autonomy individual schools have over resource allocation

Percentage of students in schools whose principals reported that only "principals and/or teachers", only "regional and/or national education authority" or both "principals and/or teachers" and "regional and/or national education authority" have a considerable responsibility for the following tasks

- **A** Selecting teachers for hire
- **B** Dismissing teachers
- **C** Establishing teachers' starting salaries
- **D** Determining teachers' salaries increases
- **E** Formulating the school budget
- **F** Deciding on budget allocations within the school

- **1** Only "principals and/or teachers"
- **2** Both "principals and/or teachers" and "regional and/or national education authority"
- **3** Only "regional and/or national education authority"

▬▬ Range between top and bottom quarter
◆ Average index

	A1	A2	A3	B1	B2	B3	C1	C2	C3	D1	D2	D3	E1	E2	E3	F1	F2	F3	Index of school responsibility for resource allocation	Variability in the index (S.D.)
OECD																				
Australia	61	20	19	43	12	45	12	5	84	13	6	81	68	16	16	93	6	0		0.9
Austria	13	35	52	5	26	68	1	0	99	1	0	99	11	9	80	84	12	4		0.3
Belgium	75	13	12	63	21	17	0	1	99	0	1	99	56	18	26	63	19	17		0.3
Canada	54	39	7	17	35	48	3	5	92	4	6	91	25	30	45	76	19	5		0.5
Chile	69	8	23	59	3	38	37	1	62	37	1	62	55	9	36	71	9	20		1.2
Czech Republic	100	0	0	99	1	0	77	15	8	65	25	11	55	36	9	75	24	1		1.2
Denmark	97	2	0	69	15	16	20	10	70	16	14	70	80	13	8	98	2	0		0.9
Estonia	98	2	0	95	5	0	7	20	73	12	33	55	37	54	9	85	15	1		0.6
Finland	32	43	25	18	19	63	8	7	84	5	15	80	36	41	23	92	6	1		0.5
France	w	w	w	w	w	w	w	w	w	w	w	w	w	w	w	w	w	w		w
Germany	29	36	34	7	14	79	3	0	97	4	15	81	29	4	67	97	2	2		0.5
Greece	0	1	99	0	2	98	0	0	100	0	0	100	34	7	59	59	7	34		0.1
Hungary	99	1	0	97	2	1	49	7	44	56	7	37	73	15	12	92	5	2		1.2
Iceland	94	6	0	93	7	0	7	13	80	4	16	80	57	30	13	77	22	0		0.5
Ireland	61	25	14	36	14	50	0	2	98	1	0	99	60	13	27	89	5	6		0.2
Israel	67	30	3	49	38	13	9	4	87	13	6	80	15	26	59	66	24	11		0.8
Italy	9	10	82	9	6	84	3	0	97	3	0	96	7	7	86	69	11	21		0.5
Japan	25	2	73	22	1	77	13	0	87	16	3	80	28	4	69	89	3	8		1.0
Korea	32	6	62	23	4	74	8	0	92	6	0	94	29	12	58	86	6	8		0.7
Luxembourg	21	41	38	19	36	45	6	0	94	6	0	94	31	57	12	78	14	8		0.8
Mexico	34	5	61	22	4	73	8	0	92	6	0	94	46	6	48	71	7	22		0.8
Netherlands	100	0	0	99	1	0	72	8	20	55	12	33	99	1	0	100	0	0		1.0
New Zealand	100	0	0	89	7	4	9	3	88	15	21	64	95	4	1	99	1	0		0.7
Norway	72	21	6	44	22	34	8	4	88	6	13	81	55	28	17	88	12	1		0.6
Poland	87	12	1	90	10	0	9	20	71	4	20	77	7	42	51	26	43	31		0.4
Portugal	13	57	30	14	0	86	5	0	94	5	0	94	63	10	27	89	3	8		0.7
Slovak Republic	98	2	0	98	2	0	39	27	34	32	33	35	45	40	15	70	27	3		1.1
Slovenia	96	4	1	88	10	1	7	11	82	13	31	56	26	49	26	78	21	1		0.6
Spain	31	3	66	32	1	67	3	2	95	3	2	95	63	4	33	93	4	3		0.6
Sweden	96	4	0	63	17	20	57	16	27	69	22	9	64	20	16	93	5	2		1.1
Switzerland	82	15	3	60	26	15	8	8	84	8	13	79	35	30	35	83	13	4		0.7
Turkey	1	1	99	2	2	96	1	0	99	1	0	99	34	19	47	56	16	28		0.2
United Kingdom	90	9	0	70	22	8	52	23	25	67	17	15	57	29	14	95	5	1		1.1
United States	88	12	0	75	19	6	17	5	78	18	6	75	54	29	16	83	13	4		0.9
OECD average	61	14	25	51	13	37	17	7	77	17	10	73	46	22	32	81	12	8		0.7
Partners																				
Albania	8	14	78	7	14	79	3	0	97	3	1	96	33	12	55	61	8	31		0.5
Argentina	44	5	51	27	3	70	2	1	97	1	4	96	22	5	73	64	12	24		0.4
Azerbaijan	40	22	38	61	17	22	35	6	59	13	3	84	5	6	89	20	4	76		0.3
Brazil	17	7	76	14	8	78	8	1	91	7	1	92	14	5	80	21	6	73		0.8
Bulgaria	93	5	2	97	2	1	66	20	14	84	12	4	73	22	5	92	7	1		1.1
Colombia	21	5	75	21	1	79	0	0	86	13	1	86	58	5	36	87	5	8		1.0
Croatia	90	10	0	84	11	5	1	1	98	2	1	97	26	34	40	68	23	9		0.4
Dubai (UAE)	65	12	23	67	9	24	62	3	34	68	1	31	75	2	22	92	3	5		1.2
Hong Kong-China	83	15	2	79	17	4	18	24	58	18	12	71	84	15	2	91	9	0		0.9
Indonesia	29	12	59	26	11	63	20	9	70	23	11	66	83	11	5	78	14	8		1.0
Jordan	6	1	93	4	1	95	1	1	98	2	0	98	83	1	17	70	2	28		0.4
Kazakhstan	88	10	2	95	4	2	17	10	73	8	10	82	8	13	79	17	19	64		0.7
Kyrgyzstan	74	14	11	68	13	19	18	4	77	13	3	84	12	7	81	19	7	74		0.6
Latvia	94	4	2	96	4	0	10	15	75	18	25	57	62	25	12	81	16	3		0.7
Liechtenstein	41	0	59	37	0	63	6	0	94	37	0	63	100	0	0	0	0	0		1.0
Lithuania	96	4	0	99	1	0	11	7	81	6	8	86	25	27	48	42	29	28		0.5
Macao-China	92	4	4	91	5	4	91	4	5	90	4	5	95	5	0	84	16	0		1.0
Montenegro	89	11	0	82	18	0	0	5	95	10	11	78	12	21	68	65	22	13		0.3
Panama	22	3	76	20	8	72	14	5	81	14	8	79	70	15	15	43	10	47		0.9
Peru	38	15	47	30	9	61	22	2	76	22	2	77	60	9	31	79	6	15		1.3
Qatar	52	3	44	54	5	41	47	3	50	47	4	50	43	4	53	52	4	44		1.2
Romania	1	9	91	4	11	86	0	2	97	1	4	95	7	25	68	40	13	47		0.1
Russian Federation	95	4	1	95	5	0	35	15	50	29	20	51	8	30	63	46	28	27		0.7
Serbia	72	28	1	64	30	7	1	8	90	16	19	65	9	27	64	74	16	10		0.3
Shanghai-China	98	2	0	99	1	0	36	5	59	43	6	51	91	2	6	98	1	1		1.1
Singapore	14	38	48	14	24	62	4	3	93	7	17	75	49	22	29	91	8	1		0.6
Chinese Taipei	73	13	14	74	14	12	18	7	75	23	7	70	50	13	37	78	8	14		1.0
Thailand	30	20	50	59	12	28	29	14	56	72	24	5	70	20	10	99	7	2		1.1
Trinidad and Tobago	17	14	69	6	4	90	2	1	96	6	5	89	46	28	26	75	12	12		0.6
Tunisia	2	0	98	1	0	99	1	1	99	1	0	99	10	18	72	78	13	9		0.3
Uruguay	17	5	78	13	1	86	3	1	96	2	1	96	13	12	75	49	16	35		0.6

-2.0 -1.5 -1.0 -0.5 0 0.5 1.0 1.5 2.0 2.5 Index points

Source: OECD, *PISA 2009 Database*, Table IV.3.5.
StatLink ᴍˢᴾ http://dx.doi.org/10.1787/888932366636

■ Figure 2.11 ■

How much autonomy individual schools have over curricula and assessments

Percentage of students in schools whose principals reported that only "principals and/or teachers", only "regional and/or national education authority" or both "principals and/or teachers" and "regional and/or national education authority" have a considerable responsibility for the following tasks

A Establishing student assessment policies
B Choosing which textbooks are used
C Determining course content
D Deciding which courses are offered

1 Only "principals and/or teachers"
2 Both "principals and/or teachers" and "regional and/or national education authority"
3 Only "regional and/or national education authority"

━━ Range between top and bottom quarter
◆ Average index

	A 1	A 2	A 3	B 1	B 2	B 3	C 1	C 2	C 3	D 1	D 2	D 3	Index of school responsibility for curriculum and assessment	Variability in the index (S.D.)
OECD														
Australia	65	33	2	92	8	0	46	40	14	75	24	1		0.9
Austria	57	27	15	94	5	1	37	40	23	32	40	29		0.8
Belgium	78	19	4	94	4	1	32	42	26	40	46	13		0.8
Canada	28	62	10	40	49	11	12	51	38	44	54	3		0.6
Chile	72	21	6	73	20	7	43	22	35	64	20	16		1.0
Czech Republic	95	5	0	89	11	1	83	16	1	88	11	1		0.8
Denmark	61	28	11	100	0	0	56	32	12	47	39	14		0.9
Estonia	63	33	3	66	32	2	66	30	4	79	20	2		0.9
Finland	50	43	7	98	2	0	32	52	16	55	39	6		0.8
France	w	w	w	w	w	w	w	w	w	w	w	w		w
Germany	71	21	9	84	13	3	21	47	32	80	18	2		0.7
Greece	20	12	68	7	8	85	1	3	96	6	5	88		0.3
Hungary	94	6	0	98	2	0	49	36	15	43	28	29		0.9
Iceland	92	8	1	93	4	3	61	26	13	48	42	10		0.9
Ireland	87	13	0	97	3	0	29	37	34	78	21	1		0.7
Israel	80	20	0	53	43	4	52	44	5	44	50	6		1.0
Italy	91	8	1	99	1	0	59	27	14	49	25	27		0.9
Japan	98	2	0	89	8	3	93	6	1	94	5	2		0.7
Korea	92	6	2	96	4	0	89	8	2	79	17	4		0.8
Luxembourg	9	33	58	13	80	7	9	72	20	18	61	21		0.6
Mexico	56	15	29	63	11	26	14	7	79	5	5	91		0.5
Netherlands	99	1	0	100	0	0	87	12	1	89	10	1		0.6
New Zealand	81	17	2	99	1	0	79	20	1	92	8	0		0.8
Norway	38	36	27	97	2	1	30	40	30	23	33	44		0.7
Poland	92	8	0	92	8	0	93	7	0	40	31	29		0.8
Portugal	35	37	28	98	2	0	5	3	92	10	5	86		0.4
Slovak Republic	76	21	3	56	39	5	48	47	5	52	48	1		1.0
Slovenia	46	48	5	72	27	1	34	59	6	28	52	20		0.8
Spain	44	34	23	95	5	0	32	31	37	30	31	39		0.8
Sweden	66	30	3	99	1	0	66	26	8	53	25	22		1.0
Switzerland	57	27	16	40	40	20	21	41	38	24	50	27		0.7
Turkey	42	29	30	14	18	68	9	15	76	14	21	65		0.4
United Kingdom	88	12	0	98	2	0	77	20	2	86	14	0		0.8
United States	46	40	13	62	28	10	36	46	18	58	37	4		0.9
OECD average	66	23	11	78	15	8	45	31	24	50	28	21		0.8
Partners														
Albania	51	16	33	91	8	1	35	7	57	35	12	53		0.8
Argentina	74	20	6	81	16	3	28	43	29	8	30	61		0.6
Azerbaijan	54	8	38	50	6	43	27	9	64	37	5	58		0.8
Brazil	47	27	26	88	9	2	35	25	40	18	17	65		0.8
Bulgaria	25	37	38	88	12	1	10	26	65	10	15	75		0.4
Colombia	39	21	39	92	3	4	69	23	8	64	14	23		0.8
Croatia	26	36	38	63	34	3	11	50	39	2	25	72		0.4
Dubai (UAE)	77	10	13	55	17	27	62	13	26	59	16	25		1.1
Hong Kong-China	93	7	0	93	7	0	81	17	2	87	13	0		0.8
Indonesia	67	28	6	80	13	7	75	18	7	49	23	28		0.9
Jordan	27	4	70	4	1	95	7	1	93	7	1	92		0.5
Kazakhstan	31	22	47	16	14	70	11	18	71	40	22	37		0.5
Kyrgyzstan	65	8	26	68	8	23	59	10	31	44	7	49		1.0
Latvia	56	40	4	71	27	2	19	46	36	30	42	28		0.6
Liechtenstein	69	25	6	54	5	40	41	0	59	53	9	38		1.1
Lithuania	75	20	5	89	11	1	50	35	15	75	20	5		0.9
Macao-China	95	0	5	100	0	0	94	6	0	81	14	4		0.8
Montenegro	40	32	28	5	30	65	5	34	61	20	36	44		0.6
Panama	41	25	34	52	26	22	41	23	36	26	23	51		0.8
Peru	75	15	10	52	12	37	53	23	24	45	18	37		1.0
Qatar	45	18	37	37	16	47	31	9	60	35	17	48		0.9
Romania	42	36	22	86	13	1	46	33	20	31	41	29		0.7
Russian Federation	63	25	12	65	27	8	21	40	39	71	22	7		0.8
Serbia	49	44	7	19	59	23	2	41	57	0	12	87		0.2
Shanghai-China	86	9	5	49	17	34	45	22	33	52	28	20		1.0
Singapore	57	41	2	72	24	3	44	38	18	66	31	4		0.9
Chinese Taipei	74	17	8	92	8	0	81	16	3	68	25	7		0.9
Thailand	79	18	2	89	10	1	89	11	0	91	8	1		0.8
Trinidad and Tobago	50	45	5	29	62	10	21	40	39	34	51	15		0.7
Tunisia	11	11	78	0	1	99	3	14	83	4	9	87		0.1
Uruguay	23	30	47	31	36	33	3	26	71	21	19	59		0.4

-2.0 -1.5 -1.0 -0.5 0 0.5 1.0 1.5 2.0 2.5 Index points

Source: OECD, *PISA 2009 Database*, Table IV.3.6.
StatLink ⇒ http://dx.doi.org/10.1787/888932366636

PISA classifies OECD countries into four groups that share similar profiles in the way they allow schools and parents to make decisions that affect their children's education. The grouping is based on the levels of school autonomy and school competition. Two categories are identified for each dimension and the interplay between these dimensions results in four groups: school systems that offer high levels of autonomy to schools in designing and using curricula and assessments and encourage more competition between schools; school systems that offer low levels of autonomy to schools and limit competition between schools; school systems that offer high levels of autonomy to schools, but with limited competition between schools; and school systems that offer low levels of autonomy to schools, yet encourage more competition between schools (Figure IV.3.5 in *PISA 2009 Results Volume IV*).

Across OECD countries, the most common configuration is the one that gives schools the freedom to make curricular decisions, yet restricts competition for enrolment among schools. These school systems have relatively limited levels of choice for parents and students and there is little competition for enrolment among schools. Private schools are not widely available in these countries. Twenty-two OECD countries, including the United States, fall into this category.

School systems that offer relatively low levels of autonomy to schools and low levels of choice to parents are also fairly common across OECD countries: four OECD countries share this configuration and 11 partner countries and economies do.

Six other OECD countries offer high levels of autonomy and choice, either in the form of a high prevalence private schools or competition among schools for enrolment. In these school systems, schools have the freedom to choose teaching methods to meet learning objectives, and parents and students can choose among a variety of schools for enrolment. Some of the variables underlying this classification are examined in greater detail below.

School choice

Students in some school systems are encouraged or even obliged to attend their neighbourhood school. However, reforms over the past decades in many countries have tended to give more authority to parents and students to choose schools that meet their educational needs or preferences best. The assumption has been that if students and parents have sound information and choose schools based on academic criteria, this will foster competition among schools and create incentives for institutions to organise programmes and teaching in ways that better respond to diverse student requirements and interests, thus reducing the costs of failure and mismatches. In some school systems, schools not only compete for student enrolment, but also for funding. Direct public funding of independently managed institutions, based on student enrolments or student credit-hours, is one model for this. Giving money to students and their families to spend in public or private educational institutions of their choice through, for example, scholarships or vouchers, is another method (Figure 2.12).

According to the responses of school principals in PISA, across OECD countries, 76% of students attend schools competing with at least one other school for enrolment. Only in Switzerland, Norway and Slovenia do less than 50% of students attend schools that compete with other schools for enrolment. In contrast, in the Netherlands, Australia, Belgium, the Slovak Republic and Japan, over 90% of students attend schools that compete with other schools for enrolment (Table IV3.8a in *PISA 2009 Results Volume IV*).

Some 13 OECD countries allow parents and students to choose public schools and also incorporate vouchers or tax credits in their school-choice arrangements. Eleven OECD countries provide for freedom in the choice of public schools, but do not offer vouchers or tax credits; two OECD countries restrict parents and students in the choice of public schools, but offer tax or voucher credits to attend other schools; and in four OECD countries, parents and students must attend the public school nearest to where they live and are not offered any kind of subsidy to attend other schools (Table IV.3.7 in *PISA 2009 Results Volume IV*).

Competition among schools, as reported by school principals in PISA, is consistent with these school-choice arrangements as reported by central and regional governments, and is greatest in school systems that grant parents and students the freedom to choose public schools and offer subsidies in the form of vouchers or tax credits to attend other schools. In countries with these characteristics, 85% of students attend schools whose principals reported that they compete with at least one other school for enrolment. The lowest levels of school competition are found in countries that restrict attendance to public schools and do not offer subsidies to attend other schools. In the average country in this category, 52% of students attend schools whose principals reported that they compete for student enrolment with at least one other school (Figure 2.12). Levels of school competition are similar in countries that restrict attendance to public schools and offer subsidies, and in countries that do not restrict attendance to public schools yet offer no subsidies. In these countries, around 75% of students attend schools whose principals reported that they compete with other schools for enrolment. The use of vouchers or tax credits and opening choice among public schools enhances school competition for students. However, competition among schools is less frequent in remote and rural areas, where public schools are usually located at greater distances from each other, making it more difficult for parents and students to choose a school other than the one that is closest to their home (Table IV.2.6 in *PISA 2009 Results Volume IV*).

■ Figure 2.12 ■

Countries in which parents can choose schools for their children

Prevalence of school competition by school choice arrangements

More freedom to choose public schools: At most one restriction on choosing public schools (region, district or other restrictions)		Less freedom to choose public schools: At least two restrictions on choosing public schools (region, district or other restrictions)	
Vouchers or Tax Credits to attend other schools: Vouchers or tax credits offered to attend public, government-dependent or private-independent schools	**No Vouchers or Tax Credits to attend other schools:** No vouchers or tax credits offered to attend public, government-dependent or private-independent schools	**Vouchers or Tax Credits to attend other schools:** Vouchers or tax credits offered to attend public, government-dependent or private-independent schools	**No Vouchers or Tax Credits to attend other schools:** No vouchers or tax credits offered to attend public, government-dependent or private-independent schools
Belgium, Chile, Estonia, France, Germany, Italy, Korea, Luxembourg, New Zealand, Portugal, Slovak Republic, Spain, United Kingdom, Lithuania, Macao-China, Montenegro, Qatar, Singapore	Austria, Czech Republic, Denmark, Finland, Japan, Hungary, Ireland, Mexico, Netherlands, Slovenia, Sweden, Bulgaria, Colombia, Hong Kong-China, Kyrgyzstan, Latvia, Peru, Shanghai-China	Poland, **United States,** Argentina, Thailand, Brazil, Chinese Taipei	Iceland, Israel, Norway, Switzerland, Croatia

Note: Bars represent the average percentages of school competition in OECD countries, by four categories of school choice arrangements.
Source: OECD, *PISA 2009 Database*, Tables IV.3.7 and IV.3.8a.
StatLink ⏵⏴ http://dx.doi.org/10.1787/888932366636

Among schools within a country, competition and performance do seem related; but once the socio-economic profile of students and schools are taken into consideration, the relationship weakens, since privileged students are more likely to attend schools that compete for enrolment (Tables IV.2.4b and IV.2.4c in *PISA 2009 Results Volume IV*). This may reflect the fact that socio-economically advantaged students, who tend to achieve higher scores, are also more likely to attend schools that compete for enrolment, even after accounting for location and attendance in private schools (Table IV.2.6 in *PISA 2009 Results Volume IV*).

Why are socio-economically advantaged students more likely to attend schools of their choice? To understand differences in how parents choose schools for their children, PISA asked a series of questions regarding school choice in the questionnaire for parents that was distributed in eight OECD countries (no data from parents are available for the United States). On average, socio-economically disadvantaged parents are over 13 percentage points more likely than advantaged parents to report that they considered "low expenses" and "financial aid" to be very important determining factors in choosing a school (Table IV.2.7 in *PISA 2009 Results Volume IV*). While parents from all backgrounds cite academic achievement as an important consideration when choosing a school for their children, socio-economically advantaged parents are, on average, 10 percentage points more likely than disadvantaged parents to cite that consideration as "very important". It is possible that there can be differences in the parent's reasons due to socio-economic status because some of the priorities are already met in schools available to advantaged parents. Still, these differences suggest that socio-economically disadvantaged parents believe that they have more limited choices of schools for their children because of financial constraints. If children from socio-economically disadvantaged backgrounds cannot attend high-performing schools because of financial constraints, then school systems that offer parents more choice of schools for their children will necessarily be less effective in improving the performance of all students.

Public and private schools

School education takes place mainly in public schools. Nevertheless, with an increasing variety of educational opportunities, programmes and providers, governments are forging new partnerships to mobilise resources for education and to design new policies that allow all stakeholders to participate more fully and share costs and benefits more equitably. Privately provided education is not only a way of mobilising resources from a wider range of funding sources, it is sometimes also considered a way of making education more cost-effective. Publicly financed schools are not necessarily also publicly managed. Instead, governments can transfer funds to public and private educational institutions according to various allocation mechanisms. Indeed, publicly funded private schools are the most common model of private education in OECD countries (see section on school choice, above).

Across OECD countries, 15% of students are enrolled in privately managed schools that are either privately or government funded, although in many countries government authorities retain significant control over these schools, including the power to shut down non-performing schools. Enrolment in privately managed schools exceeds 50% of 15-year-old students in the Netherlands, Ireland and Chile, and between 35% and 40% in Australia and Korea. In contrast, in Turkey, Iceland and Norway, more than 98% of students attend schools that are publicly managed (Table IV.3.9 in *PISA 2009 Results Volume IV*).

On average across OECD countries, privately managed schools show a performance advantage of 30 score points on the PISA reading scale (in the United States, that advantage reaches 65 score points). However, once the socio-economic background of students and schools is accounted for, public schools come out with a slight advantage of seven score points, on average across OECD countries (in the United States, public and privately managed schools do not show a difference in performance once the socio-economic background is accounted for).

Selection of students into schools, grades and programmes

While teaching and learning are at the heart of schooling, they are supported by a complex organisation responsible for everything from selecting and admitting students to schools and classrooms, to evaluating their progress, formulating curricula, promoting successful approaches to teaching and learning, creating incentives to motivate students and teachers and deciding on the distribution of financial, material and human resources – all with the aim of providing quality education. This section looks at how school systems are organised to allocate students to programmes, schools and classes.

In the high-performing benchmark countries of this volume, it is the responsibility of schools and teachers to engage constructively with the diversity of student interests, capacities and socio-economic contexts, without having the option of making students repeat the school year or transferring them to educational tracks or school types with lower performance requirements. The data from PISA show that creating homogeneous schools and/or classrooms through selection is unrelated to the average performance of education systems, but clearly associated with larger variation in student achievement and a significantly larger impact of socio-economic background on learning outcomes. In particular, the earlier in the student's career the selection occurs, the greater the impact of socio-economic background on learning outcomes. That suggests that selection tends to reinforce inequities as students from disadvantaged backgrounds tend to be exposed to lower quality learning opportunities when compared to their peers from more advantaged socio-economic backgrounds (Figure IV.2.1 in *PISA 2009 Results Volume IV*).

PISA data also show grade repetition to be not only negatively related to equity but also negatively related to the average performance of education systems. That is, school systems with high grade repetition rates tend to also be school systems with lower student performance. Moreover, the more schools group students by ability across all subjects, and the more frequently schools transfer students to other schools because of students' low academic achievement, behavioural problems or special learning needs, the lower the school systems' overall performance, even after accounting for national income. While transferring difficult students out of a school may be advantageous to the school, it seems to relate negatively to the performance of the education system as a whole, and to larger performance differences between schools (Figure IV.2.1a in *PISA 2009 Results Volume IV*). School transfers may hurt student achievement because changing schools implies a loss of social capital inasmuch students have limited access to the resources that are shared in the school they are moving out of and need to recreate support and friendship networks. Furthermore, when transfers are motivated by behavioural problems, low academic achievement and special learning needs, students that are transferred out are more likely to be received by schools with a higher prevalence of similar students. Students that are transferred for these reasons not only pay the cost in terms of lost social capital, but are also less likely to benefit from higher-achieving peers. Also, in systems where transferring students or grade repetition is commonplace, teachers and the school community have an incentive to evade problems by transferring students, rather than committing effort and resources to solving the underlying problems. They also tend to have more autonomy to adapt the learning environment in their schools (Figure 2.13). Equally important, a higher rate of student transfers also seems to be related to greater socio-economic inequities.

■ Figure 2.13 ■
School systems with low transfer rates tend to give more autonomy to schools to determine curricula and assessments

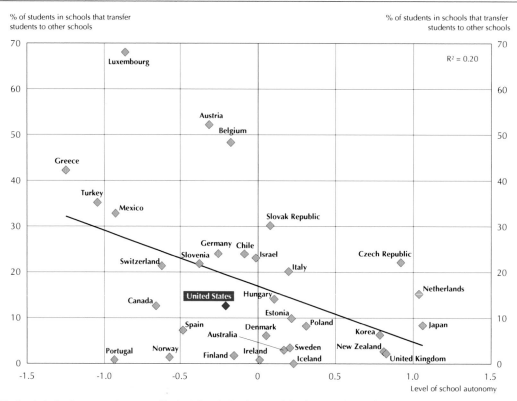

Note: The level of school autonomy is measured by the index of school responsibility for curriculum and assessment. Positive values indicate greater autonomy.
Source: OECD, *PISA 2009 Database*, Tables IV.3.3a and IV.3.6.
StatLink http://dx.doi.org/10.1787/888932366636

PISA classifies school systems attended by 15-year-old students into 12 groups according to the policies and practices they adopt concerning differentiation (Figure IV.3.2 in *PISA 2009 Results Volume IV*).[14]

Together with 12 other OECD countries, the United States is characterised by relatively low levels of formal differentiation. Students are generally not formally streamed, schools are not selective in their admissions process, and students usually do not repeat grades and few tend to be transferred to other schools. However, there is a high prevalence of informal streaming and tracking within schools in the United States, often starting in the early grades and particularly so in high schools (*e.g.* Advanced Placement courses, honours courses, etc.), which is not accounted for by this indicator. In addition, as shown above, there is also considerable socio-economic segregation between schools in the United States. And those few schools in the United States that do show high rates of grade repetition or schools transferring students with low performance or behavioural problems tend to perform more poorly and tend to be socio-economically disadvantaged schools (Tables IV.2.2b and IV.2.2c in *PISA 2009 Results Volume IV*).

School systems in six other OECD countries stratify students into different programmes based on students' academic performance, usually before they are 15 years old. Grade repetition is not common in these school systems, nor is horizontal differentiation at the school level. In five other OECD countries, school systems also provide differentiation at the system level. These school systems are characterised by their use of streaming and early selection into these programmes based on students' academic performance, but they generally do not use grade repetition or school-level differentiation.

Countries whose school systems use grade-repetition policies and similar devices to create homogeneous learning environments can be divided into two groups. While both groups make limited use of school-level horizontal differentiation, they differ in the extent to which they use vertical differentiation at the system level. While one system uses vertical differentiation and streaming of students into educational programmes (two OECD countries and three partner countries and economies), the other uses vertical differentiation as the primary and almost only form of selection and distributing students (one OECD country and four partner countries and economies).

In sum, the data suggest that in most of the countries that performed well in PISA, it is the primary responsibility of schools and teachers to engage constructively with the diversity of student interests, capacities and socio-economic contexts, without having the option of making students repeat the school year, or transferring them to educational tracks or school types with lower performance requirements. As shown in the subsequent chapters of this volume, many of the benchmark countries have developed elaborate support systems to foster the motivation of *all* students to become independent and lifelong learners. They tend to train teachers to be better at diagnosing learning difficulties so that they can be addressed through personalised instruction methods. They also help individual teachers to become aware of specific weaknesses in their own practices, which often means not just creating awareness of what they do, but also changing the underlying mindset. In addition, they seek to provide their teachers with an understanding of specific best practices and encourage teachers to make the necessary changes with a variety of incentives that goes well beyond material rewards. As noted above, the personalisation in these countries is provided in flexible learning pathways through the education system, rather than by establishing individualised goals or institutional tracking, which have often been shown to lower performance expectations for students and tend to provide easy ways for teachers and schools to defer, rather than solve, problems.

ASSESSMENT AND ACCOUNTABILITY ARRANGEMENTS

Educational standards

Fifteen-year-olds in the United States usually rate themselves comparatively highly in academic performance in PISA, even if they did not do well comparatively. This may be partly due to culture, but one interpretation is also that students are being commended for work that would not be acceptable in high-performing education systems. One trend across countries over recent years has been efforts to articulate the expectations that societies have in relation to learning outcomes and to translate these expectations into educational goals and standards. The approaches to standard-setting that OECD countries have pursued range from defining broad educational goals to formulating concise performance expectations in well-defined subject areas.

Educational standards have influenced many OECD education systems in various ways, helping them to: establish rigorous, focused and coherent content at all grade levels; reduce overlap in curricula across grades; reduce variation in implemented curricula across classrooms; facilitate co-ordination of various policy drivers, ranging from curricula to teacher training; and reduce inequity in curricula across socio-economic groups. The move by states to establish "common core standards" in the United States is a similar step that could address the current problem of widely discrepant state standards and cut scores that have led to non-comparable results. These discrepancies often mean that a school's fate depends more than anything else on where it is located and, perhaps even more important, that students across the United States are not equally well prepared to compete in the United States labour market.

Examinations

Setting performance standards has, in turn, led to the establishment of accountability systems. As discussed in the 2009 edition of *OECD's Education at a Glance* over the past decade, assessments of student performance have become common in many OECD countries – and often the results are widely reported and used in both public and specialised debate. However, the rationale for assessments and the nature of the instruments used vary greatly within and across countries. Methods employed in OECD countries include different forms of external assessment, external evaluation or inspection, and schools' own quality assurance and self-evaluation efforts. For students, tests may be the motivation needed to work harder. For teachers, student-based standardised assessments can provide information regarding the learning needs of students and may be used to personalise learning opportunities accordingly.

One aspect relating to accountability systems concerns the existence of standards-based external examinations. These are examinations that focus on a specific school subject and assess a major portion of what students who study this subject are expected to know or be able to do. Essentially, they define performance relative to an external standard, not relative to other students in the classroom or school. These examinations usually have a direct impact on students' education – and even on their futures – and may thus motivate students to invest greater efforts into learning. Other standardised tests, which may be voluntary and implemented by schools, often have only indirect consequences for students. For teachers, standardised assessments can provide information on students' learning needs and can be used to tailor their instruction accordingly. In some countries, such as Brazil, Hungary, Italy, Malaysia, Mexico, Poland and the Slovak Republic, such tests are also used to determine teachers' salaries or to guide professional development (for data, see the 2009 edition of *Education at a Glance*). At the school level, information from standardised tests can be used to determine the allocation of additional resources, and what interventions are required to establish performance targets and monitor progress.

Across OECD countries, students in school systems that require standards-based external examinations perform, on average, over 16 points higher than those in school systems that do not use such examinations (Figure IV.2.6a in *PISA 2009 Results Volume IV*).

Among OECD countries, in the Czech Republic, Denmark, Estonia, Finland, France, Hungary, Iceland, Ireland, Israel, Italy, Japan, Korea, Luxembourg, the Netherlands, New Zealand, Norway, Poland, the Slovak Republic, Slovenia, Turkey and the United Kingdom, standards-based external examinations exist throughout the systems for students attending secondary school. In Australia, they cover 81% of secondary students, in Canada 51% and in Germany 35%. In Austria, Belgium, Chile, Greece, Mexico, Portugal, Spain, Sweden and Switzerland, such examinations do not exist or exist only in minor parts of the system (Table IV.3.11 in *PISA 2009 Results Volume IV*).

ASSESSMENT POLICIES AND PRACTICES

In PISA 2009, school principals were asked to report the types and frequency of assessments used: standardised tests, teacher-developed tests, teachers' judgemental ratings, student portfolios or student assignments. An average of 76% of students in OECD countries are enrolled in schools that use standardised tests. Standardised tests are relatively uncommon in Slovenia, Belgium, Spain, Austria and Germany, where less than half of students attend schools that use standardised tests for assessments. In contrast, the use of standardised tests is practically universal in Luxembourg, Finland, Korea, the United States, Poland, Denmark, Sweden and Norway, where over 95% of students attend schools that use this assessment at least once a year (Table IV.3.10 in *PISA 2009 Results Volume IV*).

The purposes of assessments vary greatly across countries. At the school level, these assessments can be used by schools to compare themselves to other schools, to monitor progress, or to make decisions about instruction. Some 59% of students across OECD countries are in schools that use achievement data to compare their students' achievement levels with those in other schools or against regional/national benchmarks. This practice is most common in the United States, New Zealand and the United Kingdom, where over 90% of students attend schools that use achievement data for comparative purposes. In Belgium, Japan, Austria, Spain and Greece, less than one-third of students attend schools that use achievement information this way (Table IV.3.12 in *PISA 2009 Results Volume IV*).

It is more common for schools to use achievement information to monitor school progress from year to year: on average across OECD countries, some 77% of students are in schools that do so. In 21 countries, more than 80% of students attend schools that use achievement data this way. Only in Denmark, Luxembourg, Switzerland and Austria do less than 50% of students attend schools that use achievement data to monitor progress.

Data on student achievement can also be used to identify aspects of instruction or the curriculum that could be improved. Across OECD countries, 77% of students are in schools whose principals reported doing so, and over 90% of students in New Zealand, the United States, the United Kingdom, Iceland, Poland, Mexico, Chile, Spain and Israel attend schools whose principals reported using achievement data in this way. Curriculum and instructional assessment using achievement data is less common in Greece and Switzerland, where less than 50% of students attend schools that use achievement data this way.

In contrast to standards-based external examinations, PISA does not show the prevalence of standardised tests to be systematically related to performance (Figure IV.2.6b in *PISA 2009 Results Volume IV*). This may be because, in part, the content and use of standardised tests vary considerably across schools and systems. However, education systems with a higher prevalence of standardised tests tend to show smaller socio-economic inequalities between schools and consequently show a smaller impact of school socio-economic background on performance (Table IV.2.10 in *PISA 2009 Results Volume IV*). The same holds for the use of assessment data to identify aspects of instruction or the curriculum that could be improved and the high proportions of schools where achievement data is tracked over time by administrative authorities.

PISA arranges OECD countries into four groups sharing similar profiles based on two dimensions (Figure 2.14): whether achievement data are used for various benchmarking and information purposes; and whether achievement data are used to make decisions that affect the school The idea is that school systems that use achievement data for benchmarking and information purposes are more likely to use this data to compare themselves with other schools, monitor progress across time, have their progress tracked by administrative authorities, make their achievement data public, and provide parents with their child's achievement benchmarked to national or regional populations. School systems that use achievement data for decision making are more likely to use achievement data to determine the allocation of resources, make curricular decisions, and evaluate teachers' performance.

A first group of countries, composed of 16 OECD countries, including the United States, tend to use achievement data for benchmarking and information purposes and also for decisions that affect the school.

Four OECD countries use achievement data for benchmarking and information, but not for decisions affecting the school.

A third group, comprising four OECD countries, uses achievement data for decisions affecting the school, but not for benchmarking and information.

The fourth group, composed of nine OECD countries, is less likely to have schools that use achievement data for either for benchmarking and information or for decision making.

Some of the factors underlying this classification are examined in greater detail below.

■ Figure 2.14 ■
How school systems use student assessments

		Infrequent use of assessment or achievement data for benchmarking and information purposes	Frequent use of assessment or achievement data for benchmarking and information purposes
		Provide comparative information to parents: 32%	Provide comparative information to parents: 64%
		Compare the school with other schools: 38%	Compare the school with other schools: 73%
		Monitor progress over time: 57%	Monitor progress over time: 89%
		Post achievement data publicly: 20%	Post achievement data publicly: 47%
		Have their progress tracked by administrative authorities: 46%	Have their progress tracked by administrative authorities: 79%
Infrequent use of assessment or achievement data for decision making	Make curricular decisions: 60% Allocate resources: 21% Monitor teacher practices: 50%	Austria, Belgium,[1] Finland,[2] Germany, Greece, Ireland, Luxembourg, Netherlands,[1] Switzerland,[1] Liechtenstein	Hungary, Norway,[2] Turkey, Montenegro, Tunisia, Slovenia
Frequent use of assessment or achievement data for decision making	Making curricular decisions: 88% Allocating resources: 40% Monitor teacher practices: 65%	Denmark, Italy, Japan,[2] Spain, Argentina, Macao-China, Chinese Taipei, Uruguay	Australia,[1] Canada,[2] Chile, Czech Republic, Estonia,[2] Iceland,[2] Israel, Korea,[2] Mexico, New Zealand,[1] Poland,[1] Portugal, Slovak Republic, Sweden, United Kingdom, **United States,** Albania, Azerbaijan, Brazil, Bulgaria, Colombia, Croatia, Dubai (UAE), Hong Kong-China,[2] Indonesia, Jordan, Kazakhstan, Kyrgyzstan, Latvia, Lithuania, Panama, Peru, Qatar, Romania, Russian Federation, Shanghai-China,[1] Singapore,[1] Thailand, Trinidad and Tobago, Serbia

Note: The estimates in the grey cells indicate the average values of the variables used in latent profile analysis in each group. See Annex A5 for technical details.
1. Perform higher than the OECD average in reading.
2. Perform higher than the OECD average in reading and where the relationship between students' socio-economic background and reading performance is weaker than the OECD average.
Source: OECD, *PISA 2009 Database*.
StatLink ᘯᕞ∎ http://dx.doi.org/10.1787/888932366636

Accountability arrangements

While performance data in the United States are often used for punitive accountability purposes, other countries tend to give greater weight to guide intervention, reveal best practices and identify shared problems. Where school performance is systematically assessed, the primary purpose is often not to support contestability of public services or market mechanisms in the allocation of resources; rather it is to reveal best practices and identify common problems in order to encourage teachers and schools to develop more supportive and productive learning environments. To achieve this, many education systems try to develop assessment and accountability systems that include progressive learning targets that explicitly describe the steps that learners follow as they become more proficient, and define what a student should know and be able to do at each level of advancement. The trend among OECD countries here is leading towards multi-layered, coherent assessment systems, from classrooms to schools to regional to national to international levels, that: support improvement of learning at all levels of the system; are increasingly performance-based; add value for teaching and learning by providing information that can be acted on by students, teachers, and administrators; and are part of a comprehensive and well-aligned learning system that includes syllabi, associated instructional materials, matching exams, professional scoring and teacher training.

PISA 2009 collected data on the nature of accountability systems and the ways in which the resulting information was used and made available to various stakeholders and the public at large (Table IV.3.13 in *PISA 2009 Results Volume IV*). Some school systems make achievement data public to make stakeholders aware of the comparative performance of schools and, where school-choice programmes are available, to make parents aware of the choices available to them. Across OECD countries, an average of 37% of students attend schools that make achievement data available to the public; but in Belgium, Finland, Switzerland, Japan, Austria and Spain, less than 10% of students attend schools that make their data publicly available. In the United States and the United Kingdom, by contrast, more than 80% of students attend schools that make student achievement data publicly available. In seven OECD countries and nine partner countries and economies, schools whose school principals reported that student achievement data are posted publicly perform better than schools whose achievement data is not made publicly available, before accounting for the socio-economic and demographic background of students and schools; however no such relationship is seen in the United States. Moreover, since in most of the countries the schools that post achievement data publicly tend to be socio-economically advantaged schools, this performance advantage is often not observed once socio-economic background is accounted for (Figure IV.2.6b in *PISA 2009 Results Volume IV*).

School-level achievement data is often tracked over time by administrative authorities: across OECD countries, an average of 66% of students attend schools whose achievement data are tracked over time by administrative authorities. In 25 OECD countries, among them the United States, with the highest percentage (96%), more than 50% of students attend schools whose achievement data is so tracked (Table IV.3.13 in *PISA 2009 Results Volume IV*).

Achievement data can also be used to determine how resources are distributed. Across OECD countries, an average of 33% of students attend schools that use achievement data in this way. In Israel, Chile and the United States, more than 70% of students attend schools in which the principals reported that instructional resources are allocated according to the school's achievement data. This practice is least common in Iceland, Greece, Japan, Czech Republic and Finland, where less than 10% of students attend schools whose achievement data are used this way.

Some school systems make achievement data available to parents in the form of report cards and by sending teacher-formulated assessments home. Some school systems also provide information on the students' academic standing compared with other students in the country or region or within the school (Table IV.3.14 in *PISA 2009 Results Volume IV*). Across OECD countries, an average of 52% of students attend schools that use achievement data relative to national or regional benchmarks and/or as a group relative to students in the same grade in other schools; but in 17 countries, over 50% of students attend schools that do not provide any information regarding the academic standing of students in either of these ways. In contrast, in Sweden, the United States, Korea, Chile, Norway and Turkey, more than 80% of students attend schools that provide parents with this information compared with national or regional student populations.

Achievement data from students can also be used to monitor teacher practices, and an average of 59% of students across OECD countries attend schools whose principals reported doing so. Over 80% of students in Poland, Israel, the United Kingdom, Turkey, Mexico, Austria and the United States attend schools whose principals reported using achievement data to monitor teacher practices. Many schools across OECD countries complement this information with qualitative assessments, such as teacher peer reviews, assessments for school principals or senior staff, or observations by inspectors or other persons external to the school. Most schools across OECD countries use either student-derived, direct observations or reviews to monitor teachers, but school principals in Finland rarely use either to monitor teacher practices. Some 18% of students in Finland attend schools that use student assessments to monitor teachers; around 20% of students attend schools that use more qualitative and direct methods to monitor teacher practices; and only 2% of students attend schools that monitor teacher practices using observations of classes by inspectors or other persons external to the school (Table IV.3.15 in *PISA 2009 Results Volume IV*). There has also been a growing trend among OECD countries to use outstanding performance in teaching as criteria for base salary and additional payments awarded to teachers in public institutions. While in 2002 such practices were used in 38% of the 29 countries with available data, in 2008, 45% of countries with available data used such practices (Table D.3.3 in the 2010 edition of OECD's *Education at a Glance*).

RESOURCES

Effective school systems require the right combination of trained and talented personnel, adequate educational resources and facilities, and motivated students ready to learn. But performance on international comparisons cannot simply be tied to money, since only Luxembourg spends more per student than the United States. The results for the United States reflect rather a range of inefficiencies. That point is reinforced by the fact that, in international comparisons of children in primary school (TIMSS and PIRLS), the United States does relatively well by international standards, which, given the country's wealth, is what would be expected. The problem is that as they get older, children make less progress each year than children in the best-performing countries do. As discussed in the section *Equity in access to resources* above, and illustrated, in particular, in the country chapters on Canada, Finland and Shanghai-China, it is noteworthy that spending patterns in many of the world's successful education systems are markedly different from those in the United States. These countries invest money where the challenges are greatest, rather than making the resources that are devoted to schools dependent on the wealth of the local communities in which schools are located, and they put in place incentives and support systems that attract the most talented school teachers into the most difficult classrooms. They have often reformed inherited, traditional and bureaucratic systems of recruiting and training teachers and leaders, of paying and rewarding them and of shaping their incentives, both short-term and long-term.

Research usually shows a weak relationship between educational resources and student performance, with more variation explained by the quality of human resources (*i.e.* teachers and school principals) than by material and financial resources, particularly among industrialised nations. The generally weak relationship between resources and performance observed in past research is also seen in PISA. At the level of the education system, and net of the level of national income, the only type of resource that PISA shows to be correlated with student performance is the level of teachers' salaries relative to national income (Figure IV.2.8 in *PISA 2009 Results Volume IV*). Teachers' salaries are related to class size in that if spending levels are similar, school systems often make trade-offs between smaller classes and higher salaries for teachers. The findings from PISA suggest that systems prioritising higher teacher salaries over smaller classes tend to perform better. The lack of correlation between the level of resources and performance among school systems does not mean that resource levels do not affect performance at all. Rather, it implies that, given the variation in resources observed in PISA, they are unrelated to performance or equity. A school system that lacks teachers, infrastructure and textbooks will almost certainly perform at lower levels; but given that most school systems in PISA appear to satisfy the minimum resource requirements for teaching and learning, the lack of a relationship between many of the resource aspects and both equity and performance may result simply from a lack of sufficient variation among OECD countries.

Many of the high-performing countries share a commitment to professionalised teaching, in ways that imply that teachers are are accorded the same status as other highly-regarded professions. The subsequent chapters show that, to achieve this, countries often do four things well: first, they attract the best graduates to become teachers, realising that the quality of an education system cannot exceed the quality of its teachers. For example, the benchmark country, Finland, recruits its teachers from the top 10% of graduates. Second, they develop these teachers into effective instructors, through, for example, coaching classroom practice, moving teacher training into the classroom, developing strong school leaders and enabling teachers to share their knowledge and spread innovation. Singaporean teachers, for example, get 100 hours of fully paid professional development training each year; teachers in Shanghai-China get 240 hours over a five-year period. Third, countries put in place incentives and differentiated support systems to ensure that every child is able to benefit from excellent instruction. The image here is of teachers who use data to evaluate the learning needs of their students, and are constantly expanding their repertoire of pedagogic strategies to address the diversity of students' interests and abilities. Such systems also often adopt innovative approaches to staffing classrooms.

It is also important that, within school systems, much of the relationship between school resources and student performance is closely associated with schools' socio-economic and demographic profiles. This suggests the need for more consideration on how to distribute resources for schools more equitably. Across OECD countries, and considering aspects that relate to class size, instruction time, participation in after-school lessons, availability of extra-curricular activities, and the school principal's perception of teacher shortages and a lack of material resources that adversely affects instruction, only 5% of the variation in student performance is attributable solely to the differences in the educational resources available to schools. In contrast, 18% of the variation in student performance is attributable jointly to spending on education and to socio-economic and demographic background (Figure IV.2.9 and Table IV.2.12a in *PISA 2009 Results Volume IV*). Improving equity will thus require considering the disparities in resources among schools.

In other words, while much of the variation in student performance cannot be predicted solely by levels of resources, resources are closely related to the socio-economic composition of individual schools, such that socio-economically advantaged students attend schools with better resources. Whether and how long students are enrolled in pre-primary education is also an important resource consideration. Many of the inequities that exist within school systems are already present once students enter formal schooling and persist as students' progress through school. Earlier entrance into the school system may reduce educational inequities, since participation is then universal. On average across OECD countries, 72% of today's 15-year-old students reported in PISA that they had attended pre-primary education for more than one year when they were children. Attendance in more than one year of pre-primary education was practically universal in Japan, the Netherlands, Hungary, Belgium, Iceland and France, where over 90% of 15-year-old students reported that they had attended pre-primary school for more than one year. More than 90% of students in 27 OECD countries had attended pre-primary school for at least some time, and 98% or more of students in Japan, Hungary, France and the United States reported having done so. Pre-primary education is rare in Turkey, where less than 30% of 15-year-olds had attended pre-primary school for at least a year. More than one year of pre-primary education is uncommon in Chile, Ireland, Canada and Poland, where less than 50% of students had attended pre-primary school for that length of time (Table IV.3.18 in *PISA 2009 Results Volume IV*).

PISA 2009 results show that, in general, students who had attended pre-primary education perform better in reading at the age of 15 than students who had not (Figure 2.15, Figure II.5.9 and Table II.5.5 in *PISA 2009 Results Volume II*). In 32 OECD countries, students who had attended pre-primary education for more than one year outperformed students who had not attended pre-primary education at all, in many countries by the equivalent of well over a school year. This finding remains unchanged in most countries even after the socio-economic background of students is accounted for. However, across countries, there is considerable variation in the impact of students' attendance in pre-primary education on their 15-year-old reading performance. Among OECD countries, in Israel, Belgium, Italy and France, students who had attended pre-primary education for more than one year perform at least 64 score points higher in reading than students who had not attended pre-primary education, which corresponds to the equivalent of roughly one-and-a-half school years. This was the case even after students' socio-economic background was accounted for. On the other hand, in Estonia, Finland, the United States and Korea, there is no marked difference in reading scores between those students who had attended pre-primary education (for more than one year) and those who hadn't after the socio-economic background of students is accounted for. In the United States, the performance advantage of students who had attended pre-primary education for one year or less is 33 score points on the PISA reading scale – roughly the equivalent of one school year at age 15 – and the advantage of students who had attended pre-primary education for one year or more is 46 score points. However, in the United States, a large part of that advantage is explained by socio-economic characteristics, that is, students from more privileged socio-economic backgrounds tend to take greater advantage of pre-primary education. While these results underline the importance of pre-primary education, international comparisons of children in primary school show that the United States does well by international standards. The problem is that as they get older, these children make less progress each year than children in many other countries. In other words, more pre-primary education can only be part of the solution.

One hypothesis to explain the variability in the impact of pre-primary education on later school performance is the quality of pre-primary education. This hypothesis is supported by the fact that the impact of pre-primary education attendance on performance tends to be greater in education systems with a longer duration of pre-primary education, smaller pupil-to-teacher ratio in pre-primary education, or higher public expenditure per pupil at the pre-primary education level (Table II.5.6 in *PISA 2009 Results Volume II*).

When the impact of pre-primary education attendance on reading performance at age 15 is compared between different socio-economic backgrounds, no significant difference is found between students from socio-economically disadvantaged and advantaged backgrounds (Table II.5.8 in *PISA 2009 Results Volume II*). Socio-economically disadvantaged and advantaged students benefit equally from pre-primary education attendance in 31 OECD countries and 25 partner countries and economies. The United States is the only OECD country where PISA shows evidence that disadvantaged students benefit more from pre-primary education. Part of the difference in the impact of attendance in pre-primary education on the performance of students from different socio-economic backgrounds may be due to the fact that many other factors apart from attendance in pre-primary education (*e.g.* education in and out of school that students received between the ages of 6 and 15) may influence 15-year-olds' performance.

■ Figure 2.15 ■
Performance difference between students who had attended pre-primary school for more than one year and those who had not

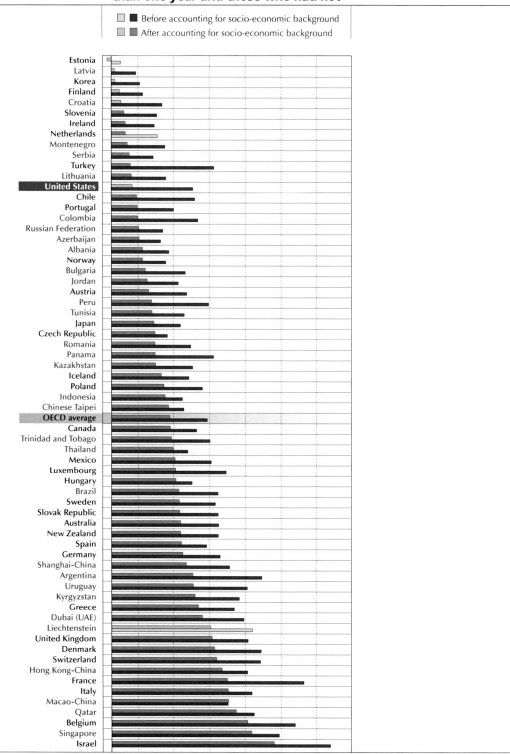

□ ■ Before accounting for socio-economic background
□ ■ After accounting for socio-economic background

Note: Score point differences that are statistically significant are marked in a darker tone.
Countries are ranked in ascending order of the score point difference between students who report having attended pre-primary school (ISCED 0) for more than one year and those without pre-primary school attendance after accounting for socio-economic background.
Source: OECD, *PISA 2009 Database*, Table II.5.5.
StatLink ⎯⎯ http://dx.doi.org/10.1787/888932366636

When the impact of pre-primary education on performance at age 15 is compared between students with immigrant backgrounds and native students, a significant difference is found in some countries (Table II.5.9 in *PISA 2009 Results Volume II*). In Finland, Ireland, Canada and the partner country Qatar, the impact of attendance in pre-primary education on performance is greater for immigrant students than for native students.

In countries that spend more public resources on pre-primary education per student, students with immigrant backgrounds tend to benefit more from pre-primary education than native students (Table II.5.10 in *PISA 2009 Results Volume II*). However, other measures of quality of pre-primary education, such as a higher enrolment rate for pre-primary education, a longer duration of pre-primary education, and smaller pupil-to-teacher ratio in pre-primary education are more closely related to the performance advantage observed by PISA.

The following chapters will describe some of the success stories of high-performing and rapidly improving education systems in detail before the concluding chapter lays out possible lessons for the United States.

■ Figure 2.16 ■
Comparing countries' performance in reading

Statistically significantly **above** the OECD average
Not statistically significantly different from the OECD average
Statistically significantly **below** the OECD average

Mean	Comparison country	Countries whose mean score is NOT statistically significantly different from that of the comparison country
556	Shanghai-China	
539	Korea	Finland, Hong Kong-China
536	Finland	Korea, Hong Kong-China
533	Hong Kong-China	Korea, Finland
526	Singapore	Canada, New Zealand, Japan
524	Canada	Singapore, New Zealand, Japan
521	New Zealand	Singapore, Canada, Japan, Australia
520	Japan	Singapore, Canada, New Zealand, Australia, Netherlands
515	Australia	New Zealand, Japan, Netherlands
508	Netherlands	Japan, Australia, Belgium, Norway, Estonia, Switzerland, Poland, Iceland, United States, Liechtenstein, Sweden, Germany
506	Belgium	Netherlands, Norway, Estonia, Switzerland, Poland, United States, Liechtenstein
503	Norway	Netherlands, Belgium, Estonia, Switzerland, Poland, Iceland, United States, Liechtenstein, Sweden, Germany, Ireland, France
501	Estonia	Netherlands, Belgium, Norway, Switzerland, Poland, Iceland, United States, Liechtenstein, Sweden, Germany, Ireland, France, Chinese Taipei, Denmark, United Kingdom, Hungary
501	Switzerland	Netherlands, Belgium, Norway, Estonia, Poland, Iceland, United States, Liechtenstein, Sweden, Germany, Ireland, France, Chinese Taipei, Denmark, United Kingdom, Hungary
500	Poland	Netherlands, Belgium, Norway, Estonia, Switzerland, Iceland, United States, Liechtenstein, Sweden, Germany, Ireland, France, Chinese Taipei, Denmark, United Kingdom, Hungary
500	Iceland	Netherlands, Norway, Estonia, Switzerland, Poland, United States, Liechtenstein, Sweden, Germany, Ireland, France, Chinese Taipei, Hungary
500	**United States**	Netherlands, Belgium, Norway, Estonia, Switzerland, Poland, Iceland, Liechtenstein, Sweden, Germany, Ireland, France, Chinese Taipei, Denmark, United Kingdom, Hungary
499	Liechtenstein	Netherlands, Belgium, Norway, Estonia, Switzerland, Poland, Iceland, United States, Sweden, Germany, Ireland, France, Chinese Taipei, Denmark, United Kingdom, Hungary
497	Sweden	Netherlands, Norway, Estonia, Switzerland, Poland, Iceland, United States, Liechtenstein, Germany, Ireland, France, Chinese Taipei, Denmark, United Kingdom, Hungary, Portugal
497	Germany	Netherlands, Norway, Estonia, Switzerland, Poland, Iceland, United States, Liechtenstein, Sweden, Ireland, France, Chinese Taipei, Denmark, United Kingdom, Hungary
496	Ireland	Norway, Estonia, Switzerland, Poland, Iceland, United States, Liechtenstein, Sweden, Germany, France, Chinese Taipei, Denmark, United Kingdom, Hungary, Portugal
496	France	Norway, Estonia, Switzerland, Poland, Iceland, United States, Liechtenstein, Sweden, Germany, Ireland, Chinese Taipei, Denmark, United Kingdom, Hungary, Portugal
495	Chinese Taipei	Estonia, Switzerland, Poland, Iceland, United States, Liechtenstein, Sweden, Germany, Ireland, France, Denmark, United Kingdom, Hungary, Portugal
495	Denmark	Estonia, Switzerland, Poland, United States, Liechtenstein, Sweden, Germany, Ireland, France, Chinese Taipei, United Kingdom, Hungary, Portugal
494	United Kingdom	Estonia, Switzerland, Poland, United States, Liechtenstein, Sweden, Germany, Ireland, France, Chinese Taipei, Denmark, Hungary, Portugal
494	Hungary	Estonia, Switzerland, Poland, Iceland, United States, Liechtenstein, Sweden, Germany, Ireland, France, Chinese Taipei, Denmark, United Kingdom, Portugal
489	Portugal	Sweden, Ireland, France, Chinese Taipei, Denmark, United Kingdom, Hungary, Macao-China, Italy, Latvia, Slovenia, Greece
487	Macao-China	Portugal, Italy, Latvia, Greece
486	Italy	Portugal, Macao-China, Latvia, Slovenia, Greece, Spain
484	Latvia	Portugal, Macao-China, Italy, Slovenia, Greece, Spain, Czech Republic, Slovak Republic
483	Slovenia	Portugal, Italy, Latvia, Greece, Spain, Czech Republic
483	Greece	Portugal, Macao-China, Italy, Latvia, Slovenia, Spain, Czech Republic, Slovak Republic, Croatia, Israel
481	Spain	Italy, Latvia, Slovenia, Greece, Czech Republic, Slovak Republic, Croatia, Israel
478	Czech Republic	Latvia, Slovenia, Greece, Spain, Slovak Republic, Croatia, Israel, Luxembourg, Austria
477	Slovak Republic	Latvia, Greece, Spain, Czech Republic, Croatia, Israel, Luxembourg, Austria
476	Croatia	Greece, Spain, Czech Republic, Slovak Republic, Israel, Luxembourg, Austria, Lithuania
474	Israel	Greece, Spain, Czech Republic, Slovak Republic, Croatia, Luxembourg, Austria, Lithuania, Turkey
472	Luxembourg	Czech Republic, Slovak Republic, Croatia, Israel, Austria, Lithuania
470	Austria	Czech Republic, Slovak Republic, Croatia, Israel, Luxembourg, Lithuania, Turkey
468	Lithuania	Croatia, Israel, Luxembourg, Austria, Turkey
464	Turkey	Israel, Austria, Lithuania, Dubai (UAE), Russian Federation
459	Dubai (UAE)	Turkey, Russian Federation
459	Russian Federation	Turkey, Dubai (UAE)
449	Chile	Serbia
442	Serbia	Chile, Bulgaria
429	Bulgaria	Serbia, Uruguay, Mexico, Romania, Thailand, Trinidad and Tobago
426	Uruguay	Bulgaria, Mexico, Romania, Thailand
425	Mexico	Bulgaria, Uruguay, Romania, Thailand
424	Romania	Bulgaria, Uruguay, Mexico, Thailand, Trinidad and Tobago
421	Thailand	Bulgaria, Uruguay, Mexico, Romania, Trinidad and Tobago, Colombia
416	Trinidad and Tobago	Bulgaria, Romania, Thailand, Colombia, Brazil
413	Colombia	Thailand, Trinidad and Tobago, Brazil, Montenegro, Jordan
412	Brazil	Trinidad and Tobago, Colombia, Montenegro, Jordan
408	Montenegro	Colombia, Brazil, Jordan, Tunisia, Indonesia, Argentina
405	Jordan	Colombia, Brazil, Montenegro, Tunisia, Indonesia, Argentina
404	Tunisia	Montenegro, Jordan, Indonesia, Argentina
402	Indonesia	Montenegro, Jordan, Tunisia, Argentina
398	Argentina	Montenegro, Jordan, Tunisia, Indonesia, Kazakhstan
390	Kazakhstan	Argentina, Albania
385	Albania	Kazakhstan, Panama
372	Qatar	Panama, Peru
371	Panama	Albania, Qatar, Peru, Azerbaijan
370	Peru	Qatar, Panama, Azerbaijan
362	Azerbaijan	Panama, Peru
314	Kyrgyzstan	

Source: OECD, *PISA 2009 Database*.
StatLink ⌐ᵐᴵᴸ↗ http://dx.doi.org/10.1787/888932366636

■ Figure 2.17 ■
Comparing countries' performance in mathematics

	Statistically significantly **above** the OECD average
	Not statistically significantly different from the OECD average
	Statistically significantly **below** the OECD average

Mean	Comparison country	Countries whose mean score is NOT statistically significantly different from that of the comparison country
600	Shanghai-China	
562	Singapore	
555	Hong Kong-China	Korea
546	Korea	Hong Kong-China, Chinese Taipei, Finland, Liechtenstein
543	Chinese Taipei	Korea, Finland, Liechtenstein, Switzerland
541	Finland	Korea, Chinese Taipei, Liechtenstein, Switzerland
536	Liechtenstein	Korea, Chinese Taipei, Finland, Switzerland, Japan, Netherlands
534	Switzerland	Chinese Taipei, Finland, Liechtenstein, Japan, Canada, Netherlands
529	Japan	Liechtenstein, Switzerland, Canada, Netherlands, Macao-China
527	Canada	Switzerland, Japan, Netherlands, Macao-China
526	Netherlands	Liechtenstein, Switzerland, Japan, Canada, Macao-China, New Zealand
525	Macao-China	Japan, Canada, Netherlands
519	New Zealand	Netherlands, Belgium, Australia, Germany
515	Belgium	New Zealand, Australia, Germany, Estonia
514	Australia	New Zealand, Belgium, Germany, Estonia
513	Germany	New Zealand, Belgium, Australia, Estonia, Iceland
512	Estonia	Belgium, Australia, Germany, Iceland
507	Iceland	Germany, Estonia, Denmark
503	Denmark	Iceland, Slovenia, Norway, France, Slovak Republic
501	Slovenia	Denmark, Norway, France, Slovak Republic, Austria
498	Norway	Denmark, Slovenia, France, Slovak Republic, Austria, Poland, Sweden, Czech Republic, United Kingdom, Hungary
497	France	Denmark, Slovenia, Norway, Slovak Republic, Austria, Poland, Sweden, Czech Republic, United Kingdom, Hungary
497	Slovak Republic	Denmark, Slovenia, Norway, France, Austria, Poland, Sweden, Czech Republic, United Kingdom, Hungary
496	Austria	Slovenia, Norway, France, Slovak Republic, Poland, Sweden, Czech Republic, United Kingdom, Hungary, United States
495	Poland	Norway, France, Slovak Republic, Austria, Sweden, Czech Republic, United Kingdom, Hungary, Luxembourg, United States, Portugal
494	Sweden	Norway, France, Slovak Republic, Austria, Poland, Czech Republic, United Kingdom, Hungary, Luxembourg, United States, Ireland, Portugal
493	Czech Republic	Norway, France, Slovak Republic, Austria, Poland, Sweden, United Kingdom, Hungary, Luxembourg, United States, Ireland, Portugal
492	United Kingdom	Norway, France, Slovak Republic, Austria, Poland, Sweden, Czech Republic, Hungary, Luxembourg, United States, Ireland, Portugal
490	Hungary	Norway, France, Slovak Republic, Austria, Poland, Sweden, Czech Republic, United Kingdom, Luxembourg, United States, Ireland, Portugal, Spain, Italy, Latvia
489	Luxembourg	Poland, Sweden, Czech Republic, United Kingdom, Hungary, United States, Ireland, Portugal
487	**United States**	Austria, Poland, Sweden, Czech Republic, United Kingdom, Hungary, Luxembourg, Ireland, Portugal, Spain, Italy, Latvia
487	Ireland	Sweden, Czech Republic, United Kingdom, Hungary, Luxembourg, United States, Portugal, Spain, Italy, Latvia
487	Portugal	Poland, Sweden, Czech Republic, United Kingdom, Hungary, Luxembourg, United States, Ireland, Spain, Italy, Latvia
483	Spain	Hungary, United States, Ireland, Portugal, Italy, Latvia
483	Italy	Hungary, United States, Ireland, Portugal, Spain, Latvia
482	Latvia	Hungary, United States, Ireland, Portugal, Spain, Italy, Lithuania
477	Lithuania	Latvia
468	Russian Federation	Greece, Croatia
466	Greece	Russian Federation, Croatia
460	Croatia	Russian Federation, Greece
453	Dubai (UAE)	Israel, Turkey
447	Israel	Dubai (UAE), Turkey, Serbia
445	Turkey	Dubai (UAE), Israel, Serbia
442	Serbia	Israel, Turkey
431	Azerbaijan	Bulgaria, Romania, Uruguay
428	Bulgaria	Azerbaijan, Romania, Uruguay, Chile, Thailand, Mexico
427	Romania	Azerbaijan, Bulgaria, Uruguay, Chile, Thailand
427	Uruguay	Azerbaijan, Bulgaria, Romania, Chile
421	Chile	Bulgaria, Romania, Uruguay, Thailand, Mexico
419	Thailand	Bulgaria, Romania, Chile, Mexico, Trinidad and Tobago
419	Mexico	Bulgaria, Chile, Thailand
414	Trinidad and Tobago	Thailand
405	Kazakhstan	Montenegro
403	Montenegro	Kazakhstan
388	Argentina	Jordan, Brazil, Colombia, Albania
387	Jordan	Argentina, Brazil, Colombia, Albania
386	Brazil	Argentina, Jordan, Colombia, Albania
381	Colombia	Argentina, Jordan, Brazil, Albania, Indonesia
377	Albania	Argentina, Jordan, Brazil, Colombia, Tunisia, Indonesia
371	Tunisia	Albania, Indonesia, Qatar, Peru, Panama
371	Indonesia	Colombia, Albania, Tunisia, Qatar, Peru, Panama
368	Qatar	Tunisia, Indonesia, Peru, Panama
365	Peru	Tunisia, Indonesia, Qatar, Panama
360	Panama	Tunisia, Indonesia, Qatar, Peru
331	Kyrgyzstan	

Source: OECD, *PISA 2009 Database*.
StatLink ᵐˢᵖ http://dx.doi.org/10.1787/888932366636

 STRONG PERFORMERS AND SUCCESSFUL REFORMERS IN EDUCATION: LESSONS FROM PISA FOR THE UNITED STATES

■ Figure 2.18 ■
Comparing countries' performance in science

	Statistically significantly **above** the OECD average
	Not statistically significantly different from the OECD average
	Statistically significantly **below** the OECD average

Mean	Comparison country	Countries whose mean score is NOT statistically significantly different from that comparison country
575	Shanghai-China	
554	Finland	Hong Kong-China
549	Hong Kong-China	Finland
542	Singapore	Japan, Korea
539	Japan	Singapore, Korea, New Zealand
538	Korea	Singapore, Japan, New Zealand
532	New Zealand	Japan, Korea, Canada, Estonia, Australia, Netherlands
529	Canada	New Zealand, Estonia, Australia, Netherlands
528	Estonia	New Zealand, Canada, Australia, Netherlands, Germany, Liechtenstein
527	Australia	New Zealand, Canada, Estonia, Netherlands, Chinese Taipei, Germany, Liechtenstein
522	Netherlands	New Zealand, Canada, Estonia, Australia, Chinese Taipei, Germany, Liechtenstein, Switzerland, United Kingdom, Slovenia
520	Chinese Taipei	Australia, Netherlands, Germany, Liechtenstein, Switzerland, United Kingdom
520	Germany	Estonia, Australia, Netherlands, Chinese Taipei, Liechtenstein, Switzerland, United Kingdom
520	Liechtenstein	Estonia, Australia, Netherlands, Chinese Taipei, Germany, Switzerland, United Kingdom
517	Switzerland	Netherlands, Chinese Taipei, Germany, Liechtenstein, United Kingdom, Slovenia, Macao-China
514	United Kingdom	Netherlands, Chinese Taipei, Germany, Liechtenstein, Switzerland, Slovenia, Macao-China, Poland, Ireland
512	Slovenia	Netherlands, Switzerland, United Kingdom, Macao-China, Poland, Ireland, Belgium
511	Macao-China	Switzerland, United Kingdom, Slovenia, Poland, Ireland, Belgium
508	Poland	United Kingdom, Slovenia, Macao-China, Ireland, Belgium, Hungary, United States
508	Ireland	United Kingdom, Slovenia, Macao-China, Poland, Belgium, Hungary, United States, Czech Republic, Norway
507	Belgium	Slovenia, Macao-China, Poland, Ireland, Hungary, United States, Czech Republic, Norway, France
503	Hungary	Poland, Ireland, Belgium, United States, Czech Republic, Norway, Denmark, France, Sweden, Austria
502	**United States**	Poland, Ireland, Belgium, Hungary, Czech Republic, Norway, Denmark, France, Iceland, Sweden, Austria, Latvia, Portugal
500	Czech Republic	Ireland, Belgium, Hungary, United States, Norway, Denmark, France, Iceland, Sweden, Austria, Latvia, Portugal
500	Norway	Ireland, Belgium, Hungary, United States, Czech Republic, Denmark, France, Iceland, Sweden, Austria, Latvia, Portugal
499	Denmark	Hungary, United States, Czech Republic, Norway, France, Iceland, Sweden, Austria, Latvia, Portugal
498	France	Belgium, Hungary, United States, Czech Republic, Norway, Denmark, Iceland, Sweden, Austria, Latvia, Portugal, Lithuania, Slovak Republic
496	Iceland	United States, Czech Republic, Norway, Denmark, France, Sweden, Austria, Latvia, Portugal, Lithuania, Slovak Republic
495	Sweden	Hungary, United States, Czech Republic, Norway, Denmark, France, Iceland, Austria, Latvia, Portugal, Lithuania, Slovak Republic, Italy
494	Austria	Hungary, United States, Czech Republic, Norway, Denmark, France, Iceland, Sweden, Latvia, Portugal, Lithuania, Slovak Republic, Italy, Spain, Croatia
494	Latvia	United States, Czech Republic, Norway, Denmark, France, Iceland, Sweden, Austria, Portugal, Lithuania, Slovak Republic, Italy, Spain, Croatia
493	Portugal	United States, Czech Republic, Norway, Denmark, France, Iceland, Sweden, Austria, Latvia, Lithuania, Slovak Republic, Italy, Spain, Croatia
491	Lithuania	France, Iceland, Sweden, Austria, Latvia, Portugal, Slovak Republic, Italy, Spain, Croatia
490	Slovak Republic	France, Iceland, Sweden, Austria, Latvia, Portugal, Lithuania, Italy, Spain, Croatia
489	Italy	Sweden, Austria, Latvia, Portugal, Lithuania, Slovak Republic, Spain, Croatia
488	Spain	Austria, Latvia, Portugal, Lithuania, Slovak Republic, Italy, Croatia, Luxembourg
486	Croatia	Austria, Latvia, Portugal, Lithuania, Slovak Republic, Italy, Spain, Luxembourg, Russian Federation
484	Luxembourg	Spain, Croatia, Russian Federation
478	Russian Federation	Croatia, Luxembourg, Greece
470	Greece	Russian Federation, Dubai (UAE)
466	Dubai (UAE)	Greece
455	Israel	Turkey, Chile
454	Turkey	Israel, Chile
447	Chile	Israel, Turkey, Serbia, Bulgaria
443	Serbia	Chile, Bulgaria
439	Bulgaria	Chile, Serbia, Romania, Uruguay
428	Romania	Bulgaria, Uruguay, Thailand
427	Uruguay	Bulgaria, Romania, Thailand
425	Thailand	Romania, Uruguay
416	Mexico	Jordan
415	Jordan	Mexico, Trinidad and Tobago
410	Trinidad and Tobago	Jordan, Brazil
405	Brazil	Trinidad and Tobago, Colombia, Montenegro, Argentina, Tunisia, Kazakhstan
402	Colombia	Brazil, Montenegro, Argentina, Tunisia, Kazakhstan
401	Montenegro	Brazil, Colombia, Argentina, Tunisia, Kazakhstan
401	Argentina	Brazil, Colombia, Montenegro, Tunisia, Kazakhstan, Albania
401	Tunisia	Brazil, Colombia, Montenegro, Argentina, Kazakhstan
400	Kazakhstan	Brazil, Colombia, Montenegro, Argentina, Tunisia, Albania
391	Albania	Argentina, Kazakhstan, Indonesia
383	Indonesia	Albania, Qatar, Panama, Azerbaijan
379	Qatar	Indonesia, Panama
376	Panama	Indonesia, Qatar, Azerbaijan, Peru
373	Azerbaijan	Indonesia, Panama, Peru
369	Peru	Panama, Azerbaijan
330	Kyrgyzstan	

Source: OECD, *PISA 2009 Database*.
StatLink ᴍᴧᴨ http://dx.doi.org/10.1787/888932366636

■ Figure 2.19 ■
United States: Profile data

Language(s)	American English
Population	304 228 300[15]
Youth population	20.2%[16] (OECD average 18.7%)
Elderly population	12.7%[17] (OECD average 14.4%)
Growth rate	0.95%[18] (OECD 0.68%)[19]
Foreign-born population	13.6%[20] (OECD average 12.9%)
GDP per capita	USD 47 495[21] (OECD average 33 732)[22]
Economy-origin of GDP	Services: 30.8%; Other: 28.2%; Finance, insurance and real estate: 18.2%; Government and government enterprises: 13%; Manufacturing: 9.7%[23]
Unemployment/youth unemployment	5.8% (2008)[24] (OECD average 6.1%)[25] 12.8% (OECD average 13.8%)[26]
Expenditure on education	5.3% of GDP; (OECD average 5.2%) 3.7% on primary, secondary and post-secondary non-tertiary 1.2% on tertiary[27] education[28] (OECD average 3.5%; 1.2% respectively) 14.1% of total public expenditure (OECD average 13.3%) 9.9% on primary, secondary and post-secondary non-tertiary 3.3% on tertiary education[29] (OECD average 9%; 3.1% respectively)
Enrolment ratio, early childhood education	46.9%[30] (OECD average 71.5%)[31]
Enrolment ratio, primary education	98.6%[32] (OECD average 98.8%)[33]
Enrolment ratio, secondary education	80.8%[34] (OECD average 81.5%)[35]
Enrolment ratio, tertiary education	23.2%[36] (OECD average 24.9%)[37]
Students in primary education, by type of institution or mode of enrolment[38]	Public: 90.3% (OECD average 89.6%) Government-dependent private: no data[39] (OECD average 8.1%) Independent, private: 9.7% (OECD average 2.9%)
Students in lower secondary education, by type of institution or mode of enrolment[40]	Public 91.1% (OECD average 83.2%) Government-dependent private: no data[41] (OECD average 10.9%) Independent, private: 8.9% (OECD average 3.5%)
Students in upper secondary education, by type of institution or mode of enrolment[42]	Public: 91.4% (OECD avg 82%) Government-dependent private: no data[43] (OECD average 13.6%) Independent, private: 8.6% (OECD average 5.5%)

Students in tertiary education, by type of institution or mode of enrolment[44]	Tertiary type B education:
	    Public: 81.1%
	    Government-dependent private: no data[45]
	    Independent-private: 18.9%
	    (OECD average Public: 61.8%
	    Government-dependent private: 19.2%
	    Independent-private: 16.6%)
	
	Tertiary type A education:
	    Public: 71.7%
	    Government-dependent private: no data[46]
	    Independent-private: 28.3%
	    (OECD average Public: 77.1%
	    Government-dependent private: 9.6%
	    Independent-private: 15%)

Teachers' salaries	Average annual starting salary in lower secondary education: USD 35 915 (OECD average USD 30 750)[47] Ratio of salary in lower secondary education after 15 years of experience to GDP per capita: 94[48] (OECD average: 1.22)[49]
Upper secondary graduation rates	77% (OECD average 80%)[50]

StatLink ⌨📊 http://dx.doi.org/10.1787/888932366636

References

OECD (2010a), *OECD Factbook 2010*, OECD Publishing.

OECD (2010b), *OECD Economic Surveys: United States 2010*, OECD Publishing.

OECD (2010c), *Employment Outlook*, OECD Publishing.

OECD (2010d), *Education at a Glance 2010*, OECD Publishing.

OECD (2010e), *Pathways to Success*, OECD Publishing.

OECD (2010f), *PISA 2009 Results, Volume I-V*, OECD Publishing.

Notes

1. Though rank 14 is the best estimate, due to sampling and measurement error the rank could be between 8 and 19.

2. Though rank 17 is the best estimate, due to sampling and measurement error the rank could be between 13 and 22.

3. Though rank 23 is the best estimate, due to sampling and measurement error the rank could be between 21 and 29.

4. Twenty-six per cent of US students in socio-economically disadvantaged schools performed at or above the average performance in Finland. Disadvantaged schools are defined as schools for which the *PISA index of economic, social and cultural status* is below the average of the United States, which is equal to -.0634 index points.

5. All figures shown in purchasing power parities.

6. This is measured by the *PISA index of economic, social and cultural status* of students. The index has an average of 0 and a standard deviation of 1 for OECD countries. The index value for the most disadvantaged quarter of students is -1.05 for the United States and -1.14 for the OECD average. The index value for the entire student population is 0.17 for the United States and 0.00 for the OECD average.

7. No such data are available for the United States.

8. Among the students in socio-economically disadvantaged schools, 2% of American students are in schools that compare with the average school in Finland.

9. Twenty-six per cent of US students in socio-economically disadvantaged schools performer at or above the average performance in Finland. Disadvantaged schools are defined as schools for which the *PISA index of economic, social and cultural status* is below the average of the United States, which is equal to -.0634 index points.

10. Students in the United States attending schools located in a city with between 100 000 and 1 000 000 inhabitants performed, on average, at 504 score points, students attending schools in towns with between 15 000 and 100 000 inhabitants reached 506 score points, and students attending schools located in a small town with between 3 000 and 15 000 inhabitants reached 502 score points.

11. Resilient students are those who come from a socio-economically disadvantaged background and perform much higher than would be predicted by their background. To identify these students, first, the relationship between performance and socio-economic background across all students participating in the PISA 2009 assessment is established. Then the actual performance of each disadvantaged student is compared with the performance predicted by the average relationship among students from similar socio-economic backgrounds across countries. This difference is defined as the student's residual performance. A disadvantaged student is classified as resilient if his or her residual performance is found to be among the top quarter of students' residual performance from all countries.

12. In the United States, one unit of the *PISA index of student-teacher relationship* is positively associated with 14.9 score points on the PISA reading scale (Table IV.4.1).

13. An average proportion of school principals in the United States report that a number of student-related factors hinder learning "to some extent" or "a lot."

14. <u>Vertical differentiation</u> refers to the ways in which students progress through the education systems as they become older. Even though the student population is differentiated into grade levels in practically all schools in PISA, in some countries, all 15-year-old students attend the same grade level, while in other countries they are dispersed throughout various grade levels as a result of policies governing the age of entrance into the school system and/or grade repetition. <u>Horizontal differentiation</u> refers to differences in instruction within a grade or education level. Horizontal differentiation, which can be applied by the education system or by individual schools, groups students according to their interests and/or performance. At the system level, horizontal differentiation can be applied by schools that select students on the basis of their academic records, by offering specific programmes (vocational or academic, for example), and by setting the age at which students are admitted into these programmes. Individual schools can apply horizontal differentiation by grouping students according to ability or transferring students out of the school because of low performance, behavioural problems or special needs.

15. OECD (2010a), *OECD Factbook 2010*, OECD Paris.

16. OECD (2010a), *OECD Factbook 2010*, OECD Paris. Ratio of population aged less than 15 to the total population (data from 2008).

17. OECD (2010a), *OECD Factbook 2010*, OECD Paris. Ratio of population aged 65 and older to the total population, (data from 2008).

18. OECD (2010a), *OECD Factbook 2010*, OECD Paris. Annual population growth rate (data from 2007).

19. OECD (2010a), *OECD Factbook 2010*, OECD Paris. Annual population growth in percentage, OECD total, (data from 2007).

20. OECD (2010a), *OECD Factbook 2010*, OECD Paris. Foreign-born population as per cent of the total population, (data from 2007).

21. OECD (2010b), *OECD Economic Surveys: United States 2010*, OECD Publishing. Data from 2009.

22. OECD (2010a), *OECD Factbook 2010*, OECD Paris, Current prices and PPPs (data from 2008).

23. OECD (2010b), *OECD Economic Surveys: United States 2010*, OECD Publishing. Origin of national income in 2009 (per cent of national income).

24. OECD (2010a), *OECD Factbook 2010*, OECD Paris. Total unemployment rates as percentage of total labour force (data from 2008).

25. OECD (2010a), *OECD Factbook 2010*, OECD Paris. Total unemployment rates as percentage of total labour force (data from 2008).

26. OECD (2010c), *Employment Outlook*, OECD Publishing. Unemployed as a percentage of the labour force in the age group: youth aged 15-24 (data from 2008).

27. The OECD follows standard international conventions in using the term "tertiary education" to refer to all post-secondary programmes at ISCED levels 5B, 5A and 6, regardless of the institutions in which they are offered. OECD (2008), *Tertiary Education for the Knowledge Society: Volume 1*, OECD Publishing.

28. OECD (2010d), *Education at a Glance 2010*, OECD Publishing. Public expenditure presented in this table includes public subsidies to households for living costs (scholarships and grants to students/households and students loans), which are not spent on educational institutions (data from 2006).

29. OECD (2010d), *Education at a Glance 2010*, OECD Publishing. Public expenditure presented in this table includes public subsidies to households for living costs (scholarships and grants to students/households and students loans), which are not spent on educational institutions (data from 2006).

30. OECD (2010d), *Education at a Glance 2010*, OECD Publishing. Net enrolment rates of ages 4 and under as a percentage of the population aged 3 to 4 (data from 2008).

31. OECD (2010d), *Education at a Glance 2010*, OECD Publishing. OECD average net enrolment rates of ages 4 and under as a percentage of the population aged 3 to 4 (data from 2008).

32. OECD (2010d), *Education at a Glance 2010*, OECD Publishing. Net enrolment rates of ages 5 to 14 as a percentage of the population aged 5 to 14 (data from 2008).

33. OECD (2010d), *Education at a Glance 2010*, OECD Publishing. OECD average net enrolment rates of ages 5 to 14 as a percentage of the population aged 5 to 14 (data from 2008).

34. OECD (2010d), *Education at a Glance 2010*, OECD Publishing. Net enrolment rates of ages 15 to 19 as a percentage of the population aged 15 to 19 (data from 2008).

35. OECD (2010d), *Education at a Glance 2010*, OECD Publishing. OECD average net enrolment rates of ages 15 to 19 as a percentage of the population aged 15 to 19 (data from 2008).

36. OECD (2010d), Net enrolment rates of ages 20 to 29 as a percentage of the population aged 20 to 29 (data from 2008). This figure includes includes all 20-29 year olds, including those in employment, etc. The Gross Enrolment Ratio (GER), measured by the United Nations as the number of actual students enrolled/number of potential students enrolled, is generally higher. The GER for tertiary education in the US in 2008 is 83% (*www.WorldBank.org*).

37. OECD (2010d), *Education at a Glance 2010*, OECD Publishing. OECD average net enrolment rates of ages 20 to 29 as a percentage of the population aged 20 to 29 (data from 2008).

38. OECD (2010d), *Education at a Glance 2010*, OECD Publishing. Data from 2008.

39. Data is not applicable because category does not apply.

40. OECD (2010d), *Education at a Glance 2010*, OECD Publishing. Data from 2008.

41. Data is not applicable because category does not apply.

42. OECD (2010d), *Education at a Glance 2010*, OECD Publishing. Data from 2008.

43. Data is not applicable because category does not apply.

44. OECD (2010d), *Education at a Glance 2010*, OECD Publishing. Data from 2008.

45. Data is not applicable because category does not apply.

46. Data is not applicable because category does not apply.

47. OECD (2010d), *Education at a Glance 2010,* OECD Publishing. Starting salary/minimum training in USD adjusted for PPP (data from 2008).

48. OECD (2010d), *Education at a Glance 2010,* OECD Publishing. Data from 2008.

49. OECD (2010d), *Education at a Glance 2010,* OECD Publishing. Data from 2008.

50. OECD (2010d), *Education at a Glance 2010,* OECD Publishing. Sum of upper secondary graduation rates for a single year of age (year of reference for OECD average: 2008).

3

Ontario, Canada: Reform to Support High Achievement in a Diverse Context

Since 2000, Canada has become a world leader in its sustained strategy of professionally-driven reform of its education system. Not only do its students perform well, they perform well despite their socio-economic status, first language or whether they are native Canadians or recent immigrants. Canada has achieved success within a highly federated system, which features significant diversity, particularly with respect to issues of language and country of origin. This chapter takes an in-depth look at Canada's success, taking the case study of the nation's largest province, Ontario.

It shows how consistent application of centrally-driven pressure for higher results, combined with extensive capacity building and a climate of relative trust and mutual respect, have enabled the Ontario system to achieve progress on key indicators, while maintaining labour peace and morale throughout the system.

INTRODUCTION

Canada is a relative latecomer to the top of the international rankings. Unlike Japan and Korea, it was not a clear leader in international assessments in the 1980s and 1990s, and it was only after the release of the PISA rankings in 2000 that Canada found itself a leader of the pack (Table 3.1). These results have been confirmed in subsequent PISA tests, which have revealed that Canada has both strong average results as well as less dispersion among its high and low socio-economic status (SES) students than many other nations (OECD, 2010).

Understanding the factors behind this strong performance is not easy for two reasons. First, Canadian education is governed at the provincial level; the federal role is limited, and sometimes non-existent. Thus each of the 10 provinces and 3 territories has its own history, governance structure and educational strategy. Second, because Canada is a newcomer to educational success, there has not yet been the array of visitors, scholars, and other interested observers who could generate the kind of secondary literature which tells a story of Canadian success as a whole. Given those limitations, this report tries to balance breadth and depth by describing the features of the system and the relatively little that is known about the reasons for the success of Canadian education as a whole, coupled with an in-depth look at the recent educational strategy of the nation's largest province, Ontario.

Table 3.1 **Canada's mean scores on reading, mathematics and science scales in PISA**

	PISA 2000	PISA 2003	PISA 2006	PISA 2009
	Mean score	Mean score	Mean score	Mean score
Reading	534	528	527	524
Mathematics		532	527	527
Science			534	529

Source: OECD (2010), *PISA 2009 Results: What Students Know and Can Do: Student Performance in Reading, Mathematics and Science (Volume I)*, OECD Publishing.
StatLink ⬛⬛ http://dx.doi.org/10.1787/888932366655

This report aims to spur further investigations into the work of additional provinces, which would allow for a more definitive assessment of the reasons for Canadian success in future years. This question is especially important because Canada has achieved success within a highly federated system, which features significant diversity, particularly with respect to issues of language and country of origin. Given that many of the other PISA leaders are relatively small and culturally homogenous countries, Canada could provide a model of how to achieve educational success in a large, geographically dispersed, and culturally heterogeneous country.

THE CANADIAN EDUCATION SYSTEM

As mentioned above, the most striking feature of the Canadian system is its decentralisation. It is the only country in the developed world that has no federal office or department of education. Education is the responsibility of its 10 provinces and 3 territories. Four of those provinces hold approximately 80% of Canada's 5 million students: Ontario (2 million), Quebec (1 million), British Columbia (610 000) and Alberta (530 000).

Responsibility within the provinces is divided between the central provincial government and more locally-elected school boards. The provincial government is responsible for setting the curriculum, determining many major policies for schools and providing the majority, if not all, of the funding for schools (funding patterns vary slightly across provinces). The minister of education is chosen by the premier from elected members of the provincial legislature, and becomes a member of the ruling party's cabinet. The deputy minister is a civil servant, who carries much of the operational responsibility for the workings of the department. Tensions can exist between the civil servants in the province's Department of Education, who generally by training and inclination are sympathetic to the views of educators, and elected officials who may have a broader reform agenda.

Local school boards are elected. They employ staff and appoint principals and senior administrators. They also set annual budgets and make decisions on some programmes. Over time, the number of districts has shrunk considerably through consolidation processes. In Alberta, for example, there were historically more than 5 000 districts, which by the end of the 20th century had been consolidated to less than 70. There is no interim level of administration between the provinces and districts in Canada – provinces and districts work directly with one another on province-wide initiatives.

Teachers are unionised in Canada, and the unit of collective bargaining varies across provinces – some bargain at the local level, some at the provincial level, and some are mixed. Teacher training takes place in universities, although the standards for certification have traditionally been set by the provinces. In 1987, British Columbia was the first to make its teachers self-governing, granting to the British Columbia College of Teachers exclusive responsibility for governing entry, discipline, and professional development of teachers. In 1996, Ontario followed suit, creating an Ontario College of Teachers which governs similar functions; on its 31 member governing council sit 17 teachers elected by the College, and 14 members appointed by the Ontario Minster of Education. In both cases, more traditional issues, such as wages, continue to fall under collective bargaining and are separate from the work of these self-regulating bodies.

The Canadian system is also internationally distinctive for its efforts to balance respect for diversity of language and religious affiliation with province-wide educational goals. For religion, Section 93 of the Constitution Act 1867 sought to protect parents' rights to send their children to Protestant and Catholic schools, subject to provincial control over funding and teachers, but using public funding. This structure means that these schools and school boards in Canada are within the public system and under partial control of the Ministry of Education, not in the private sector. These schools were named "separate schools" in Canada West and "dissentient" schools in Canada East. There is variation across provinces in exactly how these arrangements have evolved; in some provinces – like Alberta, Ontario and Saskatchewan – separate public and dissentient schools exist; in others, like Manitoba and British Columbia, parents seeking a Catholic or Protestant education have to send their children to private schools, though even these often receive some degree of public funding.

While initial struggles in Canada were around religious differences, in more recent years language has shown greater salience. Section 23 of the Canadian Charter of Rights and Freedoms protects parents who speak a minority language (English or French), gives their children the right to receive primary and secondary instruction in their native language, and allows for the establishment of "minority language educational facilities," if sufficient numbers warrant it. There has been some controversy over how many students speaking a minority language are required to invoke this right; in Quebec it has generally been interpreted to mean only one, whereas in Nova Scotia one judge felt that 50 students were too few to justify the creation of a French school. Courts have also had to adjudicate what it means to have "minority language educational facilities", with some seeing that as requiring only separate francophone programmes within existing schools, whereas others judge it necessary to create separate francophone schools. The overall consequences of the protection of both language and religious rights is that in some provinces, such as Ontario, as many as four separate systems of public schools can exist within one province (English, English Catholic, French, French Catholic).

Students in Canada are grouped by ability in ways that are very similar to the United States' system. Elementary school-aged children are often placed in ability groups within heterogeneous classrooms. Students in secondary schools are placed into tracks or streams, based on perceived ability levels. Most high schools have tracks such as general, advanced, vocational, or university entrance. These practices have faced criticism for not sufficiently challenging students in the lower tracks, but sorting by perceived ability persists.

The thumbnail history of Canadian educational reform in the post-war period shares much in common with the United States and the rest of the industrialised world. Strong economic growth in the 1950s and 1960s, combined with increasing demand for schooling, led to rapidly increasing spending on schooling between 1950 and 1970, with much of the energy focused on school construction and teacher hiring. Because of the increased demand for teachers, teacher wages rose considerably over this period. Schools and teachers were given more autonomy over what to teach, and the inspection functions of provincial ministries were delimited or eliminated. At the same time, provinces were taking increasing financial responsibility for schooling: in 1950, localities paid 64% of the costs compared to 36% from the provinces, and by 1970 the ratio had largely reversed, with provinces paying 60% and localities 40%. By 1997, eight out of the ten provinces had taken total responsibility for funding. The structure of the Canadian education system is lean and uniform, as shown in Figure 3.1.

The post-war boom of the 1950s and 1960s gave way to hard economic times in the 1970s, and the final three decades of the 20th century saw Canadian education seeking a way to cut costs while increasing educational outcomes. Globalisation and the arrival of the knowledge economy increased the importance of schooling as a matter of economic competitiveness. A neoliberal emphasis on efficiency pervaded the system, and support for greater choice, growing support for private schools, and increased state accountability became the order of the day.

While all four leading provinces increased the role of centralised testing and curriculum planning in the 1980s and 1990s, some of these efforts combined greater centralised accountability with more school-level control, under a "tight-loose" philosophy of school improvement.[1] The emphasis on testing in Canada was extensive compared to most European systems, but not nearly as prominent as in the United States.

■ Figure 3.1 ■
Canada's education system organisation

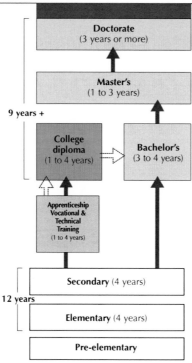

The first decade of the 21st century has seen a set of educational reforms which emphasise the centralised standards and assessments which also characterised the earlier reforms of the 1980s and 1990s. However, the new reforms include a strong effort to try to build capacity among teachers, and to generate teacher buy-in to the improvement strategy. While the earlier strategy of testing grew out of an increasing scepticism about the quality of education and a more general distrust of government, the new strategy seeks to address this distrust as a core problem and aims to generate a virtuous cycle of greater performance leading to higher levels of trust, which in turn generate more energy for continued improvement. This strategy is described in some detail below, taking the case of Ontario. But first we discuss the factors behind Canada's general successful educational performance, and especially its success at educating and integrating its immigrant children.

CANADIAN SUCCESS IN EDUCATION

When asked to explain Canada's strong nationwide PISA results, several Canadian officials and informed observers could only offer informed hunches, given the absence of any meaningful national government role in education. These hunches fell generally into three categories: Canadian culture; the Canadian welfare state; and three policy-specific factors (teacher selectivity, equalised funding, and provincial curricula).

Cultural factors

In terms of culture, observers note that parents in Canada are generally supportive of their children's education and can be seen as an asset to the schools. Comparative PISA data on the leisure reading habits of Canadian students suggest that Canadian students are more likely than any other children in the world to read daily for pleasure (Tibbetts, 2007). While culture is notoriously diffuse and difficult to measure, further exploration of its potential influence seems warranted because it could help to explain the similarity of results across provinces that differ in their educational strategies.

The welfare state

Despite its provincial educational structure, Canada does have a strong national welfare state, which was born of the crisis spurred by the Great Depression and which continued to grow in the 1960s. Observers suggest that this has had two important educational consequences. First, children and their parents have access to national health insurance, and adults are protected from the vicissitudes of capitalism by a strong social safety net. While child poverty rates in Canada are fairly high by international standards (Canada had the 7th highest child poverty rate of 23 countries measured), variation across provinces in child poverty rates are correlated with PISA outcomes (*e.g.* Alberta has the lowest rate at 11.2% and the highest PISA scores).

Second, the idea of a welfare state and a common good is much more firmly entrenched in Canada than in its more individualistic neighbour to the south (the US). The idea that health care and other social services are a right and not a privilege carries over into education, where there is a broadly-shared norm that society is collectively responsible for the educational welfare of all of its children. The combination of this norm with the protection afforded by the welfare state creates a climate in which school success is expected for all students. As Harvard Professor Richard Elmore, who has worked for years with Canadian schools, said during interviews for this report:

> While the structure and artefacts of the Canadian system look about the same as the American one (professional learning communities, resource rooms for data driven instruction), the culture in which this work takes place is entirely different. Canadian teachers feel that the state has done its part by delivering the students to the schools ready to learn, and that they, in turn, have a deeply-felt obligation and responsibility to ensure that the students do indeed get educated. (Interview conducted for this report)

Policy factors

In terms of policy, despite the lack of a national co-ordinating body, a number of respondents suggest that the provinces are quite similar in some of their key policies. The reason given was what scholars in other contexts have called "isomorphism", or the desire to acquire legitimacy by becoming similar to other organisations. Canada possesses a Council of Ministers of Education (CMEC), which is the forum through which the ministers of education in the respective provinces can meet for co-ordination purposes. While this body was consistently described as limited in its impact, because it acted only when all of the ministers agreed (infrequently), it does fulfil an important information-sharing function and enables good ideas and practices to spread across provincial lines.

Neil Guppy, a professor of sociology at the University of British Columbia and author of a textbook on Canadian education, put it this way during an interview for this report:

> My own take is that autonomy is overblown – many of the textbooks used by the provinces are identical, our teacher education programs are very similar, the arrangements of schooling (kindergarten, elementary, middle, high) are very similar, unionisation is similar, school administration personnel shuffle between provinces with little problem, etc. To my knowledge all universities treat student grades from each province as substitutable even though we do not have SAT or national exams. Imitation from, and monitoring of, other jurisdictions is high. In most English-speaking provinces you are likely to find as much variation between rural and urban as you are province to province. (Interview conducted for this report)

Three common policy factors (in addition to the welfare state and cultural reasons) were highlighted as potentially important to pan-Canadian educational success:

- The establishment of province-wide curricula. These are developed by the respective ministries of education through a process of extensive consultation with groups of teachers and subject matter experts. In some provinces these curricula are fairly detailed, whereas in others they serve more as guidelines of what should be learned and when. While there is wide variation in the degree to which these curricula actually penetrate classroom practices, they do provide basic guidance as to what should be learned by which students at what ages. In recent years, some of the smaller provinces in the west have moved towards co-ordinating these efforts to establish greater uniformity across provinces, similar to consortia of states in the United States working together towards Common Core standards. Recent PISA results have shown that Alberta is the highest-scoring province, and the Alberta Ministry ascribes this success in part to the quality of its curriculum.

- The high degree of selectivity in choosing teachers. The 2007 McKinsey report on leading PISA countries emphasised that one factor which differentiated PISA leaders from those further down the chart was the degree to which teacher education programmes were able to draw their students from the top end of the talent pool (Barber and Mourshed 2007). Ben Levin, former deputy minister in Ontario and a widely cited scholar on Canadian education, said that Canadian applicants to teachers colleges are in the "top 30%" of their college cohorts.

One Canadian teacher interviewed explained that it was difficult to get into a teachers' college in Canada, although, as he pointed out, "everyone knew that there was a loophole – you could always cross the border to the United States. Anyone can get credentialed there." The education within these teacher training institutions is seen by some to be of high quality; Levin estimates there are perhaps 50 institutions in all of Canada, as opposed to hundreds across the United States, which allows for greater monitoring of training quality. Other respondents agreed that teacher selectivity was high, but were more sceptical of the quality of the training institutions.

- Equalised funding. Because funding has shifted entirely or almost entirely to the province level, the provinces are able to provide funding to offset the greater neediness of some of their students. Funding from the provinces to districts is generally split into three categories: block grants based on number of students; categorical grants which are either used to fund particular programmatic needs (*e.g.* special education) or to help districts meet specific challenges in providing basic services (*e.g.* more remote districts need more funds for transportation); and equalisation funding, which is used in the districts that retain some local funding to equalise the poorer districts.

These factors represent the views of a small sample of Canadian officials and observers (see interviewee list at end of chapter) about how they understand their own success. However, there is clearly more research and analysis needed. There are many countries and states/provinces elsewhere that have centralised curricula without yielding these kinds of results. There is also an extensive literature debating the importance of funding, which broadly suggests that money can help, but that it all depends on how it is spent. The teacher selectivity argument carries more weight because it is one of the few factors that more generally differentiates PISA leaders from the rest. In general, the major features of the Canadian system don't look that different from many other systems that do much less well on the PISA, and thus it is particularly difficult to know the sources of Canada's success.

Similar structures can actually house very different types of work depending on the culture in which they are situated. Curriculum, funding and teacher talent are resources that provinces and schools can draw upon to create high quality schooling if they are inclined towards collaboration and are willing to take internal collective responsibility for student outcomes. One example of such practice in Ontario will be explored below. Before getting to that, however, it is important to address one unique element in Canada's performance: its education of immigrant children.

CANADIAN SUCCESS EDUCATING IMMIGRANT CHILDREN

One of the most striking things about the Canadian results is their success with immigrant children. By some estimates, Canada has the highest rates of immigration per capita in the world. It is a country of which former prime minister William Lyon MacKenzie King once famously said, "If some countries have too much history, we have too much geography," referring to the way in which Canada is a relatively young nation comprising travellers from all over the world. Canada takes in about 250 000 immigrants per year (in a country of approximately 34 million inhabitants). Given the size of the land area, the relative low density population and low birth rates, immigrants are seen in Canada as an important and needed resource. All of the major political parties currently support either sustaining or increasing rates of immigration; there is no popular support for restricting immigration.

Patterns of immigration have shifted over time. Until the 1970s, the majority of immigrants came from Europe; over the past 40 years, most have come from Asia and the developing world. In 2007, the leading source countries of Canadian immigrants were China and India (about 28 000 each), the Philippines (20 000), and Pakistan (10 000). Smaller groups of immigrants come from Algeria, Colombia, France, Iran, Romania, Russia, South Korea, Sri Lanka, the United Kingdom and the United States, each of whom sends more than 3 500 immigrants per year.[2] In total, these patterns of immigration mean that there are 40 000 newcomers to public schools each year; 80% of these students are non-English speaking, and 90% will go to school in Montreal, Toronto or Vancouver.

Immigration in Canada is organised into three classes – refugee populations (22 000 in 2008), family class sponsorships (65 000), and workers imported to fill a gap in the Canadian economy (150 000).[3] The fact that 60% of immigrants are selected on the basis of their ability to make an economic contribution creates a highly educated immigrant class. In total, 23% of Canadian workers in 2008 were born abroad, as were 49% of doctorate holders and 40% of those with masters' degrees.

PISA results suggest that within three years of arrival in Canada, immigrants score an average of 500 on the PISA exam, which is remarkably strong by international standards. For comparison's sake, in the 2006 PISA assessment of reading, Canadian first generation immigrants scored an average of 520 points, as opposed to less than 490 in the United States and less than 430 in France. Canada is also one of very few countries where there is no gap between its immigrant and native students on the PISA. (By contrast in the United States the gap in reading is 22 points, and in France and Germany it is around 60 points). Second generation Canadians perform significantly better than first generation Canadians, suggesting that the pattern is of progress by all students over time. Finally, Canada is one of the few countries where there is no difference in performance between students who do not speak the language of instruction at home and those who do.

Why has Canada done so well at educating its immigrant students? Interviewees' responses can be grouped around three factors. First and most importantly, because the majority of immigrants are selected on the basis of their ability to contribute economically, many immigrant children have highly-educated parents. A 2006 OECD report found that, on average, first generation Canadian students had parents with as many or more years of education as native-born parents. These advantages in terms of parental education and socio-economic status also translated into school resources; in the same study, Canada was one of only a few countries in which immigrant students had access to equal or greater resources than native-born students. Specifically, student/teacher ratios, physical infrastructure, classroom climate, and teacher morale were on average higher for the immigrant students sampled than for native students (OECD, 2006).

Second, Canadian multiculturalism provides a distinct philosophy that seeks to both respect the importance of native cultures while also incorporating immigrants into a distinctively Canadian identity. In practice, this has meant that immigrant students are for the most part placed into classes with native students in English and French; native language instruction primarily takes place in non-profit organisations and other work outside of schools.

Third, in some of the provinces that have had the largest influx of immigrants, an explicit policy has sought to support the success of these students. In British Columbia, for example, students participate in the regular curriculum, but the ministry provides funds for additional language support if a series of criteria are met. These include: *i)* evidence that the student lacks proficiency and will not reach it without additional support; *ii)* an annual instruction plan is prepared that meets the needs of the student; *iii)* a teaching specialist participates in the creation and review of the plan; *iv)* the school must provide pull-out and in-class support for the student, as well as support and training for the affected teachers.

All in all, Canada has a positive and reinforcing cycle when it comes to immigration and educating immigrant students. It is an attractive destination for immigrants, and immigrants are welcomed as part of both a cultural commitment and as an economic necessity. The majority of immigrants who come to the country are selected to fill economic needs. This means that they are not seen as a threat or as competing for jobs and increases the political support for their continued arrival. Immigrant students as a group have much the same advantages in terms of parental education and socio-economic status as native-born students, and they attend schools that by all measures are relatively equal. Philosophically, they are welcomed as part of Canada's commitment to multiculturalism, and some programmes are in place to supplement students' learning of English and French, although the emphasis is largely on immersion. Overall, this combination of factors creates a fairly welcoming environment for relatively advantaged immigrants, and as we have seen, they correspondingly fare extremely well by international standards.

THE ONTARIO EXPERIENCE

Education system and context for reform

From 2003 to 2010, Ontario was a world leader in its sustained strategy of professionally-driven reform of its education system. Initiated by Premier Dalton McGuinty following his election in 2003, the Ontario strategy has achieved widespread positive results in increasing elementary literacy and numeracy, improving graduation rates, and reducing the number of low-performing schools. The constellation of elements that came together to allow this strategy to succeed is described below.

Ontario is the largest province in Canada, with an area of 400 000 square miles, and a population of approximately 13 million, or 40% of all Canadians. It is a highly urbanised province, with 80% of students located in metropolitan areas. In terms of diversity, 27% of Ontario students were born outside of Canada and 20% are visible minorities. Toronto, the main city in Ontario, is one of the most diverse cities in the world.

The oversight of education in the province of Ontario is divided between the Ontario Ministry of Education, covering school-level education, and the Ministry of Training, Colleges and Universities, covering vocational and higher education.

For school-level education there are four sets of locally-elected school boards in Ontario, meeting Canada's constitutional requirements for public support of minority languages and religious minorities (Levin, 2008):

- 31 English school boards serve about 1.4 million students;
- 29 English catholic school boards serve about 590 000 students;
- 8 French catholic boards have 70 000 students; and
- 4 French public boards have 23 000 students.

This means that any given area of the province will be served by four boards, introducing some degree of choice into the system. There are about 5 000 schools in the public system; there is no public funding for private schools.

There were two major initiatives pursued by the Ontario Ministry of Education over this time period:

- The Literacy and Numeracy initiative: to increase reading and mathematics outcomes in elementary schools. Through a deep capacity-building strategy (described below), this initiative has succeeded in raising the average pass rate in provincial exams from roughly 55% (2003) to roughly 70% (2010) in reading, mathematics and writing in grade 3. Similar gains of about 10-12 percentage points are apparent in the same subjects in grade six.

- The Student Success initiative: to increase the high school graduation rate to 85%. The background to this programme was that the road to dropping out of high school starts early; by tracking students who have failed one or more courses in 9th grade, it is possible to identify potential dropouts early. By funding a "student success officer" in each school, and creating programmes of "credit recovery" through which students could make up the parts of courses that they failed, the graduation rate has increased from 68% to 79%.

Ontario benefits from a set of background conditions that helped to facilitate much of its success. Politically, the McGuinty Liberal premiership benefitted from following a conservative government that was extremely unpopular with teachers and others working in the sector. The conservative government is generally credited with having created a province-wide curriculum and instituted an accompanying assessment and accountability framework, but it alienated the education community in the process by cutting funding, reducing professional development time by half, running television ads demonising teachers, and increasing support for private schools. During this period 55 000 students left the public system, and polls suggested that more than 15% of public school parents were actively considering private school options. There were several teacher strikes, including a two-week work stoppage protesting government legislation in 1997. Morale was extremely low and the relationship between the government and teachers was highly acrimonious. Union leader Rhonda Kimberly Young, former President of the Ontario Secondary School Teachers Federation, had this to say when interviewed for this report about the years before McGuinty government took over:

> Then we got the conservatives and they came in on what they called a "Common Sense Revolution" which implied that there was going to be a miracle. They could lower everybody's taxes. They could cut waste. They could do more with less – better quality services at lower cost. Unfortunately, they were able to sell this idea to the voters. When they took office Mike Harris was the premier and the first education minister that he appointed was a high school dropout. We saw that as fairly indicative of their approach to education. [That they were not] going to be looking at pedagogy, research and those sorts of things but rather were coming in with a hammer…and they did. In 1998 we had a province wide walkout – it was a political protest. (Interview conducted for this report)

In this highly polarised environment the Liberal party made an early decision to make education the central issue in the next provincial election. As opposition leader, McGuinty made a major policy speech in 2001 committing the party to a quite specific set of reforms, including class size reductions, should they be elected. This speech was followed up by the development of a very detailed education platform with 65 policy proposals. By the time the Liberals took office in 2003 they believed they had a strong reform mandate.

McGuinty's first Education Minister, Gerard Kennedy, came in with a running start, for he had been the opposition party's education "critic," *i.e.* shadow minister. In his own words, he came into office unusually well-prepared:

> During my time as critic I visited lots of schools and school boards all across the province. I spent a lot of time in lunchrooms with teachers, in meetings after school with parent groups, and I sat down with student councils whenever I had the opportunity. I met with every key stakeholder group not only to build relationships but to engage them in the development of our policy agenda. I must have met with 6,000 people during that period.

> We needed to create a new political consensus on education. The current level of politicisation of the system was taking a huge toll on public confidence. In the preceding eight years of Conservative government hundreds and hundreds of hours of school had been lost to strikes and lockouts, and this level of disruption was at the core of public discontent with the system. We felt we had to change that dynamic if we were going to have any chance of successfully moving our reform agenda. We needed to re-establish trust between the government and the profession, and between school boards and teachers. (Interview conducted for this report)

In addition to Minister Kennedy's leadership role, the McGuinty government benefitted from the advice and leadership of a deeply knowledgeable and experienced school reformer, Michael Fullan, a University of Toronto expert who had written widely and lectured around the world on school reform. He became McGuinty's special advisor on education, and helped recruit Ben Levin, another deeply knowledgeable academic and practitioner, to come into the government as Kennedy's Deputy Minister. All of these figures shared a relatively similar vision of capacity-building system change, which helped to anchor and sustain the reforms in the years that followed. McGuinty himself also visited England to learn about somewhat similar British reforms, and the Ontario strategy drew upon the British strategy with some important modifications (described below).

Financially, funding in Ontario had shifted in 1997 so that 100% of school funding came from the province. Thus while the system does have multiple levels, province-wide funding increased the leverage of the ministry.

Leadership, goals and capacity for improvement

The literature and interviewees are all clear that the sustained leadership of Premier McGuinty has been fundamental to the success of the reforms. McGuinty ran on a platform of becoming the education premier, and through his election and re-election in 2007, he has kept a sustained focus on educational improvement. McGuinty was personally involved in the reforms, and has met repeatedly with key educational stakeholders over the course of his premiership to emphasise the importance of the reforms. Michael Fullan, who was the architect of the strategy and an advisor to the premier, said of McGuinty during interviews for this report:

> The Premier is key, obviously. If Premier McGuinty had left it would have been a different story. I said to him in the first term, when you get re-elected…. [don't] lose the plot, fail to keep the sustainability and focus on it. And the week after he got re-elected, he said to me, 'Not only am I not going to lose the plot, I'm going to intensify it, become even more committed and more confident and more impatient. (Interview conducted for this report)

In contrast to the kind of "spinning wheels" which often doom school reform efforts as systems lurch from leader to leader, or to situations where education falls off the leadership's agenda after an initial bout of enthusiasm, McGuinty has maintained an active, sustained, personal and consistent focus on education over the past seven years. Deputy Minister Costante, who took office in 2009, recalls receiving a call from Premier McGuinty on the day he took office with the following message:

> Don't get distracted. There will be a lot of people asking you to do all sorts of nice things out there, some of which may be perfectly good but will not add to our student achievement agenda. I want you to keep focused on the student achievement agenda. (Interview conducted for this report)

And just in case the new deputy thought he might have an opportunity to coast on the achievements of the past several years, McGuinty has tasked Costante with developing and implementing a new full-day kindergarten programme for four and five-year-olds in 600 schools by September 2010.

From the beginning, Ontario's theory of change centred on the fact that school systems are easily distracted and drawn into many questions and controversies that have little or no relationship to improving student learning and educational attainment. They also believed that creating systemic change across several layers of government and 5 000 schools would require a very limited number of goals that would serve as a focus for coherent effort. McGuinty had made two central commitments that guided the work of the ministry: increasing literacy and numeracy in elementary schools, and increasing the high school graduation rate. They also set ambitious, but hopefully not unrealistic, long-term quantitative targets for each of these goals: to improve the provincial passing rate in literacy and numeracy from 55% to 75%, and to increase the high school graduation rate from 68% to 85%.

To achieve these goals, they had a seemingly simple, but actually quite complex theory of action. This work was informed by a careful analysis of the failings of previous initiatives. Most top-down initiatives, they concluded, were unable to achieve deep and lasting changes in practice because: *i)* the reforms were focused on things that were too distant from the instructional core of teaching and learning; *ii)* the reforms assumed that teachers would know how to do things they actually didn't know how to do; *iii)* too many conflicting reforms asked teachers to do too many things simultaneously; and *iv)* teachers and schools did not buy in to the reform strategy. To achieve sustained change, then, would require:

- Strategies directly focused on improving the act of teaching.

- Careful and detailed attention to implementation, along with opportunities for teachers to practice new ideas and learn from their colleagues.

- A single integrated strategy and one set of expectations for both teachers and students.

- Support from teachers for the reforms.

Both province and district policies would need to be crafted with all of these goals in mind.

Of all of these points, the last one (gaining teacher support) was perhaps most important to the new strategy. To improve skills across 5 000 schools would require a continuous and sustained effort by hundreds of thousands of teachers to try to improve their practice. This, they thought, could only happen if teachers were "onside" (to use their word).

To this end, the ministry drew a sharp contrast between its capacity-building approach to reform and the more punitive versions of accountability used in the United States, and, to a lesser extent, in Britain.[4] They chose to downplay the public reporting of results, and they emphasised that struggling schools would receive additional support and outside expertise rather than be punished or closed.

It is clear that the ministry acted extremely skilfully politically to win over teachers, schools, and unions to their vision of reform. A key move was the appointment of Gerard Kennedy as Deputy Minister. He was a vigorous critic of the previous administration and widely seen as someone who supported public education and was sensitive to the needs of teachers. He met quarterly with the major teachers' unions, superintendents' organisations, and principal associations to discuss ongoing reform strategies. The ministry also created the Ontario Education Partnership Table where a wider range of stakeholders could meet with ministry officials two to four times a year. This led to Working Tables, where smaller groups of stakeholders worked in more detail on particular issues.

Very important to these efforts was the signing of a four-year collective bargaining agreement with the four major teachers' unions in 2005, covering 2004 to 2008. In this agreement, the ministry was able to negotiate several items that were consistent both with their educational strategy and with the unions' interests. Specifically, McGuinty had pledged to reduce class size in elementary schools, which created 5 000 new jobs. The ministry and the union also both wanted 200 minutes of weekly preparation time for all elementary school teachers; this created 2 000 new positions in music, arts, physical education and languages. The agreement also provided money for the hiring of a student success position, full or part-time, in each school. This agreement thus both pushed forward the educational agenda and created a sustained period of labour peace which allowed for a continued focus on educational improvement. In 2008, a second four-year agreement was signed.

To achieve these results, the ministry created a well thought-out implementation strategy. To implement the literacy and numeracy initiatives, they created a new 100-person secretariat responsible for building the capacity and expertise to do the work. This was separate from the ministry, and thus was able to start fresh without the usual bureaucratic obstacles. They also required that teams be created in each district and each school in order to lead the work on literacy and numeracy. By so doing, they paired external expertise with sustained internal time and leadership to push the initiative. Avis Glaze, who was responsible for leading the Literacy and Numeracy Secretariat, said during interviews for this report that the effort succeed in part because of its field base:

> We recruited a new team of people who had deep experience in the field – teachers, principals, subject matter specialists – people who were deeply respected by teachers and schools, and were not seen primarily as representatives of the department. This mini-organisation was largely based in the field – we had 6 regional teams plus one French language team, each of 6-8 people. This means that the majority of the people in the Secretariat were actively working in the field, building relationships with schools, principals and teachers, rather than in the home office back at the Ministry. (Interview conducted for this report)

They also tried to ensure that reform was really a two-way street, rather than simply something imposed from above. As Michael Fullan describes it, one of the lessons learned from the British model was to avoid mandating from the top:

> Michael Barber in the English strategy eventually called their strategy "informed prescription". So the idea of informed prescription was that you do your homework at the centre, you get informed and then you pretty much prescribe the curriculum and the instructional methods and use of time, including such things as the literacy hour. By contrast, when we set up our secretariat, we said to the field, to our 72 districts, don't worry, we are not going to come up with informed prescription and start advocating particular usages. Rather, what we are going to do is join in partnership with you in the field, the sector, and identify good practices and consolidate those and spread them. They might eventually come to have a certain kind of status that comes close to being non-negotiable, but we are not in the business at the centre of telling you what to do. We are in the business of jointly co-discovering it, so that's what we did and that's how we did it. (Interview conducted for this report)

The government pursued a different strategy for the Student Success initiative in high schools. Rather than sending out a team from the ministry, they gave the districts money to hire a "Student Success leader" to co-ordinate efforts in their district. The ministry also gave money for the district leaders to meet and share strategies. Again each high school was given support to hire a provincially-funded Student Success teacher and was required to create a Student Success team to identify students showing early indicators of academic struggles and design appropriate interventions.

An important element in the development of the Student Success strategy was the creation of a new programme in high schools called the High Skills Major. This aimed to take high school students who were not engaged by the traditional academic curriculum and give them a different menu of courses. While earlier approaches in this vein have justifiably been accused of tracking working class students away from higher end jobs, by working with prospective employers, the High Skill Major programme created more hands-on courses to give students practical skills to lead to employment opportunities. More than 20 000 students are now enrolled in 740 High Skill Major programmes in 430 schools.

The ministry also had a clear theory of comparative advantage in terms of who should do what during the reforms. The role of the ministry was to set clear expectations and targets, to provide funding, to create a working collective bargaining agreement that would support improved teaching and learning, to provide external expertise, and to provide support for struggling schools. The role of the district was to align its personnel and hiring policies with the overall strategy, and to support the schools as they went through continuous processes of learning. However, much of the real action necessarily had to happen in the schools, where teachers worked in communities to think about practical problems and to learn from one another. While the mission and pressure came from the top, there was a clear recognition that it was at the school level in which change had to happen, and that the role of other actors in the system was to support the learning and change occurring in the schools.

Economic and sociological theories of action: Motivation, trust and respect versus punishment and competition

The Ontario strategy differs from a number of other reform efforts, particularly in the United States, in its lack of punitive accountability, performance pay, and competition among schools. Very broadly speaking, the architects of the reforms seem to take more of a "*homo sociologicus*" than a "*homo economicus*" view of reform. The architects of the reforms drew upon organisational theorists like Peter Drucker and Edwards Deming rather than economists. From this viewpoint, the problem was more to do with lack of knowledge than lack of will, and the key to motivation was not individual economic calculations but rather the chance to be part of successful and improving schools and organisations. This meant that the key ideas were less about "hard" concepts like accountability and incentives and more about "softer" ideas like culture, leadership and shared purpose. The key challenge was to create layers of organisations directed towards systemic improvement. There is also little emphasis in the Ontario strategy on "getting better people"; instead the idea is to work with what you have and upgrade their skills. In all of these respects, the Ontario model challenges more market-based theories of reform.

The Ontario strategy is perhaps the world's leading example of professionally-driven system change. Through consistent application of centrally-driven pressure for higher results, combined with extensive capacity building, in a climate of relative trust and mutual respect, the Ontario system was able to achieve progress on key indicators, while maintaining labour peace and morale throughout the system.

LESSONS FROM ONTARIO

▪ Commitment to education and to children

The strong cultural commitment to education seems to be an important underlying national value that helps explain Canada's overall strong performance despite the absence of a national governmental role in education. The commitment to the welfare of children, as expressed in Canada's strong social safety net, helps explain why Canada's achievement gaps, while still worrisome, are nowhere near as profound as those in the United States.

▪ Cultural support for universal high achievement

The extraordinary performance of Canada's immigrant children is largely a reflection of the high expectations immigrant families have for their children, and of the fact that those high expectations seem by and large to be held by educators as well. Because Canada has historically seen its immigrants as crucial assets for the continuing development of the country, and because its immigration policies reflect those values, schools see it as their role to integrate children into the mainstream culture as rapidly as possible. If anything, the value placed on high achievement for immigrant children seems to have positive spill over effects for expectations for native-born children, rather than *vice versa*.

▪ System coherence and alignment

This is one of the big lessons from Ontario's reforms. Although some observers complained about the sheer number of initiatives launched by the McGuinty government over the years, it is apparent that the Ontario reform designers worked hard to develop and implement a systemic response to the problems and challenges they inherited. An important, often underestimated barrier to achieving system coherence is the lack of a shared understanding among key stakeholders about how key governmental leaders see the problems of the system and what lies behind the policies and programmes they have designed in response. The McGuinty government worked tirelessly to build a sense of shared understanding and common purpose among key stakeholder groups, and consequently their two major systemic initiatives – the Literacy and Numeracy Secretariat and the Student Success strategy – enjoyed broad public understanding and support.

▪ Teacher and principal quality

Ontario's reforms rested heavily on the confidence the government had in the quality of the province's teaching force. The decision by the Literacy and Numeracy Secretariat not to follow England's "informed prescription" model, but instead to put seed money into the field to encourage local experimentation and innovation, sent a strong signal that teacher-generated solutions to weaknesses in reading and mathematics performance were likely to be more successful than solutions imposed from above. The fact that teaching has historically been a respected profession in Canada, and continues to draw its candidates from the top third of secondary school graduates, meant that the government had a solid basis for believing that its trust would pay off. Given the "teacher-bashing" engaged in by the previous government, this show of trust in the competence and professionalism of the teaching force was an essential ingredient in repairing the rupture that had developed between the profession and the government.

Ontario has paid special attention to leadership development, especially for school principals. In 2008 the government initiated the Ontario Leadership Strategy that spells out the skills, knowledge and attributes of effective leaders. Among the elements of the strategy are a strong mentoring programme that has now reached over 4 500 principals and vice-principals, and a new province-wide appraisal programme for school leaders.

▪ A single capable centre with authority and legitimacy to act

The Ontario story is very much one of strong central leadership coupled with a major investment in capacity-building and trust-building in the field. The combination of skilled, sustained political leadership from the Premier and a succession of capable ministers, and very strong professional leadership from the Deputy Education Minister account for a big part of Ontario's success. While the initial decision to create the Literacy and Numeracy Secretariat outside the bureaucracy suggests that the political leadership did not have confidence that the ministry could carry out such an ambitious, high-profile initiative, one of the Deputy Education Minister's key goals was to make the department more attentive and responsive to the field. By all accounts he and his successors have made progress in that regard.

▪ Professional accountability

Ontario has managed to balance administrative and professional accountability in an admirable fashion. The McGuinty government made no attempt to dismantle or weaken the assessment regime put in place by the previous government, and it has consistently communicated the message to the field and the public that results matter, as defined by performance on the provincial assessments. However, its response to weak performance has consistently been intervention and support, not blame and punishment. One of its major successes in the early years was to reduce dramatically the number of low-performing schools, not by threatening to close them (as often happens in the US), but by flooding the schools with technical assistance and support. The underlying assumption of Ontario's leaders seems to be that teachers are professionals who are trying to do the right thing, and that performance problems are much more likely to be a product of lack of knowledge than lack of motivation. Consequently, teachers seem to take more responsibility for performance than is often the case in countries with a more punitive approach to external accountability.

WHERE IS CANADA ON THE EDUCATIONAL CONTINUUM?

Canada is an interesting case. It is more reliant than many advanced industrial countries on commodities and agricultural production. Yet it can certainly be counted among the most advanced of the industrial nations, especially its four most populous provinces. Though it has more natural resources than most industrial countries, it confounds predictions in its firm conviction that high education levels for everyone are essential to its economic future. In that sense it looks very like Finland and Singapore (Chapters 5 and 7), despite a very different economic profile.

Similarly, Canada fits the education profile of a country that is counting on its human resources for its prosperity. It recruits its teachers from the top third of the cohort. It seems, at least from the example of Ontario, to have struck a nice balance between a top-down and bottom-up approach to reform. It has clearly moved as far as any other nation towards trusting its teachers and treating them like professionals. While schools have a fair amount of discretion, they operate within a clear provincial framework of standards, assessments and accountability. In some ways the system is quite traditionally organised. Students are tracked by ability, and yet there seems to be a strong focus on students most at-risk of failure, as evidenced especially by the Student Success Initiative. In that sense, Canada has adopted the view that its future cannot be assured unless all students are performing at high levels and it has specific policies designed to assure that outcome. Canada's post-secondary enrolment rates are now among the highest in the OECD community (Annex 3.A), a clear reflection of the growing public realisation that education beyond high school will be increasingly essential in a knowledge-based economy.

FINAL OBSERVATIONS

Canada demonstrates, rather surprisingly, that success can be achieved without a national strategy. This observation runs counter to the instincts of many of those who sit in policy seats and seek to effect change, but the fact is that Canada has achieved success on PISA across its provinces despite a limited to non-existent federal role. The best explanation for this is that different jurisdictions will tend to blend in with one another. The power of ideas and the possibilities of diffusion can therefore be sufficient to generate good practice. Ironically, some Canadian leaders, including Gerard Kennedy, are now trying to mount a more national strategy, arguing that education is too important to be left entirely to the provinces.

A second observation is that too often in education policy discussions the choices are frequently framed as reform *versus* the *status quo*. The implicit idea is that there are two sides: external reformers who are pushing for progress; and existing forces – primarily teachers, administrators and unions – who are resistant. The Canadian experience suggests a more complex analysis, in which teachers are a crucial constituency who can be enlisted in a broad reform agenda. Ironically, the more they perceive the state as the hammer, the more likely they are to entrench themselves into a unionised rather than a professional association. The Ontario experience suggests instead that by treating teachers as professionals, and including them at the table, they were able to build considerable goodwill – a critical resource for long-term and sustainable change. This is not to imply that the government was naïve – it was quite aware of the standard discussion points of union negotiations, but the government was able to direct that energy towards win-win issues like providing more professional development time. Ultimately, the Ontario government created a sustainable strategy and a clear push for improved performance in a way that included teachers, rather than alienated them.

■ Figure 3.2 ■
Canada: Profile data

Language(s)	English and French[5]
Population	32 934 166 (2007)[6] (12th largest in OECD)
	13 210 667 (Ontario)[7]
Youth population	16.7%[8] (OECD average 18.7%)
Elderly population	13.6%[9] (OECD average 14.4%)
Growth rate	1[10] (OECD 0.68%)[11]
Foreign-born population	20%[12] (OECD average 12.9%)
GDP per capita	USD 38 975 [13] (OECD average 33 732)[14]
Economy-Origin of GDP	Other: 66.4%; Manufacturing: 15.8%; Construction: 6.3%; Public Administration: 5.6%; Mining and quarrying: 3.6%; Agriculture: 2.3%[15]
Unemployment	6.1% (2008)[16] (OECD average 6.1%)[17]
Youth unemployment	11.6% (2008) (OECD average 13.8%)[18]
Expenditure on education	4.9% of GDP (OECD average 5.2%)
	3.1% on primary, secondary and post-secondary non-tertiary
	1.8% on tertiary[19] education[20] (OECD average 3.5%; 1.2% respectively)
	12.3% of total government expenditure (OECD average 13.3%)
	7.8% on primary, secondary and post-secondary non-tertiary
	4.5% on tertiary education[21] (OECD average 9%; 3.1% respectively)
Enrolment rate, early childhood education	70.5%[22] (OECD average 71.5%)[23]
Enrolment rate, primary education	106.2%[24] (OECD average 98.8%)[25]
Enrolment rate, secondary education	80.2%[26] (OECD average 81.5%)[27]
Enrolment rate, tertiary education	25.4%*[28] (OECD average 24.9%)[29]
Students in primary education, by type of institution or mode of enrolment[30]	Public* (OECD average 89.6%)
	Government-dependent private* (OECD average 8.1%)
	Independent, private* (OECD average 2.9%)
Students in lower secondary education, by type of institution or mode of enrolment[31]	Public 94.2% (OECD average 83.2%)
	Government-dependent private (included in "public" figure) (OECD average 10.9%)
	Independent, private (included in "public" figure) (OECD average 3.5%)
Students in upper secondary education, by type of institution or mode of enrolment[32]	Public: 94.2% (OECD average 82%)
	Government-dependent private (included in "public" figure) (OECD average 13.6%)
	Independent, private (included in "public" figure) (OECD average 5.5%)
Students in tertiary education, by type of institution or mode of enrolment[33]	Tertiary type B education: missing data[34]
	(OECD average Public: 61.8%
	Government-dependent private: 19.2%
	Independent-private: 16.6%)
	Tertiary type A education: missing data[35]
	(OECD average Public: 77.1%
	Government-dependent private: 9.6%
	Independent-private: 15%)
Teachers' salaries	Average annual starting salary in lower secondary education: missing data* (OECD average USD 30 750)[36]
	Ratio of salary in lower secondary education after 15 years of experience to GDP per capita: missing data (OECD average: 1.22)
Upper secondary graduation rates	76% (OECD average 80%)[37]

*Data on institutional breakdown and Canadian teachers' salaries missing from *Education at a Glance 2010* (OECD, 2010).
StatLink ⟨ms⟩ http://dx.doi.org/10.1787/888932366655

Interview partners

Kevin Costante, Deputy Minister of Education, Ministry of Education, Ontario, Canada.

Leona Dombrowsky, Minister of Education, Ontario, Canada.

Richard Elmore, Anrig Professor of Education Leadership, Harvard Graduate School of Education, United States.

Michael Fullan, Professor Emeritus of the Ontario Institute for Studies in Education of the University of Toronto and Special Advisor to the Premier and Minister of Education, Ontario, Canada.

Avis Glaze, former CEO of the Ontario Ministry of Education's Secretariat for Literacy and Numeracy, Ontario, Canada.

Keray Henke, Deputy Minister, Alberta Education, Alberta, Canada.

Gerard Kennedy, currently a Member of Parliament but formerly Minister of Education, Ontario, Canada.

Rhonda Kimberly Young, former President of the Ontario Secondary School Teachers Federation, Canada.

Benjamin Levin, former Ontario Deputy Minister of Education, currently Professor and Canada Research Chair Education Leadership and Policy at the Ontario Institute for Studies in Education, University of Toronto, Ontario, Canada.

References

Barber, M. and Mourshed, M. (2007), *How the World's Best-Performing School Systems Come Out on Top*, McKinsey and Company, London, available at *www.mckinsey.com/App_Media/Reports/SSO/Worlds_School_Systems_Final.pdf*.

Bussierre, P. and F. Cartwright (2004), *Measuring Up: Canadian Results of the OECD Pisa Study*, Statistics Canada, Ottawa.

Bussierre, P., T. Knighton and D. Pennock (2007), *Measuring Up: Canadian Results of the OECD Pisa Study*, Statistics Canada, Ottawa.

Canadian Language & Literacy Research Network (2009), *Evaluation Report. The Impact of the Literacy and Numeracy Secretariat: Changes in Ontario's Education System,* final report submitted to the Ontario Ministry of Education, available at *www.edu.gov. on.ca/eng/document/reports/OME_Report09_EN.pdf*.

Davies, S. and N. Guppy (1997), "Globalization and Educational Reforms in Anglo-American Democracies", *Comparative Education Review* 41(4): 435-459.

Fullan, M. (2010), *All Systems Go: The Imperative for Whole System Reform*, Corwin Press, Thousand Oaks, CA, and Ontario Principals Council, Toronto.

Guppy, N. and S. Davies (1998), *Education in Canada: Recent Trends and Future Challenges*, Statistics Canada, Ottawa.

Leithwood, K., M. Fullan and N. Watson (2003), *The Schools We Need: Recent Education Policy in Ontario. Recommendations for Moving Forward*, Ontario Institute for Studies in Education, University of Toronto, Toronto.

Levin, B., A. Glaze and M. Fullan (2008), "Results Without Rancour or Ranking: Ontario's Success Story", *Phi Delta Kappan*, Vol. 90, No. 4, 273-280.

Levin, B. (2008), *How to Change 5000 Schools. A Practical and Positive Approach for Leading Change at Every Level*, Harvard Education Press, Cambridge, MA.

Manzer, R. (1994), *Public Schools and Political Ideas: Canadian Educational Policy in Historical Perspective*, University of Toronto Press, Toronto.

OECD (2006), *Where Immigrant Students Succeed: A Comparative Review of Performance and Engagement in PISA 2003*, OECD Publishing.

OECD (2010), *PISA 2009 Volume I, What Students Know and Can Do: Student Performance in Reading, Mathematics and Science*, OECD Publishing.

Pascal, C.E. (2009), *With our Best Future in Mind. Implementing Early Learning in Ontario*, report to the Premier by the Special Advisor on Early Learning, available at *www.ontario.ca/ontprodconsume/groups/content/@onca/@initiatives/documents/document/ont06_018899.pdf*.

Pedwell, L. *et al.* (in press). *Building Leadership Capacity Across 5000 Schools. International Handbook on Leadership for Learning,* Springer Press, Dordrecht, The Netherlands.

Supovitz, J. (2009), "Can High Stakes Testing Leverage Educational Improvement? Prospects from the Last Decade of Testing and Accountability Reform", *Journal of Educational Change*, Vol. 10, No. 2-3, pp. 211-227.

Tibbetts, J. (2007), "Canadian 4th Graders Read Up a Storm," *The Gazette* (Montreal), November 29, 2007, p. A2.

Ungerleider, C. (2008), *Evaluation of the Ontario Ministry of Education's Student Success / Learning to 18 Strategy*, final report submitted to the Ontario Ministry of Education, available at *www.edu.gov.on.ca/eng/teachers/studentsuccess/CCL_SSE_Report.pdf*.

Young, J., B. Levin, and D. Wallin (2007), *Understanding Canadian Schools: An Introduction to Educational Administration*, 4th edition, Nelson, Toronto.

Notes

1. "Tight-loose" refers to a theory of management where the central unit is "tight" or specific and uncompromising on the ends it seeks, but "loose" or flexible on the means that those closer to the ground take to achieving those ends.

2. Statistics Canada, "Report on the Demographic Situation of Canada," Table A-4,1, accessed online at *www.statcan.gc.ca/ pub/91-209-x/2004000/part1/t/ta4-1-eng.htm*.

3. Statistics Canada, "Facts and Figures 2008: Immigration Overview," accessed online at *www.cic.gc.ca/english/resources/statistics/ facts2008/permanent/01.asp*.

4. For a comparative international look at accountability, see Supovitz, (2009).

5. OECD (2008), *OECD Economic Surveys: Canada*, OECD Publishing.

6. OECD (2008), *OECD Economic Surveys: Canada*, OECD Publishing.

7. *www.statcan.gc.ca*. Data from 2010.

8. *OECD Factbook 2010*, OECD Publishing. Ratio of population aged less than 15 to the total population (data from 2008).

9. *OECD Factbook 2010*, OECD Publishing. Ratio of population aged 65 and older to the total population (data from 2008).

10. OECD (2008), *Jobs for Youth Canada*, OECD Publishing. Ontario's population growth depends largely on immigration. Ontario, Alberta and British Columbia are the only provinces in which the projected average annual growth would exceed the growth rate for Canada as a whole.

11. *OECD Factbook 2010*, OECD Publishing. Annual population growth in percentage, OECD total (year of reference – 2007).

12. *OECD Factbook 2010*, OECD Publishing. Foreign-born population as percent of the total population (data from 2007).

13. *OECD Factbook 2010*, OECD Publishing. Current prices and PPPs (data from 2008).

14. *OECD Factbook 2010*, OECD Publishing. Current prices and PPPs (data from 2008).

15. OECD (2008), *OECD Economic Surveys: Canada*, OECD Publishing. Origin of GDP, percent of total (data from 2006).

16. *OECD Factbook 2010*, OECD Publishing. Total unemployment rates as percentage of total labour force (data from 2008).

17. *OECD Factbook 2010*, OECD Publishing. Total unemployment rates as percentage of total labour force (data from 2008).

18. OECD (2010), *Employment Outlook*, OECD Publishing. Unemployed as a percentage of the labour force in the age group: youth aged 15-24.

19. The OECD follows standard international conventions in using the term "tertiary education" to refer to all post-secondary programmes at ISCED levels 5B, 5A and 6, regardless of the institutions in which they are offered. OECD (2008), *Tertiary Education for the Knowledge Society: Volume 1*, OECD Publishing.

20. OECD (2010), *Education at a Glance 2010*, OECD Publishing. Public expenditure presented in this table includes public subsidies to households for living costs (scholarships and grants to students/households and students loans), which are not spent on educational institutions (data from 2006).

21. OECD (2010), *Education at a Glance 2010*, OECD Publishing. Public expenditure presented in this table includes public subsidies to households for living costs (scholarships and grants to students/households and students loans), which are not spent on educational institutions (data from 2006).

22. UNESCO Institute for Statistics, *http://data.worldbank.org/country*, Gross enrolment ratio (data from 2006).

23. OECD (2010), *Education at a Glance 2010*, OECD Publishing. OECD average net enrolment rates of ages 4 and under as a percentage of the population aged 3 to 4 (year of reference – 2008).

24. *http://data.worldbank.org/country*, Gross enrolment ratio (data from 2007).

25. OECD (2010), *Education at a Glance 2010*, OECD Publishing. OECD average net enrolment rates of ages 5 to 14 as a percentage of the population aged 5 to 14 (year of reference – 2008).

26. OECD (2010), *Education at a Glance 2010*, OECD Publishing. Net enrolment rates of ages 15 to 19 as a percentage of the population aged 15 to 19 (data from 2007).

27. OECD (2010), *Education at a Glance 2010*, OECD Publishing. OECD average net enrolment rates of ages 15 to 19 as a percentage of the population aged 15 to 19 (year of reference – 2008).

28. OECD (2010), *Education at a Glance 2010,* OECD Publishing. Net enrolment rates of ages 20 to 29 as a percentage of the population aged 20 to 29 (data from 2007). This figure includes includes all 20-29 year olds, including those in employment, etc. The Gross Enrolment Ratio (GER), measured by the UN as the number of actual students enrolled / number of potential students enrolled, is generally higher. The GER for tertiary education in Canada in 2002 is 60%, compared to the regional avg of 70% (UIS 2010).

29. OECD (2010), *Education at a Glance 2010,* OECD Publishing. OECD average net enrolment rates of ages 20 to 29 as a percentage of the population aged 20 to 29 (year of reference – 2008).

30. OECD (2010), *Education at a Glance 2010,* OECD Publishing. Data from 2008.

31. OECD (2010), *Education at a Glance 2010,* OECD Publishing. Data from 2008.

32. OECD (2010), *Education at a Glance 2010,* OECD Publishing. Data from 2008.

33. OECD (2010), *Education at a Glance 2010,* OECD Publishing. Data from 2008.

34. Data missing from *Education at a Glance 2010* (OECD, 2010)

35. Data missing from *Education at a Glance 2010* (OECD, 2010)

36. OECD (2010), *Education at a Glance 2010,* OECD Publishing. Starting salary/minimum training in USD adjusted for PPP (data from 2008).

37. OECD (2010), *Education at a Glance 2010,* OECD Publishing. Sum of upper secondary graduation rates for a single year of age in 2007 (year of reference for OECD average – 2008).

4

Shanghai and Hong Kong: Two Distinct Examples of Education Reform in China

China has made huge strides in educating its population. During the Cultural Revolution, educated people, including teachers, were sent to rural areas to work in the fields. The teaching force was effectively destroyed. But, not three decades later, parts of the country – notably Shanghai – are among the contenders for top spots on the world's education league tables. Hong Kong reverted back to China in 1997 and has also made significant reforms to its education system.

This chapter looks at how China has made rapid progress, taking Shanghai and Hong Kong as examples of innovation. The main lessons include the government's abandonment of a system built around "key schools" for a small elite and its development of a more inclusive system in which all students are expected to perform at high levels; greatly raising teacher pay and upgrading teacher standards and teacher education; reducing the emphasis on rote learning and increasing the emphasis on deep understanding, the ability to apply knowledge to solving new problems and the ability to think creatively. All of these are reflected in deep reforms to the curriculum and examinations. These changes have been accompanied by greater curricular choice for students and more latitude for local authorities to decide on examination content, which in turn is loosening the constraints on curriculum and instruction.

INTRODUCTION

Despite China's emergence as one of the world's most influential economies, relatively little is known in other countries about China's educational system and how its students learn. People might have gained some insights either through the achievements of its students in universities abroad, or from their high scores in all kinds of tests. Otherwise, the prevailing impression is that students in China learn by rote, and that much in the schools is about memorising and cramming for examinations.

This chapter seeks to provide a more nuanced and accurate picture of education in China, using Shanghai and Hong Kong as examples. Shanghai is one of China's most developed urban areas, while Hong Kong, despite having the same cultural background, is a rather different society under the "one country, two systems" political arrangement. However, as China encompasses such a diverse spectrum of economies, societies and cultures, Shanghai and Hong Kong can provide a very powerful window into education into China, but may not be representative of all parts of the country.

Nevertheless, in both cases, student learning is the focus, with other dimensions – such as teaching and teachers, school facilities and systemic strategies – providing the context and supporting various aspects of student learning.

CHINA'S EDUCATION SYSTEM: THE CULTURAL CONTEXT[1]

China has a long tradition of valuing education highly. This began with the Civil Examination system, established in 603 AD, which was also exported to Japan and Korea later in the 7th century. It was a very competitive yet efficient system for selecting officials, and was known for its rigor and fairness. These examinations evolved over many dynasties before their abolition in 1905.

The system had three tiers of examinations, at county, provincial and national levels. There were variations, but the general mode was basically an essay test, where the candidates were confined for days in an examination cell, fed with good food, and required to write essays of political relevance. To do this, they had to be familiar with the classics, basically the *Four Books* and *Five Classics*, and refer all arguments to these works – hence the requirement for "rote-learning". Good calligraphy and writing styles were also part of the basic requirements. The final level of selection was usually held in the Examinations Department, which was often part of the imperial organisation. Whoever gained the appreciation of the Emperor, who was virtually the chief examiner, would be the champion, followed by a few runners-up. These winners were appointed to various official posts according to their examination results.[2]

A few "beauties" of this system made it sustainable for almost two centuries. First, it was simple, requiring only performance in the examinations. Teachers were only affordable by wealthy families, so no formal institutions such as schools existed. It was basically a self-study system, or a "self-motivated distance learning system", in contemporary jargon. It was low-cost for both the government and the household because it involved only an examination, and the textbooks (the standard classics) were common in household collections. Apart from the exclusion of women (Elman, 2000), which was part of the broader ideology at the time, there were no entrance requirements, so it was thought that family background would not matter. Indeed, Chinese folklore over hundreds of years, reflected in novels, operas, dramas and all art forms, includes stories about scholars from poor families who endured years of hardship and poverty, became champions in the Civil Examination, were appointed ministers, married princesses and enjoyed glorious home-coming ceremonies. The Civil Examination drove almost all families, regardless of socio-economic status, to have high hopes for their children's future (*i.e.*, the boys), and such hopes translated into hard work and adaptability to difficult learning environments. This cultural tradition exists throughout the entire Chinese population. However, it has also led to the emphasis (almost the exclusive emphasis) on examination results for validating genuine learning or knowledge. In a way, for more than 16 centuries, generation after generation of young people were trained only to face the challenges of examinations.

This cultural respect for "education" hence carries a special meaning for China: education (basically examination preparation) is viewed as the sole route for upwards social mobility, the only hope for an individual's future. This is translated into a zest for credentials and the predominance of examinations to win them.

What are the consequences of this historic cultural emphasis on exams and credentials?

- Education was seen as the major path to climb the social ladder and change one's social status. This was intertwined with the supreme status given to civil servants (officials). And because of the Civil Examination, only scholars could become officials. A circular causality is at work here, where social status, officialdom, scholarship, and education became synonymous in people's minds.

- Despite the meagre odds of moving to the top, the chances of success mobilised the entire population to take examinations. This was strongly augmented by the assumption that working hard pays off. While other factors, such as family background and innate ability, are not controllable, working hard was something anyone could do. Some corollary observations may help explain the culture of education in contemporary China and to a large extent in other East Asian cultures.[3]

- Success in examinations is therefore still seen as the only respectable success, unlike in other societies where military capacity (such as with the *samurai* in Japan), or economic wealth can also attract social respect.[4]

- As a result of this history, reading, learning and education are often taken as synonyms in Chinese. Reading is regarded as the only effective means of learning, and for that matter of memorisation. "All are low but reading" is the saying; hence the tradition of "rote learning" as perceived by outside observers.

- The reality, however, was that achievements in education were decided by the subjective favour of the emperor or the chief examiner. Therefore successful essays conveyed ideas that would appeal to authority. This tradition may help explain the cultural aspect that favours political correctness over scientific objectivity.

- The importance attached to examination results also underpins the prevailing mentality among teachers, students and parents, in which the direct relevance of the curriculum is less important than achieving high scores.

- As most research results concur, motivation in education in China (and also in Japan and Korea) is basically extrinsic, prompted by family or social expectations (Chapter 6). In most cases, intrinsic motivation or genuine interest in the subject matter *per se*, are not the driving factors.

- This also underpins the fundamental source of examination pressure. In all these East Asian societies, frequent and intense examinations and tests in schools and high-stakes public examinations prevail throughout the entire education system, leading to all kinds of private tuition and tutorial schools to prepare students for examinations.

- The Civil Examinations tradition also explains the culture of hard work and tolerance of hardship. "Only those who could tolerate the bitterest among the bitter would come out as a man above men," as the saying goes.

- This tradition also underpins the belief that effort is more important than innate ability. "Diligence can compensate for stupidity" is a common Chinese belief, a view not shared by many other cultures.

The social emphasis on education has always made it easy for Chinese-based societies (such as mainland China, Hong Kong, Chinese Taipei and Macao) to develop their education systems, as there is popular support for expanding education to reach more people. However, at the same time, genuine attention to quality learning is often a challenge for education reformers in these societies.

CHINA'S EDUCATION SYSTEM: THE HISTORICAL CONTEXT

This system has undergone several stages of development: the rather rigid Russian model of the 1950s, the period of "renaissance" in the early 1960s, disastrous damage during the Cultural Revolution (1966-1976), rapid expansion during the 1980s and 1990s, and the move towards massive[5] higher education in the 21st century. With perhaps the exception of the Cultural Revolution, education in general has trended upwards, both in scale and quality.

The Cultural Revolution: 1966 to 1976

It is essential to understand the context in which China's education reform started in the early 1980s. The death of Mao Zedong in 1976 marked the end of the Cultural Revolution. Formally the Proletariat Cultural Revolution, it was started by Mao in 1966 as a national-scale political campaign to eliminate all bourgeois influences in the country's "superstructure" (as opposed to the economic infrastructure). Violent activities sought to remove and destroy all symbols of bourgeois culture, such as music, drama, opera and novels, and to make sure their replacements were rooted in proletariat ideology. Activities in all these art forms had to start again from scratch, using a few "model" prototypes created from pure proletariat ideology. It became a social campaign and intellectuals were the most vulnerable.

Among the revolution's consequences was the closing down of conventional schools. They were replaced with schools led by political teams of workers, peasants and soldiers, and the curriculum was totally revamped to reflect the essence of "class struggle." There were several attempts to resume schooling, but with little effect. Higher education institutions were suspended, replaced by new institutions admitting only workers, peasants and soldiers regardless of their academic merits. Professors and intellectuals were sent to factories, villages and remote places to be "re-educated." The concept reflected a utopian ideal of egalitarianism, where everybody produces for the state and the state distributes its wealth equally among its citizens. But the reality was total stagnation of the economy, a society of "equal poverty", as economists recognised in hindsight. It is no exaggeration to say that China had to rebuild the entire education system in the late 1970s and early 1980s from the ruins left by the Cultural Revolution.

The reconstruction of education: Late 1970s through the 1980s

The end of the Cultural Revolution brought about unprecedented changes in China. In 1978, Deng Xiaoping started an economic reform in which peasants were given land and allowed to keep their crop surpluses. Commercial activities began to take place. Schools resumed normal activities. A milestone in education development at that time was the resumption of university admissions in 1977 (which doubled the intake) and 1978, when most of those enrolled were mature students who had been deprived of learning opportunities during the Cultural Revolution.

At the same time, peasants were eager to build their own schools in the villages. This led to a decision in 1980 to allow local non-government financing of schools as a way of mobilising community resources. This paved the way for a major reform and decentralisation of education in 1985. There was an immediate mushrooming of schools and the target of universal primary education was achieved in just a few years. The same reform also called for universal nine-year education as a national target, with benchmarks every year towards its accomplishment.

In 1986, China enacted the *Law of Compulsory Education*, which required every child to complete nine years of formal schooling – six years of primary school and three years of junior secondary school.[6] By the mid-1990s, China had basically achieved this goal.

At about the same time, in 1980, cities like Shanghai, with a large non-state enterprises sector, started pioneering new types of vocational schools that did not guarantee or assign jobs. This was a significant step away from the strict manpower planning that had been an integral part of the planned economy. By 1997, formal assignment of jobs to graduates disappeared from all levels of the education system. It was also in 1982 that China for the first time established its degree system for higher education, following the Western model.

It was not until 1988, however, that China moved away from uniform national textbooks to experiment with diversity in textbooks; until that point cultural tradition stated that these textbooks were the most essential instrument for student learning and were provided by the state almost free. (This was very different from practices in other developing countries of similar economic status). Textbook diversification allowed for diverse interpretations of the centralised syllabuses, and there were attempts, for example in Shanghai (see next section), to create new syllabi within the centralised framework.

Quantitative expansion: 1990 to the present day

China has now passed the stage of quantitative expansion in basic education. Official statistics (for 2009) show a net enrolment of 99.4% at the primary school level, the envy of many countries. The gross enrolment ratio for junior secondary school was 99%.[7] In the same year, gross enrolment at senior secondary level, both general and vocational, was 79.2%. The general (*i.e.* academic) senior secondary schools enrol 52.5% of students at this level, putting about half of senior high school students in the academic stream (Figure 3.1). However, the figures may conceal regional disparities. In most urban areas, gross enrolment at the senior secondary level is 100% or above, which means that the number of students enrolled exceeds the number in the appropriate age group.

The 1985 reform, as mentioned earlier, established the framework for decentralised local school finance and governance. Almost as a textbook example, decentralisation led immediately to huge regional disparities because of the differences in local economies. After several back-and-forth debates and adjustments about degrees of decentralisation, the *Revised Law of Compulsory Education*, enacted in 2006, established differential subsidies from the central government to different regions of varied economic capacities.[8] This marked the government's determination to sustain universal basic education, and hence paved the way for more energetic reforms in educational quality.

The 21st century: Focus on higher education

If the highlight of the 1980s and 1990s was expansion of basic education to the entire population, then the emphasis of the first decade of the 21st century has been the expansion of higher education. Starting in 1998, China broke away from its long-standing policy of restricting higher education to a small percentage of the population and launched a spectacular expansion. In 1999, all institutions across the nation were required to increase intake by 50%. This was followed by jumps of 25% in 2000 and 22% in 2001.[9]

■ Figure 4.1 ■
China's education system organisation

Tertiary	Non-formal/Lifelong			
Senior Secondary (3 years) General	Specialised	Vocational	Crafts	
Junior Secondary (3 years)				
Primary (6 years)				
Pre-School (3-4 years)				

Despite government intentions to pause this expansion, higher education has now gained its own momentum, and all kinds of non-government initiatives, such as private institutions and self-financing programmes, are flourishing at their own pace. The net result is that the higher education student population grew from less than 6 million in 1998 (before the expansion) to 29.8 million in 2009. Although the enrolment ratio still stood at a low 24.2% in 2009 (Ministry of Education, 2010a), China nonetheless has the largest number of higher education students in the world, much higher than the United States (around 18 million in 2007), which was the second largest, and above India (around 13 million in 2007) (UNESCO Institute of Statistics, 2009).

The expansion of higher education has immense implications for the entire education system. On the one hand, there is visible graduate unemployment, particularly in the major metropolitan areas, including Shanghai. Analysts often argue that this is mainly due to the unwillingness of graduates to take jobs with less satisfactory incomes or in less developed regions, and hence this should not deter further development of higher education.[10] And indeed the job situation does not appear to hamper parents' and young people's aspiration for more higher education. On the other hand, the rapid expansion of higher education has created a new level of desire for academic studies, inducing remarkably high enrolment in general (academic) senior secondary schools and lowering enrolment in vocational schools.

In all these expansions, private institutions emerge in great numbers, although in terms of percentage and student populations they are still the minority. However, the trend is irreversible. It is also noticeable that private institutions in mainland China are formally called *minban* schools, which means "community" schools, or more accurately, "non-government schools". The nomenclature is justifiable, because in China, public and private distinctions are rather blurred. For example, many private schools are headed by former government officials, or government departments may run private schools for income.

The quantitative picture would not be complete without including China's complex structure of lifelong learning, which includes full-time sabbatical study, evening spare-time programmes, distance learning programmes and self-study examinations. Such learning opportunities often lead to formal credentials such as certificates and diplomas, and sometimes to degrees. Operators range from major institutions of higher education (as their extension programmes), to individual professionals and private for-profit enterprises.

TEACHERS AND TEACHING

Teachers have always been a major issue in China. Educational expansion in the 1980s immediately led to an enormous shortage of teachers. In the Cultural Revolution, many young people with some education (such as primary or junior secondary) were branded intellectuals and sent to rural villages. They were seen as the most educated in the villages, and became teachers. Most of them were untrained, under-qualified and paid little.

They were generally called *minban* (community) teachers, but many were very competent and popular nonetheless. A policy in the 1980s aimed to retrain these teachers and put them on the public payroll. The success of this policy, however, has caused an exodus of teachers fleeing back to cities in search of better living and working conditions. Village schools now often resort to hiring even less qualified teachers using the "supply teachers" category that is meant for temporary substitutes. This is a structural problem that has yet to be solved. The disparity in competence among the vast number of China's teachers is perhaps a driving reason for the development of a comprehensive and effective system of organising teaching, as will be discussed below.

The situation in cities is more definite and positive. Since 1997, when universities began to charge fees, a state policy has given early admission to student teacher candidates. Hence, "normal" (teacher training) universities enjoy priority admissions and attract better students. In major cities, such as Beijing and Shanghai, where the economy is more open and incomes fluctuate more, teaching stands out as a preferred occupation attracting a more stable income. Over the years, because of the improvement in teachers' salary scales, teaching has risen up the ladder of preferred occupations.

It has to be added that while teachers in mainland China do not receive very high salaries, they often have other significant income on top of their salaries. This may come from additional assignments beyond normal responsibilities, income generated outside school (from private tutorials or invited talks), or school "bonuses" (*e.g.* sponsoring fees collected from students who come from other neighbourhoods or whose test scores are below the official admissions cut-off).

Class sizes in mainland China are generally large: the national norm is 50 students. However, in rural areas where good schools are sparse, it is not unusual to see classes of over 80 or in the extreme case, over 100. Parents often indicate their preference for better schools and better teachers over smaller classes. However, in major cities (and Shanghai is typical), recent drastic declines in population have forced local governments to adopt small classes so as to minimise teacher layoffs. This has significantly reduced teachers' workload and created room for student activities during lessons that would be impossible in large classes.

China has also developed a rather rigorous framework and system of teaching. At the grassroots level, subject-based "teaching-study groups" engage in study and improvement of teaching on a daily basis. For example, a physics teacher of Senior Secondary 2 (SS2) involved in a teaching-study group typically teaches 12-15 classes per week, teaching only one programme (*e.g.* SS2 Physics) and nothing else. There are timetabled sessions when the study group will meet, often with related personnel such as laboratory assistants, to draw up very detailed lesson schemes for a particular topic the following week. Teachers are expected to teach according to the scheme, which is then translated into more detailed lesson plans by and for individual teachers.

The lesson plan serves not only as a guide for the teacher during the lesson, but also as documentation of the teacher's professional performance. In many cases, teachers are observed by the school principal or by district education officers when they are being considered for promotions or awards. In short, a Chinese teacher sees a lesson more as a show or a performance, and puts in many hours of preparation to cover the standard 40-minute period.[11]

The "teaching-study group" is supervised for each of its subject areas by the "teaching-study office" in the Education Bureau (in a rural country or city district), which is in turn supervised by the relevant "teaching-study office" in the Education Department in the provincial or municipal government. Professionally, all these "teaching-study" setups work under the Basic Education Department II within the central government's Ministry of Education. The Basic Education Department II is charged with all matters related to curriculum development, textbook production, pedagogy enhancement and school management for the whole nation. In a way, teaching in China is much more centrally organised than in many other systems.

During actual teaching, teachers may observe each other or may be observed by peers (in the case of a new teaching topic because of curriculum change, for example), by new teachers (so they can learn from more experienced teachers), by senior teachers (for mentoring), or by the school principal (for monitoring or for constructive development purposes). Sometimes, teachers are expected to teach demonstration lessons (called public lessons) for a large number of other teachers to observe and comment upon. This structured organisation of teaching in China is thus not only a means for administration; it is also a major platform for professional enhancement.

Such teaching protocols are present throughout China, from remote villages to prosperous cities. These practices are taken for granted as the basic protocol for teaching. Observers may see this as a matter of quality assurance, but it serves also the fundamental purposes of professional development and pedagogical advancement. The steps are built into teachers' career ladders.

Teachers in China are classified into four grades as an indication of their professional status. Promotion from one grade to the next often requires the capacity to give demonstration lessons, contributions to induction of new teachers, publications in journals or magazines about education or teaching, and so forth. Of course, many other aspects of education are unique to China, but the teaching protocols are perhaps among the most relevant to this chapter.

This picture of teaching in China would not be complete without mentioning that almost all the officers in the government education authorities, both at municipal and district levels, started as school teachers. Most of them distinguished themselves as teachers or school principals with strong track records. This perhaps explains their devoted professional attention to teaching and learning amidst all the administrative chores and political issues they normally contend with. They manage, however, to maintain this teaching focus while at the same time relying on a strategic vision that enables them to navigate a policy arena which goes well beyond education.

CONTINUOUS CURRICULUM REFORM

Ongoing reform is another dimension in the larger context of China's education system that merits attention. China has launched a series of reforms since the early 1980s; indeed, reform is a sustained concept in education. As noted earlier, major milestones include the nationwide reform in 1985 that decentralised finance and administration; a 1988 move to encourage local production of textbooks (rather than requiring a uniform set of textbooks across the nation); a spectacular expansion in higher education in 1999, together with a major re-design of higher education entrance examination in the same year; legislation in 2002 to encourage private schools; and a major policy move in 2006 to alleviate disparity in financial support for education.

The latest initiative is a major national comprehensive campaign to improve education in the next decade – the Outline for Medium and Long-term Development and Reform of Education (announced in July 2010). This prescribes education developments up to 2020. One of its ambitions is to introduce universal pre-school education. This is likely to pose new challenges given the nation's diverse conditions and concepts about early childhood development. The strategy also highlights the need to overcome educational disparity and the importance of respect for diversity and individual needs. It is generally regarded as a strategic plan for moving into an era of quality, equity and individuality in planning education.

Examinations have long been a focus of attention in China in any attempt to reform education. Teaching and learning, in secondary schools in particular, are predominantly determined by the examination syllabi, and school activities at that level are very much oriented towards exam preparation. Subjects such as music and art, and in some cases even physical education, are removed from the timetable because they are not covered in the public examinations. Schools work their students for long hours every day, and the work weeks extend into the weekends, mainly for additional exam preparation classes. As noted earlier, private tutorials, most of them profit-making, are widespread and have become almost a household necessity. In the past two decades, the national policy agenda has sought to move the system away from examination orientation, but the call has seldom met with significant success. The most recent appeal along this line is the move to reduce students' workload, which is regarded as a major task in the coming decade of education development.

Examination pressure remains a major concern to educators, parents and policy makers. Some provinces forbid the holding of formal classes over the weekends. There is a general belief that emphasis on examinations jeopardises the genuine development of young people and is detrimental to the entire national population, but few effective solutions have emerged to reduce or minimise examination pressures. Educators jokingly describe the situation as follows: "High-sounding appeals to promote quality education, down-to-earth preparation for examinations."

Nevertheless, committed reformers continue to make great efforts to reform the curriculum at the national level. A major document issued in 2001 calls for the following changes (Ministry of Education, 2001):

• To move away from pure knowledge transmission towards fostering learning attitudes and values.

• To move away from discipline-based knowledge, towards more comprehensive and balanced learning experiences.

- To move away from pure "bookish" knowledge and to improve relevance and interest in the content of a curriculum.

- To move away from repetitive and mechanistic rote-learning towards increased student participation, real-life experience, capacity in communications and teamwork, and ability to acquire new knowledge and to analyse and solve problems.

- To de-emphasise the screening and selective functions of assessments and instead to emphasise their formative and constructive functions.

- To move away from centralisation, so as to leave room for adaptation to local relevance and local needs.

Concrete changes include dilution of the disciplined structure of "subjects" so as to re-organise content according to life-relevance and progression in learning; the introduction of new integrated contents at the cross-over between natural sciences and humanities; the creation of elective arts modules as a compulsory part of the curriculum; to change examination formats from fact regurgitation to analyses and solutions for stated problems; and so forth.

It is clear that the reform discourse is one of "student learning"; a discourse that is shared by other similar reforms in Singapore and Hong Kong at almost the same time. The reform is strongly underpinned by the concepts of constructive learning. It is not just an improvement of the existing conventional curriculum, but an overhaul of the fundamental concept of curriculum, and hence it challenges basic assumptions about education and curriculum. It means not doing what has traditionally been done, but doing more, better and differently. Hence, it is curriculum reform in the genuine sense.

Understandably, this approach has received strong opposition from leading scientists in the academic establishment. They argued that such a curriculum would damage the integrity of the disciplines and would hinder the nation in producing new scientists. The constructive interpretation of learning has also led to debates among education researchers and policy advisors. Some interpret constructive learning as pure empirical experience, which deprives students of learning from earlier learning outcomes. Others regard constructive learning as the only effective approach to human learning, and insist that it should be the core tenet of curriculum reform.

The net result is progress in curriculum reform, but its momentum is very much hampered by academics' conceptual opposition, as well as by front-line teachers who have found the new curriculum difficult to handle when preparing their students to do well in public examinations. Nonetheless, the reform is gradually gaining ground.

The following discussion focuses on education and learning in two major Chinese cities: Shanghai and Hong Kong. Both are vibrant economies and have undertaken major comprehensive education reforms in the past two decades. While they have both inherited the same cultural traditions about education, the two cities work under different political and ideological frameworks. Nevertheless, their reform efforts share a similar discourse of making student learning central, but their different assumptions about the role of government have led them to adopt rather different approaches.

■ SHANGHAI: A LEADER IN REFORM

Shanghai is the largest city in China, with a population of 20.7 million, of whom 13.8 million are permanent residents, and 5.4 million are temporary. In addition, there are around 1.5 million who are mobile (without a Shanghai home; Shanghai Municipal Statistics Bureau, 2010). The city is one of four municipalities with the status of a province (the others are Beijing, Tianjin and Chongqing). In 2009, Shanghai's GDP was USD 11 563 per capita. While its population and land account for 1% and 0.06% of the nation respectively, it contributes one-eighth of China's income (Information Office of Shanghai Municipality and Shanghai Municipal Statistics Bureau, 2010). In 2009, the contribution of the service sector to economic growth in Shanghai was around 60%, the highest in mainland China.

While Beijing is China's political centre, Shanghai is its undeniable business centre. Shanghai is also the country's most international and open city. This is attributable to its prosperous and colonial past before the change of government in 1949. It was among the first ports forced open by international powers in the mid-19th century.[12] After 1978, as China opened up to trade and began the transition to a market economy (the "socialist market economy"), Shanghai took on a new role in almost all fronts, including education.

Ahead of the pack in universal education

Shanghai is among the most internationalised cities of mainland China, but cultural traditions about education still prevail. Popular support for education means the city has had little difficulty in launching universal education. However, Shanghai also struggles with undue examination pressure, which is still a major item on the reform agenda.

Shanghai was among the first cities to achieve universal primary and junior secondary education and was also among the first to achieve almost universal senior secondary education. According to the *Shanghai Yearbook 2009* (Shanghai Municipal Government, 2010), enrolment at the age of compulsory education was above 99.9%, and 97% of the age cohort attended senior secondary school (general and vocational). It is notable that enrolment for preschool programmes was 98%, which already surpasses the new national preschool education goal for 2020.

Statistics also show that over 80% of the city's higher education age cohort are admitted into higher education in one way or another (compared to the national figure of 24%; Ding, 2010). In other words, all those who would like to attend higher education are able to do so. There were 61 higher education institutions in Shanghai in 2009, plus quite a few private institutions yet to be officially recognised. There would be higher education over-supply if only residents of Shanghai were counted,[13] but Shanghai institutes also admit students from all over the nation.[14] Indeed, Shanghai has always been a preferred place to pursue higher education, perhaps second only to Beijing, and has attracted the best students from the national pool of elite candidates.

If it were not for the admission quota put aside for Shanghai high school graduates, the city could have attracted more and better candidates from the entire nation. Graduates from Shanghai's institutions are allowed to stay and work in Shanghai, regardless of their places of origin. For that reason, many "education migrants" now move to Shanghai mainly for to educate their children.[15] Of course, many Shanghai students attend higher education in other cities, usually Beijing.

Nevertheless, Shanghai is indeed an education hub in China, and is very high on the aspiration ladder for potential candidates. This situation has greatly strengthened the competitiveness of the city's higher education institutions. What is remarkable, however, is that even with the very generous admissions quota for local students, this sense of competition is still very keen. Reformers had thought that when the system became less selective, undue competition would also be reduced. This does not seem to have happened.

There are varied interpretations of this phenomenon, which is common to many Asian societies. One is that the Chinese perceive society as a vertical hierarchy[16] and always seek to enter the best institution despite broader access to higher education in general. Indeed, institutions are ranked in parents' minds. By the same token, parents would like to see their children ranked highest in their classes, and anything less than 100% is perceived as undesirable.[17] Another interpretation is that the cultural tradition cherishes hard work, and that to "study" (or "reading books" in the ancient tradition) is their "responsibility". Parents and teachers like to keep students busy studying and do not feel comfortable if students spend less time studying. Hence, despite the increase in higher education opportunities, examination pressure persists in Shanghai as in other parts of China.

The cultural heritage also works in positive directions. Shanghai is home to quite a few experimental programmes that are seen as pioneers in developing quality education as opposed to examination pressure. One such example is "success education" (Box 4.1).

Box 4.1 **Success education**

Shanghai's Zhabei district is characterized by high crime and poor educational performance. In 1994, Liu Jinghai became the principal of the Zhabei District School No. 8, a school that had been among the poorest-performing in the district. Mr. Liu applied a strategy called "success education" that he developed through years of research. The strategy encourages teachers to instill low-performing pupils with greater confidence in their abilities to become potential achievers. This program has transformed School No. 8, placing it in rank 15 out of 30 schools in the district. Around 80% of School No. 8 secondary graduates go on to university, compared with a municipal average of 56%. In 2005 the Shanghai Education Authority asked Mr. Liu to help turn around 10 other low-performing schools in Shanghai through "commissioned administration" whereby teachers from School No. 8 work with partner schools applying administrative and pedagogical practices of success education.

Reforming exams in Shanghai

Shanghai has opted to modify the mode and contents of examinations so they serve the purpose of curriculum and pedagogy reform. In Chinese phraseology, public examinations are the baton that conducts the entire orchestra – rather than removing the baton, the alternative is to modify the baton so that it conducts good music.

In 1985, Shanghai was given the privilege of organising the higher education entrance examination for universities under its jurisdictions. Since then, a lot of effort has gone into reforming assessments and examinations. Generally, exam changes match reform expectations in curriculum and pedagogy. As an example, integrated papers are required that cross disciplinary boundaries and test students' capacity to apply their knowledge to real-life problems. As another example, examination questions provide students with information not covered in the syllabuses and so test their abilities in applying what they know to new problems. Multiple-choice questions have disappeared from the city's public examinations.

Student engagement

One of the most essential influences of China's cultural heritage is the intensity of students' engagement in learning. Typically in a Shanghai classroom, students are fully occupied and fully engaged. Non-attentive students are not tolerated. In one mathematics lesson observed for this research, a lesson which was by no means unique, students at Junior Secondary II were learning about parabolas. Students covered 15 problems at their desks, plus selected students gave blackboard demonstrations. This is rather different from classrooms in other cultures, where students may not be required to be fully engaged or attentive throughout the entire lesson. Such intense concentration is considered a student's responsibility in Chinese culture.

Student engagement in learning is not limited to lessons. Homework is an essential part of their learning activities and in a way governs their lives at home after school. Parents expect students to do homework every evening and are prepared to devote their family lives to student study, again as part of ancient tradition. Homework is such a burden to students that many local authorities in China have stipulated a maximum amount of homework (measured in hours) that schools are allowed to assign. Shanghai was among the first areas to impose such limits as a municipal policy.

The intensity of students' engagement goes well beyond the schools. A rather comprehensive "remedial system" of tutorial schools caters to the demands of exam preparation.[18] In the absence of formal statistics, it is estimated that over 80% of parents send their children to tutorial school. Such schools are mostly for-profit, operate after school hours or at weekends, and tend to use small groups to focus on particular subjects. Parents see such tutorial schools as essential for enabling students to pass the public examinations with flying colours. Teachers are not totally against such schools either, because they also think that passing examinations is the prime aim of student study. Even parents who are against examination cramming often send their children to tutorial schools, almost as a matter of insurance. Those who go to such classes are not all weak students: even very strong students like to reinforce their strengths to achieve higher scores in the examinations.

Apart from the "remedial system", there is also the "supplementary system"[19] of institutions or programmes outside schools, where young people can learn music, fine arts, sports, martial arts (gungfu) and all kinds of subjects not offered by schools. The most popular are piano, flute, ballet, Chinese calligraphy and Chinese painting. Parents are very prepared to invest in these expensive learning activities.

Students' engagement in learning does not stop at academic study. They are obliged to take part in all kinds of other activities (e.g see Box 4.2). In Shanghai schools, for example, there is a municipal requirement that every student should engage in at least one hour per day of physical education. They start with a morning exercise before class; there is an "intermission exercise" in the middle of the morning, and other physical activities are held after school. Some schools practise "eye exercises" where student massage essential acupuncture points in order to prevent eyesight deterioration. Students also engage in all kinds of extracurricular activities in sports and the arts, where they are expected to learn organisation and leadership. Students take turns at "daily duties" in cleaning the classrooms and nearby corridors, for example. Students are also assigned teamwork in keeping the campus tidy. They are also organised to visit rural villages or deprived social groups as a matter of social or service learning. All these activities are co-ordinated by the municipal education authority.

Students are often overwhelmed by all these learning activities, both within and outside schools. This is why the national 2020 planning document calls for a "reduction of student workload." Shanghai is already much more aware of this issue than many other places in China, and good schools often refrain from holding classes during evenings and weekends, and parents do not normally press for heavier workloads.

Box 4.2 **Oriental Green Ark**

A spectacular facility established by the Shanghai municipal Education Department is an education base known as the Oriental Green Ark. This huge education park occupies more than 60 000 acres and includes activity centres, physical challenge centres, military training, museums, villas and hotels, as well as a convention centre. The villas and hotels follow the concept of a global village, with each block in the style of a particular nation. Every student in Shanghai primary and secondary schools experiences the Oriental Green Ark at least once as an organised school visit. It is interesting that many parents also send their children to the Ark through individual bookings at their own cost. Children see it as an alternative amusement park.

Compared with other societies, young people in Shanghai may be much more immersed in learning in the broadest sense of the term. The logical conclusion is that they learn more, even though what they learn and how they learn are subjects of constant debate. Critics see young people as being "fed" learning because they are seldom left on their own to learn in a way of their choice. They have little direct encounters with nature, for example, and little experience with society either. While they have learned a lot, they may not have learned how to learn. The Shanghai government is developing new policy interventions to reduce student workload and to refocus the quality of student learning experiences over quantity. Challenges from a changed and changing society maintain tension between such intense engagement and genuine learning in the broader sense.

Curriculum reforms

Shanghai has always been seen as a pioneer in education reform, with reform of the curriculum taking centre stage. Curriculum reform in Shanghai follows the general framework of national reform, described earlier. But Shanghai is often given the privilege of experimenting with reforms before they are endorsed for other parts of the nation. Since 1989, Shanghai has launched two waves of curriculum reform. Their essence has been to overcome "examination orientation" practices in schools in order to build quality education (Ding, 2010).[20]

The first phase of curriculum reform started in 1988, with an attempt to allow students to select courses of personal interest. A curriculum comprising three blocks was established: compulsory courses, elective courses and extra-curricular activities. Accordingly, textbooks and teaching materials were produced and phased in.

Curriculum reform moved into its second phase in 1998, to integrate natural science with the humanities, the national curriculum with school-based curriculum, and knowledge acquisition with active inquiry. The purpose was to transform students from passive receivers of knowledge to active participants in learning, so as to improve their capacity for creativity and self-development and to fully achieve their potential. Traditional subjects were re-organised into eight "learning domains": language and literature, mathematics, natural science, social sciences, technology, arts, physical education, and a practicum. Schools were encouraged to develop their own curricula specific to their individual conditions. Museums and other "youth education bases" (such as the Oriental Green Ark, Box 4.2) have now become crucial places in which the new curriculum is also implemented.

The new curriculum has three components: the *basic curriculum*, to be experienced by all students, mainly implemented through compulsory courses; the *enriched curriculum*, which aims to develop students' potential and is realised mainly through elective courses, and *inquiry-based curriculum*, which is mainly implemented through extra-curricular activities. The inquiry-based curriculum asks students, backed up by support and guidance from teachers, to identify research topics based on their experiences. It is hoped that through independent learning and exploration, students can learn to learn, to think creatively and critically, to participate in social life and to promote social welfare. Since 2008, the new curriculum has been implemented throughout the city.

Overall, the curriculum reform involves broadening students' learning experiences, enhancing the relevance of subjects by relating them to broader human and social issues, and concentrating on the development of "capability" rather than accumulation of information and knowledge. These are reflected in the reform of examinations as well as reform in pedagogy.

The overhaul of curriculum is supported by changes in teacher education and professional development. Over the years, teachers' threshold qualifications have been significantly elevated. Twenty years ago, primary school teachers were trained in teacher-training schools at the level of senior secondary schools. Junior secondary teachers received diplomas from sub-degree programmes. Less than 20 years later, all primary school teachers now must have a sub-degree diploma, and all teachers in secondary schools are degree-holders with professional certification. Many teachers have master's degrees. Shanghai was the first district in China to require CPD (continuous professional development) for teachers. Every teacher is expected to engage in 240 hours of professional development within five years.

In order to facilitate the sharing of good practices of curriculum design, development and implementation, a web-based platform[21] was constructed and put into use in 2008. Included on the website are resources for curriculum development and learning, success stories of curriculum implementation, and research papers on teaching and learning. The draft version of Shanghai's plan for educational reform and development for 2020, which has been put out for public consultation, calls for school-based curricula and proposes a credit system at the senior secondary level to make learning more individualised and flexible.

In parallel to the curriculum reforms are changes to teaching practice. These reforms aim to change classroom reality to better facilitate student learning. One very significant change has been implemented in recent years through the slogan "return class time to students". This calls for an increase in time allocated to student activities in classes relative to teachers' lecturing. This has caused a fundamental change in the perception of a good class, which was once typified by good teaching, with well-designed presentations by the teachers. Videos of model teaching concentrated on teachers' activities. Now, model classes are filmed with two cameras, one of which records student activities. Teachers' performances are now also evaluated by the time given to student participation and how well student activities are organised. A similar slogan is "to every question there should be more than a single answer." This poses a challenge to the orthodoxy and authority of teachers over the information they teach.

These changes add up to a sea change in classroom pedagogy. The use of slogans is a Chinese tradition, and proposed changes become a campaign. The slogans are carefully crafted to capture the very essence of the proposed change and to be easily understood and followed by grassroots teachers. This is particularly powerful in the rural schools, where most theories are still foreign ideas. The use of slogans in pedagogy reform is also based on the culture of what could be called "constructive conformity" in China. That is, teachers do not mind imitating other teachers' good practices, and indeed creative practices are meant to be copied. This is very different from the meaning of creativity in, say, the United States, where practices are called creative when they are different from others.

Redesigning examinations is another crucial element of Shanghai reform. In 1985, as noted earlier, Shanghai received permission to start an independent higher education entrance examination. This was a big step forward in two senses. First, admissions to higher education are a complex annual exercise on a national scale, and setting up a separate local examination was a deviation from the uniform system. Shanghai's experiment indeed heralded a trend in exam decentralisation, which is key to localised curricula. Second, Shanghai saw public examinations (in this case the higher education entrance exam) as key in the design of any new curriculum. Moving away from the central national entrance examination allowed Shanghai to have a comprehensive platform in reforming its curriculum.

Since 2001, the entrance examination has taken the form of "3+X": the three core subjects of Chinese language, English language and mathematics, plus the "X" of any other subject(s) as required by individual institutions or faculties. The "X" component may take the form of a paper-and-pencil examination, an oral examination, a test of practical skills and so on. The content may cover one discipline, one kind of ability, or several disciplines or abilities. Individual institutions decide on the weighting of the three core subjects and the "X" component. For example, at Shanghai University for Science and Technology, the three core subjects contribute to 40% of the candidate's overall scores and the "X" component is 60%.

In 2006, Fudan University, Shanghai Jiaotong University and six vocational higher education institutions started to organise their own entrance examinations and to set their own admission requirements. The two universities admitted 578 new students through self-organised examination. In 2007, another three institutions set their own entrance examinations (Shanghai Municipal Education Commission, 2008). The overall trend and intention is to diversify higher education entrance examinations so as to reduce the pressure from a single uniform exam. To lower exam pressures further, Shanghai has moved to allow admissions based on school recommendations at both senior secondary and university entrance levels. Other selected institutions, presumably the stronger, have also been given the autonomy to set their own admission criteria and entrance examinations. More recently, students are allowed to do self-recommendation for admissions at higher levels of education.

Overcoming disparity and inequality

China has in recent years joined the international community in realising the importance of overcoming disparity and inequality in education (and indeed in society at large). This is of particular significance since success in the overall reform has been based on a break from the extreme egalitarianism that prevailed during the Cultural Revolution. The breakthrough brought about by Deng Xiaoping, architect of the reform, was partly due to the concept of "let a few become rich first." Disparity was at that time seen as an incentive to the growth of national wealth and a cure to national poverty.

There has long been the concept of "key schools" in China. Key schools are selected by education authorities to be given additional resources and assigned better teachers. National key schools are very rare now, but provincial/municipal key schools and county/city district key schools persist. There are also key universities with privileged resources, although the term is no longer used to describe them. The key schools admit better students who then do better in terms of selection into higher-level key schools or universities. A senior secondary key school may have 100% of its graduates entering good universities, while a school at the bottom of the non-key category might not send any students to such institutions. This notion is taken for granted in a society conceived as a hierarchy, as noted earlier. Parents do not question the existence of such a system; they only think how their own children might win the competition to get into key schools.

In 1982, a national policy shift sought to remove the label of key schools at the primary level, but they still exist at junior-secondary and senior-secondary levels. Even at primary levels, "experimental" schools or schools under other labels, while lacking the title of key school, are privileged with better resources and better teachers.

Because of high demand under the key school system, it became necessary to have a highly selective public examination at the end of primary schooling to allocate students to junior secondary schools of different categories, and another public examination at the end of junior secondary schooling to allocate students to senior secondary schools. This explains the examination pressure that prevails over all sectors and all levels of the education system.

Neighbourhood attendance

In 1994, Shanghai was the first jurisdiction in China to introduce neighbourhood attendance at primary and junior secondary levels, requiring students to attend their local schools and in effect eliminating the notion of key schools at these levels. This was a challenge to society and caused some uneasiness among parents, who were bewildered that their children could no longer compete for admission to the better schools. The social pressure was so great that eventually a compromise was reached: students could choose schools in other neighbourhoods by paying a sponsorship fee. This is often known as the Chinese version of "school choice," which was a hot issue in America. Parents see the additional fees as fair, because otherwise preferential admissions could go to parents with political power or personal connections.

Neighbourhood attendance also caused concern among teachers who were not used to teaching classes of mixed abilities. Now, however, teachers seem to be proud of being able to handle children of diverse backgrounds and different abilities, realising that diversity and disparity within schools are common features in contemporary societies. Neighbourhood attendance has allowed public examinations to be removed at the end of primary schooling, releasing primary teaching from examination pressure. As an immediate result, innovations and creativity now flourish in primary schools. Policy makers often see this as an essential factor in making Shanghai a champion of curriculum and pedagogy reforms.

Migrant children

Neighbourhood attendance also prepared the school system to face the challenges of migrant children, who became a major national problem in the late 1990s. In the 1980s, migrant workers flooded in from rural villages to work in urban areas. Most are low-wage labourers in factories, while others are contract workers on construction sites. Still others created small businesses to tap the urban market. Migrant workers have contributed immensely to China's economic growth, but their children and their education have become a national problem.

To date, around 30 million children of school age belong to migrant families all over China. This is 20% of the entire student population at the basic education level. In other words, one in every five school children comes from a migrant family. About 20 million are with their parents in cities, but the other 10 million have been left behind in villages without parental care. Both categories pose serious educational as well as social problems and have become a major issue on the government's agenda. They are also one of the major issues China pledged to tackle in its 2020 education plan.

Shanghai is one of the principal recipients of migrant workers because of its active industrial and commercial economies. Statistics in 2006 indicated that 80% of migrant children were of school age, and those who studied in Shanghai schools were 21.4% of the entire student population at the basic education level (Ding, 2010). Since 2002, national policy has been based on two statements (known as the policy of "Two Mainly"):[22] "Education of migrant children is mainly the responsibility of the recipient city", and "Migrant children should be educated mainly in public schools". These policies became necessary at a time when recipient cities did not want to spend local taxpayers' money on migrant children and when parents in public schools did not want to their own children to be mixed with migrant children. The national policy is interpreted differently in different cities.

Shanghai is among the cities that have dealt with migrant children with reason and sympathy. The city's spectacular economic growth can be very much attributed to the contribution of migrant workers, and it followed that their children should be well treated. Interviewees in this study also gave this reason for Shanghai's policies on migrant children's education:

Shanghai has historically always been a city of migrants. Children of the migrants today will stay on and become *bona fide* citizens of Shanghai. How they are treated today will determine how they feel towards and contribute to the future of Shanghai.[23]

An article in a recent issue of *Shanghai Education*, a very popular teachers' magazine, argued that migrant children from rural villages would have positive effects on urban children. The migrant children brought in characteristics such as frugality and perseverance, while urban children from one-child families may be quick in mind and broad in knowledge but spoilt in their personalities. Hence the article argues for "bilateral integration" so that children of all origins can benefit from each other's company.

In a way, Shanghai has established the notion that migrant children are "our children" and works constructively to include them in its educational development. Meanwhile, at the system level, the admission of migrant children to public schools helps solve the problem caused by the acute decline of school-age children among the permanent residents.

Strengthening weak schools

Another major undertaking in Shanghai has been to improve the school system by converting "weaker schools" to stronger schools. Since the 1980s, several rounds of school renovation attempted to ensure that schools were in sound physical condition. In the mid-1990s, the demographic decline began to show, which gave the government a good opportunity to further improve the schools (Jin, 2003). In 1999, Shanghai started a second wave of school renovation, upgrading school buildings and facilities according to a "standard programme." A total of 1 569 schools were either re-organised or closed, accounting for three-quarters of all schools in Shanghai. A third wave of school renovation started in 2002, and one-third of junior secondary schools in Shanghai benefited. The second and third rounds included other reform measures, such as strengthening the team of teachers or selecting a strong principal.

With the improved economy, the Shanghai municipal government has been keen to improve households' capacity to support children's education. Since 2006, all students receiving compulsory education have been exempted from tuition and miscellaneous fees. Since 2007, all students in compulsory education have been provided with free textbooks and exercise books (Shanghai Municipal Education Commission, 2009). Although basic education is free and compulsory, the quality of schools varies, and that affects the quality of education children receive. Indeed, public schools in Shanghai have long been criticised for the disparity among them.

In order to reduce this disparity, the Shanghai government has adopted several strategies.[24] The first, as mentioned earlier, is *school renovation*. The government evaluates schools in terms of their infrastructure and educational quality, and then classifies them into Levels A, B, C and D. Level A schools meet the government's standards for both infrastructure and quality, while Level D schools meet neither standard. With the decrease in the number of school-age children, quite a few Level C and D schools were closed. Others were merged into Level A or B schools or reorganised in the second and third waves of renovation. When the third renovation wave ended in 2005, Level C and D schools disappeared and all public schools became Level A or B. In junior secondary education, 64% of public schools are Level A.

The second strategy is known as *financial transfer payment*, which is the mobilisation of public funding with positive discrimination. Statistics showed that per-student expenditure in rural areas was only 50% to 60% of that in the city.

Rural schools also had far lower capital spending than downtown schools on average (Shanghai Municipal Education Commission, 2004). The strategy was then to set a minimum standard for per-student public expenditure at different levels, and to transfer public funds to the deprived areas. Between 2004 and 2008, over USD 500 million was transferred to rural schools to help them build new facilities and laboratories, update older ones, purchase books and audiovisual materials, and increase teacher salaries.

The third strategy is to *transfer teachers* from urban to rural areas and *vice versa*. It was often difficult for rural schools to recruit teachers, and they also suffered from high teacher turnover. For example, it was reported that in Qingpu District, a rural area, 160 experienced teachers in relatively poor junior secondary schools resigned between 1997 and 2002.[25] To reverse the situation, the government transferred a considerable number of teachers from urban public schools to rural schools, along with some outstanding urban principals (Shanghai Municipal Education Commission, 2008). Meanwhile, young and middle-aged principals and teachers from rural schools were transferred to urban schools. They are expected to return to the rural schools to enrich them with their new urban experiences.

The fourth strategy is to *pair off* urban districts with rural districts. In 2005, the educational authorities of nine urban districts signed three-year agreements with educational authorities of nine rural districts. The authorities exchange and discuss their educational development plans and join hands to deal with problems such as teachers' capacity building. Teachers' Professional Development Institutes affiliated to both authorities share their curricula, teaching materials and good practices. Moreover, some 91 schools paired up as sister schools, and a substantial number of teachers undertook exchange programmes among the sister schools (Shanghai Municipal Education Commission, 2009). The first round of the three-year "pairing off" programme ended in 2008, and the second round is under way.

The fifth strategy is relatively new but has gained increasing attention. It is called *commissioned administration*, a kind of school custody programme in which the government commissions "good" public schools to take over the administration of "weak" ones. Under this scheme, the "good" public school appoints its experienced leader (such as the deputy principal) to be the principal of the "weak" school and sends a team of experienced teachers to lead in teaching. It is believed that the ethos, management style and teaching methods of the good schools can in this way be transferred to the poorer school.

In 2007, the Shanghai municipal government asked 10 good schools in downtown and other educational intermediary agencies to take charge of 20 schools providing compulsory education in 10 rural districts and counties. The good schools/agencies and the rural schools signed a two-year contract that required the former to send senior administrators and experienced teachers to the latter. The city government bears the cost of the partnership (Shanghai Municipal Education Commission, 2008); Shanghai Municipal Education Commission, 2009). Such an arrangement not only benefits the poor schools; it also gives the good schools more room to promote their teachers.[26]

The sixth strategy is to establish a *consortium* of schools, where strong and weak schools, old and new, public and private are grouped into a consortium or cluster, with one strong school at the core (Box 4.3).

Box 4.3 **The Qibao Education Group**

Qibao is a suburb of Shanghai. Its secondary school, established in 1947, has become known for the humanist values that permeate all aspects of school life. It is also known for the percentage of its graduates admitted to good universities. Some graduates from Qibao have been directly admitted to Harvard University. Since the 1960s, Qibao Secondary School has been identified as an "experimental school" or a "demonstration school" because of its effective leadership, and it has been famous in the realms of science education, sports, arts and music, and technology. Under the leadership of Principal Qiu Zhonghai, the Qibao Education Group was established in 2005 with Qibao Secondary School as the core. To date it hosts six schools. Three other public schools were renamed and "adopted" by Qibao, while two private secondary schools, one junior and one senior, were newly established by the group. All six schools have demonstrated continuous improvement since becoming members of the Qibao Group.

Source: A focus group discussion with administrators of the group, 2010.

Achievements and challenges in Shanghai's education system

External observers might see the development and practice of education in Shanghai as very effective. Shanghai participated in PISA 2009 and achieved very high average results overall (Table 4.1, OECD, 2010). Although these results were not yet available at the time of this study, there was consensus among all those interviewed (see list at end of chapter) on some positive developments including some improvements on local measurements of student learning. Local experts believe that this is evidence of successful reforms, whereby students are now exposed to a much broader knowledge base and are trained to integrate their knowledge and tackle real-life problems. Students have also become used to identifying questions of interest to themselves, and to make open-ended explorations. All these changes are markedly different from the traditional Chinese pattern in which students learn subjects by heart and regurgitate such knowledge in examinations.

Table 4.1 **Shanghai-China's mean scores on reading, mathematics and science scales in PISA**

	PISA 2000	PISA 2003	PISA 2006	PISA 2009
	Mean score	Mean score	Mean score	Mean score
Reading				556
Mathematics				600
Science				575

Source: OECD (2010), *PISA 2009 Results: What Students Know and Can Do: Student Performance in Reading, Mathematics and Science (Volume I)*, OECD Publishing.
StatLink ⫘⫘ http://dx.doi.org/10.1787/888932366674

However, none of the interviewees was satisfied with the quality of Shanghai's education system. As one experienced educator insightfully expressed it, the changes in student learning were brought about chiefly by organised and structured top-down reforms, implemented either through examinations or policy shifts.[27] Such measures may be well designed, but students are still not given much autonomy in their study. Schools with outstanding characteristics are still rare, and examination pressure still prevails.

There is little expectation of any fundamental change in the near future, given that in comparison to injustice from abuses of power or payments of money, examination scores are seen to be "scientific," "reliable" and hence "fair." However, the dictates of the examinations have left students with little time and room for learning on their own. "There is an opportunity cost in terms of time and space," said the interviewee. "Students grow within narrow margins" and are not fully prepared for their lives and work in the future. This is seen as a deep crisis, exacerbated by the reality of single-child families.

■ HONG KONG'S EDUCATION SYSTEM: ONE COUNTRY, TWO SYSTEMS

Hong Kong was originally a small fishing island that was ceded to the British government in 1842 after China's defeat in the Sino-British War ("The Opium War"). In further treaties in the late 19th century, China also lost the Kowloon Peninsula and the New Territories to Britain on a 99-year lease. Hong Kong maintained its colonial status at the end of the Second World War when all other "unequal treaties" with China were terminated. In 1997 the 99-year lease ended. Following a surprise suggestion from Deng Xiaoping to British Prime Minister Margaret Thatcher, Hong Kong's sovereignty was returned to China under the "one country, two systems" notion.

Under this arrangement, China resumed its sovereignty over Hong Kong, but Hong Kong remained a separate jurisdiction, governed by a "Basic Law" and enjoying autonomy in all areas except military defence and diplomatic relations. As a Special Administrative Region of China (SAR), Hong Kong maintains an independent legislature, with a distinct currency and policies of its own, independent from the national government in Beijing. In the realm of education, for example, Hong Kong maintains its own system of education under an Education Bureau (EDB) which reports only to the Hong Kong government and Hong Kong taxpayers, without direct relations with the Ministry of Education in Beijing. Meanwhile, Hong Kong is free to engage in bilateral relations with other jurisdictions and assume membership in other international organisations for finance, commercial, education, culture and so forth. Hong Kong's education system has been and remains quite distinct from that of the rest of China, with a unique history, structure and reform trajectory.

Hong Kong has a population of around 7 million living in a small area of 1 000 square kilometres. Its average GDP per capita is often above USD 42 000, bringing it within the world's top ten richest nations on most lists.[28] The service sector of the economy accounts for 92% of Hong Kong's economic growth. Across the border on the Chinese mainland, an estimated 80 million people work for Hong Kong investors.

The population is predominantly ethnic Chinese. Caucasians from Western countries living in Hong Kong are small in number but mostly work for influential multinationals. The ethnic Chinese derive from immigrations at different periods of history. Increasingly, they come from mainland China, either as immigrants who stay on or as tourists or migrants who reside in Hong Kong temporarily. Small but significant portions of the population are from Indonesia and the Philippines, most with temporary permits to work as domestic helpers. Traditionally, residents of South Asian origin include businessmen from India, manual or service workers from Pakistan and former Ghurkas from Nepal. Hong Kong residents, both men and women, have life expectancies that are among the longest in the world.

Hong Kong hosts an education system comprising around 1 100 schools. However, the number is shrinking because of dramatic declines in population. Each age cohort has declined from around 9 000 members in the early 1980s to around 4 000 in recent years. The fertility rate is around 0.9 children per woman, far less than the "replacement" level of 2.1 children per woman.

Hong Kong's education system is very much part of the British colonial legacy. The school system still maintains the British approach of five-year secondary schooling (Forms 1-5), which ends with a Certificate of Education Examination, the crucial certification for a student's future. The certificate is a gateway for all young people, either to work or further study. It is followed by a two-year matriculation education (known as Forms 6 and 7) in preparation for the A-Level examinations, which aim at admissions to higher education (Figure 4.2a). However, this system is facing an overhaul, as we will discuss below.

■ Figure 4.2a ■
Hong Kong's education system organisation until 2012

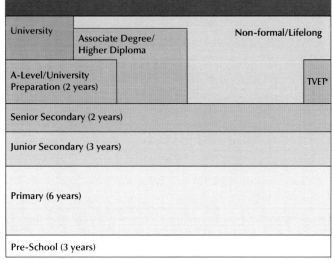

* Technical and Vocational Education and Training.

The post-war years: The foundations of an elitist system

Whilst the school system on the Chinese mainland only began after 1905 with the abolition of the Civil Examinations, Hong Kong already had schools in place long before that and they were not influenced by changes on the mainland. The leading elite Hong Kong schools followed the model of the British "public" (*i.e.*, private) schools. Nonetheless, the Hong Kong population has always been predominantly Chinese, and the schools have largely been adapted to the Chinese culture. This was also aided by British colonial localisation policies, particularly after the Second World War. Hence, it is fair to say that the Hong Kong education system is very much a hybrid of Chinese culture and British traditions and schools enjoy the best of both worlds.

Hong Kong's education remained rather elitist even after the Second World War and until the 1960s. There was only one university, the University of Hong Kong, which took in only 100 to 200 students each year. A rather stringent primary school examination later evolved into the Secondary Schools Entrance Examination, so that the traditional examination pressure prevailed at the primary level, even though primary schooling was already widespread. The post-war baby boom caused school attendance to soar, but secondary schools remained very selective.

There have never been many government schools in Hong Kong. However, since the 1950s, the government has been subsidising non-government school-sponsoring bodies (mainly churches, charitable organisations and other associations or agencies) and with them formed a public school system. Many such schools once operated under marginal conditions (such as on the rooftops of public housing), but were given land and buildings in the 1970s and 1980s. Now they enjoy state-of-the-art facilities. In brief, the Hong Kong government provides most of the capital cost and almost the full recurrent cost of public schools, but expects the non-government sponsoring bodies to run them. The sponsoring bodies abide by a Code of Aid, a kind of contractual agreement with the government. In a way, the "aided schools" are near to the US concept of charter schools, except that the Code of Aid governs operational procedures rather than performance.

Hong Kong still has quite a few elite schools whose graduates are favoured candidates for admission to the best universities in the world. It is notable that such students are not necessarily from wealthy families. Hong Kong strongly exemplifies the Chinese belief that young people achieve because of hard work, regardless of family background. However, its schools are not only strong in academic achievements; often they are also champions in sports and music, and most graduates have become leaders in higher education, mainly because of their vibrant and autonomous student organisations. The Hong Kong schools breed leaders.

Private schools, many of them for-profit, mushroomed in the 1970s to respond to the shortage of school places. Such schools tended to offer low-quality education and as a result gradually disappeared during the 1980s because of expansion in the public sector. Since the turn of the century, however, a new breed of elite private schools has been established as international schools, though admitting mainly local students.

The push for universal education: 1960s onwards

In 1965, new legislation introduced compulsory six-year primary education. Actual primary enrolment was already near 100%.[29] This was followed by heated debate about whether to offer three years of free schooling after the primary level. There was tension between government expansion plans and escalating social aspirations for more education. The tug-of-war was about the speed of expansion. Government plans, bold as they were, attempted to maintain a pyramidal structure in response to the manpower needs of the manufacturing industrial economy, the main thrust of Hong Kong's economic "miracle" in the 1970s and 1980s. That is, the government maintained a very small percentage in the enrolment of higher education, while steadily expanding senior secondary education and providing universal education for primary and junior secondary. Meanwhile, social equity goals emerged in the 1970s, leading to calls for universal secondary education. Due to international pressures, mainly from the General Agreement on Tariffs and Trade (GATT), Hong Kong introduced nine-year compulsory education in 1978.[30]

The next step was to abolish the Secondary Schools Entrance Examination. This could be regarded as an historic first step to release the schools from formal public examinations, at least at the primary level. However, schools remain different in their standards. The replacement for exams as placement mechanisms was a "scientific" approach that combined school internal assessments, an aptitude test to scale the internal assessments across schools, a classification of students into five capacity bands, and parental choice after random picks by computers. In the end, however, the best students were still admitted to the best schools. The public examination was gone, but schools still managed to create all kinds of tests as a tangible yardstick for performance. Drilling survived, and the situation did not change until the comprehensive reform discussed below.

The aspiration for education did not stop at the introduction of nine-year compulsory schooling. It was a textbook example of how increased supply led to increased demand. Without much intervention from the government, enrolment in secondary education was again near universal by the end of the 1980s. This was augmented by a rather sophisticated system of vocational education (programmes for apprenticeship, craftsmen and technicians) with the milestone establishment of the Vocational Training Council in 1982.

The next battle was for higher education expansion. Until the early 1980s, Hong Kong maintained a small gross enrolment ratio of 1-2%, with a 3% increment in the intake each year. Local enrolments were limited to two universities, and those who could afford it would go abroad to study in overseas institutions. There were several attempts to expand access to higher education, but government determination to do so came only in 1988. That year saw an exodus of emigrants because of the forthcoming handover in sovereignty to China, as well as other political change. This situation prompted the Hong Kong government to expand its formal higher education intake to 18% of the eligible population. Another tug-of-war ensued between government policies and social aspirations, now focused on this tertiary education level. By the early 1990s, however, the 18% target was achieved.

The 1990s to the present day: The movement towards comprehensive education reform

From the late 1990s the discourse in Hong Kong shifted from one of expansion to one of "what should education offer." A comprehensive education reform began in 1999. This initiative emerged at a time of rather comprehensive dissatisfaction with the education system. Parents were not satisfied with the education schools were providing and were often upset by unpleasant experiences their children were undergoing, particularly in the newer public schools. For example, children were working on homework until almost midnight, and most of what they did was little more than regurgitation. They subjected their children, unwillingly, to tough competition in order to move to better schools. Those who could afford it sent their children to international schools that were liberal in their philosophies and where children seemed happier. Teachers in turn were dissatisfied with their students, thinking standards and motivation were declining. Employers were also dissatisfied with the quality and calibre of graduates from local institutions, finding them less prepared to engage in an increasingly complex workplace. They were turning to recruiting returnees from studying overseas.

In hindsight, this dissatisfaction can be explained by a few crucial factors. First, schools were unprepared for an intake that suddenly changed from a select few to almost everybody. The system now had greater student "mixability", but teachers still maintained approaches generally used for teaching the elite, in which only the capable students would benefit and the slower students were abandoned. Second, the sense of responsibility changed following the introduction of compulsory education. While students could be blamed for performing poorly in schools they had struggled to enter, when education became compulsory blame was laid on schools and teachers, even though they had been badly prepared. Third, although there had been successful reforms in curriculum and pedagogy (such as the introduction of integrated science in junior secondary schools and the change to an "activities approach" in primary classes, both in the 1970s), the general environment still favoured a conventional curriculum and didactic teaching. This was reinforced by the highly competitive public examinations and keen selection process for higher education. Fourth, and perhaps most fundamentally, employment patterns had undergone major changes. While young people with only a nine-year education could previously easily find employment as blue-collar unskilled labourers in manufacturing plants, such factories had mostly moved across the border into southern China where labour costs were much cheaper (thanks to China's open policies). The corresponding expansion of Hong Kong's service sector was accompanied by an expectation of higher knowledge in its labour force.

In sum, at the end of the 20th century Hong Kong's education system faced a multitude of structural crises, partly due to the efforts to accommodate more children and partly due to changes in society's expectations for education.

Seen from this perspective, the apparent failure of the system at that time was less a problem of government incompetence or ill-management than a demonstration of the widening gap between a rapidly changing society and the static approaches to education. The solution was not to do more and better of what schools had been doing, but to put education in a different framework. That was the starting point for Hong Kong's comprehensive education reform which began in 1999 and continues today.

The reform was led by the Education Commission, the overseeing advisory body in education policies. The Commission's core comprised four people: the Chair, who was head of a major international bank; a university professor with world-wide experience; an insightful school principal; and the Permanent Secretary for Education, who was a committed reformer.

The reform started with a "mobilisation phase". Some 800 community leaders were invited to a major gathering to air their concerns. The meeting started with a presentation titled "Questioning Education," which asked over 100 questions with no answers. Participants assumed the roles of parents, employers and corporate citizens, and expressed such anger that they fuelled the Education Commission with determination to never go back to the old ways. A subsequent campaign encouraged every school to establish a paper "tree of hope" onto which students hung tags with statements beginning, "I have a hope: Education should be ..."

The design phase followed. A document that asked questions about the "Aims of Education" was published. It described recent changes in society and proposed a list of fresh aims for education. Upon public invitation, more than 40 000 suggestions were submitted. It became a community campaign and greatly enriched the Education Commission's understanding of how society was changing and its implications for education.

Meanwhile, as part of the learning process, the Education Commission carried out a series of innovative consultations to aid their decision making. Major professional bodies were interviewed to solicit their views. A typical example was the Society of Accountants, which suggested that the best action for a university to take towards accounting was to "not teach it".[31] Another study looked at manpower aspirations among small and medium enterprises (SMEs) that were becoming the backbone of Hong Kong's economy. This was a genuine learning process for the Education Commission, which was discovering that fundamental changes were occurring in society and the workplace, but that the general design for education had not kept pace.

The Education Commission also studied education reform in other systems, as well as patterns of lifelong learning in OECD countries,[32] and supply and demand in the local market for lifelong learning. The Commission looked at ways to retrain the newly unemployed and visited trade unions in order to understand the trends of employment in various industries.

By the end of this stage, it was relatively clear that the reform, despite its comprehensive nature, would have to concentrate on three aspects: the system's structure, its curriculum and assessments. Subcommittees were established to design these different aspects of the reform.

In 2001, as a first step in the reform, public assessments after primary schooling were abolished with immediate effect. This caused some confusion among school principals and teachers, who had to seek new frames of reference. However, the move has proved critical to primary schools, allowing teachers to develop more relevant school-based learning activities and changing the general discourse in primary schools from one of examinations and drills to one of learning. As a result, in less than a decade, secondary schools are seeing more active learners coming out of primary schools, with improvements in student performance as assessed in consecutive international comparisons in reading literacy. For example, in PIRLS (Progress in International Reading Literacy Study), Hong Kong's primary schoolchildren's performance in reading literacy was elevated from 14th in 2001 to 2nd in 2006 in the international rankings (Mullis *et al.*, 2006). At the secondary school level, PISA measures learning outcomes for 15 year-olds, showing fairly consistent and high results across the three skills tested, including reading (Table 4.2; OECD, 2010).

Table 4.2   **Hong Kong-China's mean scores on reading, mathematics and science scales in PISA**

	PISA 2000	PISA 2003	PISA 2006	PISA 2009
	Mean score	Mean score	Mean score	Mean score
Reading	525	510	536	533
Mathematics		550	547	555
Science			542	549

Source: OECD (2010), *PISA 2009 Volume I, What Students Know and Can Do: Student Performance in Reading, Mathematics and Science*, OECD Publishing.
StatLink ⎌ http://dx.doi.org/10.1787/888932366674

In 2002, a crucial reform document – *Learning to Learn* – was published (Curriculum Development Institute, 2001). The title carries two major messages: the change of focus from "teaching" to "learning," and a new emphasis on the process of learning rather than memorising facts. This document, still the basic reference for the entire reform effort, was informed by the contemporary theories of learning. In layman's language, these theories hold that:[33]

- Learning is the active construction of knowledge by the learner.
- Learning is a process, achieved through activities called learning experiences.
- Similar experiences may lead to the construction of different kinds of knowledge, *i.e.* to people learning differently.
- Learning is for understanding.
- Understanding is demonstrated by the effective application of the knowledge thus constructed.
- Effective learning experiences often require integration of knowledge.
- Learning is therefore best in real-life experiences with actual effects.
- Learning is also a social action, best achieved in groups.
- Human learning is motivated by a sense of improvement.

This is just a synopsis of the general principles of theories of constructive learning. The reform exercise in Hong Kong incorporates the common denominator of theories about learning, rather than committing itself to any particular school of "constructivism."

The consequences of reform for secondary school and higher education

Although the change in curriculum was at all levels, the consequences have been most noticeable at senior secondary level:

- The secondary school curriculum is designed according to what learning experiences students need, rather than being guided by manpower needs in the economy.

- The curriculum is decided in secondary schools before seeking endorsement from universities. The latter's concern is to select the best students, while the curriculum reform aims for lifelong benefits for students.

- The secondary school curriculum is framed around eight key learning areas (KLA), rather than "subjects": Chinese Language, English Language, Mathematics, Science and Technology, Social Science and Humanities, Sports and Arts, Applied Learning (to allow students to gain real-life workplace experiences) and Other Learning Experiences (including service learning, workplace visits and overseas experiences). The latter two are new to both teachers and schools.

- A long process of negotiation with higher education institutions resulted in a compromise in which secondary school students going on to university are expected to perform in four areas: Chinese, English, Mathematics, and a new subject called Liberal Studies (see next point). Institutions and programmes may also ask for one other "subject." This reflects a change among higher education institutions from basing their student selections on the number of subjects studied (as if that would guarantee better academic performance) to understanding the benefit of requiring less and allowing broader learning experiences among their candidates.

- Liberal Studies has introduced a new area of assessment in secondary education in Hong Kong: a learning experience with timetabled slots and no syllabus – only broad topics. Assessment is meant to be flexible. In effect, teachers allow students to design their own learning schemes in which they rely mostly on current affairs and non-textbook information, and develop high-order or critical thinking. This includes asking sensible questions; finding directions for analysis, synthesis and conceptualisation; and proposing hypotheses or theories.

All these overhauls to the curriculum are carried out in the context of structural change to the school system, where junior-secondary, senior-secondary and higher education will shift from 5 years + 2 years + 3 years (following the British model) to 3 years + 3 years + 4 years, so that achieving a bachelor's degree will now take four years instead of three (Figure 4.2b).

■ Figure 4.2b ■
Hong Kong's education system organisation after 2012

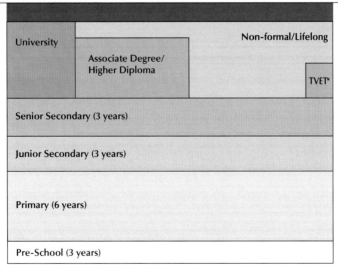

* Technical and Vocational Education and Training.

The focus in higher education now is how to make the best use of the additional year in the new system. Almost all institutions have decided not to extend specialised studies in the additional year but to offer alternative learning experiences, following the spirit of the reform in secondary curricula. Such alternative learning experiences include a new common core curriculum, all kinds of experiential learning and expansion of overseas exchanges.

It is conceivable that after 2012, the higher education scene will be very different. After years of discussion and design, the New Senior Secondary (NSS) curriculum was launched towards the end of 2009 in anticipation of a new public examination in 2012, when university entrance requirements will change accordingly. As this chapter is being written, both secondary and higher education institutions are busy preparing for the change.

Critical to the reform is construction of a new assessment system to facilitate the changes in curriculum and pedagogy. This is underway, and faces the dual task of reflecting the new philosophy of learning and gaining international recognition for university admissions.

Key factors in managing the reform

The Hong Kong education reform has benefited from a long lead time, well-designed preparations and good management of perceptions.

Preparation

Starting in 2005, four years before implementation of the new curriculum, the government organised meticulous activities to prepare schools for it. In a typical exercise, representatives from 12 schools would gather in a hotel for at least one whole-day "retreat". Each delegation would have six members: the supervisor, one school board member, the principal, the vice-principal and two senior teachers. The retreat usually started with a talk from a prominent community leader on how "society has changed". The Curriculum Development Institute then outlined the curriculum reform, and each school delegation was asked to discuss their initial strategies for implementing it. The school groups then exchanged views.

Forty-five such sessions were held and all schools were covered. The government then went on to do similar training sessions with middle managers, such as subject department heads. Such perception-management exercises have eased schools into the changes, allowed them to develop ownership of the reforms, and minimised unnecessary resistance during the long reform process. This was essential given that the increased workload and disturbance for schools were by no means trivial. The bulk of preparation for the reform stayed with the schools. The reform could be seen as a combination of centralised design, school-based implementation and professional support.

Managing perceptions

Another crucial factor has been the inclusion of the media in the entire process. At the early stages of designing the reform, seminars were held for reporters on the fundamental principles of the reform philosophy. There were constant interactions with chief editors of the major media to involve them in engaging the public in the reform. However, since the process has already taken 11 years, changes in personnel both in government and the media have required a special effort to sustain the relationships.

Media relations are only one aspect of "perception management" for the reform. Through the years, despite the different reform phases, consistent themes have been *i)* societal change; and *ii)* concentration on student learning. In the earlier years of consultation and design, many documents started with the phrase "Society has changed!" People from all walks of life contributed to the theme. Meanwhile, emphasis on student learning and sustained discussions continuously enriched that theme. Numerous seminars and conferences were held on various aspects of education, but these two themes remained constant.

However, there is no uniform model of reform implementation. Indeed, its very core was respect for individual needs, and hence the evolution of schools into more autonomous entities. Under the general theme, and with the pulling force of the public and university entrance exams, schools have developed rather diverse approaches to implementing the reform. Nonetheless, because of the change led by the reform, schools across the board have developed their own mechanisms of collective decision making and division of labour which respect their individual school cultures.

ACHIEVEMENTS AND CHALLENGES IN HONG KONG'S EDUCATION SYSTEM

The Hong Kong education system has been reformed several times, but people tended to shun the word "reform" until the most recent overhaul. Overall, the Hong Kong government is known for its philosophy of positive non-intervention, although that has often been challenged in recent years. In the two decades after the war, the Hong Kong government did not intervene in the school system beyond providing subsidies. Even in later years, when government action in developing and reforming education became significant, the general understanding remained that government intervention should be minimal. This philosophy could be called the "governmentality" of Hong Kong, to use Foucault's term.[34] This is fundamentally different from other jurisdictions where governments see themselves as the comprehensive controllers of all things happening in schools. However, the notion is very much challenged by critics who not only do not believe in the concept but also doubt whether it is actually practised by the Hong Kong government. However, the vaguer notion of "small government, great market" is still something that Hong Kong honours.

The philosophy of "positive non-intervention" becomes a challenge because Hong Kong celebrates school autonomy and denounces anything that would downplay school-based endeavours. The result is great disparity among its schools. Another consequence is that unlike practices in Shanghai and Singapore, where weaker schools are often the focus of attention and measures are taken to strengthen them, Hong Kong is reluctant even to rank schools. The result has been that some public schools receive standard public funding yet deliver sub-standard educational services. Parents see this as unfair. Changing the situation may not be straightforward, however, because it entails a different kind of accountability to allow the government to actively intervene.

Nevertheless, Hong Kong's comprehensive reform is succeeding because of its strong rationale: fundamental change in society requires new ways of looking at human learning. The reform challenges the very basics of student learning and how such learning can best be achieved.

LESSONS FROM SHANGHAI AND HONG KONG

Shanghai and Hong Kong represent two different approaches to education, which makes it worthwhile to look at them separately. Yet despite the differences, the students of both cities consistently perform well in international comparisons, as the PISA results testify. It is interesting to compare some of the common features of the two cities: they share a cultural heritage that treasures education, yet their students suffer from tremendous examination pressure. They share a colonial past, although colonial rule in Hong Kong lasted much longer. Both are major metropolitan centres in China, and indeed in Asia, and both prosper because of the vibrant cultures produced by highly-educated citizens.

However, the cities have followed very different development paths over the past six decades. Shanghai became a major industrial centre under the government of the People's Republic, and later, at the opening of China, moved on to become the city with the most remarkable development in the service sector. Before 1997, Hong Kong remained outside China, and hence was relatively immune from its political fluctuations. It hosts the country's freest market and has become the centre of finance and management for the whole of Asia.

Both societies felt the need for fundamental reforms of their education almost at the same time. The reform in Shanghai was part of a national undertaking. The reform in Hong Kong was, however, due to specific needs within the local system.

Shanghai belongs to an organised society and approached education reform in an organised way. It would be inaccurate to describe the Shanghai reform as top-down, because unmistakable and remarkable initiatives emerged from the grassroots. However, the municipal government did not only design the reform but also effectively intervened in the process, for example in running schools and improving teaching.

Hong Kong is almost the opposite. Its reform provides schools with a platform, supports them with resources and modifies the public examination as well as university admissions, but leaves the process of reform to the schools. Teachers may find this difficult because changes in the curriculum and examinations have made their familiar paths invalid. But the reform has pushed schools and teachers to take a professional stand, exercise professional autonomy and adapt the changes to best fit their respective student bodies.

Hence, reform in the two cities has given us a very good opportunity to observe two systems of education, both strong in international comparisons and assessments, to showcase a whole spectrum of possibilities.

This section discusses factors not analysed in the preceding sections because they are less explicit and are largely taken for granted by the Chinese themselves, but very important for those who might be interested in learning from the Chinese experience.

▪ Building legitimacy

Both Shanghai and Hong Kong aim high in their educational ambitions, both as a systemic target goal and to meet individual aspirations. They both use statements about education to guide their reforms, which take a moralistic approach. In the 1990s, Shanghai used the slogan of "first class city" and added "first class city, first class education". Although the definition of "first class" remains vague, the concept drives the development of education and keeps education high on the policy agenda.

Hong Kong has always felt insecure in international competitions, and much of its competitive edge is being challenged by mainland China and by other jurisdictions in the vicinity, such as Singapore, Malaysia, and even Macao. Hong Kong has identified "six pillars" for its further development, and building an "education hub" is one of them.[35]

The sustained emphasis on education carried in these statements attracts the attention and support of the entire society. It underpins the allocation of substantial government resources to education and helps mobilise community resources. And as good education cannot be achieved only by teachers, the statement is an appeal to support from all parts of society. In other words, a consistent continuous movement creates and reinforces the legitimacy of educational development.

A recent example is China's *Outline of the Medium and Long Term Plan for Development and Reform of Education* (Ministry of Education of the PRC, 2010b), a blueprint for education in 2020 and perhaps beyond. The initial "consultation" draft, published in February 2010, took more than 18 months to produce. The process involved thousands of professionals and experts and more than 23 000 seminars and forums for brainstorming, and was accompanied by technical reports totalling more than five million words. It received 2.1 million submissions from all walks of society.

After the consultation draft launch in February, further discussion and revisions included provisional plans for interpretation and implementation. The exercise was chaired by Prime Minister Wen Jiabao and went through the State Council and then received endorsement from the Central Committee of the Chinese Communist Party and eventually the Politbureau, just to make sure of its high priority in the political arena. Such a strong effort in legitimacy-building is unusual, but will guarantee that the educational reform movement will carry huge momentum.

However, legitimacy means very different things in other societies and systems. There are diverse ways that governments can build and enhance the legitimacy of their policies. While the approaches in Shanghai and Hong Kong may not apply to other societies, the attention they gave to building legitimacy for education is of crucial importance.

▪ Reform to break ranks with tradition

It is difficult to say which of the factors observed are due to cultural heritage and which are due to policy interventions and practices. They are intertwined. However, in both Shanghai and Hong Kong, deep cultural influences in values surrounding education (such as the emphasis on exams) have been perceived as problems and have provoked a reaction in order to modernise the system: moving from elite to massive popular education, from emphasis on teaching to emphasis on learning, from fact memorisation to development of learning capacities, and from economic needs to individual needs. In both cases, the change in the nature and orientation of the entire education system involves struggles against the culture.

Hence, if we really want to understand anything useful from the two systems in Shanghai and Hong Kong, the first is the sense of *reform* as a value. Both Shanghai and Hong Kong have resorted to fundamental and comprehensive reforms in education, and without much mutual communication they started almost at the same time. This sense of *reform* is also shared by Singapore (Chapter 7), which started its comprehensive education reforms in the late 1990s. It was also the intention of the reforms in Japan (Chapter 6) and South Korea[36] in the mid-1980s. The degree of success in these reforms varies, but intolerance of the ill effects of cultural heritage was a common factor.

▪ Root and branch reform versus superficial improvement

These experiences show us that reform is not equivalent to improvement. "Improvement" means doing what the system has been doing all along, but more and better. "Reform" involves paradigm shifts. In other words, the notion of a *reform* entails an awareness that further development of education is not only a matter of remedying perceived shortcomings; it is an understanding that more fundamental issues exist where education has to catch up with changes in society. Without such an understanding, any "improvement" of the system and practices only reinforces what might have gone wrong. This is perhaps the problem with education policies in many other systems. Often, worries surround students' under-performance in visible areas such as language and mathematics but pay no attention to the fact that the entire curriculum and pedagogy could be obsolete. "Improvement" would then mean the repetition and reinforcement of obsolete approaches to education.

So the legitimate questions a country could ask itself are: *Education for all, but for what purpose? Quality assurance in education, but what quality is expected?*

▪ The importance of instruction for learning

A key factor behind the accomplishment of the two cities' systems is that they took *learning* as the core concern in their educational reforms. It might sound odd that we should remind educators and policy-makers that learning should be the core business of education. However, reforms in some other systems emphasise systemic planning or finance, school management or accountability, without actually looking at the causes, environments and processes of student learning. It is easy to forget that structure, policy, standards, finance and so on make no difference at all unless they affect the instruction that students get and what they ultimately learn. In this sense, both systems are to be congratulated for moving away from the tradition in which education (based on examination preparation) is reaffirmed without actually understanding the process of learning.

The core position of *learning* comes into play only when one understands how the changes in society and the economy affect the function of education. In a typical industrial society, the prime function of education is to prepare manpower and provide the relevant credentials. Once in the workplace, individuals are protected by orders, procedures, rules and regulations, regardless of their personal knowledge and characteristics. This function is now diminishing as the pyramidal structure collapses, replaced by small work units where individuals have to face clients, to solve problems, to design products or solutions, to endure risks and to face moral and ethical dilemmas. Knowledge and personality are of prime importance, and education has to prepare young people for this.

It is noticeable that in both Shanghai and Hong Kong, the attention to learning is not so much a matter of puritan educational ideals but rather an awakening to the future needs of society. Attention to social change and attention to learning are two sides of the same coin. Hence, to reinforce the point made in the last section, genuine reform in education has to start with an analysis of society and its changes.

By the same token, both systems have made tremendous efforts to understand human learning. This includes *i)* a body of scholars concentrating on the "sciences of learning"; *ii)* a framework based on learning that shapes the curriculum; *iii)* professional discussions among educators in the form of debates, seminars, forums, conferences and experiments, where theories of learning are interpreted and translated into grassroots practices; *iv)* effective methods of dissemination (such as slogans in Shanghai) among grassroots teachers; and *v)* perception management to convince parents and the media of the value of the changes. All these dimensions have to be strategically co-ordinated and synchronised, and this in turn requires champions who are committed to the concepts.

Because of the usual confusion between learning, study and education, it is often essential to roll out the education reforms in phases. The beauty of a campaign is that there are milestones and phased targets, so that reform activities do not deteriorate in bureaucratic hands that might turn them into administrative routines. This could also explain many failures of education reform elsewhere which, despite a dramatic start, quickly become conventional.

▪ Reform that looks at the whole system and the whole student

Both Shanghai and Hong Kong have engaged in comprehensive approaches to education reform.

Reforms in the two cities do not concentrate only on certain aspects of education. Students are complex human beings, and the improvement in their educational achievement can be accomplished only when all the complex contextual factors are considered and changed. The reforms perceived education as the development of the student as a whole. Students' academic achievements are not separate from the other aspects of their personal development physical, cultural, spiritual, and so on. Extra-curricular experiences, for example, are treated in both systems as an essential element of students' comprehensive learning experiences and holistic development.

The reforms also try to mobilise all sectors of society and are seen as an undertaking that concerns everyone. As mentioned earlier, they started with different frameworks: The Shanghai reform was launched as "first-rate city, first-rate education" and regarded education as part of a comprehensive aim of building a world-class city. Education reform was sold as a way to increase Shanghai's competitiveness in the global arena. The Hong Kong reform started with the awareness that "society has changed" and young people had to be prepared for a totally new society and precarious future developments. But both societies positioned education as a core element in the city's future. Hence, the reforms not only received priority consideration on the governments' agenda, but all sectors of society are expected to participate and give support.

▪ A capable centre with authority and legitimacy to act

Decentralisation is the overwhelming focus for the current literature on education planning and governance, but the subject may deserve a more nuanced look. Without suggesting that centralisation is a virtue, finding a balance between central and local control, or choosing a degree of decentralisation, is perhaps something all governments must handle carefully. Education is no exception. Such a balance is perhaps contingent on the specific circumstances and popular beliefs of societies at particular times of social development. This is reflected in the two contrasting set-ups in Shanghai and Hong Kong. A single government organ, the Education Bureau, co-ordinates all matters concerning education in Hong Kong and administers more than 1 000 schools. This centralised set up has the advantage of equal distribution of research funding and equal student unit expenditures. Schools are also not left on their own or in small clusters where reforms might not be straightforward. Shanghai, whose population is larger than Hong Kong, is divided into city districts that each runs its own schools using local finance. However, the municipal government retains its policy-making and co-ordinating authority, and maintains strong monitoring to ensure parity among schools. Each approach appears to have its unique virtues.

▪ The public examinations: a positive way to facilitate learning

Policy makers and curriculum reformers see attitudes towards the public examinations as a major hurdle in opening doors for broader learning experiences for students. Hence, as discussed earlier, much of the reform effort seeks to counteract the adverse effects of the public examination.

Nevertheless, it is also true that the exam provides a basic infrastructure for learning, especially imparting knowledge, without which schools and teachers and even parents would feel bewildered. It might be over-simplistic to argue that public examinations are a necessary evil, but ways might be found to explore the positive function of public assessments. The PISA exercises and reformed public examinations in Shanghai, Hong Kong and Singapore all provide experimental ground for using public examinations in a positive way to facilitate learning.

The question is how assessments and evaluations can be revised to monitor the output of education *as a system*, as well as ensuring the quality of student learning. For example, public examinations could be coupled with school-based assessments, one-off examinations could be augmented by comprehensive and time-sensitive student portfolios and so forth. Many such dimensions are being experimented with in many systems, Shanghai and Hong Kong included.

▪ Accountability

The term accountability is pervasive in the literature on education policies. Sometimes packaged as quality assurance, it is on every government's agenda. However, often people may have taken procedures of quality assurance as assurance of quality. This could be a gross misunderstanding. First, as noted above, defining quality and the standards we expect should precede methods for assuring this quality. In other words, if we set a rather low quality standard, any quality assurance mechanism will only assure low quality. Second, quality assurance works only in a culture that has internalised high quality as a norm. This is the only way that there will be active efforts towards and understanding of quality across the board.

Shanghai and Hong Kong both have social norms which value quality in education. First, both have systems of quality assurance in the managerial sense, as understood elsewhere. There is no shortage of performance indicators and appraisal mechanisms, and there is no phobia of such technicalities in these societies. Second, both education systems are basically transparent. Parents in these societies are not used to intervening in school activities as they do in many Western societies. However, parents have very powerful influence on schools, either through their choice of schools or through the media, which run constant reports on schools (often their discrepancies). The vibrant cyber-community has added to the tremendous pressures on schools to maintain a high quality of education. In Shanghai, schools and parents have very close relations, to the extent that information flows both ways on cell phones. In Hong Kong, most leading newspapers have education pages that deal on a daily basis with policy debates as well as disputes in schools.

Principals and teachers therefore face a constant daily struggle to balance administrative accountability, client accountability and professional accountability. Dealing with the larger environment is not seen as an extra chore but as an integral part of professional responsibilities. This sense of accountability is built into programmes of teacher preparation, teachers' continuing professional development and training for school leadership. Hence, unlike in other cultures, accountability in Shanghai and Hong Kong is not regarded as a separate machinery to assure quality. Instead, accountability is built into the system as social expectations, as fundamental in school leadership, as well as an essential part of teachers professionalism. It is not about procedures and indicators.

FINAL OBSERVATIONS

China entered the global economy very late in the game, but has been making progress at breakneck speed ever since. It is hardly surprising that one can find almost everything somewhere in China, from examples of pre-industrial agricultural society to some of the most advanced industrial production sites in the world.

This chapter reflects this compressed development progression (see Chapter 1) in its account of the recent history of China's education system. The cultural background shared by the two case study societies no doubt explains elements of their common success. Yet both societies have been dissatisfied with some of the problems caused by that culture and both have sought to overcome them in their own ways. Both societies aim high and aspire to perform well in many areas of social development. Their ambitions are augmented by their prospering economic and financial sectors. However, both societies also regard human resources as the only resources they can rely on, and hence they have made substantial investments in education. This is a virtuous circle. Their spectacular reforms in education have made possible a no less spectacular economic success, which has in turn made it possible to continue to ratchet up the quality of their education systems. Their cultural heritage has played an important role in these successes, but that heritage has been constantly modernised.

In all these ways, the Chinese experience reflects the kind of progression in education development that appears to be taking place worldwide as the economy globalises, but the rate of these changes appears to be faster in China than in most other parts of the world.

■ Figure 4.3 ■
Shanghai-China and Hong Kong-China: Profile data

Language(s)	Official: Standard Mandarin (Shanghai) Standard Cantonese; English (Hong-Kong)
Population	1 328 million (2008)[37] 12 million (2007)[38] (*Shanghai*) 6 977 million (2008)[39] (*Hong Kong*)
Youth population	20.5%[40] (OECD 18.7%; World 27.4%)
Elderly population	7.9%[41] (OECD 14.4%; World 7.4%)
Growth rate	0.63%[42] (OECD 0.68%; World 1.19%)
Foreign-born population	0.1% Immigrants (2010)[43]
GDP per capita	USD 5 962 (2008)[44] USD 11 361 (2009)[45] (*Shanghai*) USD 39 062 (2008)[46] (*Hong-Kong*)
Economy-Origin of GDP	Manufacturing, mining, utilities and construction 48.6%; Services 40.1%; Agriculture, forestry, fishing 11.3% (2008)[47] Manufacturing, auto making, chemical processing, steel manufacturing, biomedicine (*Shanghai*)[48] Manufacturing, finance, trade, other services, other sectors (*Hong Kong*)[49]
Unemployment	5.7%[50] (OECD average 6.1%)[51]
Expenditure on education	3.3% of GDP (OECD average 5.2%)[52] *3.3% of GDP (Hong Kong)*[53] 16.3% of total government expenditure (OECD average 13.3%)[54] *23% of total government expenditure (Hong Kong)*[55]
Enrolment ratio, early childhood education	44% (2008) (regional average 49%)[56]
Enrolment ratio, primary education	113% (2008) (regional average 110%)[57]
Enrolment ratio, secondary education	76% (2008) (regional average 77%)[58]
Enrolment ratio, tertiary[59] education	23%[60] (regional average missing)
Students in primary education, by type of institution or mode of enrolment[61]	Public: 93.8% (OECD average 89.6%) Government-dependent private: 6.2% (OECD average 8.1%) Independent, private (included in "Government-dependent private" figure) (OECD average 2.9%)
Students in lower secondary education, by type of institution or mode of enrolment[62]	Public 92.9% (OECD average 83.2%) Government-dependent private: 7.1% (OECD average 10.9%) Independent, private (included in "Government-dependent private" figure) (OECD average 3.5%)
Students in upper secondary education, by type of institution or mode of enrolment[63]	Public: 85.9% (OECD average 82%) Government-dependent private: 14.1% (OECD average 13.6%) Independent, private (included in "public" figure) (OECD average 5.5%)
Students in tertiary education, by type of institution or mode of enrolment[64]	Tertiary type B education: missing data[65] (OECD average public: 61.8% Government-dependent private : 19.2% Independent-private: 16.6%) Tertiary type A education: missing data[66] (OECD average Public: 77.1% Government-dependent private : 9.6% Independent-private: 15%)
Teachers' salaries	Average annual starting salary in lower secondary education: no data (OECD average USD 30 750)[67] Ratio of salary in lower secondary education after 15 years of experience (minimum training) to GDP per capita: no data (OECD average: 1.22)[68]
Upper secondary graduation rates	Data missing (OECD average 80%)[69]

StatLink ᘎᔛᕐᑜ http://dx.doi.org/10.1787/888932366674

Interview partners (Shanghai)

Shanghai Academy of Educational Science

Lu Jing, Associate professor, Vice director, Shanghai Institute for Basic Education Research and Shanghai PISA Centre, Shanghai Academy of Educational Sciences.

Gu Ling-yuan, professor, master teacher, former vice director of Shanghai Academy of Educational Sciences. He was honoured Shanghai Education Hero in 2003.

Dr. Wang Jie, Associate Professor, Director of Teacher Education Centre, Shanghai Academy of Educational Sciences.

Interviews at China Pu Dong Cadre College

Shen Zu-yun, Director of Shanghai Educational News Centre.

Wang Mao-gong, Director of Education Bureau in Xuhui District, a central district in Shanghai.

Yin Hou-qin, Vice director general, Shanghai Municipal Education Commission.

Zhang Min-sheng, professor, Shanghai Education Society, former Vice Director General of Shanghai Municipal Education Commission.

Dr. Zhang Min-xuan, Professor, Vice Director General, Shanghai Municipal Education Commission, PGB and NPM of Shanghai PISA 2009.

Zhu Jian-wei, Director of Education Bureau in Minhang District, a suburb district in Shanghai.

Shanghai Teaching Research Institute

Tan Yi-bin, Assistant Director, master teacher, teaching researcher in Chinese, Shanghai Teaching Research Institute, Leading Expert of PISA 2009 Reading Expert Group in Shanghai.

Xu Dian-fang, Director, Shanghai Teaching Research Institute.

Teachers and Principals

Bai Bin, principal, Chinese teacher, Wen Lai Middle School, PISA School Co-ordinator in PISA 2009 Field Trial, which is held on April 25, 2008.

Ding Yi, Vice Principal, Middle School affiliated to Jing 'an Teacher Education College.

Li Xiao-yu, vice principal charges on teaching, Chinese teacher, Qibao High School.

Qiu Zhong-hai, Master teacher and master principal, Shanghai Qibao High School, he was honoured Shanghai Education Hero in 2008.

Shi Ju, mathematics teacher, Wen Lai Middle School.

Wang Hong, Chinese teacher, Wen Lai Middle School.

Xu Feng, vice principal, politics teacher, Wen Lai Middle School.

Mr Zhou. Vice Principal, Wen Lai High School.

Zhou Ming-jun, English teacher, Wen Lai Middle School.

(Hong Kong)

The material for the section on Hong Kong is based on the experience of Professor Kai-ming Cheng, Chair of Education, University of Hong Kong (1995 to present), Senior Advisor to the Vice-Chancellor, University of Hong Kong (2003 to present), and former Vice-Chancelor, University of Hong Kong 1997-2003.

References

Bransford, J.D. (ed.) (2000), *How People Learn: Brain, Mind, Experience, and School,* National Academy Press, Washington, DC.

Bray, M. (2009), *Confronting the Shadow Education System: What Government Policies for What Private Tutoring?* UNESCO/International Institute for Educational Planning, Paris.

Cheng, K.M. (1987), *The Concept of Legitimacy in Educational Policy-making: Alternative Explanations of Two Policy Episodes in Hong Kong,* PhD Thesis, University of London Institute of Education, London.

Cheng, K.M. (1996), *The Quality of Primary Education: A Case Study Of Zhejiang Province, China,* UNESCO/International Institute for Educational Planning, Paris.

Cheng, K.M. (1997), "The Meaning of Decentralisation: Looking at the Case of China", in W.K. Cummings & N.F. McGinn (eds.), *International Handbook of Education and Development: Preparing Schools, Students And Nations For The Twenty-first Century,* Pergamon, Oxford.

Cheng K.M. (2000), "Education and Development: The Neglected Dimension of Cross-Cultural Studies", in R. Alexander, M. Osborn And D. Philips (eds.), *Learning From Comparing: New Directions in Comparative Educational Research,* Vol 2: Policy, Professionals and Development, Symposium Books, Oxford, pp. 81-92.

Cheng, K.M. (2004), "Turning a Bad Master into a Good Servant: Reforming Learning in China", in I. Rotberg (ed.), *Balancing Change and Tradition in Global Education Reform,* Scarecrow Education, Washington, DC.

Cheng, K.M. (2007), "Reforming Education Beyond Education", in Y.M. Yeung (ed.), *The First Decade of the HKSAR,* The Chinese University Press, Hong Kong, pp. 251-72.

Cheng, K.M. (2010), "Developing education beyond manpower", in UNDP (2010), *Capacity is Development, UNDP,* New York, available at *www.capacityisdevelopment.org/doccs/capdev_research/Developing%20Education%20Beyond%20Manpower.pdf.*

Cheng, K.M. and H.K. Yip (2007), *Facing the Knowledge Society: Reforming Secondary Education in Shanghai and Hong Kong,* working paper, World Bank, Washington, DC.

Curriculum Development Institute (2001), *Learning to Learn: The Way Forward in Curriculum,* Curriculum Development Institute, Hong Kong, available at *www.edb.gov.hk/index.aspx?langno=1&nodeID=2365.*

Ding, X. (2010), *Educational Reform and Development in Shanghai,* paper commissioned by the Shanghai Academy of Education Research for this present study.

Elman, B.A. (2000), *A Cultural History of Civil Examinations in Late Imperial China,* University of California Press, Berkeley.

Fei, H.T. (1947), *Xiang Tu Zhong Guo* (Earth-bound China), reprinted 2006, Shanghai People's Press, Shanghai. English translation: G.G. Hamilton, and Z Wang (1992), *From the Soil: The Foundations of Chinese Society,* University of California Press, Berkeley.

Illich, I. (1971), *Deschooling Society,* Calder and Boyars, London.

Information Office of Shanghai Municipality and Shanghai Municipal Statistics Bureau (2010), *2010 Shanghai Basic Facts,* Shanghai Literature and Art Publishing Group, Shanghai.

Jin, Ke (2003), *The Project of Standardization of Primary and Secondary Schools was Completed in Three Years and 1569 Schools were Upgraded,* in Chinese, SINA, Beijing, available at *http://sh.sina.com.cn/news/20030102/08432422.shtml.*

OECD (2010), *PISA 2009 Volume I, What Students Know and Can Do: Student Performance in Reading, Mathematics and Science,* OECD Publishing.

Min, W. (2008), "Higher Education Financing in East Asia: Policy Implications for China", in J.Y. Lin and B. Pleskovic (eds.), *Higher Education and Development,* World Bank, Washington, DC, pp. 41-46.

Ministry of Education of the PRC (People's Republic of China) (2010a), *National Statistics of Education Development in China 2009,* Ministry of Education, Beijing, available at *www.moe.edu.cn/publicfiles/business/htmlfiles/moe/moe_633/201008/93763.html.*

Ministry of Education of the PRC (2010b), *National Outline for Medium and Long-Term Education Reform and Development 2010-2020,* in Chinese, Ministry of Education, Beijing, *www.gov.cn/jrzg/2010-07/29/content_1667143.htm.*

Ministry of Education of the PRC (2001), *Guidelines for Curriculum Reform in Basic Education,* draft, Ministry of Education, Beijing.

Mullis, I.V.S. *et al.* (2006), *PIRLS 2006 International Report: IEA's Progress in International Reading Literacy Study in Primary School in 40 Countries,* International Association for the Evaluation of Educational Achievement (IEA), Boston College, Chestnut Hill, MA.

Sawyer, K. (ed.) (2006), *The Cambridge Handbook of the Learning Sciences*, Cambridge University Press, Cambridge.

Shanghai Municipal Education Commission (2004), *Shanghai Education Yearbook 2004*, Shanghai Educational Publishing House, Shanghai.

Shanghai Municipal Education Commission (2008), *Shanghai Education Yearbook 2008*, Shanghai Educational Publishing House, Shanghai.

Shanghai Municipal Government (2010), *Shanghai Yearbook 2009*, Shanghai Municipal Government, Shanghai.

Shanghai Municipal Statistics Bureau (2010), *Shanghai Statistical Yearbook 2010*, China Statistics Press, Shanghai.

Shao, S. (2010) "Social Stratification and the Education of Migrant Children: A Sociological Analysis of the Policy Decisions of "Two Mainly", *Research in Education Development*, November 2010, available at *www.cnsaes.org/homepage/html/magazine/jyfzyj/jyfzyj_jyysh/2674.html*.

Solomon, R.H. (1971), "Confucianism and the Chinese Life Cycle", in *Mao's Revolution and the Chinese Political Culture*, University of California Press, Berkeley, pp. 28-38.

Stevenson, H.W. and J.W. Stigler (1992), *The Learning Gap: Why Our Schools are Failing and What We Can Learn from Japanese and Chinese Education*, Summit Books, New York.

Tsang, D. (2009), *Embracing new challenges. Policy Address 2009-10*, Hong Kong Government, available at *www.policyaddress.gov.hk/08-09/eng/policy.html*.

UNESCO Institute of Statistics (2009), *Global Education Digest, 2009: Comparing Education Statistics Across the World*, UNESCO, Paris.

Yang, R. (2004), "Toward Massification: Higher Education Development in the People's Republic of China since 1949," in J. Smart (ed.) *Higher Education: Handbook of Theory and Research*, Springer, Dordrecht.

Notes

1. This section describes the general situation in mainland China. The set up in Hong Kong is different and is described in the section on Hong Kong.

2. See detailed discussions in Elman, 2000.

3. South Korea, Japan, Macao, Vietnam and North Korea, though not all of them have the same results.

4. In ancient China, the general understanding of the social hierarchy went from scholars (at the top), to farmers, then artisans and finally merchants.

5. "Massive" is defined by an enrolment ratio of over 25%. The enrolment ratio in 2009 was 23%, very near to the "massive" threshold.

6. Despite minor variations in parts of the nation, 6+3+3 is the basic pattern for primary, junior secondary and senior secondary schooling. Vocational schools of various types normally operate at the senior secondary level.

7. Gross enrolment ratio is used here because of age staggering at that level.

8. An 80% subsidy towards student unit costs from the central government in underdeveloped provinces, 60% for provinces of medium economies and no subsidy for developed provinces.

9. See more detailed discussion in Yang 2004.

10. This is the argument, for example, of Professor Weifang Min, the Party Secretary of Peking University and leading economist of education at the World Bank conference held in 2007 in Beijing.

11. The curriculum reform reduced a class period to 35 minutes for primary school and 40 minutes for secondary school in Shanghai. In most of the other provinces in China, a class period is 40 minutes for primary school and 45 minutes for secondary school (Ding, 2010).

12. This was due to the Nanking Sino-British Treaty of 1842, after China's defeat in the Opium War.

13. This is comparable with South Korea and Japan, where the number of places in higher education exceeds the number of high school graduates.

14. Institutes in Shanghai belong to different categories in terms of their relations with the central and municipal governments, with different degrees of sponsorship from the two authorities. Accordingly, they are assigned admission quotas of different mixes between local and national candidates.

15. To contain such education migrants, national stipulations require migrant children who attend basic education in the hosting city (*e.g.* Shanghai) to return to their places of origin for application to higher education institutions. In other words, they are not allowed to occupy a seat in the Shanghai quota.

16. The best presentation of this cultural assumption is by Fei Hsiao-tung, a student of Malinovsky and the first renowned anthropologist in China. According to Fei, society is perceived by the Chinese in a "hierarchical configuration" that is vertical and structured, as opposed to the Western view of society as an "association configuration" that is flat and *ad hoc*. This was best presented in the lecture series *Earthbound China* (1947).

17. This is also among the observations made by Stevenson and Stigler (1992).

18. This point was made succinctly by Mr Zhang Minsheng, former Director of the Education Commission of Shanghai, during a recent interview.

19. *Ibid.*

20. The following three sections are extracted and modified from a commissioned paper by Ding (2010).

21. See *http://wljy.sherc.net/kgpt/*.

22. This is a policy started in 2002, widely quoted. One of the most recent discussions can be found in Shao, 2010.

23. Interview with Gu Lingwan, former Deputy Director of the Shanghai Academy of Educational Research, a renowned teacher and reformer in mathematics education.

24. These are extracted and modified from Ding (2010).

25. *Ibid.*

26. Data from a group interview with good public school leaders.

27. This is from an interview with Mr Gu Lingyuan, a nationally famous mathematics teacher turned researcher, who is influential in education reforms in Shanghai.

28. USD 42 748 (7th) according to International Monetary Fund; USD 43 957 (4th) according to the World Bank.

29. The gross enrolment ratio in 1965 was actually over 100%. This was due to the staggered ages at which children started school.

30. At this time Hong Kong's legal labour age was 14, one year less than the international norm of 15, so the city was barred from joining major trade treaties. The decision about nine-year compulsory education came almost overnight to rescue Hong Kong from this major trade crisis. See Cheng (1987).

31. The Society of Accountants' representative made the point that what had been taught in universities was not useful in the workplace, and hence graduates have to unlearn what they have learned. They'd rather they were not taught accounting, which they could learn on-the-job in a matter of months. The interview was carried out in 2000.

32. Including a special session with Dr Albert Tuijmann, then member of the OECD education team, in June 2000.

33. For the best summaries of these theories see Sawyer (2006) and Bransford *et al. (*2000).

34. This is a concept development by Foucault in his later years. A brief introduction to the concept can be found in *www.policyaddress.gov.hk/08-09/eng/policy.html*.

35. This is one of the main themes of the Chief Executive's Policy Speech in 2009 (Tsang, 2009).

36. South Korea launched a few reforms in the 1980s which went against the elitist tradition of calling for equalisation of secondary schools and mass admission to higher education. See Cheng 2010.

37. OECD (2010), *OECD Economic Surveys: China 2010*, OECD Publishing.

38. OECD (2010), *OECD Economic Surveys: China 2010,* OECD Publishing. Non-agricultural and total inhabitants (year of reference – 2007).

39. World Bank, World Development Indicators.

40. OECD (2010), *OECD Factbook 2010*, OECD Publishing. Ratio of population aged less than 15 to the total population (data from 2008).

41. OECD (2010), *OECD Factbook 2010*, OECD Publishing. Ratio of population aged 65 and older to the total population (data from 2008).

42. OECD (2010), *OECD Factbook 2010*, OECD Publishing. Annual population growth rate (data from 2007).

43. China is a sending country, with an estimated diaspora of 35 million worldwide (International Organisation for Migration, *www.iom.int*).

44. OECD (2010), *OECD Economic Surveys: China 2010*, OECD Publishing. PPP (data from 2008).

45. National Bureau of Statistics of China, *www.stats.gov.cn/english/*.

46. In current US dollars, derived from World Bank national accounts data, and OECD National Accounts data files. World Bank, World Development Indicators.

47. OECD (2010), *OECD Economic Surveys: China 2010*, OECD Publishing. Percentage of GDP 2008.

48. Shanghai municipal government.

49. Hong Kong Census and Statistics Department, *www.censtatd.gov.hk*.

50. OECD (2010), *Employment Outlook 2010*, OECD Publishing. Measured as a percentage of the estimated urban non-agricultural labour force (data from 2008).

51. OECD (2010), *OECD Factbook 2010*, OECD Publishing. Total unemployment rates as percentage of total labour force (data from 2008).

52. OECD (2010), *Education at a Glance 2010*, OECD Publishing (year of reference – 2007).

53. UIS Statistics in Brief: Hong Kong (China) SAR 2010 (year of reference – 2008).

54. OECD (2010), *Education at a Glance 2010*, OECD Publishing (year of reference – 2007).

55. UIS Statistics in Brief: Hong Kong (China) SAR 2010 (year of reference – 2008).

56. UNESCO-UIS (2010), *UIS Statistics in Brief: China*. Percentage represents gross enrolment rate for MF; 2008 (regional average 49%).

57. UNESCO-UIS (2010), *UIS Statistics in Brief: China.* Percentage represents gross enrolment rate for MF; 2008 (regional average 110%).

58. UNESCO-UIS (2010), *UIS Statistics in Brief: China.* Percentage represents gross enrolment rate for MF; 2008 (regional average 77%).

59. The OECD follows standard international conventions in using the term "tertiary education" to refer to all post-secondary programmes at ISCED levels 5B, 5A and 6, regardless of the institutions in which they are offered. OECD (2008), *Tertiary Education for the Knowledge Society: Volume 1*, OECD Publishing.

60. UNESCO-UIS (2010), *UIS Statistics in Brief: China.* Percentage represents gross enrolment rate for MF; 2008.

61. Data from UNESCO Institute for Statistics, Data from 2008, cited in OECD (2010) *Education at a Glance 2010,* OECD Publishing.

62. Data from UNESCO Institute for Statistics, Data from 2008, cited in OECD (2010) *Education at a Glance 2010,* OECD Publishing.

63. Data from UNESCO Institute for Statistics, Data from 2008, cited in OECD (2010) *Education at a Glance 2010,* OECD Publishing.

64. Data from UNESCO Institute for Statistics, Data from 2008, cited in OECD (2010) *Education at a Glance 2010,* OECD Publishing.

65. Data missing from *Education at a Glance 2009* (OECD, 2009).

66. Data missing from *Education at a Glance 2009* (OECD, 2009).

67. Starting salary/minimum training in USD adjusted for PPP, *Education at a Glance 2010* (OECD, 2010).

68. Starting salary/minimum training in USD adjusted for PPP, *Education at a Glance 2010* (OECD, 2010).

69. OECD (2010), *Education at a Glance 2010*, OECD Publishing. Sum of upper secondary graduation rates for a single year of age (year of reference for OECD average – 2008).

5

Finland: Slow and Steady Reform for Consistently High Results

Finland is one of the world's leaders in the academic performance of its secondary school students, a position it has held for the past decade. This top performance is also remarkably consistent across schools. Finnish schools seem to serve all students well, regardless of family background, socio-economic status or ability. This chapter looks at the possible factors behind this success, which include political consensus to educate all children together in a common school system; an expectation that all children can achieve at high levels, regardless of family background or regional circumstance; single-minded pursuit of teaching excellence; collective school responsibility for learners who are struggling; modest financial resources that are tightly focused on the classroom and a climate of trust between educators and the community.

INTRODUCTION

Since the publication of the first PISA results in 2001, Finland is now seen as a major international leader in education (Table 5.1; OECD, 2010). It has consistently ranked in the very top tier of countries in all PISA assessments over the past decade, and its performance has been especially notable for its remarkable consistency across schools. No other country has so little variation in outcomes between schools, and the gap within schools between the top and bottom-achieving students is extraordinarily modest as well. Finnish schools seem to serve all students well, regardless of family background or socio-economic status. For these reasons, Finnish schools have become a kind of tourist destination, with hundreds of educators and policy makers annually travelling to Helsinki to try to learn the secret of their success.

Table 5.1 **Finland's mean scores on reading, mathematics and science scales in PISA**

	PISA 2000	PISA 2003	PISA 2006	PISA 2009
	Mean score	Mean score	Mean score	Mean score
Reading	546	543	547	536
Mathematics		544	548	541
Science			563	554

Source: OECD (2010), *PISA 2009 Results: What Students Know and Can Do: Student Performance in Reading, Mathematics and Science (Volume I)*, OECD Publishing.
StatLink ⟟⟟⟟ http://dx.doi.org/10.1787/888932366693

Prior to 2000 Finland rarely appeared on anyone's list of the world's most outstanding education systems. This is partly explained by the fact that while Finland has always done well on international tests of literacy, its performance in five different international mathematics or science assessments between 1962 and 1999 never rose above average. But it was also because Finland's path to education reform and improvement has been slow and steady, proceeding gradually over the past four decades. Its current success is due to this steady progress, rather than as a consequence of highly visible innovations launched by a particular political leader or party.

As described in this chapter, the evolution of Finland's education reform is closely intertwined with the country's economic and political development since the Second World War, and cultural factors are clearly an important part of the Finnish success story. However, they are by no means the whole story. There are Finnish education policies and practices from which others seeking to emulate Finland's success might learn.

Some international observers argue that the Finnish success story can be explained primarily by its specific national history and culture. They are unsure that other countries could learn anything from Finland that is applicable to them. For example, these sceptics point out that Finland is culturally homogenous. This is true, although there are now schools in Helsinki where nearly half the students are immigrants. They observe Finland's overall economic health, with its flourishing IT sector, but neglect to note that its average per pupil expenditure is well below that of the highest spending countries, including the United States. They note that primary school teaching is now the most popular profession among Finnish young people, attracting the top quartile of high school graduates into its highly competitive teacher training programmes, without asking whether this has always been so or whether the country took special steps to upgrade the status of teachers and teaching.

HISTORY OF THE FINNISH EDUCATION SYSTEM[1]

Finland is a relatively young country, having only established its independence from the Soviet Union in 1917. Finland had to fight long and hard to preserve that independence through the Second World War. For a nation with a population of less than 4 million, the cost of the war was devastating: 90 000 dead; 60 000 permanently injured and 50 000 children orphaned. Additionally, as part of the 1944 peace treaty with the Soviet Union, Finland was forced to cede 12% of its land, requiring the relocation of 450 000 Finnish citizens. A Soviet military base was established on a peninsula near Helsinki, and the communist party was granted legal status.

The first post-war elections in 1945 produced a parliament in which the seats were almost evenly divided between three political parties: the Social Democrats, the Agrarian Centre Party, and the Communists. In the 1950s the Conservatives gained sufficient strength to also be included in major negotiations. Multi-party systems typically require the development of a political consensus in order to move any major policy agenda forward, and one priority around which such a consensus developed was the need to rebuild and modernise the Finnish education system.

The education system that the new post-war parliament inherited was still unequal and more reflective of the needs of a predominantly rural, agricultural society than of a modern industrial society. Although the country was still in fact 60% rural as late as 1960, the urbanisation process really began right after the war and over the next decades accelerated to the point where Finland is now two-thirds urban.

In 1950 most young Finns left school after six years of basic education; only those living in towns or larger municipalities had access to a middle grade education. There were two types of middle grade education: civic schools, run by some municipalities, which offered two or three additional years of schooling, and could lead to further vocational education for those fortunate enough to live in a town large enough to support such a school; and grammar schools,[2] which offered five additional years of schooling and typically led to the academic high school (*gymnasium*) and then to university. Only about a quarter of young Finns in 1950 had access to the grammar school path, and two-thirds of the grammar schools were privately governed.

Over the next decade there was explosive growth in grammar school enrolments, which grew from 34 000 to 270 000. Most of this growth took place in the private schools, which in the 1950s began to receive government subsidies and come more under public control. This growth reflected the aspirations of ordinary Finns for greater educational opportunity for their children, a message that the country's political leaders heard as well. In the post-war decade, parliament created three successive reform commissions, each of which made recommendations that helped build public support and political will to create an education system that would be more responsive to the growing demand for more equitable educational opportunities for all young people in Finland.

The first of these commissions, launched in 1945, focused on the primary school curriculum, and offered a compelling vision of a more humanistic, child-centred school, in contrast to the Germanic, syllabus-driven model of schooling that characterised most Finnish schools. This commission also conducted field studies in 300 schools as part of its work, offering an example of how research might guide the development of policy.

The second commission, launched in 1946, focused on the organisation of the system, and advocated for the creation of a common school (covering grades 1-8) that would serve all students. However, this report produced such opposition from the universities and the grammar school teachers that its recommendations quickly died.

A decade later, however, the idea of the common or comprehensive school resurfaced in the recommendations of the Commission on School Programs, and this time the idea gained traction. The commission recommended that compulsory education in Finland should take place in a nine-year (grades 1-9) municipally-run comprehensive school, into which existing private grammar schools and public civic schools would ultimately merge (Figure 5.1). This proposal triggered a very substantial debate about core values and beliefs. Could all students be educated to a level that only those who currently had access to grammar schools were expected to achieve? Did society really need all young people to be educated to a high level? Did all young people really need to know a third language in addition to Finnish and Swedish (a requirement of grammar schools), and was it fair to expect this of them? Over the next several years these debates continued, but as Finland's ambitions grew to become more economically competitive, and as the demand for social and economic equality grew, pressure on parliament built up to move forward with the recommendation to create the new comprehensive school. In November 1968 parliament finally enacted legislation, by a substantial majority, to create a new basic education system built around a common, comprehensive school for grades 1-9.

The reason for dwelling at some length on the political evolution of the comprehensive school idea is that most Finnish analysts believe that the comprehensive school (*peruskoulu*, in Finnish) is the foundation upon which all subsequent reforms rest. As Pasi Sahlberg, Director of the Center for International Mobility and Co-operation, and an interpreter of Finland's education story to the outside world put it during an interview for this report "The comprehensive school is not merely a form of school organisation. It embodies a philosophy of education as well as a deep set of societal values about what all children need and deserve."

The transition from a parallel form of school organisation to the single comprehensive system was challenging, and consequently was phased in slowly and carefully. Implementation did not begin until 1972, initially in northern Finland and only gradually spreading to the more populated municipalities and towns in the south. The last southern municipality to implement the new comprehensive system did so in 1977.

■ Figure 5.1 ■
Finland's education system organisation

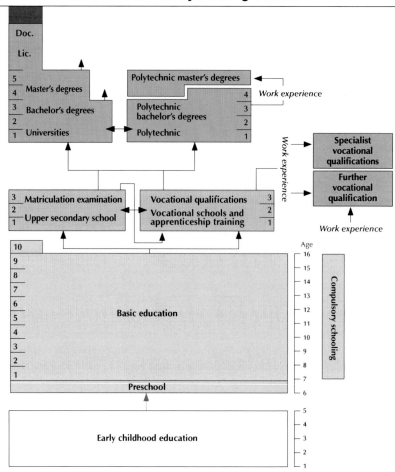

Jukka Sarjala, who spent 25 years in the Ministry of Education (1970-1995) before becoming Director-General of the National Board of Education, described the task he faced as the person in the ministry with lead responsibility for planning the implementation of the new law:

> My challenge was to develop a plan that guaranteed that this reform would ultimately be implemented in every Finnish community. There were lots of municipalities that were not eager to reform their system, which is why it was important to have a legal mandate. This was a very big reform, very big and complicated for teachers accustomed to the old system. They were accustomed to teaching school with selected children and were simply not ready for a school system in which very clever children and not so clever children were in the same classes. It took several years, in some schools until the older teachers retired, for these reforms to be accepted. (Interview conducted for this report)

A major vehicle for addressing the anxieties of veteran teachers and resolving some of the difficulties inherent in merging the formerly parallel sets of schools into a unified system was the development of a new national core curriculum for the comprehensive school. The process for developing the curriculum engaged hundreds of teachers and took place over a five-year period (1965-1970). One important decision that allayed the fears of some of the critics of the comprehensive school was to allow some differentiation in the upper grades to accommodate perceived differences in ability and interests, especially in mathematics and foreign languages. Schools could offer three levels of study in these subjects: basic, middle, and advanced, with the basic level corresponding to what had been offered in civic schools and advanced to what had been offered in the old grammar schools. This form of ability grouping persisted into the mid-1980s, when it was finally abolished.

Perhaps the most significant and long-lasting consequence of the shift to the comprehensive school was the recognition that to create a school system that could serve all students equally well, regardless of family background, would require a teaching force with a very high level of knowledge and skills. To quote Pasi Sahlberg again:

> In the early 1970s policy makers realised that if we were to successfully implement this very ambitious comprehensive school reform, bringing all Finnish students into the same school and expecting them to master the same curriculum, it would require not only different systems of support but a very different level of understanding and knowledge from each and every teacher. (Interview conducted for this report)

This recognition led to a sweeping set of reforms that significantly raised the bar for aspiring teachers by moving teacher preparation from the *seminarium* (the Finnish equivalent of teacher college) into the university, and ultimately requiring all teachers, primary through upper secondary, to obtain a masters degree as a condition of employment. The design and content of the new teacher preparation programmes are described in more detail below. Finland also has a long tradition of in-service teacher training that developed over the years as national curricular changes have been implemented. During the intensive adaptation to the new educational structure from 1972 to 1977, Finland instituted a special, comprehensive, compulsory in-service training programme for all teachers in all municipalities.

A third major effect of the implementation of the comprehensive grade 1-9 basic school was to greatly heighten demand for upper secondary education. In 1970 only 30% of Finnish adults had obtained at least an upper secondary diploma. That percentage is now over 80%, and among 24-35 year olds it is 90%. This extraordinary growth is in part due to a radical set of reforms enacted in 1985, in which the traditional set structure of the academic upper secondary school was replaced with a much more flexible, modular structure, which injected significantly more choice into the system. In recent years the modernisation of the academic secondary school has been mirrored in the vocational secondary school (known as vocational education and training or VET), which has been significantly strengthened and expanded to the point where it now enrols 42% of graduates from the comprehensive school. One reason for the increasing popularity of the vocational secondary option is that Finland has in recent years created a set of polytechnic colleges, thereby creating a pathway into tertiary education for vocational students. Today vocational upper secondary education gives eligibility to university studies as well. So the way into tertiary education is totally open to VET students. VET has thus become a trusted pathway to tertiary education. Consequently, 43% of young Finns in their twenties are enrolled in tertiary education, well above the OECD average of 25%, and the highest percentage in Europe. Moreover, much has been done in Finland to increase work-based learning initiatives, creating strong links between VET and professional life.

Economic development and the cultivation of the schooling culture in Finland

The story of the evolution of the Finnish education system over the past two decades is inextricably linked to the development of the modern Finnish economy. The rise of the comprehensive school in the 1970-1990 period needs to be seen in the context of the development of the Finnish welfare state and the national push for much greater social and economic equality. However, the less visible but equally profound changes in Finland's schools over the past two decades need to be seen in the context of the deep changes taking place in the Finnish economy.

Two major events occurred in the early 1990s that triggered a significant shift in the economic development strategy promulgated by Finland's governmental and private sector leaders. The first was the initiation of the accession process that led to Finland's acceptance into the European Union in 1995. With the collapse of the Soviet Union (a major trading partner), Finland had no choice but to diversify its export strategy and begin to move away from its historic reliance on forest products and other traditional industries. The second and more powerful stimulus was a major economic recession in the early 1990s, set off by a collapse of the financial sector reminiscent of the banking crisis the US has recently experienced. Unemployment in Finland approached 20%; gross domestic product (GDP) declined by 13% and public debt exceeded 60% of GDP.

The government used this crisis as an opportunity to develop a new national competitiveness policy designed to support private sector innovation and focused heavily on the development of the telecommunications sector, with Nokia as the central player. In a remarkably short time, Finland managed not only to dig itself out of recession but to reduce its historical reliance on its natural resources and transform its economy into one based on information and knowledge. Investments in research and development provided the fuel for this growth. In 1991 only 5 Finnish workers out of 1 000 were in the research and development (R&D) labour force. By 2003 this number had increased to 22, almost three times the OECD average. By 2001 Finland's ranking in the World Economic Forum's global competitiveness index had climbed from 15th to 1st, and it has remained at or near the top in these rankings ever since.

The impact of this new focus on innovation and R&D not only led to the development of new partnerships between tertiary education and industry in Finland, but also had a profound effect on the primary and secondary education sector. Finnish employers sent very strong signals to the schools about the kinds of knowledge, skills and dispositions young people needed in order to be successful in the new economy. Finnish industry leaders not only promoted the importance of mathematics, science and technology in the formal curriculum, but they also advocated for more attention to creativity, problem-solving, teamwork and cross-curricular projects in schools. In spite of some criticism in the 1990s, one example of the kind of message that corporate leaders were delivering to the schools is this statement from a senior Nokia manager whom Sahlberg interviewed during this period in his role as chair of a task force on the national science curriculum:

> If I hire a youngster who doesn't know all the mathematics or physics that is needed to work here, I have colleagues here who can easily teach those things. But if I get somebody who doesn't know how to work with other people, how to think differently or how to create original ideas and somebody who is afraid of making a mistake, there is nothing we can do here. Do what you have to do to keep our education system up-to-date but don't take away [the] creativity and open-mindedness that we now have in our fine *peruskoulu*. (Sahlberg, forthcoming)

Implicit in this last sentence is the Nokia manager's belief that the comprehensive schools were already paying attention to developing at least some of the traits that employers in the new Finnish economy were seeking. In fact, it is hard to imagine how an information and knowledge-based economy could have grown up so quickly in the 1990s if the Finnish schools hadn't already been producing graduates with the kind of flexibility and openness to innovation that industry was demanding. The development of these kinds of qualities is at least as much a function of the culture and climate of schools as of the formal curriculum.

FINNISH SUCCESS IN EDUCATION

While it is important to note the key legislative landmarks that have created the policy framework within which Finnish schools have become world-class over the past decade, these do not provide a full explanation for Finland's remarkable success story. After all, Finland is not the only northern European country to have abolished tracking and created a unified basic school structure. Other countries have revamped and upgraded their teacher education programmes and have taken steps similar to Finland's to modernise secondary education. So what else accounts for Finland's success? One way to explore this question is to outline some of the most salient characteristics of Finland's comprehensive schools as described by the Finnish informants for this study.

A system involving more than education

The first thing to note is that these schools offer more than education. These are full-service schools. They provide a daily hot meal for every student. They provide health and dental services. They offer guidance and psychological counselling, and access to a broader array of mental health and other services for students and families in need. None of these services is means-tested. Their availability to all reflects a deep societal commitment to the well-being of all children.

Support for children with special needs

A second, related characteristic is the role of the "special teacher". Finland prides itself on its commitment to inclusion. While 8% of Finland's children are deemed as having special education needs, only half of them are placed in special schools; the other half are mainstreamed. Finnish educators believe that if schools focus on early diagnosis and intervention, most students can be helped to achieve success in regular classrooms. Its principal mechanism for supporting struggling students in a timely fashion is the "special teacher", a specially trained teacher assigned to each school. Their job is to work closely with the class teachers to identify students in need of extra help and to work individually or in small groups with these students to provide the extra help and support they need to keep up with their classmates.

Furthermore, it is not left solely to the discretion of the regular class teacher to identify a problem and alert the special teacher. Every comprehensive school has a "pupils' multi-professional care group," as described by Riitta Aaltio, principal of a 360-student primary school in Kerava, just outside Helsinki. The group meets at least twice a month for two hours. The group consists of the principal, the special education teacher, the school nurse, the school psychologist, a social worker, and the teachers whose students are being discussed. The parents of any child being discussed are contacted prior to the meeting and are sometimes asked to be present. Principal Aaltio describes the group's function as follows:

> In each meeting we usually have enough time to discuss two classes of pupils with their class (*i.e.* homeroom) teacher, plus any "acute cases". First, we talk about the class and how things are going in general. If there are

any concerns – learning, teaching, social climate – or some problems with individual students we try to decide what kind of support we can provide. If we believe a pupil needs professional help beyond what we can provide at the school, we help the family get that kind of help be it medical, psychological, or social.

These measures are available to all students – social background makes no difference – because health care, like education, is free in Finland. This functional support system is a very important part of our education system. It helps explain why we have such small gaps in student achievement. (Interview conducted for this report)

Significant responsibility for teachers and students

Both regular class teachers (grades 1-6) and subject teachers (7-9) exercise an enormous degree of professional discretion and independence. While there is a national core curriculum in Finland, over the past 20 years it has become much less detailed and prescriptive. It functions more as a framework, leaving education providers and teachers latitude to decide what they will teach and how. Teachers select their own textbooks and other instructional materials, for example. Because the only external testing in comprehensive schools is done on a sampling basis and is designed to provide information on the functioning of the system as a whole, assessment in Finnish schools is a classroom responsibility. Teachers are expected to assess their own students on an ongoing basis, using the assessment guidelines in the national core curriculum and textbooks. However, a major focus in Finnish classrooms is also on helping students learn how to assess their own learning. In Principal Aaltio's school, this emphasis begins as early as first grade.

Finnish classrooms are typically described by observers as learner-centred. As the emphasis on student self-assessment would suggest, students are expected to take an active role in designing their own learning activities. Students are expected to work collaboratively in teams on projects, and there is a substantial focus on projects that cut across traditional subject or disciplinary lines. By the time students enrol in upper secondary school (grades 10-12), they are expected to be able to take sufficient charge of their own learning to be able to design their own individual programme. Upper secondary schools are now mostly based on individual study plans. There is no longer a grade structure; each student proceeds at his or her own pace within the modular structure. Every student constructs his or her own study plan, which consists of different courses in various subjects according to each student's individual choices.

The focus on helping students take increasing responsibility for their own learning is not accidental; it reflects a key value underpinning the national core curriculum for the comprehensive school, as described below:

> The learning environment must support the pupil's growth and learning. It must be physically, psychologically, and socially safe, and must support the pupil's health. The objective is to increase pupils' curiosity and motivation to learn, and to promote their activeness, self-direction, and creativity by offering interesting challenges and problems. The learning environment must guide pupils in setting their own objectives and evaluating their own actions. The pupils must be given the chance to participate in the creation and development of their own learning environment. (Preamble, National Core Curriculum for Basic Education, 2004)

Social and cultural factors

As with all education systems that achieve good results, Finland's success is a function of the interaction of several different factors that work together to create a coherent approach that supports consistent system-wide performance. Some of these factors are cultural. As Sahlberg points out, Finland's history and geography – "caught between the huge kingdom in the west and the even bigger empire in the east" – compelled it to put the nation's interest first and not allow education policy to become victim to partisan politics:

> We are a small nation that the rest of the world sees as a strange place that speaks a language nobody else understands. Over the last half-century we developed an understanding that the only way for us to survive as a small, independent nation is by educating all our people. This is our only hope amid the competition between bigger nations and all those who have other benefits we don't have. (Interview conducted for this report)

While Finland has jealously guarded its hard-won independence, in many areas of social policy it has been much influenced by its Scandinavian neighbours, especially Sweden. As noted above, the idea of the comprehensive school emerged in Finland as part of a larger movement in the 1960s for more social and economic equality, and over the next two decades the Finns adopted many features of the Swedish welfare state. Consequently, Finnish schools are embedded in a society with strong social safety nets and a broad and deep commitment to the healthy development and well-being of children, as reflected in Principal Aaltio's description of the pupils' care group in her school.

Another reflection of Finnish society's deep commitment to its children can be found in its school buildings. In the period following the Second World War, municipalities and towns all over Finland embarked on a major effort to rebuild schools that had been destroyed and build new ones where none had existed. Consequently, most children in Finland attend schools that are small enough for each child to be known by all the adults in the school (although more than 50% of school children go to schools that have more than 300 pupils). While the school buildings are not intended to be architectural statements, they are typically light, airy and functional. Their small size allows for a degree of personalisation and individual attention that is one of the hallmarks of Finnish education.

Finnish society is also characterised by a degree of social cohesion and trust in government that is partly a function of size and relative cultural homogeneity, but which also reflects the national temperament. Social cohesion and trust are difficult factors to isolate and quantify, but they clearly are part of the explanation for why teaching has become such an attractive profession for talented young people in Finland, at least on a par with medicine and law. Finnish primary teacher education programmes are able to attract *ten applicants for every slot*. Olli Luukkainen, President of the Finnish Teachers Union comments on the trust factor in discussing the status of teaching in Finland:

> Teachers in Finland are very independent. They can decide almost everything: how they will teach, what they will select from the basic (national) curriculum, when they will teach each particular topic. The fact that teachers have so much independence and respect influences young people as they are deciding what program they will follow in the university. If they choose teacher education they know they will be entering a profession that enjoys broad trust and respect in the society, one that plays an important role in shaping the country's future. (Interview conducted for this report)

Exceptional teacher quality

The trust that teachers enjoy in Finnish society is deserved and reflects the very high quality of their training. For example, Finnish teachers have earned the trust of parents and the wider society by their demonstrated ability to use professional discretion and judgement in the way they manage their classrooms and respond to the challenge of helping virtually all students become successful learners.

The quality of teachers and teaching lies at the heart of Finland's educational success, and the factors responsible for producing that quality can be found at the intersection of culture and policy. One policy aspect was the 1979 decision to move teacher preparation into the universities and make it substantially more rigorous. Another was the subsequent decisions of governments in the 1980s to devolve increasing levels of authority and responsibility for education from the Ministry of Education to municipalities and schools. This movement was largely an expression of ideology, of a growing scepticism in the West about the role of central governments and their ability to know what works best in the field. However, the effect of these decisions was to extend even greater responsibility and trust to educators in the schools.

Prior to devolution, the central administration had two primary tools for regulating the quality of education: the national core curriculum, and a national school inspectorate. As mentioned above, the national core curriculum has become much less detailed and prescriptive – there are now only 10 pages devoted to basic school mathematics – and the current version acknowledges that the curriculum plan adopted by each municipality will incorporate locally-developed priorities and reflect community aspirations and values. Even more striking, the inspectorate was abolished, leaving only the periodic sampling of student learning in grades 6 and 9 as the central administration's vehicle for assessing and monitoring school quality. Nevertheless, municipalities are legally obliged to evaluate the education provided by their schools.

Those responsible for designing the reforms following the establishment of the common school in Finland are likely to have followed a rationale similar to this:

> *If* we can somehow manage to recruit highly talented young people to enrol in our teacher preparation programmes and then redesign those programmes to equip all incoming teachers to differentiate instruction, diagnose learning problems, and assess student progress; and *if* we can create the conditions in schools that allow teachers to exercise professional judgement and discretion in selecting materials and designing instruction tailored to the needs of their students; and *if* we can create school cultures in which teachers take collective responsibility for the learning and well being of their students; and *if* we can create in every school mechanisms that provide access to extra support for children and families most in need; *then* we can be reasonably confident that virtually all students in virtually all schools will thrive.

Because this theory of change rests so heavily on the quality of the teaching force, we now turn to the role of teacher preparation in Finland.

Finnish practices in teacher recruitment and preparation

Teaching has long been a respected occupation in Finland, but until the teacher education reform act of 1979, there was little sense that teachers required much advanced training. After completing upper secondary school, prospective primary and secondary teachers enrolled in a *seminarium* (teacher college) for two or three years of mostly practical training and then moved straight into the classroom. This model of preparation was hardly unique to Finland. Its premise was that as long as students had a solid foundation of subject matter knowledge from their upper secondary schooling, they could be taught enough about pedagogy, child development and classroom management in two or three years to become effective teachers. The *seminaria* presumably screened their applicants to ensure that they had the requisite character and personality traits to become teachers, but their admissions criteria were understandably much less rigorous than those of the universities.

All this changed with the movement of teacher education from the teacher colleges into the university, and especially with the decision to require even primary school teachers to obtain a master's degree before receiving a teaching qualification. As was the case with the creation of the comprehensive school, this decision was not without controversy. University leaders initially resisted the idea that teaching was anything more than a semi-profession and feared that advocates for other semi-professions like nursing and social work would now clamour to give their training programmes university status. Their real worry was that the admission of teacher education candidates would lead to a dilution of academic standards and a consequent loss of status.

Over time, however, as the new university-based teacher education programmes were designed and built, these fears were not borne out. In fact, university-based teacher education programmes are now highly selective and teacher education units in the university faculties have autonomy in the selection process.

In 2010 over 6 600 applicants competed for 660 available slots in primary school preparation programmes in the 8 universities that educate teachers. The admissions process occurs in two stages. The initial paper screen is based on the applicant's Matriculation Exam score, upper secondary school record, and out-of-school accomplishments. Those who pass that screening must then take a written exam; be observed in a teaching-like activity in which their interaction and communication skills can be assessed; and finally be interviewed to assess, among other things, the strength of their motivation to teach.

The teacher education programmes for prospective primary and upper grade teachers are somewhat different in structure, but not in rigor. Primary grade teachers major in education, but they are expected to minor in at least two of the subjects included in the primary school curriculum. This means, for example, that they are studying mathematics in the mathematics department, not in the education department. Upper grade teachers major in the subject they will be teaching, but they do substantial work in education as well, either in an integrated five-year programme or in a concentrated fifth year after they have completed their work in their subject field. It is also possible for a master's degree holder to take one year of pedagogical studies in the faculty of education to gain a formal teacher qualification.

Teacher education in Finland has at least four distinguishing qualities:

- Research based. Teacher candidates are not only expected to become familiar with the knowledge base in education and human development, but they are required to write a research-based dissertation as the final requirement for the masters degree. Upper grade teachers typically pick a topic in their subject area; primary grade teachers typically study some aspect of pedagogy. The rationale for requiring a research-based dissertation is that teachers are expected to engage in disciplined inquiry in the classroom throughout their teaching career.

- Strong focus on developing pedagogical content knowledge. Traditional teacher preparation programmes too often treat good pedagogy as generic, assuming that good questioning skills, for example, are equally applicable to all subjects. Because teacher education in Finland is a shared responsibility between the teacher education faculty and the academic subject faculty, there is substantial attention to subject-specific pedagogy for prospective primary as well as upper-grade teachers.

- Good training for all Finnish teachers in diagnosing students with learning difficulties and in adapting their instruction to the varying learning needs and styles of their students.

- A very strong clinical component. Linda Darling-Hammond, a leading US scholar and practitioner of teacher education, describes this aspect of Finnish teacher preparation:

Teachers' preparation includes both extensive course work on how to teach – with a strong emphasis on using research based on state-of-the-art practice – and at least a full year of clinical experience in a school associated with the university. These model schools are intended to develop and model innovative practices, as well as to foster research on learning and teaching. …

Within these model schools, student teachers participate in problem-solving groups, a common feature in Finnish schools. The problem-solving groups engage in a cycle of planning, action, and reflection/evaluation that is reinforced throughout the teacher education program and is, in fact, a model for what teachers will plan for their own students, who are expected to use similar kinds of research and inquiry in their own studies. Indeed, the entire system is intended to improve through continual reflection, evaluation, and problem-solving, at the level of the classroom, school, municipality, and nation. (Darling-Hammond, 2010)

In summary, raising the bar for entry into teaching has made this an even more attractive career option than previously, enabling teacher preparation programmes to select from the top quartile of secondary school graduates. The significantly lengthened and strengthened preparation of teachers has equipped them to rise to the increasing professional autonomy and control challenge thrown down to them by government. The autonomy and trust that teachers enjoy has only enhanced their status in the society, thereby assuring that teacher preparation programmes should continue to attract a steady flow of highly talented and motivated applicants.

Finnish teachers: autonomy, quality assurance and accountability

One of the most striking facts about Finnish schools is that their students have fewer hours of instruction than students in any other OECD country. This means that Finnish teachers teach fewer hours than their peers. In lower secondary schools, for example, Finnish teachers teach about 600 hours a year – 800 lessons of 45 minutes each, or four lessons per day. By contrast, US middle school teachers teach about 1 080 hours, or six daily lessons of 50 minutes. Teaching hours per day also depend partly on the number of teachers in a given school and teaching loads vary according to the level of education being taught. Nevertheless, the number of teaching hours is generally fewer than in many other countries. Leaving aside the important question of how Finnish 15-year-olds manage to outperform peers in other nations despite the equivalent of three less years of schooling, the relevant question here is what Finnish teachers are doing when they are not engaged in classroom teaching.

With the professional autonomy Finnish teachers enjoy comes very substantial responsibility for tasks that in other systems are typically handled more centrally. Chief among these are curriculum and assessment. As described above, the national core curriculum is really a framework rather than a roadmap, leaving teachers an enormous amount of discretion to interpret that framework, select their own textbooks and other curriculum materials, and then design their own lessons, all of which require time. In some schools the process of curriculum development is undertaken collaboratively by teams of teachers, while in smaller schools the responsibility might fall largely on each individual teacher.

The 2004 National Core Curriculum offers some broad criteria for student assessments, but again it is teachers who have the principal responsibility for building systems to continuously assess the progress of students. Teachers are also expected to be in close communication with parents, and many schools have an elaborate structure of staff committees to deal with various aspects of school life. Although Finnish teachers in theory are allowed to leave school when they are not teaching, teaching is clearly a full-time profession.

When it comes to professional development in Finland, the situation seems highly variable. This is in large part because Finnish schools are primarily funded at the municipal level, and municipal authorities attach varying degrees of importance to professional development. Municipalities are required to fund three days annually of mandatory professional development for each teacher, but some municipalities do much more. On average, Finnish teachers report spending seven days a year on professional development, some of which are in their own time. Some larger municipalities organise common professional development activities for all their schools, while others allow each school to design its own programme.

According to Olli Luukkainen, this highly variable approach to professional development is a weakness of the Finnish system:

Our system of continuing education and professional development for teachers is not good enough. It differs too much from one part of the country to another and one group of teachers to another. Teachers in vocational schools, for example, have much better support for continuing education than do primary teachers. (Interview conducted for this report)

Recently, however, the union, ministry and other partners have come together to develop a national programme to try to provide more equitable access to professional development. The ministry allocated EUR 20 million to support this programme in 2010.

Assessing progress

Beyond the periodic sampling assessments administered at different grades by the National Board of Education, there is no national mechanism for monitoring the performance of schools. There is a national evaluation council, but its role seems to be focused more on the evaluation of national policies than the performance of schools. There is a National Matriculation Exam taken at the end of upper secondary school, but its function is to certify what the student knows, not to assess the quality of his or her school. Perhaps the most frequent question asked of Finnish policy makers is, therefore, "How, in the absence of annual external assessments and any form of outside inspection, do you assure that all students in all schools are receiving a quality education?" This question comes most frequently from visitors from countries like the US and the UK, which invest heavily in external accountability systems designed to produce more equitable outcomes. Even so, their results pale in comparison to the Finnish system.

There is no obvious, single answer to the quality assurance question. The ability of Finnish schools to produce high achievement with so little variation between or within schools is the result of the confluence of factors, cultural and educational, outlined throughout this chapter. One factor cited by Principal Aaltio is, paradoxically, the heavy Finnish emphasis on student assessment. While the Finns do not assess for school accountability purposes, they do an enormous amount of diagnostic or formative assessment at the classroom level. When asked how she knows how well the students in any particular class are learning, Principal Aaltio's answer is that there is so much assessment data at her disposal that there is no way she would not know if a teacher was failing to teach her students. She also reports that, in her school at least, the parents keep a close eye on how their children are progressing and would alert her if there were problems. As described above, there are also the twice-monthly meetings of the pupil's care group to bring class as well as individual problems to light.

Lines of accountability

Accountability in the Finnish system is built from the bottom up. Teacher candidates are selected in part based on their ability to convey their belief in the core mission of public education in Finland, which is deeply moral and humanistic as well as civic and economic. The preparation they receive is designed to build a powerful sense of individual responsibility for the learning and well-being of all the students in their care.

The next level of accountability rests with the school. Again, the level of trust that the larger community extends to its schools seems to engender a strong sense of collective responsibility for the success of every student. While every comprehensive school in Finland reports to a municipal authority, authorities vary widely in the quality and degree of oversight that they provide. They are responsible for hiring the principal, typically on a six or seven-year contract, but the day-to-day responsibility for managing the schools is left to the education professionals, as is the responsibility for assuring student progress.

Given the very substantial level of autonomy that schools enjoy, one might expect that the system would focus the same kind of attention on recruiting and developing a corps of highly effective principals as it does on preparing teachers. However, there is little evidence of this. As in many countries, the role of the principal in Finland is changing, but the very independence of teachers in Finland poses some special challenges according to Professor Jouni Välijärvi of the University of Jyvaskyla, lead researcher for the analysis of Finland's PISA results:

> Historically, the principal in Finland has simply been head teacher, first among equals as a member of the teaching staff with the added responsibility of representing the faculty to the rest of the society. But given the degree to which school budgets have been decentralised, the job is now much more demanding, for principals now have financial responsibility along with responsibility for the care and well-being of the students.

> Because Finnish teachers are highly educated and are accustomed to being in full control of their own classroom, we have no tradition of principals actively visiting classes to monitor the quality of teaching in their schools. In fact, given our small school sizes, most principals are themselves teaching at least a few hours a week, so their role is a mixed one, with confusing and sometimes contradictory demands. (Interview conducted for this report)

While some universities, including Välijärvi's, have now mounted professional development programmes for principals, this does not seem to be seen as a major problem or need.

FUTURE CHALLENGES FOR FINNISH EDUCATION

The big question all high-performing systems need to face is whether or not the policies and practices that have brought about their current high performance will be sufficient to sustain them in a rapidly changing, globalising world. In the case of Finland this question is a particularly intriguing one, for the big policy shift that most observers credit with bringing about Finland's current level of performance took place 40 years ago. Unlike many other high-performing countries, Finland's reforms have evolved slowly and carefully over decades, have enjoyed broad and sustained political support across many changes in government, and are so intertwined with deep cultural factors that they are firmly institutionalised in the fabric of everyday life in schools. They are not the result of bold new policies or big programmatic initiatives that one can identify with a particular government or political leader. Rather, they are now almost taken for granted as the way schooling is done in Finland.

Given its history and development, what particular challenges might the future hold for Finland's education system? The first is not unique to Finland – the challenge of successfully absorbing increasing numbers of children of immigrants into its schools. This is a problem many European nations have struggled with, some more successfully than others. Although children of immigrants only make up about 3% of Finland's students, this percentage is growing, and as stated above there are already some schools in Helsinki that are nearly half immigrant. Until now Finland has been committed to providing immigrant children the option of continuing to study in their mother tongue and to teach all immigrant children their own language. However, this practice could be a problem going forward, as Jouni Välijärvi observes:

> Traditionally we have stressed that immigrant students can be taught in their own language. We have done this for reasons having to do with our own history, when we were part of Sweden and wanted the right to be taught in Finnish. Even today, when Swedish is the native language of only 5% of our population, we have extended them the same right to be taught in their language. But when you have a growing number of languages, it may not be possible to continue to be able to provide this right to be taught in your own language. And then there is this larger question of how to balance respect for your native language with the importance of learning the Finnish language to be able to function in Finnish society. We have been critical of Sweden for its insistence that newcomers integrate into Swedish society, but given the expense and difficulty of finding enough teachers to teach all immigrant children in their own language, we may be forced to move in this direction as well. (Interview conducted for this report)

A second question one might ask about Finland's future has to do with the extraordinary degree to which its system relies on its continuing ability to draw its teachers from the top end of the talent pool. Can one imagine circumstances under which teaching might begin to lose its allure among young Finns? Professions undergo cycles in which their relative status in a society can rise or fall. Suppose, as some observers fear, the pendulum begins to swing back to more centralised control of schooling in Finland. If other countries begin to surpass Finland on PISA or other international measures of performance, will there be calls for the ministry to step in and take a stronger hand in guiding Finnish education? If that were to happen, would young people continue to find teaching so attractive?

A third question concerns the future of the current upper secondary divide between academic and vocational education. While there seems to be a strong societal consensus that supports the division of upper secondary education into tracks, at least one respected and deeply experienced former education official wonders whether the principle of the common comprehensive school might someday be extended into upper secondary education. Jukka Sarjala asks whether in the future the needs of academic and vocational education students will really be so different from one another:

> If we ask what foreign language skills young people will need in the future, won't everyone need at least English in addition to Swedish, and many people in different lines of work might also need French or German or Russian. And what about mathematics? Won't everyone need some form of advanced mathematics? Wouldn't it make sense to combine academic and vocational programs in the same institution while allowing students to develop their own individual programmes? (Interview conducted for this report)

Current education policy strongly encourages co-operation between the two types of upper secondary education in order to provide students with a wider and more flexible selection of studies. Jouni Välijärvi believes that the rising popularity of vocational education among young people is likely to create increasing pressure at the municipal level for greater collaboration between the two types of schools:

> Many academically oriented upper secondary schools are having trouble today attracting students. Because they are funded based on student enrolment, in some smaller municipalities this is a serious threat to their survival.

We are now starting to see some of these schools close, a brand new phenomenon in our system. At the same time a growing number of very talented students are leaving comprehensive school and choosing vocational studies, thereby increasing the popularity of vocational schools. In the coming years this will mean that unless the academic schools learn to collaborate on a deeper level, many more are likely to close, since most of our 450 academic upper secondary schools are very small and cannot sustain a continuing loss of students. (Interview conducted for this report)

A final worry or challenge is best articulated by Pasi Sahlberg at the end of his unpublished manuscript, *Finnish Lessons*. In Sahlberg's view, the Finnish reform movement over the last few decades has been animated by what he calls "the Big Dream," a unifying vision of a more equitable society in which even students in the most isolated rural schools would receive a strong enough educational foundation in the first nine years of schooling to equip them for further education, and in which young people from all walks of life would be prepared to live and work together through a common schooling experience. Is there now a need for a new vision, one more reflective of the changes taking place in today's society and responsive to what young people will need in the coming decades, a vision powerful enough to fuel the next generation of reforms?

LESSONS FROM FINLAND

For all of Finland's perceived advantages of size, relative cultural homogeneity, and (in recent years) economic strength, it is important to remember that as recently as 1970 only 30% of Finnish adults had completed upper secondary school, and as recently as 1993 Finland was in near economic collapse. Finland's ascent into the very top tier of educational performance was by no means inevitable: it was at least as much the result of a set of policy decisions deliberately taken, implemented thoughtfully, and sustained over a very long period of time as of factors endemic to the country's culture and history.

▪ Commitment to education and to children

The commitment to education and to the well-being of children has deep roots in Finland's culture, and provides the bedrock upon which the comprehensive school movement rests. One of the striking things about Finland's reform story is that the political consensus achieved 50 years ago – that children should be educated together in a common school system – has remained intact across numerous changes of government.

▪ Cultural support for universal high achievement

The underlying belief behind the creation of the comprehensive school was that all children could be expected to achieve at high levels, and that family background or regional circumstance should no longer be allowed to limit the educational opportunities open to children. It is important to note, however, that the Finns have a significantly broader definition of "high achievement" than just performance in two or three subjects on standardised tests. The Finns pride themselves on offering a broad, rich curriculum to all students, even those who choose the vocational pathway in upper secondary school.

▪ Teacher and principal quality

Many countries pay lip-service to the importance of attracting and retaining a high-quality teacher force, but few have pursued this goal as single-mindedly as Finland. Finland has managed to make teaching the single most desirable career choice among young Finns through a combination of raising the bar for entry into the profession and granting teachers greater autonomy and control over their classrooms and working conditions than their peers enjoy elsewhere. Consequently, teaching is now a highly selective occupation in Finland, with highly-skilled well-trained teachers spread throughout the country. The quality of the teaching force seems very likely to be the major factor that accounts for the high level of consistent performance across Finnish schools.

Until recently, Finland does not seem to have paid the same kind of attention to the recruitment, training, and ongoing development of principals, but it is hard to believe that Finnish schools could perform so well without solid leadership, especially given the degree of autonomy that Finnish schools enjoy.

▪ Accountability

Accountability clearly matters in Finland, but it is almost entirely a professional model of accountability. The strongest manifestation of that accountability can be seen in the degree to which Finnish schools are organised to take collective responsibility for struggling learners. Finnish teachers are trained to identify children who are having difficulty and to intervene before these children get discouraged and fall too far behind their classmates. The fact that every school has a specially trained intervention specialist – the special teacher – means that the regular classroom teacher has easy access to support and that struggling children are much less likely to go unnoticed or to fall through the cracks. The small size of Finland's schools is an important factor here, as is the co-ordination of resources, embodied in the pupils' care group. Again, this combination of elements helps explain why the gap between the top and bottom performing schools and students in Finland is so narrow compared with virtually all other nations.

▪ How money is spent

Finland is by no means the highest spender per pupil among OECD countries, so money cannot be an important factor in explaining Finland's success. Teacher salaries are in the middle range for European countries. Schools are quite small in size, but they have minimal administrative overheads. Even in larger schools, principals are expected to teach, and the resources of the school are tightly focused on the classroom. Because of their commitment to the inclusion model, the costs of special education are significantly lower than in countries that rely more heavily on separate classrooms for special education students. Finally, because Finnish schools are mostly a function of municipal government, there are no separate school districts and no intermediate education units sitting between the municipalities and the ministry. Therefore, except for the costs of the national educational administration, virtually all of the money spent on education in Finland is focused on schools and classrooms.

▪ Instructional practice

The decision three decades ago to move teacher education into the universities and upgrade the rigor and length of the training was taken largely in response to the challenge of meeting the needs of diverse learners in a common school. Part of the challenge, as described above, was equipping teachers to diagnose learning difficulties and design timely interventions. But the larger challenge, especially with the abolition of tracking in 1989, was helping them learn to differentiate instruction sufficiently well to engage all students in heterogeneously grouped classrooms. By all reports Finnish teacher preparation programmes focus intensively on helping teachers develop these skills, especially in the extended clinical portion of their training under the supervision of master teachers in the university-run model schools.

▪ School organisation

This, of course, was *the* central insight that has driven Finland's reform agenda over the past several decades. According to virtually all observers and Finnish policy makers, the single most important education policy decision taken since Finland established its independence in 1917 was to create a common, untracked comprehensive school system that would serve students from all walks of life.

All the other policy decisions that together help account for Finland's dramatic ascent to a position of international leadership in education in the last decades flow from that basic organisational decision. Obviously, creating the comprehensive school structure in itself was no guarantee of improvement. Rather, it has been the steady, thoughtful way in which the new structure has been implemented that is mostly responsible for the extraordinarily high and equitable achievement of Finnish students. Of particular note are the investments made in recruiting and developing a teaching force committed to the values that underlie the comprehensive school and capable of meeting the needs of diverse learners in that setting.

▪ Sequencing of reforms to economic development

In many ways what is most distinctive and impressive about Finland is the degree to which its education system has developed in close alignment with its economy and social structure. As described above, the story of the development of Finland's education reforms cannot be told without reference to the development of the welfare state in the 1960s and 1970s and the high-tech, information-based economy of the last two decades. Finland is at the furthest end of the development continuum outlined in the first chapter of this report. Its economy is driven by continuing investments in innovation and R&D. Finnish teachers are drawn from the top quartile of upper secondary graduates. Teachers are highly professional knowledge workers, and are treated as such. Accountability is almost entirely professional, as evidenced by the elimination of the inspectorate and the absence of external assessments. The curriculum framework and instructional guidance is designed to encourage an inquiry-based approach to learning.

▪ Cultivating behaviours for the knowledge economy

Finnish schools work to cultivate in young people the dispositions and habits of mind often associated with innovators: creativity, flexibility, initiative, risk-taking and the ability to apply knowledge in novel situations. Some sceptics attribute Finland's consistently high performance on PISA to the degree of alignment between the kind of learning PISA measures and the values and the goals of the Finnish education system. There is clearly some truth to this observation, but this hardly constitutes a criticism of the Finnish system. The Finns are not the least bit apologetic about their focus on preparing people for an economy in which innovation and entrepreneurship will continue to be drivers of progress.

FINAL OBSERVATIONS

Here are two final observations, both related to the degree to which the Finnish education system is aligned with and reflects qualities in the larger culture. The first has to do with the very nature of education reform in Finland. Most governments enact education reform through new programmes – *e.g.* smaller class sizes, more ambitious external assessments, and increased professional development. Reforms like these do not tamper with the basic features of the system. The Finnish reforms, by contrast, especially the creation of the comprehensive school, created a sector that functioned in a radically different way. It is the shape of this new sector, not continued programmatic initiatives from a central government, that accounts for Finland's success. One critical observer suggested that Finland doesn't really have a reform strategy, by which he meant that there were no central initiatives that the government was trying to push through the system. From a longer term, more sectoral perspective, however, Finland does have a strategy, one that has propelled it to the top of the international rankings. Other countries might benefit from adopting this perspective on their reform work.

The second observation has to do with the importance of trust. Trust, of course, cannot be legislated. Consequently, this lesson may be the least useful to others wanting to learn from Finland, especially if one views trust as a precondition for the kinds of deep institutional reforms embodied in the development of the comprehensive school. But in the case of the relationship between teachers and wider society, one can argue that trust is at least as much a consequence of important policy decisions as it is a pre-existing condition. Given the respect that teachers have historically enjoyed in Finland, there was a solid base on which to build. But the combination alluded to above – much more rigorous preparation, coupled with the devolution of much greater decision-making authority over things like curriculum and assessment – enabled teachers to exercise the kind of professional autonomy other professionals enjoy. This granting of trust from the government, coupled with their new-found status as university graduates from highly selective programmes, empowered teachers to practise their profession in ways that deepened the trust afforded them by parents and others in the community. The fact that there seems to be very little interest in Finland in instituting the assessment and external accountability regimes that have characterised the reform strategies of many OECD countries, most prominently the US and the UK, is perhaps the best evidence of the fundamental trust that seems to exist between the educators and the community. Given the extraordinary performance of the Finnish system over the past decade, this is a lesson others might want to study.

■ Figure 5.2 ■
Finland: Profile data

Language(s)	Finnish and Swedish[3]
Population	5 326 000[4]
Youth population	16.8%[5] (OECD average 18.7%)
Elderly population	16.6%[6] (OECD average 14.4%)
Growth rate	0.43%[7] (OECD 0.68%)[8]
Foreign-born population	3.8%[9] (OECD average 12.9%)
GDP per capita	USD 35 918[10] (OECD average 33 732)[11]
Economy-Origin of GDP	Electronics, machinery, vehicles and other engineered metal products, forestry and chemicals. Services: 70.6%; Industry and construction: 24.6%; Agriculture, forestry and fishing: 4.9%[12]
Unemployment	6.4% (2008)[13] (OECD average 6.1%)[14]
Youth unemployment	15.7% (OECD average 13.8%)[15]

Expenditure on education	5.9% of GDP; (OECD average 5.2%)
	  3.7% on primary, secondary and post-secondary non-tertiary
	  1.9 % on tertiary[16] education[17] (OECD average 3.5%; 1.2% respectively)
	
	12.5% of total government expenditure[18]
	  7.9% on primary, secondary and post-secondary non-tertiary
	  3.9 % on tertiary education[19] (OECD average 9%; 3.1% respectively)

Enrolment ratio, early childhood education	48.2%[20] (OECD average 71.5%)[21]
Enrolment ratio, primary education	95.5%[22] (OECD average 98.8%)[23]
Enrolment ratio, secondary education	87.2%[24] (OECD average 81.5%)[25]
Enrolment ratio, tertiary education	42.6%[26] (OECD average 24.9%)[27]
Students in primary education, by type of institution or mode of enrolment[28]	Public: 98.6% (OECD average 89.6%) Government-dependent private: 1.4% (OECD average 8.1%) Independent, private: no data[29] (OECD average 2.9%)
Students in lower secondary education, by type of institution or mode of enrolment[30]	Public 95.7% (OECD average 83.2%) Government-dependent private: 4.3% (OECD average 10.9%) Independent, private: no data[31] (OECD average 3.5%)
Students in upper secondary education, by type of institution or mode of enrolment[32]	Public: 86.1% (OECD average 82%) Government-dependent private: 13.9% (OECD average 13.6%) Independent, private: no data[33] (OECD average 5.5%)

Students in tertiary education, by type of institution or mode of enrolment[34]	Tertiary type B education:
	  Public: 100%
	  Government-dependent private[35]
	  Independent-private: no data[36]
	  (OECD average Public: 61.8%
	  Government-dependent private : 19.2%
	  Independent-private: 16.6%)
	
	Tertiary type A education:
	  Public: 89.3%
	  Government-dependent private 10.7%
	  Independent-private: no data[37]
	  (OECD average Public: 77.1%
	  Government-dependent private : 9.6%
	  Independent-private: 15%)

Teachers' salaries	Average annual starting salary in lower secondary education: USD 32 513 (OECD average USD 30 750)[38] Ratio of salary in lower secondary education after 15 years of experience to GDP per capita: 1.15 (OECD average: 1.22)[3]
Upper secondary graduation rates	93% (OECD average 80%)[40]

StatLink 🔗 http://dx.doi.org/10.1787/888932366693

Interview partners

Riitta Aaltio, Principal, Kerava Primary School, Kerava, Finland.

Sakari Karjalainen, Department for Education and Science Policy, Ministry of Education, Finland.

Hanna Laakso, Senior Adviser, International Visits, National Board of Education, Finland.

Timo Lankinen, Director General, National Board of Education, Finland.

Olli Luukkainen, President, Trade Union of Education in Finland (OAJ).

Ray Marshall, Professor Emeritus of Economics and Public Affairs, LBJ School of Public Policy, University of Texas at Austin, United States.

Pasi Sahlberg, Director General, Centre for International Mobility and Co-operation (CIMO), Finland.

Jukka Sarjala, Former Director General, National Board of Education, Finland.

Jouni Välijärvi, University of Jyvaskyla, Institute for Educational Research, Finland.

Henna Virkkunen, Minister of Education, Finland.

References

Aho, E., K. Pitkanen and **P. Sahlberg** (2006), "Policy Development and Reform Principles of Basic and Secondary Education in Finland since 1968", prepared for the *Education Working Paper Series*, World Bank, Washington, DC. *http://www.pasisahlberg. com/downloads/Education%20in%20Finland%202006.pdf.*

Burridge, T. (2010), "Why Do Finland's Schools Get the Best Results?" *BBC News* [Online] 7 April, Retrieved from *http://news.bbc. co.uk/2/hi/8601207.stm.*

CIA World Factbook (2010), *Finland: Country Background Information*, [Online] Retrieved from *www.cia.gov/library/publications/ the-world-factbook/geos/fi.html.*

Darling-Hammond, L. (2010), *The Flat World and Education,* Teachers College Press, New York.

Eurydice (2008), *Organisation of the Education System in Finland*, Education, Audiovisual and Cultural Executive Agency (EACEA P9 Eurydice), Brussels.

Eurydice (2009), *Finland*, National Summary Sheets on Education Systems in Europe and Ongoing Reforms, Education, Audiovisual and Cultural Executive Agency (EACEA P9 Eurydice), Brussels.

Eurydice (2010), *Structures of Education and Training Systems in Europe: Finland*, Eurybase, Brussels.

FNBE (Finnish National Board of Education) (2008), *Education in Finland*, FNBE, Helsinki, available at *www.oph.fi/download/124278_ education_in_finland.pdf.*

FNBE (2010), Structures of Education and Training Systems in Europe, FNBE, Helsinki, available at *http://eacea.ec.europa.eu/ education/eurydice/documents/eurybase/structures/041_FI_EN.pdf.*

Gamerman, E. (2008), "What Makes Finnish Kids So Smart?", *The Wall Street Journal*, Feature Article, 29 February.

Gardner, W. (2010), "Are Quality and Quantity Possible in Teacher Recruitment?", *Education Week* [Online], 26 February, available at: *http://blogs.edweek.org/edweek/walt_gardners_reality_check/2010/02/are_quality_and_quantity_possible_in_teacher_recruitment.html.*

Grubb, W.N. (2007), "Dynamic Inequality and Intervention: Lessons from a Small Country," *Phi Delta Kappan International*, Vol. 89, No. 2, available at *www.pdkintl.org/kappan/k_v89/k0710gru.htm.*

Hargreaves, A., G. Halász and **B. Pont** (2007), *School Leadership for Systemic Improvement in Finland*, OECD, Paris, available at *www.oecd.org/dataoecd/43/17/39928629.pdf.*

Kaiser, R. (2005), "In Finland's Footsteps", *The Washington Post* [Online], available at *www.washingtonpost.com/wp-dyn/content/ article/2005/08/05/AR2005080502015.html.*

Kupiainen, S., J. Hautamäki, and **T. Karjalainen** (2009), *The Finnish Education System and PISA*, Ministry of Education Publications, Helsinki University Print, Helsinki.

Meisalo, V., et al. (2010), *ICT in Initial Teacher Training, Country Report: Finland*, OECD Publishing. *http://www.oecd.org/ dataoecd/4/43/45214586.pdf.*

Ministry of Education, Finland (2008), *Education and Research 2007-2012: Development Plan*, Helsinki University Print, Helsinki.

Ministry of Education, Finland (2009), *Finnish Education System in an International Comparison*, Ministry of Education Policy Analyses, Helsinki.

OECD (2010), *PISA 2009 Results: What Students Know and Can Do: Student Performance in Reading, Mathematics and Science (Volume I)*, OECD Publishing.

Sahlberg, P. (2007), "Education Policies for Raising Student Learning: The Finnish Approach", *Journal of Education Policy*, Vol. 22, No. 2, pp. 147-171.

Sahlberg, P. (forthcoming), *Finnish Lessons, What can the world learn from educational change in Finland?*, forthcoming.

Sahlberg, P. (2006), "Raising the Bar: How Finland Responds to the Twin Challenge of Secondary Education?", *Revista de Curriculum y Formación del Profesorado*, Vol. 10, No. 1.

Notes

1. The historical material in this report draws heavily on Sahlberg (forthcoming).

2. To which students could apply after the 4th or the 5th grade of elementary school

3. "Population according to language and the number of foreigners and land area km² by area". *Statistics Finland's PX-Web databases.* Helsinki: Statistics Finland. 2008-12-31.

4. OECD (2010), *OECD Economic Surveys: Finland 2010,* OECD Publishing. Data from 2009.

5. OECD (2010), *OECD Factbook 2010,* OECD Publishing. Ratio of population aged less than 15 to the total population (data from 2008).

6. OECD (2010), *OECD Factbook 2010,* OECD Publishing. Ratio of population aged 65 and older to the total population (data from 2008).

7. OECD (2010), *OECD Factbook 2010,* OECD Publishing. Annual population growth rate (data from 2007).

8. OECD (2010), *OECD Factbook 2010,* OECD Publishing. Annual population growth in percentage, OECD total (year of reference – 2007).

9. OECD (2010), *OECD Factbook 2010,* OECD Publishing. Foreign-born population as percent of the total population (data from 2007).

10. OECD (2010), *OECD Economic Surveys: Finland 2010,* OECD Publishing.

11. OECD (2010), *OECD Factbook 2010,* OECD Publishing. Current prices and PPPs (data from 2008).

12. OECD (2010), *OECD Economic Surveys: Finland 2010,* OECD Publishing.

13. OECD (2010), *OECD Factbook 2010,* OECD Publishing. Total unemployment rates as percentage of total labour force (data from 2008).

14. OECD (2010), *OECD Factbook 2010,* OECD Publishing. Total unemployment rates as percentage of total labour force (data from 2008).

15. OECD (2010), *Employment Outlook,* OECD Publishing. Unemployed as a percentage of the labour force in the age group: youth aged 15-24 (data from 2008).

16. The OECD follows standard international conventions in using the term "tertiary education" to refer to all post-secondary programmes at ISCED levels 5B, 5A and 6, regardless of the institutions in which they are offered. OECD (2008), *Tertiary Education for the Knowledge Society: Volume 1,* OECD Publishing.

17. OECD (2010), *Education at a Glance 2010,* OECD Publishing. Public expenditure presented in this table includes public subsidies to households for living costs (scholarships and grants to students/households and students loans), which are not spent on educational institutions (data from 2006).

18. OECD (2010), *OECD Economic Surveys: Finland 2010,* OECD Publishing.

19. OECD (2010), *Education at a Glance 2010,* OECD Publishing. Public expenditure presented in this table includes public subsidies to households for living costs (scholarships and grants to students/households and students loans), which are not spent on educational institutions (data from 2006).

20. OECD (2010), *Education at a Glance 2010,* OECD Publishing. Net enrolment rates of ages 4 and under as a percentage of the population aged 3 to 4 (data from 2008).

21. OECD (2010), *Education at a Glance 2010,* OECD Publishing. OECD average net enrolment rates of ages 4 and under as a percentage of the population aged 3 to 4 (year of reference – 2008).

22. OECD (2010), *Education at a Glance 2010,* OECD Publishing. Data from 2008 on net enrolment rates of ages 5 to 14 as a percentage of the population aged 5 to 14.

23. OECD (2010), *Education at a Glance 2010,* OECD Publishing. OECD average net enrolment rates of ages 5 to 14 as a percentage of the population aged 5 to 14 (year of reference – 2008).

24. OECD (2010), *Education at a Glance 2010,* OECD Publishing. Net enrolment rates of ages 15 to 19 as a percentage of the population aged 15 to 19 (data from 2008).

25. OECD (2010), *Education at a Glance 2010,* OECD Publishing. OECD average net enrolment rates of ages 15 to 19 as a percentage of the population aged 15 to 19 (year of reference – 2008).

26. OECD (2010), *Education at a Glance 2010*, OECD Publishing. Net enrolment rates of ages 20 to 29 as a percentage of the population aged 20 to 29 Data from 2008). This figure includes all 20-29 year olds, including those in employment, etc. The Gross Enrolment Ratio (GER), measured by the UN as the number of actual students enrolled / number of potential students enrolled, is generally higher. The GER for tertiary education in Finland in 2008 is 94%, compared to the regional avg of 70% (UIS 2010).

27. OECD (2010), *Education at a Glance 2010*, OECD Publishing. OECD average net enrolment rates of ages 20 to 29 as a percentage of the population aged 20 to 29 (year of reference – 2008).

28. OECD (2010), *Education at a Glance 2010,* OECD Publishing. Data from 2008.

29. Data is not applicable because category does not apply.

30. OECD (2010), *Education at a Glance 2010,* OECD Publishing. Data from 2008.

31. Data is not applicable because category does not apply.

32. OECD (2010), *Education at a Glance 2010,* OECD Publishing. Data from 2008.

33. Data is not applicable because category does not apply.

34. OECD (2010), *Education at a Glance 2010,* OECD Publishing. Data from 2008.

35. Magnitude is either negligible or zero.

36. Data is not applicable because category does not apply.

37. Data is not applicable because category does not apply .

38. OECD (2010), *Education at a Glance 2010,* OECD Publishing. Starting salary/minimum training in USD adjusted for PPP (data from 2008).

39. OECD (2010), *Education at a Glance 2010,* OECD Publishing (year of reference – 2008).

40. OECD (2010), *Education at a Glance 2010,* OECD Publishing. Sum of upper secondary graduation rates for a single year of age (year of reference – 2008).

6

Japan:
A Story of
Sustained Excellence

Japan has been at or near the top of the international rankings on education surveys since those surveys began. This chapter explores how Japan may have achieved this consistent standing and what other countries might be able to learn from the Japanese experience. The Japanese education system is grounded in a deep commitment to children that is concrete and enduring. The research also attributes Japan's success to a first-rate teaching force, superb family support for Japanese students at home, the way resources are focused on instruction and the strong incentives the system provides for students to take tough courses and study hard in school. The school curriculum in Japan appears very coherent, carefully centred on core topics, with a clear goal of fostering deep conceptual understanding. The academic programme follows a logical sequence and is set at a very high level of cognitive challenge. Though it is applied nationwide, Japanese teachers have a remarkable level of autonomy in its application. The entire approach is aided by the shared belief that effort and not ability is what primarily explains student achievement. There is no tracking in Japanese schools, classes are heterogeneous and no student is held back or promoted on account of ability. The system has a great deal of inherent accountability – to one's parents, one's peers and so on. While entrance exams are deeply important for progression to Japanese higher education, the system of teacher accountability in schools is interestingly not based on student assessments. These, and many other factors, have combined to produce one of the world's best-educated and most productive workforces.

INTRODUCTION

The performance of Japan's students in mathematics and science compared with those in the other OECD countries is impressive, and its comparative performance on the PISA reading survey, though not in the very top ranks, is also impressive (Table 6.1). There is nothing new about this consistently good performance; Japan has placed at or near the top of the international rankings on all such surveys since they began.[1]

Some seasoned observers report that average Japanese high school graduates who enter colleges compare favourably with average American college graduates in terms of what they know and what they can do. Less generous observers suggest that they compare favourably to American college students with two years of college. Other observers note that many Japanese high school graduates know more about the geography and history of many other countries than natives of those countries.

Table 6.1 **Japan's mean scores on reading, mathematics and science scales in PISA**

	PISA 2000	PISA 2003	PISA 2006	PISA 2009
	Mean score	Mean score	Mean score	Mean score
Reading	522	498	498	520
Mathematics		534	523	529
Science			531	539

Source: OECD (2010g), *PISA 2009 Volume I, What Students Know and Can Do: Student Performance in Reading, Mathematics and Science*, OECD Publishing.
StatLink ⬛🖻 http://dx.doi.org/10.1787/888932366712

It is tempting to believe that these comparisons are due to the achievement of only a small elite of students, but that is not the case – 95% of the age cohort completes high school in Japan (Figure 6.2).

This has repercussions for daily life. Newspaper articles in Japan routinely assume that their readers can understand sophisticated statistical tables and highly technical scientific topics. Factory managers allocate manuals that assume knowledge of calculus to teams that include recent high school graduates.

The advantage of this level of knowledge and skill to a country, in both citizenship and economic terms, is incalculable. The question asked in this chapter is: How did they do it? And the corollary to that question is: What can other countries learn from Japan that might transcend any cultural differences?

THE JAPANESE EDUCATION SYSTEM: HISTORICAL AND SOCIAL CONTEXT

Japan is a mountainous island nation. The proportion of arable land to population is among the lowest in the industrialised world. Its inhabitants crowd together in the mountain valleys and along the coasts in densely populated enclaves. Japan is also subject to regular frequent disasters such as typhoons and earthquakes, and the regular possibility of crop failure. And, finally, these islands contain very little in the way of readily extractable natural resources. Instead, they have achieved a high level of success through their education system.

A long history in such a challenging environment has had a profound effect on Japanese culture; people developed very strong co-operative ties as a collective survival mechanism. Society recognised early on that a lack of natural resources meant that the best way to succeed was through developing human capital. The result is a culture in which great value is placed on education and skills on the one hand, and on the group and social relations on the other. In Japan there is a shared belief that if the individual works tirelessly for the group, the group will reciprocate. But if one flouts the group, one can expect very little from society. Below we look briefly at how historical factors have shaped Japan's educational philosophy.

The Tokugawa era: 1603 to 1868

Prior to the Tokugawa era, Japanese culture had been a warrior culture. The Samurai had the highest social status in the nation for a long time. During the Tokugawa era, for about 250 years up until the middle of the 19th century, Japan was at peace. From the middle of the 19th century the Samurai, while retaining their social status, replaced their swords with pens to become the bureaucrats who ran the country. Largely isolated from the outside world, Japan prospered and enjoyed a rich culture. By 1850, at least a quarter of the Japanese were literate, putting Japan about even with Europe, although it lagged behind the Europeans in technology and finance.

Towards the end of the Tokugawa era, Japan's government was beset by endemic corruption and incompetence. When the American Admiral Matthew Perry's "Black Ships" appeared in 1853, Japan was wholly unprepared to resist Perry's demands that Japan open for trade on terms favourable to the West. The tottering Tokugawa regime was overthrown in 1868 by a rebellion led by lower-ranked bureaucrats rebelling against the incompetence of the dying regime. The emperor was restored to the throne in the Meiji Restoration.

The Meiji Restoration: 1868 to 1912

During an interview for this report, Robert Fish of the Japan Society described the leadership goals at the time of the Meiji era:

> They were determined to do whatever was necessary to establish a relationship of equals with the Western nations that had entered and humiliated Japan. The new government sent an enormous delegation to the Western nations to rewrite the unequal treaties that had been imposed on Japan. When nearly half of the leadership of the new government crossed the seas, they were astonished at what they saw. Realising that advanced education, science and technology had made possible the industrial strength that had made the "opening" of Japan to the West possible, these Japanese officials came back to Japan determined to match the achievements of the West in education, science and technology and upgrade their military. (Interview conducted for this report)

With almost total consensus across leaders from all sectors, the Japanese determined to modernise their country in order to survive in the new world order. In the field of education, the Japanese scoured the West for ideas that they could adapt to the pressing needs of Japan. Today they continue to compare themselves to their competitors, making national benchmarking arguably one of the most important reasons for their great success in education. The so-called "temple schools" found all over Japan at the end of the Tokugawa era, as well as the elite schools created for the children of the Samurai bureaucrats, provided a strong base on which the new leaders could build the world-class education system to which they aspired.

Meiji Japan borrowed the administrative scheme for its new education system from the French, which could be characterised as centralised and very orderly. From Germany they adopted the idea of an educational system built around a few elite national universities. England provided Japan with a model of schools founded on strong national moral principles (such as "public" schools like Eton and Harrow). And the United States provided a powerful pedagogical paradigm in the teachings of John Dewey – an American philosopher, psychologist and educational reformer – that resonated deeply with the Japanese notion that a school should be responsible for developing the whole child (Dewey, 1902).

The new government, moving quickly to make a modern nation state, decreed universal, compulsory education and abolished the rigid class distinctions in the education system that they believed had crippled the old regime. They needed every Japanese citizen to be as well educated as possible. Therefore, there was to be no tracking or segregation of students by ability or social class in Japanese education. This turned out to be a critical decision, laying the basis for what would become possibly one of the world's most meritocratic societies.

The Imperial Rescript: 1880s to 1940s

In the 1880s there was a reaction against the Meiji government's determination to implement ideas from elsewhere in the world. It aroused deep fears that the essence of what it meant to be Japanese would be lost. The *Imperial Rescript of Education*, released in 1890, was a ringing declaration of the primacy of Japanese values in guiding the evolution of the new compulsory education system. Emphasising the Confucian virtues of loyalty, respect for one's elders, the importance of relationships with other family members, one's spouse and friends, it reminded its readers of the importance of modesty and moderation, the obligation to educate oneself to the fullest, and the duty to obey the constitution and laws. Ever since the *Rescript* was issued, Japanese education policy has been anchored at one end by benchmarking Japan against the world's best education systems and, at the other end, by a firm grounding in traditional Japanese values.

The Second World War to the present day: An emphasis on merit and values

After the Second World War, under American occupation, Japan made nine years of education compulsory (Figure 6.1), provided financial assistance for those students who needed it, and made it possible for every high school graduate to take the college entrance examinations. Previously, only a limited number of special high school graduates had been allowed to take these examinations. These policies reinforced the drive towards the highly meritocratic system that had already begun.

■ Figure 6.1 ■
Japan's education system organisation

Age	Grade	Educational institutions				
3-4		Kindergarden				
4-5						
5-6						
6-7	1	Elementary School (Compulsory Education)				Special Education
7-8	2					
8-9	3					
9-10	4					
10-11	5					
11-12	6					
12-13	1	Junior High School/Lower Secondary School (Compulsory Education)				
13-14	2					
14-15	3					
15-16	1	High School/Upper Secondary School				
16-17	2					
17-18	3				College of Technology	
18-19		University – Undergraduate	Specialised Higher Education	Community College Vocational School		
19-20	Associate					
20-21						
21-22	Bachelor					
22-23		University – Master				
23-24	Master					
24-25		University – PhD	Medical School			
25-26			Veterinary School			
26-27	Ph.D		Dentistry School			
27-28	Ph.D		Pharmaceutical School			

As noted earlier, Japan's challenging environment and living conditions may have shaped the high values placed by the Japanese on the welfare of the group over that of the individual and on group harmony (White, 1988). This sense of being enveloped by the uncritical love of a group is called "*wa*" – a vitally important concept in Japanese society. Critical to happiness, *wa* is sought at every stage of life: first with one's mother, then with the rest of one's family, friends at school and college, and colleagues and superiors at work.

In this environment, individuals gain esteem by doing things that the group values; if a person's actions threaten group harmony, social sanctions follow with wide-ranging repercussions. If one loses the respect of one group, establishing *wa* with other groups can be more difficult. This cultural factor explains why the Japanese work hard to maintain good relations with the groups to which they belong. It also lies behind the good educational performance in Japan.

In Japan a school's reputation depends on the academic performance of the students and on their behaviour. Society holds the school responsible for both aspects in a way that has no parallel in the West. For example, if a student violates the law, the law enforcement authorities call that student's homeroom teacher as well as the mother and all faculty members apologise for the student's behaviour. It is not surprising therefore that Japanese students tend to develop a strong sense of obligation to the faculty and strive to perform well academically and to stay within the limits of the law when not in school. Indeed, the same idea applies to a student's relationship to the other students at school. To fail is to let the group down. Therefore most members of this society will work very hard to do as well as possible, and are always working towards higher goals, because that is the way to earn acceptance and gain status.

The same values permeate the workplace. It is often said that people work very hard in Japan largely to earn the respect and admiration of their colleagues. They do not work hard for personal distinction, but rather for the good of the group. Workers do not "slack off" in Japan, not only because the boss is watching, but also because their peers or staff members of a lower rank are watching. If an employee gives their all, the firm – as with a family – is expected to give back. Japanese firms frequently provide housing, trips, education and even funeral expenses to their employees as part of a remuneration package.

Unlike many societies where advancement depends mainly on connections and clans, Japan is more steadfastly meritocratic according to many observers (Stevenson and Stigler, 1992; White, 1988). While children from wealthier families are statistically more likely to get higher paying jobs than less wealthy children, in Japan this seems to be due to greater financial investment in a child's education and less due to social connections. Typically, people work their entire adult life for the same firm they joined after school or university, although this is beginning to change. A person's employment in a particular firm is usually a function of the high school or university they attended prior to joining that firm; this is unusual elsewhere. In turn, the high school or university a person attends is based entirely on how a student does in entrance exams.

A mother is judged on her success in supporting the education of her children. In practice, a mother is judged first by the high school that her son or daughter gets into, and then the university to which her child is admitted. Though the trend is changing, few Japanese mothers work outside the home as commonly as mothers in Western countries. Sociologists describe how Japanese mothers are expected by society to make sacrifices for their children who, in return, are expected to perform well in school (White, 1988).

Thus advancement in Japan is a function of merit and determined by examination. This ought not to work, because there are many other important skills which are not measured by Japanese examinations. The exams emphasise memorising and accumulating facts and mastering procedures, rather than analytical thinking, creativity or the capacity for innovation. However, it does work because Japanese employers are mainly interested in three things: applied intelligence, the capacity to learn, and the capacity to work hard and persist in the face of difficulty.

Because Japanese firms generally believe that they will employ people for a long time, there is a strong willingness to invest heavily in the continuing education and training of employees. It is not uncommon for a Japanese firm to send new university recruits overseas during their early years of employment to pursue a foreign graduate programme or as an intern in a foreign plant. Research shows that Japanese firms value candidates who are not just highly intelligent, but ready to learn whatever they need to learn.

Japanese employers want to know not just whether a candidate is smart, but whether he can do something with his intelligence. Employers are interested in *applied intelligence*. Japanese exams are designed to find out how much applied intelligence students can demonstrate and the degree to which they can use their intelligence to do something of value. It is impossible to do well in Japanese exams without working very hard, over long periods of time. This takes discipline and persistence. Many countries talk about the importance of "learning to learn." Japan has done much more than talk about it; the country has built an education system around it.

In summary, from this historical and social background, three points emerge that help to frame the Japanese education context:

- In this persistently meritocratic society, the high school entrance and university entrance exams represent gateways to status in Japanese society.
- The Japanese widely believe that how well one does in these exams depends much more on studying hard than on innate intelligence.
- Exam success does not only reflect on the individual, but also on their mother, the other family members and teachers. This constellation of support shares the responsibility for failure and creates pressure to succeed.

With this background in mind, the chapter will now look more closely at the specific features of the Japanese education system for more clues to the reasons behind its outstanding performance.

THE KEY FEATURES OF JAPAN'S EDUCATION SYSTEM TODAY

A standard and demanding national curriculum

Ryo Watanabe, Director of International Research in the National Institute for Education Policy Research, believes that "Japanese students have done so well on PISA because of the curriculum. Japan has national curriculum standards, or courses of study that define the content to be taught by grade and subject, and every ten years they re-devise this curriculum. Throughout the country, teachers teach based on the national curriculum standards." (Interview conducted for this report)

In theory the curriculum is set by the Japanese Ministry of Education, Culture, Sports, Science and Technology (MEXT) with advice from the Central Council for Education. In reality, the key figures involved in setting the curriculum are university professors and ministry staff. While the curriculum defined by MEXT is only for "guidance", the prefectures (a unit of government in between the county and province level) are also funded by MEXT and so generally closely follow the guidance. The guidance curriculum is long and detailed, so MEXT also publishes explanatory booklets, subject by subject, by school level. The curriculum is revised following a regular schedule.

Until recently, there was very little flexibility in the Japanese curriculum, and very little time in the school day for anything but the official national curriculum. In most Japanese high schools, roughly 70% of total available time was devoted to just five subjects: Japanese, social studies, mathematics, science, and foreign language (mostly English). The remaining hours were devoted to gym, music, art, homeroom and other elective subjects.

Even with the recent liberalisation (see section on "How Japan's education system is changing"), there is still less choice for students in the Japanese curriculum than is typically the case in any Western country. This curriculum, combined with the fact that Japanese students spend much more time at school, means that Japanese students have much more time to go into greater depth in these core subjects than in most other countries. They are also very focused on the core subjects in the curriculum because they are not distracted by subsidiary courses.

The curriculum is very demanding. It is also highly coherent, in the sense that it progresses step by step in a very logical fashion from year to year, concentrating in each year on the topics that must be mastered in order to understand the material presented in the following year. Essential subjects are given plenty of time. Each topic is carefully developed and in great detail. In mathematics and science, the emphasis throughout is on the fundamental underlying concepts, which are presented clearly and straightforwardly. Secondary school students routinely master topics in mathematics and science that are beyond secondary school students in other countries. The curriculum could be characterised as being narrow but very deep.

The curriculum requires students at all levels to master a great deal of factual material, such as the different kinds of coal mined or location of rivers in countries on the other side of the world, or the dates of events that occurred long ago outside Japan.

The faithful implementation of this curriculum in every corner of Japan makes it much easier for everyone to hold the system accountable for results. The fact that *all* students are expected to master this very challenging curriculum, and at the same pace, adds to this transparency.

Textbooks in Japan are very lean and compact compared to their counterparts in other industrialised countries. They are very inexpensively produced paperbacks. There is a separate book for each semester, each under 100 pages. The central feature of these textbooks is their attention to the central concepts underlying the course. Teachers do not pick which parts of the text they will use. They are expected to teach the entire textbook, which is the surest sign that all Japanese students are expected to learn to the same standards. Until recently, MEXT had to approve all textbooks used in Japanese schools. Its role in textbook review has recently been significantly curtailed; now it only makes sure that the texts are neutral in content and that they treat the correct topics for the grade level for which they are written. However, given the clear, detailed and coherent nature of the Japanese curriculum, it is not surprising that the textbook publishers still stick very closely to it.

Teaching approaches: An emphasis on student engagement

At first glance, the Japanese approach to instruction violates the most common sense principles. The classes are large by Western standards – 35 to 45 students in a class – and most instruction is for the whole class. There is less instructional technology than in many other countries and fewer instructional aids of other kinds. Students are not separated into ability groups; there are no special classes for the gifted, nor are students pushed ahead by a grade or more if they are perceived to be exceptionally able. Similarly, students are not held back if they are having difficulty. Many students requiring special education are also assigned to the heterogeneous regular classrooms. The job of the teacher is to make sure that all students keep up with the curriculum and they manage to do this. Teachers meet frequently with one another to discuss students who are having difficulty and provide as much individual attention to those students as they can within the regular school day. It is not unusual for students who are not doing well in certain subjects to get extra instruction after school.

Some of the highest student performances in the world emerge from these classrooms. How do they do it? The primary goal of Japanese teachers is student engagement. Many people outside Japan imagine Japanese schools as quiet, intense places where students quietly copy down everything the teacher says. But that is not the reality. Visitors to Japanese elementary schools report that the level of noise is often well above that found in Western classrooms and the sound of laughter and intense conversation fills the school. Students can often be heard excitedly talking with one another as they tackle problems together. The visitor walks down the halls of these schools seeing students acting in plays, playing musical instruments alone and in ensembles or working through a tea ceremony.

The more engaged the students and the more students who are engaged, the happier are Japanese teachers. One might wonder how it could be possible for one teacher to engage 35 or more students in a wildly heterogeneous classroom when it is so hard for teachers in many other parts of the world to engage 25 students in more homogeneous classrooms. The answer is a major key to the success of Japanese education.

Maximising student engagement is central to the Japanese approach to classroom instruction. Japanese teachers put a great deal of thought into their lesson planning. For example, the lesson will often begin with the presentation of a practical problem (Box 6.1). Japanese teachers spend little time on drill or lecturing to their classes. The drilling is done at home or in cram school.

Box 6.1 **Engaging attention**

Harold Stevenson and Jim Stigler, in their classic and still relevant book *The Learning Gap* (1992), describe the beginning of a fifth grade Japanese mathematics class this way:

> The teacher walks in carrying a large paper bag full of clinking glass. Her entry into the classroom with a large paper bag is highly unusual, and by the time she has placed it on her desk, the students are regarding her with rapt attention…. She begins to pull out items… She removes a pitcher and a vase. A beer bottle evokes laughter and surprise. She soon has six containers lined up on her desk. The children watch intently. The teacher…poses a question: "I wonder which one would hold the most water?"

The rest of the class is devoted to answering that question. The students decide that the only way to answer it is to fill the containers with something, and they decide on water. They fill up buckets with water and the teacher asks what they should do next. Eventually the students decide that they should identify a small container and then find out how many small containers full of water it will take to fill each of the containers the teacher brought to class. They settle on a drinking cup. The teacher then divides the class into smaller groups. Each group fills its cups, measures how many cups it takes to fill the containers and records the results in a notebook. The teacher then records the answers in the form of a bar drawn to scale under each of the containers she brought to class. The bars form a bar graph when she is done. She never defines terms. She did not use the class to illustrate a concept or procedure she had already put on the blackboard.

As Stevenson and Stigler say:

> The lesson almost always begins with a practical problem [either of the sort just described] or with a word problem written on the blackboard….It is not uncommon for a…teacher to organise an entire lesson around a single problem. The teacher leads the children to recognise what is known and what is unknown, and directs the student's attention to the critical parts of the problem. Teachers attempt to see that all the children understand the problem, and even mechanics, such as mathematical computation, and are presented in the context of solving the problem. Before ending the lesson, the teacher reviews what has been learned and relates it to the problem she posed at the beginning of the lesson.

The point of a Japanese teacher's questions is not to get the right answer but to make her students think. The point of the lesson is not to cover the ground for the test – there is no test – but to stimulate real understanding.

Source: Stevenson, H. and J. Stigler (1992), *The Learning Gap*, Summit Books, New York.

Another very important feature of Japanese instruction, which also has implications for the use of whole group instruction, is the approach to mistakes. In many Western countries, mistakes are something to be avoided. Students who produce right answers quickly are rewarded and those who do not are often ignored or punished.

In Japan, a teacher will present a problem and ask her students to work on it. As they do so, she walks up and down the rows looking at the approaches taken by the students to the solution of the problem she posed. After a while, she will call on several children to go to the front of the classroom and copy their work onto the blackboard. Some of those that she picked will produce the right answer and some will not. She will ask the class to offer their views on the approach picked by the student at the board. If a student thinks it will not work, that student is asked why and must give an answer that is grounded in mathematical reasoning. The students discover that some answers are wrong for interesting reasons and these reasons are discussed at length. Sometimes they discover that there is more than one approach to answering the question posed and they discuss why some solutions are more efficient than others, but others might be more interesting. In this way, they arrive at a much deeper understanding of the mathematics that underlie the solution to the problem and become much more adept at using mathematics to solve problems.

School-home communication

Japanese students have a homeroom teacher and spend an hour a day in homeroom. The homeroom becomes that student's family in the school. Japanese homeroom teachers at elementary schools teach all subjects except specialised subjects like music and crafts. These homeroom teachers typically follow their classes through the grades for several years. They are required to regularly visit their students' families. Students often go to their teachers' homes on their teachers' birthdays. In the upper grades, the teachers are expected to provide academic and career and job counselling.

Teachers at elementary schools maintain communication with parents by means of a notebook that students shuttle between school and home. Even if a student has a non-academic problem, the teacher will communicate the nature of the problem to the parents, who are expected to provide appropriate support at home. If that is not sufficient, the teacher will advise the parents to consult other services available at municipal offices.

This entire approach is aided by the belief that effort and not ability is what primarily explains student achievement. If a student falls behind, it is not because he is not good at school work; it is because he is not working hard enough and the system has a solution to change this. It is also aided by the idea that many people, not just the student, are responsible for the poor performance of that student and poor performance student reflects badly on those people, too. This motivates both parent and teacher to do everything possible to make sure the student gets back on track.

During the American occupation of Japan after the Second World War, the Americans required Japan to start Parent-Teacher Associations of the kind that are common in the United States. In the ensuing years, while these organisations have grown less strong in the United States, in Japan they have grown stronger, providing parents with a real voice in education policy and local practice. They are not only organised at school level, but also at prefectural and national levels, with a seat on the Central Council on Education.

Long schooling hours and additional schooling

Time is an important factor in the good academic performance of Japanese students. Until recently, Japanese children went to public school six days a week. In addition, Japanese school children have several hours of homework a day. They have six weeks of vacation during the summer, which is less than students in many other parts of the world. Students often do their own research during vacations. The majority of Japanese students also spend considerable time in various forms of private instruction after the regular school day. These private schools range from offering help to students who are behind to catch up, to offering more advanced study than is available in the public school, to offering extracurricular activities or one-to-one or small group tutoring for some combination of these purposes.

The combined effect of all this additional study is that Japanese students have the equivalent of several more *years* of schooling by the time they finish high school than, say, the typical American student. And because of the briefer summer vacation, they retain much more of what they have learned as they go into the next year.

However, it is not all work and no play for Japanese students. Not all these extra hours are for instruction. Observers believe that one reason Japanese students seem more engaged when they are in class than students in many other countries is that they are given more breaks from instruction (*e.g.* see Stevenson and Stigler, 1992). Several times a day, students go outdoors, play, do exercises and let off plenty of steam. Nonetheless, they do hit the books more than students in many other countries and it shows.

Teacher quality

Surely one of the most important keys to the quality of education in Japan is the quality of its teachers. In many industrialised countries, teaching lies on the boundary between professional work and blue collar work. Having a teacher in the family is an emblem of the family's breakthrough from the lower middle-class to the middle class.

When the Meiji Restoration got underway in Japan and the state modernised the education system, most of the teachers were Samurai from Samurai schools, members of Japan's upper classes. In the Confucian tradition, great honour went to the teacher. As the modern era began and classless schools were created for the first time in Japan, those schools were staffed in significant numbers by members of the upper classes, and from that time forward, teaching has been a desirable occupation in Japan.

According to Teiichi Sato in an interview for this report, "After WWII, as incomes began to rise across the board, the government worried that respect for teachers would decline. Prime Minister Tanaka decided to raise compulsory school teacher salaries to 30% higher than other public servants. While this has gradually eroded, teachers' salaries are on par with other civil servants. This made a difference in the quality of teachers ever since." Teachers are still, by law, among the highest paid of Japan's civil servants. When they start their service, they are paid as well as novice engineers. But it is not the pay alone that attracts competent young people to teaching; it is primarily the high regard in which teachers are held. Teaching is a highly desirable job – there are seven applicants for every teaching position in Japan.

To become a teacher, students must attend a ministry-certified teacher education programme at a university or junior college. Japan also has some national teacher training universities with model schools attached to support teacher training for new teachers. Teaching practice is a common part of all teacher education programmes.

Prefectures, like other employers in Japan, are prepared to make major investments in their new teachers to make sure they have the necessary skills to succeed. They assume that these new employees come to them with the necessary applied intelligence but not necessarily the required job skills. So, similar to other employers, they take responsibility for providing an induction programme that provides a sustained opportunity to apprentice with experienced master teachers before being expected to teach full time. The induction period lasts a full year, and the master teachers are given the year off from their teaching jobs to supervise their apprentices. Once a teacher is inducted into the regular teaching work force, the law requires teachers to take certain additional training (after 10 years of service). Teachers can also apply for paid leave to take masters' degrees at graduate schools. The ministry also offers various training programmes for prefectural trainers at its national centre.

The most interesting aspect of teacher development occurs on the job. In addition to the central importance of the design of the lesson in Japanese instruction, "lesson study" in the development of the Japanese teaching profession is also crucial.

> [From the time they begin their career right to its end, Japanese teachers] are required to perfect their teaching methods through interaction with other teachers....Experienced [teachers] assume responsibility for advising and guiding their young colleagues. Head teachers [principals] organise meetings to discuss teaching techniques.... Meetings at each school are supplemented by informal district-wide study groups... [Teachers work together designing lesson plans.] After they finish a plan, one teacher from the group teaches the lesson to her students while the other teachers look on. Afterward, the group meets again to evaluate the teachers' performance and to make suggestions for improvement...Teachers from other schools are invited to visit the school and observe the lessons being taught. The visitors rate the lessons, and the teacher with the best lesson is declared the winner. (Stevenson and Stigler, 1992)

This practice is entirely consistent with the way teams work in private industry. It also reflects the Japanese focus on relying on groups to get work done. But it has a profound impact on the practice of teaching. Indeed, it is the best hope for the continual, sustained improvement of teaching practice. It brings the work of teaching out from behind the closed door of the classroom and the individual teacher and opens it up for inspection and critique by colleagues. There is very strong teacher accountability in Japan, not in the form of formalised accountability to the bureaucracy, but instead an intimate and very real accountability to one's colleagues. Because they do not want to let the group down, teachers work hard to develop superior lesson plans, to teach them well, and to provide sound and useful critiques when it is their colleague's turn to demonstrate their lesson plans to them.

Carefully-targeted financial resources

The Japanese spend less on their schools than a number of other OECD countries (Figure 6.2), but get better results. One reason is that they spend their money differently. Japanese schools are built to ministry designs – they are perfectly functional but very plain. They are not architectural symbols of community pride and lack many of the special features found in schools in other advanced industrial countries. School administration is typically confined to a principal, an assistant principal, one janitor and a nurse. There is no cafeteria – students serve the meals from a central kitchen to their teacher and classmates in the classroom. The students are also responsible for cleaning their classrooms. As noted above, textbooks are very simply produced in paperback format and are much smaller than in many other industrialised countries. At every point, the Japanese have made sure that the money they spend on educating their children goes as much as possible on teachers and on instruction, so it is no surprise that a much greater proportion of total funding is spent on these factors than is the case in many other countries (Stevenson and Stigler, 1992).

A focus on equity

It has already been pointed out that there is no tracking in Japanese schools, classes are heterogeneous and no student is held back or promoted on account of ability. Furthermore, all are expected to master the same demanding curriculum. This is a powerful formula for equity in terms of outcomes. What is particularly impressive about this approach is that the expected outcomes are not set at the lowest common denominator, but at the top of the range of possible outcomes worldwide.*

There is a widely-shared belief in Japan that these policies achieve the greatest good for the greatest number and the results bear this out. The system is set up so that high-achieving students can help lower-achieving students within a group, within a classroom and within a school. The research literature shows that all students are helped by this approach, because the students who teach and tutor learn as much or nearly as much in the process of tutoring as the recipient of the tutoring (Cohen *et al.*, 1982). This approach is consistent with Japanese values and contributes greatly to the generally high level of Japanese achievement.

Japanese teachers and principals are often reassigned to different schools by the prefectures. This is done, among other reasons, to make sure that the distribution of the most capable teachers among schools is fair and equitable. As Robert Fish remarked during his interview, "teachers and administrators are transferred regularly every few years so the same people are not in the same schools all of the time – there is a lot of levelling among schools."

All these and many other factors, including school finance, make for a high degree of equity in Japanese education.

A different approach to accountability and tests

The Japanese have virtually none of the trappings of formal Western accountability systems and they do not need them. Ryo Watanabe, Advisor to the Ministry of Education, Sports, Science and Technology, explains that until a few years ago there were no national tests in Japan. When Japan became concerned about the possibility of being overtaken in education accomplishment by the Koreans and Chinese, they instituted a national test of every student at the sixth grade and the ninth grade, but they have since decided to administer the test only to a sample of students to monitor the performance of the system.

The only tests are the entrance exams for high school and university. Everything hinges on a student's performance in these tests. Because newspapers publish results regularly everyone knows the rankings of these institutions as well as the record of each compulsory and middle school in getting their students into the right high schools and universities. The newspapers are full of statistics for each school, much like the statistics for popular sports teams in other parts of the world. Magazine articles are written about changes in the rankings and what they mean and why they occurred. Other stories are written about students who succeeded against all odds in the exams and others who did not.

But that is only half the story. As pointed out earlier, in Japanese society the burden for the fate of the student is shouldered in part by the family, the teachers, the faculty and even the students' classmates. Teachers' reputations among their peers rest on the success of their students in a way that has no parallel in many Western countries.

The system of homeroom teachers brings another level of accountability. Because these teachers follow the students through the grades, and because they are involved in their students' lives outside of school and are in constant communication with the parents, they are accountable to the parents in a unique way. This cannot be duplicated in countries where teachers do not follow students through the grades and where they are responsible for only one or a few subjects.

. . . .

* Note that there is no immigration policy in Japan. The very small number of people regarded as immigrants, mostly Koreans and Chinese, are not counted in the national education statistics. They make up less than 2% of the Japanese population. The one group thought of as a minority group is virtually indistinguishable from ethnic Japanese.

"It's always about what students are learning, agreeing on that, and holding yourself accountable and each other accountable by engaging in meaningful reviews of how students are doing," said Jim Stigler during his interview for this report. This is a system with a great deal of accountability, but it is not a system of administered accountability.

Some countries provide very strong incentives to students to take tough courses and to study hard in school, others do not, and many are somewhere in between. Japan is a leader in the first camp, and most observers believe that this factor is a major contributor to Japan's place in the international education league tables.

The Japanese system creates clear, powerful and tangible rewards for student academic success. In the short term, these come from parents, whose praise is highly valued by children. In the medium term, they come in the form of admission to the right high school or university, which is of paramount importance to the student and to everyone around her. And, finally, in this highly meritocratic society, they come from the value that employers and the society at large place on academic achievement.

All of this, of course, contributes mightily to "exam hell", the well-known pressure cooker that young people in Japan go through at exam time. People elsewhere in the world vow never to institute such high pressure exams because of the supposed high suicide rate of young Japanese people going through exam hell. The Japanese themselves say they don't like exam hell and would like to stop it.

Nevertheless, the suicide rate among young people among high school students is significantly higher in the United States than in Japan. And, in the OECD surveys of students, Japanese students tell the researchers that they are happier in school than students in most other OECD countries. It turns out that the image that much of the rest of the world has of Japanese students under relentless pressure to produce and somehow being robbed of their childhood in the process, is not a view that is shared by the Japanese students themselves. It is possible, it seems, to construct a system in which students are highly motivated to succeed in school without depriving them of a happy school experience.

HOW JAPAN'S EDUCATION SYSTEM IS CHANGING TO MEET TODAY'S CHALLENGES

No country's education system stands still for very long. Over the last two decades, there has been a rising chorus of criticism about Japan's education system, especially concerns over a deficit in encouraging creativity and innovation and whether Japan can maintain its top place in the international league table of student achievement. Other concerns centre on an apparent erosion of moral and group values. We will deal with each in turn.

Creativity and the group versus the individual

Many experts from Western nations visited Japan shortly after the 1995 Third International Mathematics and Science Study (TIMSS) revealed that it was among a handful of East Asian nations that topped the charts (Mullis, et al., 1998). The Western experts came to learn more about this success. But Japan was worried that such performance might still not translate into success in the business arena. Where, they asked, are our Nobel Prize winners? Where are the people with the kind of breakthrough ideas that create a new Microsoft or Apple, or even whole new industries? This made them wonder whether they should find out how the Western nations teach creativity.

However, the difference between Japan and the Western nations is not in how or whether they teach creativity. It is that the latter put more value on the individual than on the group, unlike Asian nations.

The idea that the emphasis on the individual is responsible for Western creativity can be uncomfortable to many Asians. They value social order highly and see the high crime rates and general social disorder in many Western nations as simply unacceptable. On the other hand, many people in the West are not willing to pay the price Asians pay for their high levels of student achievement if it means giving up their "personal freedom".

But it is possible that this analysis is much too oversimplified and one-dimensional. It may be true that Asians are less likely than people from some Western countries to make breakthroughs and chart whole new courses for their industry or even create new industries. And this might well be because Asians typically defer to their elders and superiors publicly even if they have private reservations about their judgement, wait to take their moment in the sun until after their superiors are gone, do not like to criticise others openly, prefer to be modest rather than sing out their achievements, and value contribution to the group more highly than solo achievements. In Asia there is a saying that "the nail that sticks out gets hammered down".

Nevertheless, Japan has built one of the best educated, most flexible, fastest learning and uniformly high calibre workforces in the world. The nation is brilliant at the continuous improvement of products and processes and capable of very high quality production on a vast scale. Who is to say which is more important, the occasional breakthrough or continuous improvement of almost all aspects?

And we should unpack a little further the assumption that Japan is short on creativity and innovation. After all, Japan ranks very highly on the Global Innovation Index, falling just behind South Korea and the United States in the latest report (INSEAD, 2010).

In any case, Japan is responding to the criticism by demanding high student achievement, as measured by assessments like PISA, and a greater measure of capacity for creativity and innovation.

Maintaining the social fabric and student enthusiasm

The creativity issue, while important, was not the only education challenge on the minds of the Japanese over the last decade or so. Other concerns centred on signs that the strong sense of family and group values were becoming weaker. Some of these concerns are described below:

> [There is]…a spreading tendency among youth to neglect society. This tendency is not totally unrelated with young people's declining association with society. It can be traced partially to a social trend placing too much emphasis on individual freedom and rights….At home children have their own private room and…mobile phones and other information equipment allow them to avoid getting closely involved with family members… [T]here seems to be increasingly less time spent in peer groups outside and more time spent playing video games at home. This phenomenon of the thinning socialisation of children is thought to be leading to a decline in young people's sense of respect for rules and models and further aggravating their tendency to neglect society or recede into a "world of solitude". (Ministry of Education, Culture, Sports, Science and Technology, 2002)

These concerns combined with perceptions of an alarming decline in the educational functions of the family, leading to bullying, disruptions in the classroom, student absenteeism and even violence in the schools. While the incidence of these kinds of student behaviour was small compared to many Western countries, their increased presence in Japan was being noticed.

Other concerns were to do with:

> [T]he standardisation of education due to excessive egalitarianism and the cramming of too much knowledge into children has tended to push aside education geared more to fit the individuality and capabilities of children…,making classroom lessons boring to children with a quick understanding and difficult for children who need longer to understand. (Ministry of Education, Culture, Sports, Science and Technology, 2002)

And, finally, the Japanese were become alarmed by a threat to their continued dominance in generating and exploiting advanced technologies. They noted that while Japanese students continued to do as well as ever in international comparisons of achievement in mathematics and science, they were appearing to like science less than other students in similar countries the further they went in their schooling (Ministry of Education, Culture, Sports, Science and Technology, 2002).

A new reform agenda for the 21st century

These concerns eventually led to major new education policy initiatives in the early years of the 21st century. These included a sweeping piece of education reform legislation dubbed "Zest for Living", as well as the passing in 2006 of a new Fundamental Education Law – the first revision in 60 years.[2]

Zest for Living was a reaction against the Japanese's previously strict insistence on uniformity, specificity and direction from the top. The reform turned some of the functions of the ministry over to lower levels of government, reduced the number of credits that must be earned from required courses from 38 to 31, increased the amount of time given to optional courses, reduced the school week from six to five days (though schools are still open on Saturdays for extra-curricular activities and extra school work for those who want it), and reduced the curriculum emphasis on rote learning and memorisation in favour of experimentation, problem finding and problem solving.

The reform has also made it possible for the best students to enrol in university early and take college courses in high school. It has also allowed the use of criteria other than entrance exams results to determine entrance to Japanese colleges.

Schools were given greater discretion over their budgets and personnel. New measures were taken to evaluate teachers, and, especially, to commend and reward excellent teachers while transferring teachers with questionable track records to non-teaching positions.

Though the set curriculum has been shrunk overall, an important new required course has been added at all school levels, the Period of Integrated Study. The aim of this course is to:

i) foster children's ability and quality to find a theme, think, judge and solve a problem on their own; and *ii)* enable children to think about their own life, urging them to explore subjects with creativity and subjectivity and to solve problems through their own ways of learning and thinking. To this end, the Period of Integrated Study actively introduces experiential learning such as experience in nature, social life experience, observations, experiments, field study and investigation as well as problem-solving learning to learn about cross-sectional, comprehensive subjects like the environment, international understanding, information, health and welfare as well as subjects that interest students. (Ministry of Education, Culture, Sports, Science and Technology, 2002)

In order to maintain enthusiasm for mathematics and science, the Japanese felt the need to *i)* put more emphasis on experiential, problem-solving learning through observations, experiments and project studies; *ii)* reach out to universities, research institutes and museums for help in engaging students' interest in science; and *iii)* make the images of leading scientists and engineers more visible and appealing to students thinking about what careers they might pursue.

Overall, there has been a general loosening up of what many perceived to be a very rigid system. But the overall structure is still very much in place and the move towards more freedom has been made cautiously.

In order to address the fear about the dilution of Japanese values, not just among students, but also in Japanese families where the principal responsibility for Japanese education lies, the Japanese government rewrote the Japanese Fundamental Law of Education. The first Fundamental Law (of 1947) had put forward four principles:

- The idea of education seeking the "accomplishment of character building".

- Equal opportunities of education and equality of the sexes.

- A democratic and single track school system.

- Free, compulsory education under the 6-3 school system (six years of elementary school, three of middle school).

Implementing these principles took many years, but the result was the much-admired system described earlier. The new Fundamental Law on Education, passed in 2006, reflected on how much had changed since the last one. Life expectancy for men had gone from 50 to 79 years, for women from 54 to 85. The fertility rate had dropped from 4.5 to 1.3. The high school attendance rate had gone from 43% to 98%. University attendance had climbed from 10% to 49%. From a context in which 49% of workers were employed in agriculture and 30% in manufacturing and related industries, fewer than 5% were now employed in agriculture and more than 67% in manufacturing and related industries.

While acknowledging how much had changed, the new law reaffirms that Japanese values remained the same. In doing so, it lays out the ways in which education policy could enable Japan to adapt to the needs of the next century. It reaffirms the characteristically Japanese approach – so evident in the Meiji reforms – of learning what those countries with the best education systems are doing to adapt to changing requirements, of bringing attractive ideas back and adapting them to the Japanese context while remaining faithful to Japanese values.

It will take time before the Japanese know whether their new policies will yield the results they hope for. They continue to worry that other nations are catching up and might surpass them. They worry about slipping down the OECD PISA rankings. When it appears that that might be happening, critics want to revoke the reforms, while others advocate for patience.

LESSONS FROM JAPAN

This analysis has helped to identify principles and practices that may be universally instructive. The biggest hazard in borrowing ideas from different systems is the fact that so many system features work the way they do because of a specific context. Keeping a student in school for more hours will not work as well in a system with poor instructional practices as it does in a system with effective instructional practices. Recruiting better teachers will not work very well if they flee schools that are oppressive to work in, and so on.

With these cautions in mind, some observations about what might be learned from the Japanese experience are presented below. It is true that many features of the Japanese system can also be found in other East Asian countries, particularly those that share a common Confucian heritage. However, some are uniquely Japanese. The lessons derived from Japan's experience with education are useful for analytical purposes, but risk obscuring a very important aspect of the Japanese educational system. The deeper purposes of the system appear to go way beyond the development of students' cognitive capacities, to the development of members of a society with values based on ethical behaviour, meritocratic advancement and social cohesion. The entire system is aligned not just to produce high student achievement, but to help the whole country realise the values it holds most dear.

▪ Shared belief that education is the key to the country's future

Japan's total commitment to children is not just rhetoric, but a concrete and enduring priority, for which individuals and the nation as a whole are prepared to make real sacrifices. It is the main reason that Japan has access to a first rate teaching force, that Japanese students are superbly supported at home, and that the schools are well resourced. This commitment is the foundation of the Japanese system.

▪ Consistent international benchmarking

Japan is committed to continuous international benchmarking of education systems. From the Meiji government to the present, Japan has succeeded in no small measure because of its determination to know what the best performers are doing, and to adapt the best of what they find to the Japanese setting, weaving them together into a coherent and powerful whole.

▪ Incentives count – not just for teachers, but especially for students

Japanese students, from the youngest age and all the way through their entire working life, have very strong incentives to take tough courses and to work hard at them. Doing well in exams is a paramount requirement for getting a good job. In some ways, this is the core story of the Japanese education system. If those incentives were not present in Japan, the outcome would be very different. It is worth noting that other countries provide equally strong incentives for their students to take tough courses and work hard in school, but do not have students who are as happy in school as Japanese students are. These two factors together make for a nation full of people who want to learn all their lives.

▪ A coherent and focused curriculum

The Japanese have paid more attention to the details of the national curriculum than most other countries and they have insisted that this curriculum is actually taught. The curriculum is coherent, carefully focused on core topics and their deep conceptual exploration, logically sequenced, and set at a very high level of cognitive challenge. The result is that Japanese high school graduates have a level of mastery of the subjects that rivals that of college graduates in many Western countries.

▪ Effort and expectations

The Japanese, like most East Asians, believe that academic achievement is more a matter of effort than natural (genetically-endowed) ability. They therefore demand that the effort be made and have high expectations of all their students. Students of whom much is expected – all students – achieve well.

▪ Resource allocation priorities

The Japanese spend less on education than other industrialised nations, but they get more for that money. One of the many reasons for this is the careful way they allocate that money. Compared to other advanced industrial nations, they spend more on teachers and less on school buildings and facilities, non-teaching staff, central office specialists and administrators, full colour glossy textbooks and so on.

▪ Organisation of instruction

Unlike teachers in the rest of the world, Japanese teachers believe student performance is better with bigger classes, at least in certain subjects. This is because more students are likely to come up with a wider range of problem-solving strategies from which other students can learn. And the variety of ideas generated by more students can be used to spark lively discussions. In science classes, for example, there will be a wider range of outcomes from lab experiments that also can be used to explore problem solving strategies and promote deeper understanding of the topics under study. This also makes it possible for Japanese teachers to have more time to plan, to work with other teachers, to work one on one with students who need individual help, and to engage in lesson study, all of which also improve the outcome for students.

▪ High expectations for students of all abilities

Like most East Asian countries, Japan has roughly half the proportion of the student cohort assigned to special education as is the case in some Western countries. Some in the West have decried this as inattention to students who need and deserve extra help. That may be true in some cases, but there is a lot of evidence that many students assigned to special education classes in the West have very low levels of achievement despite being the recipients of much more spending, simply because their teachers have very low expectations for their achievement (see, for example, Gartner and Lipsky, 1989).

The description above of the Japanese approach to classroom instruction makes it clear that Japanese teachers, as in many other East Asian systems, work hard to adjust instruction to individual needs. The underlying assumption is that *all*, or very nearly all, students can learn to high standards. In many Western countries, where the assumption is that student achievement is a function of inherited learning capacity, some students who could be achieving at much higher levels do not do so because they are given a more diluted curriculum. In the case of special education students this can be taken to an extreme.

▪ Professional development of teachers: a powerful engine for student performance

Japan is a laboratory for the idea of continuous improvement of teaching practice. The incarnation of that idea in Japanese schools is lesson study. This practice undoubtedly contributes in important ways to the high quality of instruction in Japanese schools.

▪ Careful attention to school-to-work transition

Japan has an unusual and highly effective system for moving students into the workforce. The idea of lifetime employment makes it worthwhile for employers to invest heavily in the continued education and training of young people joining their workforce fresh from school or university. This system results in low rates of youth unemployment, and works well because students are already accustomed to working hard. It also produces workers who are used to being loyal team members, working collaboratively with others, showing up on time and working to deadlines. It produces students who know how to learn and are eager to learn and come to work with a prodigious set of skills. Other nations interested in workforce development might consider exploring how this system works in detail.

▪ A moral education for life

Again and again, the Japanese have asserted that the most important dimension of their system is the moral dimension: how people should behave and how they should relate to one another. The entire curriculum is suffused with the moral education agenda of the Japanese government. Though there are courses on moral education in primary schools, this agenda extends far beyond them. Even in high schools, where there are no specific courses on moral education, the national curriculum emphasises that all activities should take moral education into consideration. Everywhere in schools there is evidence of efforts to reward hard work and persistence, to praise students who take on a challenge, to engage students in serving their school and fellow students and to take responsibility for helping others, to reward modesty and to give others credit for one's own good work. In many different ways, students are taught to respect their elders and their teachers, to do what is right, to be orderly and organised. It is not hard to imagine how this sort of attention to common moral standards can affect many aspects of social life, from business ethics to health care, sustainable environment to crime. Some countries do this explicitly, some implicitly, but it is worth considering what might happen to a country that ignores this aspect of their children's education.

▪ Social capital as a powerful accountability mechanism

Some outside observers may believe that Japan has no formal accountability system because it does not use national tests to enforce accountability (test-based system of accountability). But there is very strong accountability in Japan. Students are very accountable to teachers and parents. Teachers are accountable to each other in a system in which all the teachers in the school know just how good or bad the other teachers' teaching really is because of lesson study process. Everyone knows how the high schools and universities are ranked and so everyone knows how to rank the institutions and teachers who prepare students for those high schools and universities. The performance of the students on those entrance exams is there for all to see in a world in which those results matter hugely.

WHERE IS JAPAN ON THE EDUCATIONAL CONTINUUM?

Japan is clearly among the world's most advanced industrial economies. It is among the world leaders for the development and application of the most advanced technological systems. This was one of the goals Japan set for itself in the Meiji Restoration; those who launched it realised from the start that those aims would not be achieved without a first rate, highly inclusive, aggressively meritocratic education system.

Japan has not followed exactly the education continuum described in Chapter 1 (Figure 1.1). It skipped the typical slow upgrading of teacher quality, having inherited a system from the Tokugawa era in which the Samurai class staffed the schools. It also bypassed the typical slow progression from a system of school organisation based on the usual feudal orders straight to one that makes it possible for students from every social class to gain access to elite education opportunities.

Japan was also ahead of many other nations in embracing at least some aspects of modern industrial work organisation, especially in how teachers work with one another in teams to improve instruction, and in the professional norms governing the work of teachers.

On the other hand, Japan has been reluctant to devolve authority to schools as aggressively as some other countries, and it also found it harder to create schools that develop independent, creative students than other countries. This may reflect a clash between the demands of a creative culture in which individual initiative is highly valued, and the Japanese culture in which the approval of the group is typically sought before aggressively advancing one's own ideas. Japan has found a distinctive path which is congruent with its values and commensurate with the economic and societal progress it desires to achieve.

While there may be specific features of the Japanese system that are unpalatable, it is a system which bears careful scrutiny. It has contributed to a country with very high levels of school and academic achievement. Its students enjoy school more than most. It has produced one of the world's best-educated and most productive workforces. It has exceptionally low crime rates and a very strong social order. It has high rates of citizen participation and a citizenry that has an unusually sophisticated grasp of political issues. Parents in Japan participate in their children's education and partner with teachers to an unusual degree. The country has one of the world's most admired curriculums. Though the system continues to evolve, the methods used to build this system should surely be considered by any country that wants to match its achievements.

■ Figure 6.2 ■
Japan: Profile data

Language(s)	Japanese (national language – not official language)
Population	127 567 900[3]
Youth population	13.3%[4] (OECD average 18.7%)
Elderly population	22.1%[5] (OECD average 14.4%)
Growth rate	0.06%[6] (OECD average 0.66%)[7]
Foreign-born population	1.7% (OECD average 12.9%)[8]
GDP per capita	USD 34 132[9] (OECD average 33 732)[10]
Economy-Origin of GDP	Service: 63.9%; Manufacturing: 18.6%; Other: 14.3%; Agriculture and forestry: 3.8% (2008)[11]
Unemployment	4.0% (2008)[12] (OECD average 6.1%)[13]
Youth unemployment	7.2% (2008) (OECD average 13.8%)[14]

Expenditure on education	3.4% of GDP (OECD average 5.2%)
	  2.5% on primary, secondary and post-secondary non-tertiary
	  0.6% on tertiary[15] education[16] (OECD average 3.5%; 1.2% respectively)
	
	9.4% of total government expenditure[17] (OECD average 13.3%)
	  6.8% on primary, secondary and post-secondary non-tertiary
	  1.7% on tertiary education[18] (OECD average 9%; 3.1% respectively)

Enrolment ratio, early childhood education	86%[19] (OECD average 71.5%)[20]
Enrolment ratio, primary education	100.7%[21] (OECD average 98.8%)[22]
Enrolment ratio, secondary education	98.3%[23] (OECD average 81.5%)[24]
Enrolment ratio, tertiary education	58%[25] (OECD average 24.9%)[26]
Students in primary education, by type of institution or mode of enrolment[27]	Public: 99% (OECD average 89.6%) Government-dependent private: no data[28] (OECD average 8.1%) Independent, private: 1% (OECD average 2.9%)
Students in lower secondary education, by type of institution or mode of enrolment[29]	Public 92.9% (OECD average 83.2%) Government-dependent private: no data[30] (OECD average 10.9%) Independent, private: 7.1% (OECD average 3.5%)
Students in upper secondary education, by type of institution or mode of enrolment[31]	Public: 69.2% (OECD average 82%) Government-dependent private: no data[32] (OECD average 13.6%) Independent, private: 30.8% (OECD average 5.5%)

Students in tertiary education, by type of institution or mode of enrolment[33]	Tertiary type B education:
	  Public: 7.3%
	  Government-dependent private: no data[34]
	  Independent-private: 92.7%
	  (OECD average Public: 61.8%
	  Government-dependent private : 19.2%
	  Independent-private: 16.6%)
	
	Tertiary type A education:
	  Public: 24.6%
	  Government-dependent private no data[35]
	  Independent-private: 75.4%
	  (OECD average Public: 77.1%
	  Government-dependent private : 9.6%
	  Independent-private: 15%)

Teachers' salaries	Average annual starting salary in lower secondary education: USD 27 545 (OECD average USD 30 750)[36] Ratio of salary in lower secondary education after 15 years of experience (minimum training) to GDP per capita: 1.44[37] (OECD average: 1.22)[38]
Upper secondary graduation rates	95% (OECD average 80%)[39]

StatLink ⌨ http://dx.doi.org/10.1787/888932366712

Interview partners

Robert Fish, Education Specialist, Japan Society.

Steve Heyneman, Professor, International Education Policy, Vanderbilt University.

Teiichi Sato, Advisor to the Ministry of Education, Culture, Sports, Science and Technology, Former (Administrative) Vice Minister of Education Culture, Sports, Science and Technology.

Andreas Schleicher, Head of Indicators and Analysis Section, OECD Education Directorate.

Jim Stigler, Professor, University of California Los Angeles.

Ryo Watanabe, Director of International Research and Co-operation, National Institute for Educational Research, Advisor to the ministry of Education, Sports, Science and Technology (and Former Administrative Vice Minister of Education, Sports, Science and Technology.

Correspondence in writing:
David Janes, Director of Foundation Grants and Assistant to the President, US-Japan Foundation

References

Arani, M. and **T. Fukaya** (2009), *Learning Beyond Boundaries: Japanese Teachers Learning to Reflect and Reflecting to Learn*, Child Research Net website, *www.childresearch.net/RESOURCE/RESEARCH/2009/ARANI.HTM*.

Auslin, M. (2009), "Can Japan Thrive – or Survive?", *American Enterprise Institute for Public Policy Research* (AEI), Vol. 1, No. 2, AEI, Washington, DC.

Channel News Asia (2010), *Japan Ruling Party Banks on Firebrand Female Minister for Votes*, Channelnewsasia.com, 8 July 2010, *www.channelnewsasia.com/stories/afp_asiapacific/view/1068283/1/.html*.

CIA (Central Intelligence Agency) (2010), *Japan: Country Background Information*, CIA World Factbook (online), Central Intelligence Agency, Washington DC, available at *www.cia.gov/library/publications/the-world-factbook/geos/ja.html*.

Cohen, P.A., J.A. Kulik and **C.L.C. Kulik** (1982), "Educational Outcomes of Tutoring: A Meta-Analysis of Findings," *American Educational Research Journal*, Summer 1982, Vol. 19, No. 2, pp. 237-248.

Crowell, T. (2010), "Japan's New Prime Minister Faces the Voters", *Asia Sentinel*, 6 July 2010.

Dewey, J. (1902), *The Child and the Curriculum*, The University of Chicago Press, Chicago.

Gartner, A. and **D. Lipsky** (1989), *The Yoke of Special Education: How to Break It*, monograph, National Center on Education and the Economy, Rochester, New York.

INSEAD (2010), *Global Innovation Index Report 2009-2010*, INSEAD Business School and the Confederation of Indian Industry, INSEAD, Fontainebleau, France.

Ito, H. and **J. Kurihara** (2010), "A Discourse on the New Kai'entai: A Scenario for a Revitalized Japan", *Cambridge Gazette*, Politico-Economic Commentaries No. 3, 17 March, Cambridge, MA.

Jansen, M. (2000), *The Making of Modern Japan*, Harvard University Press, Cambridge, MA.

Kaneko, M. (1992), "Higher Education and Employment in Japan: Trends and Issues", *RIHE International Publication Series* No. 5, Research Institute for Higher Education (RIHE), Hiroshima.

Kaneko, M. (1997), "Efficiency and Equity in Japanese Higher Education", *Higher Education*, No. 34, pp. 165-181.

Lehmann, J. (2010), "Corporate Japan is a Little Lost in Communication", *Taipei Times* 17 April, available at *www.taipeitimes.com/News/editorials/archives/2010/04/17/2003470763*.

Ministry of Education, Culture, Sports, Science and Technology (2002), *Educational Reform for the 21ˢᵗ Century*, White Paper, Ministry of Education, Culture, Sports, Science and Technology, Tokyo.

Mizukoshi, T. (2007), *Educational Reform in Japan: Retrospect and Prospect*, Osaka University, Osaka, available at *http://unpan1.un.org/intradoc/groups/public/documents/apcity/unpan011543.pdf*.

Ministry of Economy, Trade and Industry (2010), *The New Growth Strategy: Blueprint for Revitalizing Japan*, METI Cabinet Decision, 18 June, 2010.

MEXT (Ministry of Education, Culture, Sports, Science and Technology in Japan) (2005), *Redesigning Compulsory Education: Summary of the Report of the Central Council for Education*, National Education Policy, MEXT, Tokyo.

MEXT (2010), *Elementary and Secondary Education*, MEXT website, *www.mext.go.jp/English/shotou/index.htm*.

Monahan, A. (2010), "Japan Data Show Fragile Economy", *Wall Street Journal*, 9 July, available at *http://online.wsj.com/article/SB10001424052748703636404575353664100091340.html*.

Mullis, I.V.S., *et al.* (1998), *Mathematics and Science Achievement in the Final Year of Secondary School: IEA's Third International Mathematics and Science Study (TIMSS)*, TIMSS & PIRLS International Study Center, Boston College, Chestnut Hill, MA.

Mullis, I.V.S., *et al.* (2008), *TIMSS 2007 International Mathematics Report: Findings from IEA's Trends in International Mathematics and Science Study at the Fourth and Eighth Grades*, TIMSS & PIRLS International Study Center, Boston College, Chestnut Hill, MA.

Newby, H. *et al.* (2009), *OECD Reviews of Tertiary Education – Japan*, OECD Publishing.

OECD (2008), *Tertiary Education for the Knowledge Society: Volume 1*, OECD Publishing.

OECD (2009), *OECD Economic Surveys: Japan 2009*, OECD Publishing.

OECD (2010a), "Japan: Country Note", *Economic Policy Reforms: Going for Growth*, pp. 122-123, OECD Publishing.

OECD (2010b), "Japan – Economic Outlook 87 Country Summary", *OECD Economic Outlook,* No. 87, OECD Publishing.

OECD (2010c), *Supporting Japan's Policy Objectives: OECD's Contribution*, OECD Publishing.

OECD (2010d), *OECD Factbook 2010*, OECD Publishing.

OECD (2010e), *Employment Outlook*, OECD Publishing.

OECD (2010f), *Education at a Glance 2010*, OECD Publishing.

OECD (2010g), *PISA 2009 Volume I, What Students Know and Can Do: Student Performance in Reading, Mathematics and Science*, OECD Publishing.

Qi, J. (2009), "Globalization, Citizenship and Education Reform", paper presented at the *Annual Meeting of the American Educational Research Association*, San Diego, 13-17 April, 2009.

Rohlen, T. (1983), *Japan's High Schools*, University of California Press, Berkeley.

Siegel, A. (2004), "Telling Lessons from the TIMSS Videotape: Remarkable Teaching Practices as Recorded from Eighth-Grade Mathematics Classes in Japan, Germany, and the U.S.", in W. Evers and H. Walberg (eds.), *Testing Student Learning, Evaluating Teaching Effectiveness*, Hoover Press, Stanford, CA.

Stewart, D. (2010), "Slowing Japan's Galapagos Syndrome", *HuffPost Social News* website at *www.huffingtonpost.com/devin-stewart/slowing-japans-galapagos_b_557446.html*, 21 July, 2010.

Stevenson, H. and Stigler, J. (1992), *The Learning Gap*, Summit Books, New York.

White, M. (1988), *The Japanese Educational Challenge: A Commitment to Children*, The Free Press, New York.

Wieczorek, C. (2008), "Comparative Analysis of Educational Systems of American and Japanese Schools: Views and Visions", *Educational Horizons*, Vol. 86, No. 2, pp. 99-111.

Wong, A. *et al.* (2010), *Japanese Science and Technology Capacity: Expert Opinions and Recommendations*, RAND Technical Report, RAND Corporation, Santa Monica, CA, available at *www.cgi.rand.org/pubs/technical_reports/TR714/*.

Notes

1. For example, see Mullis *et al.* (2008).

2. This legislation had its origins in a 1996 Ministry of Education report called *Japanese Education in the Perspective of the 21st Century*. It focused on the need for problem solving capacity in students to think proactively and act autonomously.

3. OECD (2010d). Data from 2008.

4. OECD (2010d). Ratio of population aged less than 15 to the total population (data from 2008).

5. OECD (2010d). Ratio of population aged 65 and older to the total population (data from 2008).

6. OECD (2010d). Annual population growth rate (data from 2005; data not available for 2006-2007).

7. OECD (2010d). Annual population growth rate (data from 2005).

8. OECD (2010d). Foreign-born population as percent of the total population (data from 2007).

9. OECD (2010d). Current prices and PPPs (data from 2008).

10. OECD (2010d). Current prices and PPPs (data from 2008).

11. OECD (2009). Measured as percentage distribution of workers.

12. OECD (2010d). Total unemployment rates as percentage of total labour force (data from 2008).

13. OECD (2010d). Total unemployment rates as percentage of total labour force (data from 2008).

14. OECD (2010e). Unemployed as a percentage of the labour force in the age group: youth aged 15-24.

15. The OECD follows standard international conventions in using the term "tertiary education" to refer to all post-secondary programmes at ISCED levels 5B, 5A and 6, regardless of the institutions in which they are offered (OECD, 2008).

16. OECD (2010f). Public expenditure presented in this table includes public subsidies to households for living costs (scholarships and grants to students/households and students loans), which are not spent on educational institutions (data from 2006).

17. OECD (2010f).

18. OECD (2010f). Public expenditure presented in this table includes public subsidies to households for living costs (scholarships and grants to students/households and students loans), which are not spent on educational institutions (data from 2006).

19. OECD (2010f). Net enrolment rates of ages 4 and under as a percentage of the population aged 3 to 4 (data from 2008).

20. OECD (2010f). OECD average net enrolment rates of ages 4 and under as a percentage of the population aged 3 to 4 (year of reference – 2008).

21. OECD (2010f). Net enrolment rates of ages 5 to 14 as a percentage of the population aged 5 to 14 (data from 2008).

22. OECD (2010f). OECD average net enrolment rates of ages 5 to 14 as a percentage of the population aged 5 to 14 (year of reference – 2008).

23. EDStats *http://web.worldbank.org/*, gross enrolment ratio (data from 2008).

24. OECD (2010f). OECD average net enrolment rates of ages 15 to 19 as a percentage of the population aged 15 to 19 (year of reference – 2008).

25. EDStats *http://web.worldbank.org/*, gross enrolment ratio (data from 2008).

26. OECD (2010f). OECD average net enrolment rates of ages 20 to 29 as a percentage of the population aged 20 to 29, year of reference 2008. This figure includes all 20-29 year olds, including those in employment, etc. The gross enrolment ratio (GER), measured by the UN as the number of actual students enrolled/number of potential students enrolled, is generally higher. The GER for Japan in 2008 is 58%. (UIS).

27. OECD (2010f). Data from 2008.

28. Data is not applicable because category does not apply.

29. OECD (2010f). Data from 2008.

30. Data is not applicable because category does not apply.

31. OECD (2010f). Data from 2008.

32. Data is not applicable because category does not apply.

33. OECD (2010f). Data from 2008.

34. Data is not applicable because category does not apply.

35. Data is not applicable because category does not apply.

36. OECD (2010f). Starting salary/minimum training in USD adjusted for PPP (data from 2008).

37. OECD (2010f). Data from 2008.

38. OECD (2010f). Data from 2008.

39. OECD (2010f). Sum of upper secondary graduation rates for a single year of age (year of reference for OECD average – 2008).

7

Singapore: Rapid Improvement Followed by Strong Performance

Singapore is one of Asia's great success stories, transforming itself from a developing country to a modern industrial economy in one generation. During the last decade, Singapore's education system has remained consistently at or near the top of most major world education ranking systems. This chapter examines how this "tiny red dot" on the map has achieved and sustained so much, so quickly. From Singapore's beginning, education has been seen as central to building both the economy and the nation. The objective was to serve as the engine of human capital to drive economic growth. The ability of the government to successfully match supply with demand of education and skills is a major source of Singapore's competitive advantage. Other elements in its success include a clear vision and belief in the centrality of education for students and the nation; persistent political leadership and alignment between policy and practice; a focus on building teacher and leadership capacity to deliver reforms at the school level; ambitious standards and assessments; and a culture of continuous improvement and future orientation that benchmarks educational practices against the best in the world.

INTRODUCTION

When Singapore became independent in 1965, it was a poor, small (about 700 km²), tropical island with few natural resources, little fresh water, rapid population growth, substandard housing and recurring conflict among the ethnic and religious groups that made up its population. At that time there was no compulsory education and only a small number of high school and college graduates and skilled workers. Today, Singapore is a gleaming global hub of trade, finance and transportation. Its transformation "from third world to first" in one generation is one of Asia's great success stories (Yew, 2000).

All children in Singapore receive a minimum of 10 years of education in one of the country's 360 schools. Singapore's students were among the top in the world in mathematics and science on the Trends in International Math and Science Study (TIMSS) in 1995, 1999, 2003 and 2007. They came fourth in literacy in the 2006 Progress in International Reading Literacy Study (PIRLS). Their excellence is further underlined by the fact that Singapore was one of the top-performing countries in the 2009 PISA survey (Table 7.1 and Figure 7.1), the first PISA survey in which it participated. Singapore was rated as one of the best performing education systems in a 2007 McKinsey study of teachers (Barber and Mourshed, 2007), and was rated first in the 2007 *IMD World Competitiveness Yearbook* (IMD, 2007) for having an education system that best meets the needs of a competitive economy. At the higher education level, the National University of Singapore was ranked 34th in the world and 4th in Asia in the *Times Higher Education Supplement* Rankings of World Universities in 2010 (*Times Higher Education Supplement*, 2010). How has this little red dot on the map, as Singaporeans frequently refer to their country, a nation that is not even 50 years old, evolved from a backwater undeveloped economy into a world economic and educational leader in such a short period of time? What education policies and practices has Singapore employed? And are the lessons from Singapore's experience relevant for other countries? This chapter attempts to provide some answers to these questions. First, however, we look at the broader context.

Table 7.1   **Singapore's mean scores on reading, mathematics and science scales in PISA**

	PISA 2000	PISA 2003	PISA 2006	PISA 2009
	Mean score	Mean score	Mean score	Mean score
Reading				526
Mathematics				562
Science				542

Source: OECD (2010), *PISA 2009 Volume I, What Students Know and Can Do: Student Performance in Reading, Mathematics and Science*, OECD Publishing.
StatLink ᴍᴦˢᴾ http://dx.doi.org/10.1787/888932366731

Under British colonial rule, from 1819 onwards, Singapore developed as a major seaport at the mouth of the Malacca Straits, on the shipping lanes between Britain, India and China. During this period, it attracted large numbers of immigrants, primarily from southern China, India and the Malay Archipelago. At independence from Britain in 1959 and then separation from Malaysia in 1965, Singapore had no assets other than its deepwater port. There was no real economy, no defence, and simmering tensions with neighbouring countries. Moreover, it had to import most of its food, water and energy. The Republic of Singapore seemed an unlikely candidate to become a world-class economic and educational powerhouse.

The risks facing this nation at birth – the sense of political and economic vulnerability to larger countries and global changes – created a sense of urgency which influences policy to this day. Lee Kuan Yew, Singapore's first Prime Minister, set out two overarching goals: to build a modern economy and to create a sense of Singaporean national identity. He recruited the best and brightest people into his early government and sought to promote economic growth and job creation. In the 1960s, the emphasis was on attracting labour-intensive foreign manufacturing to provide jobs for its low-skilled workforce. In the 1970s and 1980s, a shift to more skill-intensive manufacturing led to an emphasis on technical fields. From the mid-1990s on, Singapore has sought to become a player in the global knowledge economy, encouraging more research- and innovation-intensive industry and seeking to attract scientists and scientific companies from around the globe. The results of the government's economic policies have been stunning – rapid economic growth to reach developed country levels and a per capita income in 2009 estimated at current market prices to be about SGP 52 000 (USD 39 000). One of the so-called Asian Tigers, Singapore is a free market, business-friendly and globally-oriented economy, shaped by an active and interventionist government.

The government of Singapore is a highly efficient, honest and flexible meritocracy with a strong focus on integrated strategic planning and detailed execution. "Dream, Design, Deliver" aptly characterises its approach to policy development and implementation. Singapore's small size and political stability (the same People's Action Party has ruled Singapore since Independence) have kept the vision of making Singapore a great global city constant, but have also enabled it to be versatile in responding to rapidly changing environments. With a small limited domestic market, Singapore has had to become highly integrated in the global economy. To survive several global recessions and the ever-present uncertainties of the global economy, continuous innovation has been essential.

With respect to Lee Kuan Yew's second goal of nation-building, early race riots led to a profound commitment to creating a multi-racial and multi-ethnic society. At independence, Singapore had multiple religious groups (Buddhist, Muslim, Taoist, Hindu and Christian); multiple ethnic groups (Singapore's population is about 74% Chinese, 13% Malay, 9% Indian and 3% other); and no common language. Nor did it have a common school system or a common curriculum. A series of measures were gradually put in place to realise the Singapore pledge: "One united people regardless of race, language or religion". Singapore recognises and teaches four official languages – Chinese, English, Malay and Tamil – although English is the language of government and, since 1978, the medium of instruction in schools.[1] Two years of compulsory national service unite different ethnic groups, as does the policy of mixing each group within the government-built housing where most Singaporeans live. This has helped avoid the racial and ethnic segregation that afflicts many countries. Schools play a major role in inculcating Singaporean values and character, and civic and moral education play a major role in schools. Honesty, commitment to excellence, teamwork, discipline, loyalty, humility, national pride and an emphasis on the common good have been instilled throughout government and society.

Lacking other resources, human resources were and still are seen as the island republic's most precious asset. Education was seen, from the beginning, as central to building both the economy and the nation. Its job was to deliver the human capital engine for economic growth and to create a sense of Singaporean identity. The economic goals of education have given education policy a very pragmatic bent and a strong focus on scientific and technical fields. Singapore's education system has evolved over the past 40 years in tandem with the changing economy.

SINGAPORE'S EDUCATION SYSTEM: THE PATH TO BECOMING A LEARNING NATION

Over the past 40 years, Singapore has been able to raise its education level from one similar to that of many developing countries to match the best in the OECD. The current system did not emerge perfectly-formed, but has developed in three broad phases as it was adapted to changing circumstances and ideas:

Survival-driven phase: 1959 to 1978

According to then Prime Minister Lee Kuan Yew, the aim of Singaporean education in its early days was to "produce a good man and a useful citizen". This first phase of education has been dubbed the "survival-driven" phase. In the late 1950s, 70% of GDP was from port and warehousing activities. This was not enough to sustain, let alone grow, the economy which was suffering from high population growth and significant unemployment. The government decided that there was a need to expand the industrial base and, because of the small size of the domestic market, to make it export-oriented. It set about trying to attract foreign manufacturers who needed low-skilled labour (*e.g.* textiles, garments, wood products), both to provide jobs and to gain expertise.

Prior to independence, only the affluent were educated. At independence, most of Singapore's two million people were illiterate and unskilled. Therefore the focus of this "survival" period was on expanding basic education as quickly as possible. Schools were built rapidly. Teachers were recruited on a large scale. The schools that had been established by different ethnic groups were merged into a single Singaporean education system. A bilingual policy was introduced so that all children would learn both their own language and English. A textbook agency was created to provide textbooks. The expansion was so rapid that universal primary education was attained in 1965 and universal lower secondary by the early 1970s. By the end of the "survival-driven phase", Singapore had created a national system of public education.

However, the quality of education was not very high. In the early 1970s, out of every 1 000 pupils entering primary grade one, only 444 reached secondary grade four after 10 years. And of these, only 350 (35% of the cohort) gained three or more passes in O-level examinations. A significant report by Dutch economic advisor Dr Albert Winsemius estimated that every year between 1970 and 1975, Singapore would be short of 500 engineers and 1 000 technical workers and would have a severe shortage of people with management skills (Lee, *et al.*, 2008). The oil crisis of 1973 and the increasing competition from other Asian countries for low-skilled, labour-intensive industry led to a growing realisation that Singapore's comparative advantage was eroding and that it needed to evolve to a higher-skill economy. However, a large number of policy changes and changes of ministers for education caused confusion. Teacher morale was low and there was considerable attrition. Although there were attempts to expand vocational education, it had low status and was viewed as a dumping ground. In 1979, a watershed education report highlighted the high dropout rates and low standards and ushered in the next phase of reform (Goh, 1979).

Efficiency-driven phase: 1979 to 1996

During this phase of education, the focus shifted. The government's economic strategy was to move Singapore from a third-league, labour-intensive economy to a second-league, capital and skill-intensive country. So in January 1979, a new education system was introduced. Singapore moved away from its earlier one-size-fits-all approach to schooling that would create multiple pathways for students in order to reduce the drop-out rate, improve quality and produce the more technically-skilled labour force needed to achieve the new economic goals. Streaming (tracking) based on academic ability was introduced, starting in elementary schools, with the goal of "enabling all students to reach their potential while recognising that all students do not grow academically at the same pace" (Ho Peng, interview conducted for this report). Students could have more time, for example, to complete different stages of schooling. The multiple pathways included three types of high school: *i)* academic high schools, which prepared students for college; *ii)* polytechnic high schools that focused on advanced occupational and technical training and that could also lead to college; and *iii)* technical institutes that focused on occupational and technical training for the lowest fifth of students. The Curriculum Development Institute of Singapore was established to produce high-quality textbooks and instructional materials for the different pathways. While streaming was unpopular when it was introduced, drop-out rates did, in fact, decline significantly: by 1986, only 6% of students were leaving school with fewer than 10 years of education.[2] The range of efforts to raise standards also yielded results: performance in the O-level English examinations went from a 60% failure rate to a 90% pass rate by 1984, and by 1995 Singapore led the world in mathematics and science on TIMSS.

As Singapore sought to attract companies with a more sophisticated technological base (*e.g.* silicon wafers, computers), a major goal of this second phase was to produce technical workers at all levels. Concerned about the low status of blue-collar jobs, from 1992 Singapore invested significantly in the Institute for Technical Education (ITE; Box 7.2). With a number of campuses around the city, the ITE provides high-quality technical and vocational education, with high-tech facilities and amenities that are comparable to those of modern universities elsewhere. Each technical field is advised by industries in that sector to keep it current with changing demands and new technologies. New programmes can be built for multinational companies looking to locate in Singapore. There has been strong market demand for ITE graduates, and it is possible for the top graduates from the ITE to go on to polytechnics and then to university. As a result of these changes, the image and attractiveness of vocational education vastly improved. At the top end of the technical workforce, the number of university and polytechnic places was also expanded during this period to increase the pool of scientists and engineers.

Ability-based, aspiration-driven phase: 1997 to the present day

By the early 1990s, the efficiency-driven education system had yielded clear results. But, as became clear during the Asian financial crisis of 1997, the world economy was shifting to a global knowledge economy. The competitive framework of nations was being redefined and national progress would increasingly be determined by the discovery and application of new and marketable ideas. The growth of the global knowledge economy required a paradigm shift in Singapore's education system towards a focus on innovation, creativity and research.

A key instrument as Singapore intentionally navigated towards the global knowledge economy has been the government Agency for Science, Technology and Research (A* Star), which provides generous funding for research and aims to attract top scientists and scientific companies. One million foreign nationals with scientific, technical or managerial skills have been encouraged to work in Singapore in international corporations and in higher education. Singapore's three universities, and especially the National University of Singapore and Nanyang Technological University, have research partnerships with leading universities around the world with a focus in selected fields, including bioinformatics, information sciences and medical technologies.

At the school level, Singapore created a new educational vision, "Thinking Schools, Learning Nation". This major milestone in Singapore's education journey recognised Prime Minister Goh Chok Tong's belief that "A nation's wealth in the 21st century will depend on the capacity of its people to learn" (Goh, 1979). "Thinking Schools represented a vision of a school system that can develop creative thinking skills, lifelong learning passion and nationalistic commitment in the young. Learning nation is a vision of learning as a national culture, where creativity and innovation flourish at every level of society" (Lee *et al.*, 2008).

Thinking Schools, Learning Nation encompassed a wide range of initiatives over a number of years that were designed to tailor education to the abilities and interests of students, to provide more flexibility and choice for students and to transform the structures of education. Career paths and incentives for teachers were revamped and teacher education upgraded, as described in more detail later. Curricula and assessment changes put greater emphasis on project work and creative thinking. A major resource commitment, involving three successive master plans, was made to information and communication technology (ICT) as an enabler of new kinds of self-directed and collaborative learning. A broader array of subject matter courses was created for students and a portfolio of different types of schools has been encouraged, specialising in arts, mathematics and science, and sports, as well as a number of independent schools. "We need a mountain range of excellence, not just one peak, to inspire all our young to find their passions and climb as far as they can," explained Tharman Shanmugaratnam, then minister for Education (cited in Lee *et al.*, 2008).

Major changes were also made in the management of schools. Moving away from the centralised top-down system of control, schools were organised into geographic clusters and given more autonomy. Cluster Superintendents – successful former principals – were appointed to mentor others and to promote innovation. Along with greater autonomy came new forms of accountability. The old inspection system was abolished and replaced with a school excellence model. It was felt that no single accountability model could fit all schools. Each school therefore sets its own goals and annually assesses its progress towards them against nine functional areas: five "enablers", as well as four results areas in academic performance (Ng, 2008).[3] Every six years there is an external review by the School Appraisal Branch of the ministry of Education. Greater autonomy for schools also led to a laser-like focus on identifying and developing highly effective school leaders who can lead school transformation. This is also described in more detail later.

In 2004, Prime Minister Lee Hsien Loong introduced the idea of "Teach Less, Learn More" as the next step under the Thinking Schools, Learning Nation umbrella. Its aim was to open up more "white space" in the curriculum to engage students more deeply in learning. Despite the system's widely-recognised successes, learners were still seen as too passive, overloaded with content, driven to perform, but not necessarily inspired. Teach Less, Learn More aims to "touch the hearts and engage the minds of learners by promoting a different learning paradigm in which there is less dependence on rote learning, repetitive tests and instruction, and more on engaged learning, discovery through experiences, differentiated teaching, learning of lifelong skills, and the building of character through innovative and effective teaching approaches and strategies." (Ho Peng, interview conducted for this report) Further moves in this direction were made in 2008 with an envisioning exercise that led to Curriculum 2015. According to Ho Peng, Director General of Education in the Singapore ministry of Education, this review asserted that the Singapore education system had strong holding power and important strengths in literacy, mathematics and science, and that these should remain. However, it needed to do better on the soft skills that enable future learning. In addition, "the overload of information has put a premium on the ability to do critical analysis. Working across cultures will require language skills and a larger world view" (Ng, 2008).

A review of primary schools in 2009 focused on the question of how each child's learning can be driven by their innate curiosity and love of play. Art, music and physical education (PE) are also being enhanced in the curriculum. Finally, Curriculum 2015 re-emphasises that education must be rooted in values: "Without a moral and ethical compass, all learning will come to nought. We must rebalance content, skills and character development to achieve a more holistic education," (Ng, 2008).

Current structure

In Singapore's education system today, students receive six years of primary education, and four to five years of secondary education, followed by two years at junior college, polytechnic or the Institute for Technical Education (Figure 7.1).[4]

Primary education consists of a four-year foundation stage during which all students follow a common curriculum that emphasises English, mother-tongue language and mathematics. Science is introduced from primary 3. Other subjects taught in primary school are civics and moral education, social studies, health, physical education, art and music.

■ Figure 7.1 ■
Singapore's education system organisation

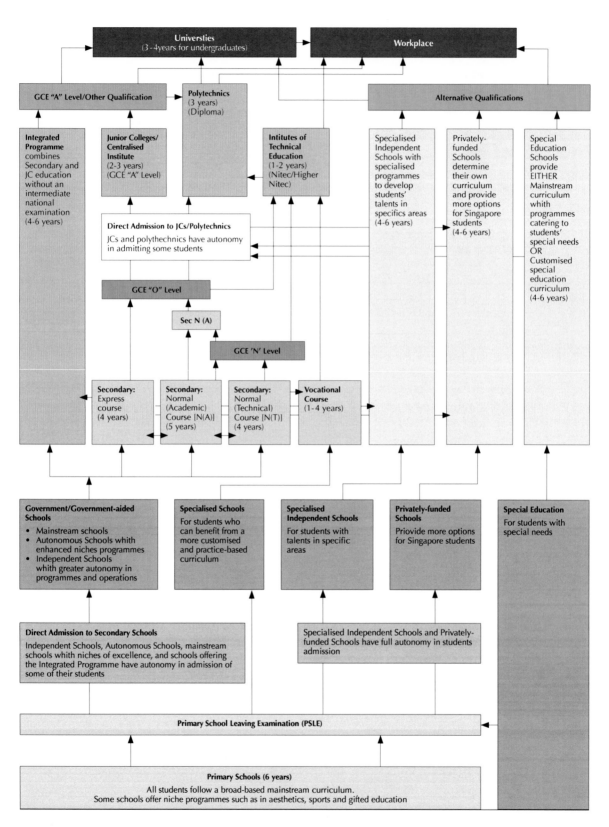

Source: Singapore Ministry of Education website: *www.moe.gov.sg/education/*.

Streaming, which was a key feature of the Singapore education system, was designed to allow students to progress at their own pace from primary 5 onwards. However, in 2008, streaming was replaced with subject-based banding. At the end of primary 6, all students sit for the Primary School Leaving Examination in English, mathematics, mother-tongue language and science. Based on the results of this examination, students are admitted to an express (60% of students), normal academic (25%) or normal technical (15%) course in secondary school.

Students in the express course follow a four-year programme culminating in the general certificate of education (GCE) O-level exam. Students in the normal academic course follow a four-year course to GCE N-level and may sit for O-levels in year five (Figure 7.2). The normal technical programme prepares students for technical higher education, jobs or the postsecondary ITE after a four-year programme leading to the GCE-N level. In recent years, more choice has been offered to students in secondary school, with a wider range of subjects at O-level and elective modules. Students who are clearly of university calibre may study in Integrated Programme Schools where they can skip O-levels; this arrangement allows them to engage in broader learning experiences that develop their leadership potential and capacity for creative thinking. There is now more horizontal mobility between courses, and students who do well are allowed to transfer between streams. The ratio among streams is further enhanced with students being able to follow subjects from a different stream. Schools specialising in sports, art and mathematics and science are also available, as well as a small number of independent schools.

After 10 years of general education, students go to post-secondary education, either junior colleges (31% of students), polytechnics (43%) or ITE (22%). Academically inclined students can take A-levels during this period and then proceed to university. Students may also take diploma courses in technical or business subjects at polytechnics. Many polytechnic graduates who have done well also go on to university. Students with GCE O- or N-levels can take skill-based certificates in technical or vocational subjects at ITE. Outstanding ITE graduates can also go on to polytechnics or universities. About 25% of a cohort goes on to university in Singapore (the number of places will rise to 30% in 2015). Many students also go abroad to university.

SINGAPORE'S SUCCESS IN EDUCATION

Singapore has pursued its vision of a high-quality education system over a long period of time and has accomplished significant improvements at each stage of its journey. What are some of the key features that have helped Singapore become so successful?

A forward-looking, integrated planning system

In modern Singapore, education has consistently been the building block for economic and national development. As Prime Minister Goh Chok Thong famously stated: "The wealth of a nation lies in its people."

Since the founding of the republic, the high value placed on education as the key to economic development and national cohesion in a country with no natural resources is evident in the statements of Singapore's senior leaders. But the statements about "nurturing every child" are not just political rhetoric. They have been accompanied by willingness at each stage to invest considerable financial resources in education. Education spending rose to 3.6% of GDP in 2010, approximately 20% of total government expenditure and second only to defence (Annex 7.A).

The linkage to economic development is tight and is driven from the top of the government. As Singapore evolved from an economy based on port and warehousing activities, through a low-wage, labour-intensive manufacturing economy, and then to a more capital and skill-intensive industry and finally to its current focus on knowledge-intensive industrial clusters, the education system was expected to ramp up the quality of its education and the supply of specific skills needed to make Singapore globally competitive.

Singapore has a uniquely integrated system of planning. The Manpower ministry works with various economic agencies (such as the Economic Development Board) responsible for promoting specific industry groups to identify critical manpower needs and project demands for future skills. These are then fed back both into pre-employment training and continuing education and training. In other countries, labour and education markets make these adjustments slowly over time, but the Singapore government believes that its manpower planning approach helps students to move faster into growing sectors, reduces oversupply in areas of declining demand more quickly, and targets public funds more efficiently for post-secondary education. The ministry of Education and the institutions of higher and post-secondary education then use these skill projections to inform their own education planning, especially for universities, polytechnics and technical institutes.

In short, the ability of the government to successfully manage supply and demand of education and skills is a major source of Singapore's competitive advantage. As Singapore seeks to become a global scientific hub, it is bringing together all aspects of the government – the finance ministry, economic development board, manpower ministry, education ministry, urban and environmental planning bodies, housing and immigration authorities – to create the next platform for Singapore's growth.

Singapore demonstrates strong alignment among policies and practices. One of the most striking things on visiting Singapore is that wherever one visits – whether the ministries of manpower, national development, community development, or education or the universities, technical institutes, or schools – he or she hears the same clear focus on the same bold outcomes: careful attention to implementation and evaluation, and orientation towards the future. "Milestone" courses bring together top officials from all the ministries to create a shared understanding of national goals. And a focus on effective implementation is shared throughout government. Because of the value placed on human resource development and the understanding of its critical relationship to economic development, Singapore's government provides a very clear vision of what is needed in education. This means that the ministry of Education can then design the policies and implement the practices that will meet this vision.

Close links between policy implementers, researchers and educators

At the institutional level, both policy coherence and implementation consistency are brought about by the very close tripartite relationship between the ministry of Education, the National Institute of Education (NIE, the country's only educator training institution), and the schools. The ministry is responsible for policy development, while NIE conducts research and provides pre-service training to educators. NIE's research is fed back to the ministry and is used to inform policy development (Box 7.1). Since NIE professors are regularly involved in ministry discussions and decisions, it is relatively easy for NIE's work to be aligned with ministry policies. NIE is Singapore's only institution for training prospective teachers, but professional in-service development for teachers comes from various institutions/sources besides NIE.

Box 7.1 **Integration in action**

An example of the benefits of close tripartite co-operation is demonstrated by how Singapore moved from a purely knowledge-transmission education model to one that emphasised creativity and self-directed learning ("Thinking Schools, Learning Nation" and "Teach Less, Learn More"). This was advanced through ministry of Education policy directives, through the regular monthly meetings of cluster superintendents with principals, and through the frequent professional development opportunities for teachers. The government also funded a long-term Centre for Research in Pedagogy and Practice at NIE, which examined current teaching practices in Singapore classrooms, piloted new approaches and fed back the necessary changes to the ministry. Recently, NIE has revamped its teacher education model to produce teachers who themselves have such 21st century literacy (Low, 2010) and can create learning environments that enable their students to develop them too. Changing pedagogy is always difficult, but in Singapore there is much less of a gap than in other countries between policy and classroom delivery, and between the intended and the actual curriculum.

Policies with the means to implement them

According to David Hogan, Senior Research Scientist at NIE and interviewed for this report, the degree of institutional alignment in Singapore is very unusual in global terms. Singapore is a "tightly coupled" system in which the key leaders of the ministry, NIE, and the schools share responsibility and accountability. Its remarkable strength is that no policy is announced without a plan for building the capacity to meet it. And while there is variation in performance within schools, there is relatively little variation between schools. By contrast, more loosely-coupled systems have a much harder time bringing about reform initiatives and are often typified by an endless parade of new, sometimes conflicting policies, without building the capacity to meet them. The teacher preparation programmes in universities are also often not aligned with the reform policies. Consequently, practitioners become cynical and wait for successive reform waves to pass. There are usually also large discrepancies between schools in the extent to which reforms are carried out.

In recent years, Singapore has loosened its tight coupling somewhat. More autonomy has been given to schools so as to encourage more innovation, and NIE has the appropriate independence for an institute in a modern research-oriented university. However, there are still strong alignment among the curriculum, examinations and assessments; incentives for students to work hard; and accountability measures for teachers and principals. This makes policy making and implementation much easier and more effective than in loosely-coupled systems, like the US's system.

The advantages of a small scale

In trying to understand Singapore's success, it is also important to remember its small size. Singapore's national education system is more like that of a city or a small state, with approximately 522 000 students and 360 schools. Professor Lee Sing Kong, Director of the NIE, likens it to "turning around a kayak rather than a battleship". The stability of the government and the broad popular consensus on the purposes of education also make it possible to pursue policies for long enough to see if they have any impact.

Commitment to equity and merit

Singapore has demonstrated an unfailing commitment to equity and meritocracy. Meritocracy was a cornerstone philosophy of Lee Kuan Yew's government from the beginning. He believed it was the most efficient way to run a government and the only way to create a peaceful multi-ethnic society. The system of education during colonial times was highly elitist and separated by ethnicity and religion; he sought to replace it with a universal state-funded system in which talent and hard work would prevail.

At independence, there were large attendance and achievement gaps between the Chinese population, on the one hand, and the Tamil and Malay populations on the other. These gaps threatened the political stability of Singapore, as well as its economic development. In the first education phase, the survival phase, rapid expansion of schooling led to universal elementary and lower secondary education by the early 1970s. In the second phase, streaming was introduced to reduce the high drop-out rates from the system; although controversial, it was successful. Today, with a secondary school graduation rate of 98% (10th grade), the gaps in educational attainment have been substantially reduced. However, there is more work to be done. In the TIMMS results, for example, Singapore has very high mean achievement scores in mathematics and science but there is also a long tail to the achievement distribution. On other measures too, socio-economic status has a significant impact on achievement.

According to Professor Lee, the measures Singapore has taken to reduce the achievement gap have been both social and educational. Believing that the causes of underachievement lie in social structures such as single-parent families, Singapore has developed a system of local town and community councils that identify families in need and can provide a range of support, including financial assistance. In addition, each of the ethnic communities has a self-help community group, the Malay *Mendaki*, Indian *Sinda* and Chinese CDAC. These organisations are funded by members of each community and support children in need.

It would be interesting to explore whether Singapore's housing policies have an impact on its small achievement gap; 80% of people live in government-built, but self-owned apartments and ethnic groups are deliberately mixed in each housing block. When asked about this during interviews for this report, Professor Lee said that he did not know of any empirical studies, but thought that it seemed plausible that being in a community with high expectations for academic achievement would have an overall positive effect on children.

On the educational side, children who require additional support in learning to read are identified through screening tests at the start of first grade. These children are provided with daily systematic intervention by teachers in small groups (8-10 students) in learning support programmes so that they do not fall behind. About 12-14% of children need such support for reading. The curriculum includes phonics and English language development since many of the children speak languages other than English at home. Learning support programmes also exist in mathematics. In addition, while most preschools in Singapore are privately funded, the government provides funding support to preschools that cater for low-income students.

In recent years, Singapore has replaced streaming in elementary schools with subject matter banding. It has also created more opportunities for students to move horizontally between streams at the secondary level and beyond – to create more flexibility in the system and to recognise "late bloomers". Another remarkable feature of the Singapore education system is the value, attention and resources it devotes to lower level achievers, not just high achievers. This focus on "levelling up", so that the lowest stream gets very high quality training, exemplifies the "many pathways" approach and is discussed in the section below on the Institute for Technical Education. The resources devoted to vocational and technical training are immense and the vocational and technical system is perhaps the best in the world – a significant element of the Singapore success story.

The goal of the education system is to nurture every child, no matter what their ability or achievement level. The ecology of education reform rests on these shared values. Parents want good opportunities for their children, high levels of social mobility and rising levels of income. The government has delivered them, so most parents believe in the fairness of the system.

We have avoided the large disparities in educational standards seen elsewhere, between schools for the privileged and those for the masses. We have achieved high standards across a spectrum of abilities, allowing a large proportion of Singaporeans to proceed to high-quality post-secondary and tertiary education". (Tharman Shanmugaratnam, former minister of Education, cited in Lee, *et al.,* 2008)

A strong focus on mathematics, science and technical skills

Singapore has focused on the universal development of strong mathematics, science and technical skills (Box 7.2). The country's solid foundation in mathematics and science for all students in the elementary grades seems to be a core part of students' later success. At the primary and secondary levels, mathematics and science are core subjects that every student must take. Mathematics begin when students enter school in primary 1 and science is taught from primary 3 onwards. Students have specialist teachers in mathematics and science from upper primary onwards. Deployment of teachers is a school-based decision. Some schools deploy specialist teachers in mathematics and science, although often teachers teach English, mathematics and science. From upper secondary onwards, there is a range of specialised mathematics courses at higher levels for those students who are interested. At the tertiary level, more than half the programmes are oriented towards science and technology.

Box 7.2 **Valuing technical education: The Institute for Technical Education**

In many countries, technical education is looked down upon as a dead-end option, of low quality and typically out of step with the changing needs of employers. But vocational education has been an important pathway in Singapore's journey to educational excellence. In 1992, Singapore took a hard look at its own poorly-regarded vocational education and decided to transform and reposition it so that it was not seen as a place of last resort. Dr Law Song Seng led the creation of the Institute for Technical Education (ITE), which transformed the content, quality and image of vocational education. Its goal was to build a world-class technical education institution that is "effective, relevant and responsive to the knowledge-based economy" (Lee *et al.,* 2008). ITE's founders brought in leaders with a broad vision and staff committed to caring for students. They completely revamped the curriculum and workforce certification system, developed courses in new industries and consolidated existing technical campuses into three mega campuses with a sophisticated technology base and close ties to international corporations. To combat the societal prejudice against less academically-inclined students, ITE promoted and rebranded its kind of "hands-on, minds-on, hearts-on" applied learning. The result has been a doubling of enrolment since 1995, and ITE students now constitute about 25% of the post-secondary cohort. More than 82% of students in 2009 completed their training and are placed in jobs. Pay levels for ITE graduates have also been strong, and the ITE track is now seen by students as a legitimate path to a bright future. Part of the reason for the success of the technical education at ITE is that students get a strong academic foundation early in their academic careers so they can acquire the more sophisticated skills required by leading edge employers. The ITE received the IBM Innovations Award in Transforming Government, given by the Ash Center for Democratic Governance and Innovation at the Harvard Kennedy School and has been recognised world-wide as a global leader in technical education.

The Singapore approach to mathematics is distinctive and has become well-known because of Singapore students' success. Developed in the 1980s from reviews of mathematics research around the world, and refined several times since, the Singapore national mathematics curriculum is based on the assumption that the role of the mathematics teacher is to instil "maths sense". In a Singapore classroom, the focus is not on one right answer; rather the goal is to help students understand how to solve a mathematics problem. The Singapore "Model Method" also makes extensive use of visual aids and visualisation to help students understand mathematics. The concrete-pictorial-abstract model used is based on an understanding of how children learn mathematics rather than on language considerations. Teachers cover far less material than in many other countries, but cover it in depth: the goal is to master mathematics concepts (Hong *et al.,* 2009). The level of mathematics in the Primary School Leaving Examination (grade 6), is approximately two years ahead of that in most US schools (Schmidt, 2005). Singapore mathematics also blurs the distinction between algebra and geometry. These concepts are integrated into basic mathematics instruction before students reach high school. Singapore teachers are all trained in how to teach the national mathematics curriculum and meet regularly to fine tune exercises and hone lessons.

The Singapore national science curriculum in primary and lower secondary grades focuses on developing the idea of science as inquiry through three domains: 1) knowledge, understanding and application; 2) skills and processes; and 3) ethics and attitudes. To awaken students' interest in science as a useful skill, inquiry projects are based on the roles played by science in daily life, society and the environment. Co-curricular activities such as mathematics and science fairs, competitions and learning trails (applying mathematics and science subjects in outdoor settings) are designed to generate interest among students. The DNA Centre at the Singapore Science Center develops hands-on activities for learning life sciences, and the government science agency A*STAR exposes students to research done by working scientists.

Human resource management which matches the demands of the system

The high quality of Singapore's workforce today is the result of deliberate policy actions, especially dating from the 1990s onwards. Since then, high-quality teachers and school leaders have formed the cornerstone of the education system and are a major reason for its high performance. Rather than focusing on just one element, Singapore has developed a comprehensive system for selecting, training, compensating and developing teachers and principals, thereby creating tremendous capacity at the point of education delivery. Key elements of that system are described below:

- *Recruitment:* Prospective teachers are carefully selected from the top one-third of the secondary school graduating class, by panels that include current principals. Strong academic ability is essential, as is commitment to the profession and to serving diverse student bodies. Prospective teachers receive a monthly stipend that is competitive with the monthly salary for fresh graduates in other fields. They must commit to teaching for at least three years. Interest in teaching is seeded early through teaching internships for high school students; there is also a system for mid-career entry, which is a way of bringing real-world experience to students.

- *Training:* All teachers receive training in the Singapore curriculum at the National Institute of Education (NIE) at Nanyang Technological University. They take either a diploma or a degree course depending on their level of education at entry. There is a close working relationship between NIE and the schools, where all new teachers are mentored for the first few years. As NIE's primary purpose is training all Singapore teachers, there are no divisions between arts and sciences and education faculties. Thus, according to Lee Sing Kong, the conflicting priorities that plague many Western teacher education programmes are less significant and there is a stronger focus on pedagogical content. NIE has put in place a matrix organisational structure whereby programme offices (*e.g.* Office for Teacher Education) liaise with individual academic groups in drawing up initial teacher training programmes. This means that these programmes are designed with the teacher in mind, rather than to suit the interests of the various academic departments. As such, there is a stronger focus on pedagogical content and greater synergies among modules within each programme.

- *Compensation:* The ministry of Education keeps a close watch on occupational starting salaries and adjusts the salaries for new teachers to ensure that teaching as seen as equally attractive as other occupations for new graduates. Teacher salaries do not increase as much over time as those in private sector jobs, but there are many other career opportunities within education for teachers. Teaching is also regarded as a 12-month position. There are retention bonuses and high-performing teachers can also earn significant amounts in performance bonuses.

- *Professional development:* In recognising the need for teachers to keep up with the rapid changes occurring in the world and to be able to constantly improve their practice, they are entitled to 100 hours of professional development per year. This may be undertaken in several ways. Courses at the National Institute of Education focus on subject matter and pedagogical knowledge and lead towards higher degrees or advanced diplomas. Much professional development is school-based, led by staff developers. Their job is to identify teaching-based problems in a school, for example, with a group's mathematics performance; or to introduce new practices such as project-based learning or new uses of ICT. Each school also has a fund through which it can support teacher growth, including developing fresh perspectives by going abroad to learn about aspects of education in other countries. Teacher networks and professional learning communities encourage peer-to-peer learning and the Academy of Singapore Teachers, was opened in September 2010 to further encourage teachers to continuously share best practices.

- *Performance appraisal*: Like every other profession in Singapore, teachers' performance is appraised annually by a number of people and against 16 different competencies. Included in this Enhanced Performance Management System is teachers' contribution to the academic and character development of the students in their charge, their collaboration with parents and community groups, and their contribution to their colleagues and the school as a whole. Teachers who do outstanding work receive a bonus from the school's bonus pool. This individual appraisal system sits within the context of great attention to the school's overall plan for educational excellence, since all students in Singapore have multiple teachers, even in primary school.

- *Career development*: Throughout Singapore, talent is identified and nurtured rather than being left to chance. After three years of teaching, teachers are assessed annually to see which of three career paths would best suit them – master teacher, specialist in curriculum or research or school leader. Each path has salary increments. Teachers with potential as school leaders are moved to middle management teams and receive training to prepare them for their new roles. Middle managers' performance is assessed for their potential to become vice principals, and later, principals. Each stage involves a range of experience and training to prepare candidates for school leadership and innovation.

- *Leadership selection and training*: Singapore has a clear understanding that high-quality teaching and strong school performance require effective leaders. Poor quality leadership is a key factor in teacher attrition in many countries (Ng, 2008). Singapore's approach to leadership is modelled on that found in large corporations. The key is not just the training programme, but the whole approach to identifying and developing talent. This differs from the US or UK approach, for example, in which a teacher can apply to train as a principal or school head, and then apply for a position in a school. In Singapore, young teachers are continuously assessed for their leadership potential and given opportunities to demonstrate and learn, for example, by serving on committees, then being promoted to head of department at a relatively young age. Some are transferred to the ministry for a period. After these experiences are monitored, potential principals are selected for interviews and go through leadership situational exercises. If they pass these, then they go to NIE for six months of executive leadership training, with their salaries paid. The process is comprehensive and intensive and includes an international study trip and a project on school innovation. Only 35 people per year are selected for the executive leadership training. Asked why Singapore uses the "select then train" rather than the "train then select" model, Professor Lee Sing Kong said that while the US/UK approach is feasible, it carries a higher risk. Singapore is very confident that they consistently have the best possible leaders for their schools and that there is a wide range of inputs into their selection. Principals are transferred between schools periodically as part of Singapore's continuous improvement strategy.

By putting its energy in the front end of recruiting high-quality people and giving them good training and continuing support, Singapore does not have the massive problems of attrition and persistently ineffective teachers and principals that plague many systems around the world. Teaching has developed into a competitive and well-regarded occupation. It is also now considered to be an honour to be a teacher in Singapore.

Finally, another critical aspect of the human resource capacity of the Singapore system is the civil service. Lee Kuan Yew's philosophy of governance was to recruit very high quality people into public service. Singapore has an extremely competent civil service, including in the ministry of Education. Top civil servants are carefully selected, well-trained (many at the best universities in the world), pragmatic, hard-working and well-paid. They have a global outlook, paying attention to education developments around the world, and are accustomed to using data and evidence in decision making. They have clear responsibility for the efficiency and effectiveness of the Singapore education system.

A system which is continuously being improved

While Singapore has devolved considerable authority to schools in recent years, it is still a centrally-driven government system. In many countries, government bureaucracies are sclerotic and move about as fast as molasses. But Singapore has inculcated an attitude and developed mechanisms for continuous improvement. In addition to the ties to economic planning that drove the major shifts in educational goals between the three major phases, there is a multitude of smaller changes and improvements being made, seemingly constantly.

Officials from the ministry and NIE frequently visit schools and have a good informal idea of what is going on, unlike the remote government departments and universities in many countries. They also pay a great deal of attention to data such as the School Cockpit and Student Hub data systems (internal ministry data systems).

There is now also a high level of investment in research relative to the size of the country (Hogan, interview conducted for this report). The publication of the policy document, "Thinking Schools, Learning Nation" in 1997 led to a national education research agenda costing SGP 50 million (about USD 38 million). A wide range of different types of research has been carried out, with research design decided by researchers not the government. One major set of studies was carried out by David Hogan, former Dean and now Senior Research Scientist at the Centre for Research on Pedagogy and Practices at NIE (and an interview partner for this report). This six-year effort aimed to understand to what extent modern pedagogical practices were being used in Singapore classrooms. It piloted interventions to demonstrate how to move classrooms from a predominantly knowledge transmission model to a 21st century model where students engage in complex knowledge construction. This research does not just sit on a shelf, but is regularly referred to in the ministry's deliberations.

Singapore has also made extensive use of international benchmarking as a tool for improvement and to move up the educational value chain. Staff of the ministry, NIE, and the schools all visit other systems and explore international best practice. Typically, the visits and research focus on very specific issues and on what does and doesn't work in implementing particular policies. For example:

- Singapore's mathematics curriculum was developed after reviewing mathematics research and practice from around the world.

- Recently, ministry of Education personnel visited the United States and other countries to examine language teaching to non-heritage speakers (heritage speakers of a language are those who learn it at home).

- Ministry staff have also visited a number of countries, including Hong Kong, Australia, Scotland and Sweden, to examine new kinds of assessments.

As a result, Singapore classrooms incorporate a wide range of pedagogical styles. Principals and master teachers are also encouraged to examine innovations in other countries and explore how they could be adapted for use in Singapore schools. A couple of years ago, a Washington Post reporter covered a visit by a group of Singapore principals to several schools in northern Virginia. "Why," she asked, "since Singapore is best in the world on the TIMSS international mathematics and science assessments, was a group of Singapore principals visiting science classes in northern Virginia schools?" The Singapore response: "There is no perfect system in the world. There are pockets of excellence in many places; the key is how to adapt them to the local context and implement them well."

Whenever Singapore seeks to create a new institution, it routinely benchmarks its planning to the best in the world. If Singapore is not in a position to create a world-class institution in a particular field, it will try to import the expertise. For example it did this in its recent partnerships with Duke University to create a new medical centre, and with Yale University to create a liberal arts college. All Singapore educational institutions – from the National University of Singapore ("A global university centred in Asia") to individual schools – are being encouraged to create global connections in order to develop "future-ready Singaporeans".

FUTURE CHALLENGES FOR SINGAPORE'S EDUCATION SYSTEM

While all these features have helped to make Singapore the world-class education system it is today, no system should rest on its laurels. Singapore educators are certainly not complacent. As a small country in an information- and innovation-driven globalised economy, it is always vulnerable to the actions of larger players. The education system is now expected to provide the kind of high-skilled creative, flexible workers needed for the 21st century economy. And the education system is responding through a wide variety of initiatives flowing from the "Thinking Schools, Learning Nation" paradigm shift. However, one constraint is the assessment system, which sets high standards but also inhibits innovation. The Singapore ministry of Education recognises the need for change but there is, as yet, no agreed approach for measuring the new kinds of complex 21st century skills. Just as importantly, it is difficult for teachers, themselves trained in a teacher-dominated pedagogy, to fundamentally change their practice. Singapore leaders worry that as the economy continues to grow and change and as these new demands are being placed on teachers, it may become harder to recruit the kind of top-level people into teaching that are needed to support the new kinds of learning. Finally, the economic changes associated with globalisation are increasing the levels of inequality in Singapore, as in many other countries. While Singapore has significantly closed its achievement gaps and focused on bringing up the lowest achievers, there is still a stronger correlation between socio-economic status and achievement than Singapore education leaders would like.

Still, Singapore has "built a system in which students are routinely taught by well-prepared teachers who work together to create high-quality curriculum, supported by appropriate materials and assessments that enable ongoing learning for students, teachers and schools alike" (Darling-Hammond, 2010).

LESSONS FROM SINGAPORE

Singapore is both a "rapid improver" and a "continuing high performer". To those who believe that large-scale change in educational performance is not possible, Singapore has shown several times over that significant change *is* possible. Singapore has developed a high-quality system in terms of educational retention, quality and efficiency. To become and remain high-performing, countries need a policy infrastructure that drives performance and builds the capacity for educators to deliver it in schools. Singapore has developed both. Where Singapore is today is no accident. It is the result of several decades of judicious policy and effective implementation. On the spectrum of national reform models, Singapore's is both comprehensive – the goal has been to move the whole system – and public policy-driven.

While the small-scale and tightly-coupled nature of the education system in Singapore may make its approaches seem inapplicable elsewhere, in fact, Singapore is the size of many states/ provinces or large cities in other countries. Many of its principles and practices *are* applicable to countries of a different scale and governance structure, although their implementation would have to take a different form. Some of the key lessons learned from Singapore are as follows:

▪ Vision and leadership

Leaders with a bold long-term vision of the role of education in a society and economy are essential for creating educational excellence. Changing any system takes five to ten years – where there are frequent changes of political leadership, a guiding coalition needs to be created to keep the vision moving forward rather than having a change of direction with every change of government.

▪ Alignment of the education system to economic development goals

The strong link between education and economic development in Singapore has kept investment in education a central priority, made education policies highly pragmatic, led to high-quality mathematics and science and also to world-class vocational/technical education – an area where most countries fail. It has also kept education dynamic, expecting to change as conditions change rather than being mired in the past. While the tightness of the link may not be possible in less planned economies, bringing together economic and education policy makers, business and education leaders to continually assess changes in economic conditions and how education and economic development could better work together would strengthen both.

▪ Coherence of the education system

In many countries there is an enormous gap between policies and their implementation at the school level. In Singapore, whenever a policy is developed or changed, there is enormous attention to the details of implementation – from the ministry of Education, to the National Institute of Education, cluster superintendents, principals and teachers. The result is a remarkable fidelity of implementation and relatively little variation across schools. While different mechanisms would be needed in larger, more multi-layered or decentralised systems, finding ways to bring greater alignment and to make all the parts work together is essential for producing results in the classroom in other nations' systems.

▪ Clear goals, rigorous standards and high-stakes gateways

Singapore's education system is extremely rigorous. The academic standards set by its Primary School Leaving Examination and O- and A-levels are as high as anywhere in the world. Rigour is the watchword. Students, teachers and principals all work very hard towards these important gateways. All students have a strong early foundation in the core subjects of mathematics, science, and literacy in two languages.

▪ Curriculum, instruction and assessment to match the standards

Singapore does not just establish high standards and then leave it to individual teachers to figure out how to achieve them. Serious attention to curriculum development has produced strong programmes in mathematics, science, technical education and languages, in particular, and has ensured that teachers are well-trained to teach them. Having been very successful as a knowledge transmission education system, Singapore is now working on curriculum, pedagogy and assessments that will lead to a greater focus on high-level, complex skills.

▪ High-quality teachers and principals

In earlier times, Singapore often had teacher shortages and was not always able to attract the highest quality people into teaching. In the 1990s, Singapore put in place a comprehensive and intensive human resource system to obtain high-quality teachers and school leaders who could meet its ambitions for its students. The system rests on active recruitment of talent, accompanied by coherent training and serious and continuing support. Education policies in Singapore today are less focused on structure and more on maintaining and increasing the quality of the educational professions. In 2007, it introduced the GROW package, consisting of measures to promote teacher Growth, Recognition, Opportunity and Well-Being.

▪ Strong central capacity and authority to act

The ministry of Education in Singapore is staffed by knowledgeable, pragmatic individuals, trained at some of the best universities in the world. They function in a culture of continuous improvement, constantly assessing what is and isn't working using both data and practitioner experience. They respect and are respected by professionals in the schools. Whilst countries vary in whether the locus of authority is at the national state/province or local level, whoever is charged with developing strategy and holding authority would do well to emulate the competence and capacity of the Singapore ministry of Education.

▪ Accountability

Singapore runs on performance management. Teachers, principals, ministry and NIE staff, students – all have incentives to work hard. To maintain the performance of teachers and principals, serious attention is paid to setting annual goals, to garnering the needed support to meet them and to assessing whether they have been met. Data on student performance are included, but so too are a range of other measures, such as contribution to school and community, and judgements by a number of senior practitioners. Reward and recognition systems include honours and salary bonuses. Individual appraisals take place within the context of school excellence plans. While no country believes it has got accountability exactly right, Singapore's system uses a wide range of indicators and involves a wide range of professionals in making judgements about the performance of adults in the system.

▪ Meritocratic values

Underpinning the whole Singaporean system is the belief – for students of all ethnic backgrounds and all ranges of ability – that education is the route to advancement and that hard work and effort pay off. The government has developed a wide range of educational and social policies to advance this goal, with early intervention and multiple pathways to education and career. The success of the government's economic and educational policies has brought about immense social mobility that has created a shared sense of national mission and made cultural support for education a near-universal value.

Lee Kuan Yew's greatest fear was that his little country would fall prey to the kinds of ethnic and religious rivalries that have thwarted the development of so many other societies. He realised that what happens in the schools could be one of the most important antidotes to this threat. So the schools became a theatre in which the country would do everything possible to give all students the skills and knowledge needed to succeed, independent of their socio-economic status. Singapore makes sure that every school has a fair share of the best teachers, and assigns their best teachers to the students who are struggling. They have been especially successful at training their teachers to diagnose student challenges and figure out how to address those challenges successfully. The belief that achieving high standards is a function of effort is stoutly embraced in Singapore and extends to the great emphasis put on raising the quality of the educators. Singapore is exemplary in the professional way that its teachers view their responsibilities. All these elements of policy have combined to produce a remarkably well-performing education system.

▪ Adaptation of proven practices from abroad

The design of Singapore's education system owes a lot to lessons from other parts of the world. Focused and universal use of international benchmarking and, more recently, significant funds for research, have enabled Singapore to move up the value chain and foster a culture in which it never stands still. This system recognises the rapidity of change around the world and has the capacity and inclination to learn and adapt. Singapore fosters a global outlook for everyone – teachers, principals, and students – who are expected to have "global awareness and cross-cultural skills" and to be "future-ready". In the words of Tan Chorh Chuan, President of the National University of Singapore, Singaporeans must be ready to "scale new heights in a changed world."

While the specific details of Singapore's education system remain particular to Singapore, the lessons from its education journey to excellence can be generalised for other settings. Success requires a clear vision and belief in the centrality of education for students and the nation; persistent political leadership and alignment between policy and practice; a focus on building teacher and leadership capacity to deliver reforms at the school level; ambitious standards and assessments; broad support in the population; and a culture of continuous improvement and future orientation that benchmarks educational practices against the best in the world.

WHERE IS SINGAPORE ON THE EDUCATIONAL CONTINUUM?

Singapore could be the "poster child" for the education development continuum described in Chapter 1 of this report (Figure 1.1). From a standing start in 1960, this small country has steadily advanced to the point at which it is now widely recognised as having one of the world's leading economies and most advanced and successful education systems. As this chapter has pointed out, that was no accident. Singapore's leaders were determined from the beginning not just to attract foreign business investment with low-cost labour, but to raise incomes in Singapore as rapidly and widely as possible. They knew that education and training had to be key elements in their strategy. More than any other country in the world, Singapore has aggressively pursued a policy of advancing in education and other arenas by systematically benchmarking the world's best performance and creating a world class education system based on what they have learned through their benchmarking.

■ Figure 7.2 ■
Singapore: Profile data

Language(s)	English (official language); Malay (national); Mandarin Chinese; Tamil[5]
Population	4 987 6006
Growth rate	5.3%[7] (OECD 0.68%; World 1.19%)[8]
Foreign-born population	Chinese: 74%; Malay: 13.4%; Indian: 9.2%; Other: 3.2%[9]
GDP per capita	USD 37 293[10]
Economy-Origin of GDP	Electronics, petroleum refining, chemicals, mechanical engineering and biomedical sciences sectors[11] Manufacturing: 26% (2005)[12]
Unemployment	3.2% (2008)[13] (OECD average 6.1%)[14]
Youth unemployment	Females (15-24 year-olds): 11.1%; Males (15-24 year-olds): 6.9% (2007)[15] (OECD average 13.8%)[16]
Expenditure on education	2.8% of GDP[17]; (OECD average 5.2%)[18]
	15.3% of total public expenditure[19], (OECD average 13.3%)[20] of which: 21% on primary education 33% on secondary education 34% on tertiary education 12% on unknown[21]
Enrolment ratio, early childhood education	No data (regional average 49%)[22]
Enrolment ratio, primary education	106.2% (2007)[23] (regional average 110%)[24]
Enrolment ratio, secondary education	76.4% (2007)[25] (regional average 77%)[26]
Enrolment ratio, tertiary[27] education	No data (regional average missing)[28]

StatLink ᘕᗕᔜ http://dx.doi.org/10.1787/888932366731

Interview partners

Ho, Peng, Director General of Education, Ministry of Education, Singapore

David Hogan, Principal Research Scientist, National Institute of Education, Singapore

Lee Sing Kong, Director, National Institute of Education, Singapore

Pang, Elizabeth. Programme Director, Literacy Development, Curriculum Planning and Development Division, Ministry of Education, Singapore

Wong, Siew Hoong, Director of Schools, Schools Division, Ministry of Education, Singapore

Representatives from the Economic Development Board, Housing Development Board, Ministry of Manpower, National University of Singapore, Ministry of National Development, NUS School of Science and Math, Victoria High School, Chongfu Primary School, Assumption Pathway School, Institute of Technical Education, National Institute of Education, A*Star, Keppel Offshore and Marine, and Marshall Cavendish who met with a delegation from North Carolina State Board of Education, January 2010.

References

Asia Society (2007), *Learning in a Global Age: Knowledge and Skills for a Flat World*, Asia Society, and New York.

Asia Society and Council of Chief State School Officers (2010), International Perspectives on U.S. Policy and Practice, Asia Society, New York, available at *http://asiasociety.org/files/learningwiththeworld.pdf*.

Barber, M. and Mourshed, M. (2007), *How the World's Best-Performing School Systems Come Out on Top*, McKinsey and Company, London.

Darling-Hammond, L. (2010), *The Flat World and Education*, Teachers College Press, New York.

Goh, K.S. (1979), *Report on the Ministry of Education 1978*, Singapore National Printers, Singapore.

Ng, E.H. (2008), *Speech by Dr Ng Eng Hen*, minister for Education, ministry of Education website, *www.moe.gov.sg*.

Hong, K.T., Mei, Y.S., and J. Lim (2009), *The Singapore Model Method for Learning Mathematics*, Curriculum Planning and Development Division, ministry of Education, Singapore.

IMD (2007), *IMD World Competitiveness Yearbook*, IMD, Lausanne.

Quek, G., *et al.* (eds) (2007), *TIMSS Encylopedia: A Guide to Mathematics and Science Education Around the World*, Vol 1, TIMSS, International Association for the Evaluation of Educational Achievement, Boston College, MA.

Lee, S.K., *et al.* (eds) (2008), *Toward a Better Future: Education and Training for Economic Development in Singapore since 1965*, The World Bank, Washington, DC.

Low, E. (2010), *Educating Teachers for the 21st Century: The Singapore Model*, National Institute of Education, Singapore.

National University of Singapore (2009), *State of the University 2009*, National University of Singapore, Singapore.

Ng, P.T. (2008), "Developing forward-looking and innovative school leaders: the Singapore Leaders in Education Program", *Journal of In-Service Education*, 34:2, 237-255.

OECD (2010), *PISA 2009 Volume I, What Students Know and Can Do: Student Performance in Reading, Mathematics and Science*, OECD Publishing.

Schmidt, W. (2005), "The Role of Curriculum", *American Educator* 23, No. 4.

Sclafani, S. and Lim, E. (2008), *Rethinking Human Capital in Education: Singapore as a Model for Human Development*, Aspen Institute, Washington, DC.

Stewart, V. (2010), *Dream, Design, Deliver: How Singapore Developed a High-Quality Teacher Workforce*, Phi Delta Kappa International, Bloomington, IN.

Times Higher Education Supplement (2010), *Rankings of World Universities 2010*, available online at *www.timeshighereducation. co.uk/world-university-rankings/*.

Yew, L.K. (2000), *From Third World to First*, Harper Collins, New York.

Notes

1. This evolution from four languages to English was a result of parental choice, rather than government decree.

2. This figure dropped to 4% in 2000, 2% in 2006 and 1.2% in 2009.

3. The five enablers are leadership, staff management, strategic planning, resources and student-focused processes. The four result areas are outcomes of holistic development of students (which includes academic results), staff well-being results, administrative and operational results and results of engagement with partners and community.

4. Polytechnic education lasts three years, leading to a diploma; ITE education lasts two to three years, depending on the qualifications sought.

5. "Republic of Singapore Independence Act". *http://statutes.agc.gov.sg/non_version/cgi-bin/cgi_getdata.pl?actno=1997-REVED-RSI&doctitle=REPUBLIC%20OF%20SINGAPORE%20INDEPENDENCE%20ACT%0A&date=latest&method=whole.*

6. *Population (Mid Year Estimates) & Land Area.* 2009. Statistics Singapore, *www.singstat.gov.sg/stats/keyind.html#popnarea.*

7. Annual population growth rate, 2008, *http://data.worldbank.org/country.*

8. OECD (2010), *OECD Factbook 2010*, OECD Publishing. Annual population growth rate (data from 2007).

9. http://www.singstat.gov.sg/

10. Singapore". International Monetary Fund. *http://www.imf.org/external/pubs/ft/weo/2010/01/weodata/weorept.aspx?sy=2007&ey=2010&scsm=1&ssd=1&sort=country&ds=.&br=1&c=576&s=NGDPD%2CNGDPDPC%2CPPPGDP%2CPPPPC%2CLP&grp=0&a=&pr.x=43&pr.y=11.*

11. Gross Domestic Product by Industry" (PDF). Singapore Department of Statistics. 2007. *http://www.singstat.gov.sg/stats/themes/economy/ess/essa11.pdf.*

12. Gross Domestic Product by Industry" (PDF). Singapore Department of Statistics. 2007. *http://www.singstat.gov.sg/stats/themes/economy/ess/essa11.pdf.*

13. *http://data.worldbank.org/country.*

14. OECD (2010), *OECD Factbook 2010*, OECD Publishing. Total unemployment rates as percentage of total labour force (data from 2008).

15. *http://data.worldbank.org/country.*

16. OECD (2010), *Employment Outlook*, OECD Publishing. Unemployed as a percentage of the labour force in the age group: youth aged 15-24, data from 2008.

17. UNESCO-UIS (2010), *UIS Statistics in Brief: Singapore*, data from 2008.

18. OECD (2010), *Education at a Glance 2010*, OECD Publishing.

19. UNESCO-UIS (2010), *UIS Statistics in Brief: Singapore*, data from 2008.

20. OECD (2010), *Education at a Glance 2010*, OECD Publishing.

21. UNESCO-UIS (2010), *UIS Statistics in Brief: Singapore*, data from 2008.

22. UNESCO-UIS (2010), *UIS Statistics in Brief: Singapore*. Percentage represents gross enrolment rate for MF; 2008 (regional average 49%).

23. *http://data.worldbank.org/country,* from UNESCO-UIS.

24. UNESCO-UIS (2010), *UIS Statistics in Brief: Singapore*. Percentage represents gross enrolment rate for MF; 2008 (regional average 110%).

25. *http://data.worldbank.org/country,* UNESCO-UIS (2010).

26. UNESCO-UIS (2010), *UIS Statistics in Brief: Singapore*. Percentage represents gross enrolment rate for MF; 2008 (regional average 77%).

27. The OECD follows standard international conventions in using the term "tertiary education" to refer to all post-secondary programmes at ISCED levels 5B, 5A and 6, regardless of the institutions in which they are offered. OECD (2008), *Tertiary Education for the Knowledge Society: Volume 1*, OECD Publishing.

28. UNESCO-UIS (2010), *UIS Statistics in Brief: Singapore*, data from 2008.

8
Brazil:
Encouraging Lessons
from a Large Federal System

Brazil has come a long way from its colonial days where education of the local population had not been a priority. This chapter describes how modern Brazil has extended public basic education to over 95% of the population; established assessment systems using an internationally benchmarked index that measures the progress of each school against a baseline; created student-based funding formulas that distribute funds fairly within states; used conditional cash transfers to lift poor families out of poverty through education; and encouraged states and municipalities to take actions to improve education in individual schools. Brazil has enjoyed 15 years of economic and political stability that has enabled it to develop a range of solid industries that now export to the world. Consumption is up among its citizens and this continues to fuel the Brazilian economy.

Average PISA scores for Brazil have improved in all subjects measured over the last ten years. While these scores are well below the OECD average and obviously do not place Brazil among the high-performing countries, such gains do suggest that Brazil has put in place federal policies based on a coherent vision that appear to be generating some consistent improvements. The challenge now is to raise the level of education of its citizens high enough to enable them to take commerce and industry to competitive levels in a global marketplace.

INTRODUCTION

In the early 1990s, Brazil suffered from hyperinflation and many of the other economic problems common to Latin American countries. Over the last 15 years Brazil has put its economic house in order, and has made enormous strides towards becoming a major player on the global economic scene.

But the poor quality of education of its people is holding Brazil back. Not until the 1990s did the people of this developing nation of 193 million inhabitants begin to believe in the importance of high quality public education for more than a small minority of its population.

The logic of economic development has forced the issue. As Brazil's economic position improves, it can no longer depend on cheap labour. Companies can train workers for basic functions, but moving from an economy based on commodities to one based on adding value to raw materials requires a much better educated workforce.

Since 1995, Brazil has developed education policies that have started to produce real improvement in student achievement. It has invested dramatically more resources in education, from 4% of GDP in 2000 to 5.2% of GDP in 2009 (Figure 8.2). And it is spending that money much more equitably than in the past. The addition of federal funds to states with poor resources has given their schools resources more comparable to those available to schools in wealthier states.

Average PISA scores for Brazil have improved in reading from 396 in 2000 to 412 in 2009; mathematics scores improved from 356 in 2003 to 386 in 2009; and science scores improved from 390 in 2006 to 405 in 2009 (Table 8.1, OECD, 2010). While these scores are well below the OECD average of 500 and obviously do not place Brazil among the high-performing countries, such gains do suggest that Brazil has put in place federal policies based on a coherent vision that appear to be generating some consistent improvements.

Table 8.1 **Brazil's mean scores on reading, mathematics and science scales in PISA**

	PISA 2000	PISA 2003	PISA 2006	PISA 2009
	Mean score	Mean score	Mean score	Mean score
Reading	396	403	393	412
Mathematics		356	370	386
Science			390	405

Source: OECD (2010), *PISA 2009 Volume I, What Students Know and Can Do: Student Performance in Reading, Mathematics and Science*, OECD Publishing.
StatLink ▄▜▄ http://dx.doi.org/10.1787/888932366750

This chapter explores some of the factors contributing to the improvement in Brazil's school system. Not all states are making significant progress, but this report will focus on three of those that are – Acre, Ceará and São Paulo – and look at how they have accomplished that. But first we look back at certain aspects of Brazil's history in order to grasp the scale of the obstacles that are being overcome and the size of the achievement.

BRAZIL'S EDUCATION SYSTEM: A BRIEF HISTORY

Four hundred years of slavery and dictatorship

When Portuguese explorers reached Brazil in 1500, there were around 4 million native Brazilians. Unfortunately, the Portuguese were more interested in extracting value from their conquest than colonising the new country. The new settlers were not accompanied by their families, so the society was run as a business, with little concern for the lives of the workers. Settlers conscripted the indigenous people to cut down trees for sending wood back to Europe and to build their plantations. One hundred years later, half the Indians were dead, so African slaves were imported from Guinea, Nigeria and Angola to work the land and to mine the gold.

When Brazil declared independence from Portugal in 1822, only very limited freedoms were provided to the slaves, and one million additional slaves were brought to Brazil in the 19th century. Brazil did not finally abolish slavery until 1888, the last country in the Americas to do so. Hence Brazil grew out of a slave-based agricultural system that did not require an educated population beyond the elite 10% who ran the country.

During the late 19th and early 20th centuries, five million Europeans from Germany, Japan, Italy, Poland, Portugal, and Spain emigrated to Brazil and settled primarily along the coast. Some had been given free land by large landowners to increase the agricultural workforce in the country after slavery was abolished, and others came as indentured servants to work on the plantations. Of the current population of 193 million, 53% are of European descent; 39% are of mixed European, African and Amerindian descent; 6% are of African descent; 0.5% are of Asian descent; 0.5% are Amerindians; and the remaining 1% are of other descent.

The beginnings of an education system: 1930s to 1980s

Brazil first created a Federal ministry of Education and Culture in 1930. School administration was left to the states and municipalities. At that time, education for children aged 7 to 10 was supposed to be universal and mandatory (Schwartzman, 2004). However, most did not attend school. The first state-owned university was established in São Paulo in 1934. Faculties of law, medicine and engineering had existed since 1822, and in 1937, several of these faculties in Rio de Janeiro came together as the first federal university, hundreds of years later than many other countries. The ministry established a curriculum for high schools as preparation for college, although few students were able to reach high school. In an economy based on raw materials and commodities, few thought there was any need for the majority of students to receive more than a few years of a very limited form of practical education.

In the 1950s, 64% of the population still lived in rural areas and over 50% were illiterate. Over the next 50 years, the population of the country nearly quadrupled, with many moving from rural to urban areas, but the quality of education did not improve much. In 1972, Brazil expanded mandatory education to include children from 7-14 years of age.

The foundations of a democratic system: 1980s to the present day

Throughout the 20th century Brazil has alternated between dictatorships and democracy. A military dictatorship lasting from 1964 to 1985 repressed political dialogue, and many intellectuals left the country. At the end of the dictatorship, the workers and intellectuals joined together with politicians and businessmen to create the constitution of 1988, which re-established a democratic structure with independent executive, legislative and judicial branches. The current minister of Education, Haddad, describes its goal as the establishment of a fair and just society, the eradication of poverty and marginalisation, the reduction of regional inequalities and the well being of all without any form of discrimination. The new constitution ensured the right to a free education for every child from 7 to 15 years of age, establishing 8 years of mandatory education. It called for greater decentralisation of finance and decision making to the school level. In addition, it fixed the minimum to be spent on education as 25% of state and municipal revenues and 18% at the federal level. Nevertheless, the schools still offered only three to four hours of instruction each day, in two or three shifts, to make the most of very limited resources.

The Brazilian economy was closed and highly protected until the early 1990s when globalisation began to have an impact. Government policies to encourage the development of new technologies and new industries required better-educated workers. The model of a small, highly-educated elite and uneducated masses no longer worked once Brazil opened itself to world trade and competition and the demand grew for social mobility through education.

However, Maria Pilar, Brazil's current Secretary of Basic Education, pointed out in interviews for this report that economic problems in the early 1990s led to the education budget being slashed by BRL 11 billion each year, so there was no money to expand educational opportunities. Jobs for the less educated were limited. Some unemployed and uneducated young people emigrated to Japan, Portugal, the United States and England to find better opportunities. She noted that recently many of these emigrees returned and started pressuring for the better quality education they had seen in other countries. However, their numbers were too low to have an impact on the system.

President Fernando Henrique Cardoso was elected in 1994 in part because, as minister of Finance in the former administration, he had created an economic plan that curbed the hyperinflation from 2000% down to less than 20%. His first action as president focused on putting the economy back on track. Cardoso privatised state businesses and used some of the funds to implement desperately-needed social reforms, especially in education. By 1995, 90% of all children were enrolled in primary school at age seven, but just half of these completed eighth grade. And it took them on average 12 years to complete grade eight because of high rates of grade repetition and dropout. As a result, in 2000 13.6% of the adult population were still totally illiterate. Nearly 75% were not functionally literate, meaning they were not able to read long texts, follow subtitles, compare two texts, carry out inferences and syntheses, solve mathematics problems, or understand maps and graphics.

Brazil faced enormous challenges after returning to democratic rule. The size of the country and the federal system made national reforms difficult. Repeated grade retentions across Brazil meant that the classes often had students whose ages spanned six years. This made day-to-day teaching more difficult and improving education outcomes more complex. While it was clear that economic development required a better-educated workforce, a focus on quantity of education without an equal focus on improving the quality of education would not enable the country to become competitive with developed countries across the world.

The context for reform: Poverty, poor quality teaching and an irrelevant curriculum

Given this backdrop, education has taken a prominent place in national, state and municipal agendas since the mid 1990s. But, while the country's leaders were making the improvement of education an important priority, simply getting by was a higher priority for many of the nation's households. The desire on the part of parents to provide their children with more education than they had had was competing with the need to put their children to work at an early age to help support the family. Child labour for children under 16 was outlawed in the constitution, but is still an important problem. In 2005, UNESCO reported that 88% of children aged between 5 and 15 were in school and did not work; however, 8.4% were going to school and working too, an average of 19 hours per week. The remainder were only working or staying at home. The northeast, north and south of the country had the highest percentages of working children, mainly in agriculture.

When secondary-aged children were surveyed in 2004 about why they were not in school, large numbers said they simply did not want to go to school (Neri and Buchmann, 2007). Simon Schwartzman, a leading political scientist in Brazil, explains that it is not the lure of jobs, but the poor quality of teaching and irrelevant curriculum that drive students out of school. One of the major problems is the high rate of grade repetition. In the beginning of each year the 7-14 age cohort is fully enrolled, but in the second semester students begin to abandon school when they see they have no chance of being promoted. Maria Helena Guimarães de Castro, former president of the National Institute for Educational Studies and Research Anísio Teixeira (INEP) and former Secretary of Education in São Paulo, noted that grade repetitions are the real problem. Data from *Pesquisa Nacional por Amostra de Domicílios* (PNAD), Brazil's main rural and urban household survey, show that dropouts begin in 6th grade. When students are 14 years old and are not in the grade corresponding to their age, they began to abandon school.

Even when children do go to school, parents who have had little or no education themselves find it hard to know if the quality of education is good or bad. So, while many parents have started to push for entry into schools, they make few demands for quality. Reynaldo Fernandes, former president of INEP, says that in the late 1990s the greatest pressure for improvements in the quality of education came from the elites even though they had no children in public schools. This was because they understood that the future development of the country depended upon a well-educated workforce and citizenry. But Jeffrey Puryear, Director of the Inter-American Dialogue's Partnership for Educational Revitalisation in the Americas, points out that without a broader demand from society for improved quality, policy making will be dominated by the professional educators who make their living in the system. They are more likely to resist changes to the *status quo* than to push for the reform required to lift student performance.

REFORM TAKES SHAPE

The election of Cardoso as President of Brazil in 1994 set the stage for real change in education policy. A number of important reforms were introduced by his federal Education minister Paulo Renato Souza. The 1996 Law of Directives and Bases of National Education (LDB) was developed with the involvement of professional educators and other stakeholders. It clarified the roles of the municipal, state and federal education systems. The federal government had responsibility for oversight of the entire education system and the states were responsible for the quality of education in the state. That said, municipalities were responsible for running schools for grades 1-4 (lower primary) and the state was responsible for grades 5-8 (upper primary) and high school (Figure 8.1). Because principalships were usually a political appointment awarded regardless of educational expertise, the LDB called for the democratisation of school governance, including involvement of the community in the election of principals. The law also provided schools with more autonomy by decentralising funding and decisions, by making curricula more flexible, and by encouraging higher teacher qualifications.

Increasing school funding

In 1996, Constitutional Amendment Number 14 created the Fund for Primary Education Administration and Development and for the Enhancement of Teacher Status, or FUNDEF. This was a major step towards a more equitable distribution of state and municipal tax funds. It replaced a population density formula that left the majority of funds in large cities, leaving little funding for small municipalities and their schools. With the addition of federal funding for resource-poor states, FUNDEF raised all elementary schools to minimum per-pupil allocations. Many politicians feared that schools would pad their numbers to get more money, so the federal government established a data system to collect and monitor enrolment figures. With the additional funds, poor states in the north and northeast could expand their school offerings and move towards universal elementary education. In addition, the federal government provided BRL 1 billion to support high schools by compensating the poorest states for their contribution to FUNDEF. With assistance from the Inter-American Development Bank, the Cardoso administration created the PROMED, a BRL 850 million fund from which grants were given to states to support high school education.

■ Figure 8.1 ■
Brazil's education system organisation

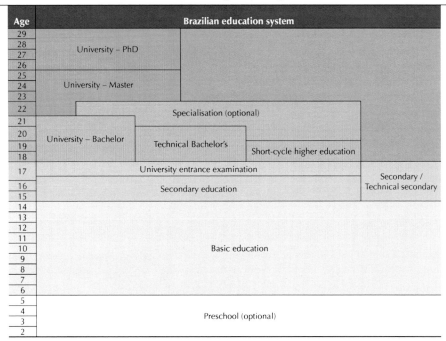

A second part of the FUNDEF reforms raised elementary school teachers' salaries by requiring that 60% of the funds going towards elementary education should be for salaries. Salaries rose on average 13%, but in the poor northeast they went up 60%. FUNDEF is therefore credited with increasing the years of teacher preparation and the number of working teachers as well as the enrolments in rural areas.

To address the problem posed by parents who preferred putting their children to work rather than sending them to school, the Cardoso government established a conditional cash transfer programme in 2001 (*Bolsa Escola*) which provided income subsidies to those parents who sent their children to school and got them essential medical checkups. It was limited to children aged 7-14, a fact which many criticised because the vast majority of these children were already in school. In fact, Schwartzman's study showed that *Bolsa Escola* did not increase student enrolment (Schwartzman, 2005). The real impact of this law, which everyone agreed was important, was to raise the poorest families up above subsistence level. This gave them the hope of continued social mobility and added to their interest in their children receiving an education. Teachers also found it a useful tool for enhancing attendance; they could threaten parents with withdrawal of the bonus if their children's attendance slipped.

In 2006, FUNDEF was renewed by the National Congress as the National Fund for the Maintenance and the Development of Basic Education (FUNDEB) which expanded the focus from elementary schools and high schools to include early childhood education and out-of-school youth and adult education. Getting this passed by the legislature involved major public campaigns supported by public-spirited groups. The creation of FUNDEF in 1996 had increased the resources dedicated to education from BRL 35.2 billion to BRL 50.7 billion per year.

The government of Luiz Ignacio Lula da Silva (known as Lula) added increased federal contributions from BRL 314 million in 2006 to BRL 4.5 billion in 2009. That raised total resources for education to BRL 55 billion, 5.2% of GDP (Figure 8.2). According to Fernandes, support for education is so strong that the legislature would have increased funding even further had the Finance minister not warned against the risk of inflation.

In 2004 the Lula presidency amalgamated the *Bolsa Escola* programme and a number of conditional cash transfers for health and nutrition under one programme, *Bolsa Família*, and increased the total amount of funding available. It is estimated that 5.7 million families were participating in the programmes by 2002; today the number has grown to 11 million. In other words, the programme has help shift 40 million people out of the lowest income level, along with higher minimum wages and better salaries due to economic growth. *Bolsa Família* added stipends for children aged between 15 and 17, which encouraged higher enrolment and attendance in high schools, where attendance is lowest. The combination of *Bolsa Família* and FUNDEB have made high school education a priority on both the supply and the demand sides.

Tackling teacher quality

One of the key problems in Brazilian education is the quality of its 1.5 million teachers. Since free public education for all students has been a recent development in Brazil, the teaching profession has not experienced the long tradition of development that occurred in developed countries over the last two centuries. In many areas of the country, teachers had only a high school education themselves, and that is still the case in some places. Reynaldo Fernandes, former president of INEP, says that it is difficult to attract trainee teachers from middle and upper class backgrounds because of the low pay, low standards and low status of the occupation. Working conditions include teaching two shifts a day, often in two different schools. Teacher absenteeism is high, partly because of the difficulty of getting from one school to the other, either in city traffic or along rural roads.

However, increases in teacher salaries since the introduction of FUNDEF have made teaching more attractive. Teachers now make almost 50% more than the average Brazilian worker, though they still make less than others with a secondary school education or better. The higher salaries, however, created a dual financial problem for states and municipalities: i) the increased cost of the salaries themselves; and ii) the increases in the cost of teacher pensions, which are generous and start being paid out after 25 years of service for women and 30 for men. It was estimated in 2000 that teacher pensions take up as much as half of some state education budgets.

The public universities saw teaching as a low status subject and buried it in their least competitive colleges. Much of the coursework was theoretical with an ideological focus that convinced teachers that societal problems, not poor teaching, were the primary source of student failure.

The 1996 Law of Directives and Bases of National Education (LDB) mandated that all teachers should have a university qualification by 2006. This law raised the educational requirements to become a teacher, and made both pre-service and in-service teacher training free. Still, much of the in-service teacher training offered is of low quality and done through instructional television and other forms of distance learning sent to the schools or through private colleges funded by the federal government. The options for increased credentials were a way for in-service teachers without degrees to get the additional credits needed, but it is not clear what it added to the teachers' knowledge and skills. The number of lay teachers without post-secondary credentials fell by 40% between 1995 and 2000. São Paulo Secretary of Education Souza says that today (2010) nearly half of the teachers in São Paulo are temporary teachers who have not met the full requirements for contract status.

The quality of teachers remains a major issue and a priority for the ministry. Minister Haddad is now trying to create standards for a career path based on credentials and a new examination that covers both content and pedagogy. Candidate teachers would have to pass it before entering into the teaching profession – a form of accreditation for new teachers. The examination will not be required for current teachers, but will lead to a better teacher corps in the future. The ministry has also collaborated with the federal universities to fund 100 000 teacher places at university, with a focus on mathematics and science teachers. While the federal government cannot dictate classroom-level changes in teacher preparation programmes because of universities' tradition of academic freedom, former INEP President Fernandes expects that the new examinations will influence the programmes to move from a philosophical and ideological focus to an emphasis on the knowledge and skills needed for success in the classroom. De Castro believes that the additional spaces should have been contingent upon changes in the curriculum for teacher training.

Setting curriculum standards

The federal government focused on improving the curriculum in 1996 by recommending curriculum parameters for all eight years of elementary education, as well as early childhood and youth and adult education. The specification of what students should know and be able to do at each grade level is left to states and municipalities. The federal government also provided new academic curriculum standards for 75% of the high school curriculum, leaving the other 25% to be defined locally in non-academic areas. At the high school level, the federal government formalised the trend in states to end the separation between academic and technical education programmes because the technical programme did not prepare students for the workplace and had simply become a home for students deemed unqualified for the academic programme. Instead states were to create comprehensive high schools for all students and provide options for short technical courses during or after high school for students and adults. While this is recommended by the federal government, it is up to states to transform current high schools or build and staff new high schools as needed.

Increasing high school completion

Although the 1996 education amendments called for moving to universal high school education, it was not until 2006 that 11 years of schooling became mandatory (this is now 12, because of the extension of primary school by one additional "year" prior to first grade). Unfortunately, even though many students have nine years of education, they often have only completed the requirements for grade 8 because of having to repeat years. Under the 1996 legislation, the states were encouraged to offer high school education. But given how long it took most students to complete eight grades – between 9 and 12 years – it is not surprising that most had had enough of school. Enrolment in high schools stands at about 70% of the cohort, even with *Bolsa Família* having added stipends to families for students between 15 and 17 years old. About 30% of students never finish basic education, and about half don't finish the three-year high school programme. A number of foundations in Brazil, notably the Instituto Airton Senna and the Roberto Marinho Foundation, have worked with states to create acceleration programmes for middle schools and high schools. These programmes work with over-aged students to ensure they develop basic academic skills, work skills, and citizenship skills before they leave school. Some states have created similar programmes at grade 9 to provide intensive interventions to raise students' skills to the level required for success in high school.

Focusing on quality

Reynaldo Fernandes, former President of INEP, says that there have been two major movements in education in the last 20 years: the efforts after the 1988 constitution concentrated on putting students in schools and avoiding grade repetition, while in the 2000s the battle was for quality. Participation in the 2000s in international comparative assessments of student achievement in Latin America and in PISA revealed clearly the low performance of Brazil's students. Maria Helena Guimarães de Castro, President of INEP in the administration of President Cardoso, describes how in 1999 President Cardoso was trying to decide whether to participate in TIMSS or PISA. He suspected that Brazil would come out at the bottom on PISA, but thought the country would benefit from participating in an assessment that tested students' ability to apply what they had learned in school and out of school. As an astute politician, he also understood the value of coming last for mobilising the country to demand better education.

Cardoso was right. Brazil was the lowest performing country on PISA 2000, coming in below Mexico. Over 50% of the students scored at or below Level One and less than 1% scored at the top level. Because grade repetitions meant that 15 year olds in Brazil might be in any grade from 5 to 11, INEP analysed scores for the 15 year olds who had completed grade 9 (modal grade) to see if student performance looked any better. It still found that only 25% of Brazilian students aged 15 at the end of 9th grade achieved at Level 3 or above on reading, as compared to 76% for South Korea, 59% for Spain and 30% for Mexico. The 2003 results were no better. In mathematics, fewer than 30% scored at Level 2 or above.

A large part of the problem is the absence of full-day schools. While the school year is 200 days long, the daily schedule is four hours long, with many schools holding two or three shifts a day. This does not give teachers sufficient time to teach the curriculum to a highly heterogeneous group of students of varying ages or to provide the individual attention that many students need, especially those who have already repeated one or two grades. FUNDEB provides a 25% increase in the per-student allocation for full-day schools, but that does not pay for the infrastructure costs of doubling the number of school buildings and hiring additional teachers. Some states are trying to move to full-day schools, but as Minister Haddad says, nationwide full-day schools will have to be the focus of the next ten-year plan. Mobilising the infrastructure and human resources will require an investment that is not currently feasible.

Creating accountability and setting targets

One of the most critical pieces of the 1996 reforms was to transform the National Institute for Educational Studies and Research into an independent statistical organisation responsible for national assessment and evaluation of education. It created the quality assurance programme for the country and made the results transparent to educators at the local, state and national levels as well as to parents, community members and the business community. It revised an earlier assessment system to create the Evaluation System for Basic Education (SAEB) for grades 4, 8 and 11 as well as the National Secondary Education Examination (ENEM) in Grade 11, which provides a qualification for further study or entry into the labour market.

The SAEB assessment system changed over time from a sample examination that was given to a representative group of students to a census examination called *Prova Brazil*, taken by all students in grades 4 and 8 in public urban schools. Only a sample of grade 11 students is assessed and so aggregate results for grade 11 in the public schools can be reported at the state, regional and national levels only. The use of promotion rates from grade to grade for each school ensures that students will not be held back or encouraged to drop out so that they don't bring down the average achievement scores. SAEB ensured that schools, municipalities and states would receive data that would tell them how their students fared on an examination of the curriculum standards in Portuguese and mathematics set by the federal government. In some states, such as São Paulo, training was provided to teachers so that they could use the test results to analyse individual classroom as well as grade and school-wide performance and develop strategies to improve teaching and learning.

In 2005 Education Minister Haddad led a national campaign of national and regional conferences and meetings to mobilise educators, governors and municipal officials to improve the quality of student achievement. Minister Haddad described his Education Development Plan as increasing funding for education, creating a base salary for teachers, establishing management guidelines for schools, and putting in place an evaluation system that would provide information on the achievement level of individual schools. Mandatory school attendance requirements were expanded to include 9th grade, but, more important, all municipalities signed on to a synthetic education index created and administered through INEP. The Basic Education Development Index (Box 8.1) tracks achievement on the *Prova Brazil* school results in grades 4 and 8 for public schools, and the SAEB results for private schools in grades 4, 8 and 11 and public schools in grade 11, as well as the promotion rates from grade to grade for each school. Leaders of each school know their targets and discuss strategies for improvement with teachers and the community as well as with their municipal supervisors. It is only after they have developed their strategies that they can effectively use the additional resources to achieve their targets.

Box 8.1 **The Basic Education Development Index: A major step forward for accountability**

Educators in Brazil see the Basic Education Development Index (IDEB), established in 2005, as a major step in increasing education accountability and providing a strong impetus for improving schools nationwide. Building on the technically well-regarded, sample-based, student assessment system (SAEB) launched in the 1990s (see above), the federal government launched IDEB as a census-based national assessment of Portuguese and mathematics achievement in grades 4 and 8. These data on learning outcomes are combined with assessment data for grade 11 students and student flow data (promotion, repetition and graduation rates) for Brazil's 200 000 schools. Each school's data are scaled as an index score from one to 10, with the levels aligned to scores on PISA. The use of the two factors, achievement and promotion to the next grade, ensures that schools are not given incentives to hold back students from the tested grades or to encourage them to drop out of school. The goal is to reach the average score on PISA in 2021, the year before the 200th anniversary of Brazilian independence.

The beauty of IDEB is that it is set individually for each primary school in the country, and will create a trajectory from a baseline in 2005 to where the school ideally reaches average PISA performance in 2021. For secondary schools, IDEB results are only aggregated at the state level, as the grade 11 assessment is sample-based. Educators accept the system because they believe it is fair to compare a school's performance against its past performance, rather than set one arbitrary score all schools should reach each year. Unlike many other countries, Brazil includes both public and private schools in the SAEB/*Prova Brazil* testing and the IDEB targets. The national performance has risen from 3.8 to 4.6 for primary schools (grades 1-4) between 2005 and 2009, outperforming the target of 4.2; from 3.5 to 4.0 in intermediate schools (grades 5-8), outperforming the target of 3.7; and from 3.4 to 3.6 in high school (grades 9-11), outperforming the target of 3.5. Further information on IDEB results is available from INEP.

According to Joaquim José Soares Neto, President of INEP, the real catalyst for school improvement in Brazil has been the setting of targets for each school through IDEB. Using IDEB, the federal government set targets for every two years for schools based on each school's trajectory, which begins where the school was in 2005 and ends at its expected arrival at OECD PISA average performance by 2021 (Box 8.1). The targets are the product of the rate of promotion and the average Portuguese and mathematics scores on SAEB/*Prova Brazil*. It results in a number from 1 to 10. It is the responsibility of each school, working with the municipality and monitored by the state, to develop a strategic improvement plan for progressing at the rate required by the trajectory which addresses the challenges the school currently faces.

The results of IDEB are published broadly, by school, by municipality, by state and for the nation as a whole, and parents and community members are aware of their school's ratings. The target and the actual performance are compared to see which schools are outperforming their targets. This has added public pressure to the push for improved school performance. Maria Pilar, Secretary of Basic Education at the ministry, recounted a visit to a school in a difficult area of Rio de Janeiro where 1 000 parents and community members were celebrating the release of the IDEB scores. Schools that show great progress are given more autonomy, while schools that remain low performers are given additional attention and assistance. In 2008, the ministry of Education prioritised work with the 1 827 lowest-performing municipalities, providing resources and technology.

The use of IDEB has changed the relationship between the ministry and municipalities and states, explained Jose Henrique Paim, Executive Secretary at the ministry. States have to diagnose the problems in low-performing schools and develop an improvement plan to send to the ministry. The plans organise the needs of the municipalities and identify the technical and financial resources needed from the ministry. In many cases, the focus of technical assistance is on improved management of the school and teacher training.

At the request of the ministry and in return for additional resources, the federal universities work with low-performing schools in their municipalities to assess the needs of individual schools and provide teacher training and assistance. The ministry also assists rural schools by providing equipment and materials, transportation services and technology to assure teacher training through the Open University. While the Open University courses are open to anyone with limited access to tertiary education, primary teachers have priority.

Rural schools account for 15% of the students in the country. Currently the one and two-classroom rural schools – those that have fewer than 30 students in all grades combined – are not included in the testing and accountability programmes. However, according to Paim, some were included in the 2009 testing to give the federal government some indication of the quality of the smallest rural schools.

Paim believes that for the first time IDEB allows the ministry to have a national map of performance from which to identify vulnerabilities and provide technical and monetary assistance. The ministry tracks the progress of the states to identify best practices that can be shared with other states. As in the United States, the argument is made that the states are laboratories of innovation in policies and practices. Monthly meetings of the state secretaries of education with the minister of Education provide a forum in which common issues and innovative solutions are discussed. Accountability extends to the secretaries as well, who are called in to talk with the federal ministry when the IDEB, SAEB and *Prova Brazil* results in their states are not improving.

The public nature of IDEB provides a real incentive for states to use effective strategies and improve student achievement. And it makes clear to parents where education is succeeding and where it is not. And since there is no choice of public schools in Brazil, parents in low-performing schools have an incentive to pressure the school to improve.

Given the low levels of achievement documented through IDEB and the lack of choice of public schools, most parents in the upper middle and elite classes opt for private schools. Overall 12% of Brazilian students attend private schools, with the largest numbers in the high schools, where they prepare for the university entrance examinations. The percentage of students in private high schools rises in wealthy areas and stands at over 20% in Brasilia, the federal district where average per capita incomes are highest.

To meet demand, private universities continue to grow and now represent nearly 90% of the higher education institutions and 75% of the higher education enrolment in Brazil. Even with that expansion, the limited number of university spaces enables only 15% of students to attend university; only 10% graduate because of their poor preparation in basic and secondary education. This is one more reason why it is difficult to motivate young people to strive for education excellence in high school.

INDUSTRY PERSPECTIVES ON EDUCATION IN BRAZIL

In Brazil's economy today, the most innovative and internationally-competitive companies are in aeronauticals, petro-chemicals, natural gas, mining, steel, paper and pulp, ethanol and meats. They have a workforce that averages nine years of education, with on-the-job education provided for the workers. For less competitive companies that do not export products or innovate, the workforce averages less than seven years of education. In the pharmaceutical industry, according to Cristalia's President, Ogari Pacheco, the production line workers can function with the training provided by the company; however, the challenge is finding the scientists who can create the compounds the company currently imports from China and India.

The Embraer corporation (Empresa Brasileira de Aeronáutica S.A.), a manufacturer of jet aircraft and Brazil's largest exporter from 1999 to 2001 and the second largest in 2002, 2003 and 2004, employed more than 16,000 people in 2009 of whom nearly 95% are based in Brazil. Eunice Rios, from Embraer's Human Resources Department, is more optimistic about recent graduates joining the firm:

> Employees who are newly hired bring a broader and more solid background as well as technical training and a more comprehensive world view. They are more connected to global trends and demonstrate a greater concern towards a job that makes sense for them and for their careers. They demonstrate a high level of ambition as well as energy and determination to achieve their goals. (Interview conducted for this report)

Embraer has created internal training programmes for employees at all levels of the organisation. For engineering graduates it has an 18-month specialisation programme to prepare aeronautical engineers. Since 2001, 1 100 engineers have completed the programme. When asked if universities are preparing graduates to be able to lead innovation efforts, she indicated that this was an area that needed improvement although it was at least on the universities' agendas. Finally, Rios noted that the link between education and development is critical to Brazil's future in a competitive global environment, and the *status quo* cannot get the country where it needs to go.

CASE STUDIES OF STATE EDUCATION REFORM

The states of Acre, Ceará, and São Paulo have seen significant growth in their IDEB scores in the last five years because they have built upon the federal mandates with their own state policies and services. While the funding from FUNDEF, and especially FUNDEB, had given them the required resources, each state recognised that it had to create instructional systems, teacher training and accountability systems with school support if it was going to improve student achievement. All three states have had highly effective leaders in key positions in the state secretariats. In some cases, they followed political appointees who had previously just maintained the *status quo*. All three states have had the benefit of consistent educational policies and leadership for a number of years: 11 years for Acre, 16 years for Ceará and 8 years for São Paulo. Not all states have professionalised their education systems. Many still select secretaries of education on a patronage basis and leave municipalities and state schools to their own devices. Since states have the legal authority to run their education systems as they see fit, the federal government cannot interfere. It can and does offer assistance to individual municipalities whose IDEB scores are the lowest in the country, but it cannot create effective state secretariats from the federal level.

State of Acre

Acre is one of the smallest states in Brazil, located in the far northwest in the Amazon forest. Over half of the population of 690 000 lives in two cities, Rio Bronco and Cruzeiro do Sul. The rest of the population lives in small cities and isolated areas. Acre was initially part of the Bolivian territory, and the annexation to Brazil was accomplished through diplomatic means in 1903. In the early 1900s immigrants fleeing droughts in northeastern Brazil settled in Acre. It owes its initial development to Goodyear's discovery of the process for making rubber into tyres and that remains one of its main areas of commerce. As competition from other countries reduced demand for rubber, development slowed. Acre finally became a Brazilian state in 1962. For the last 48 years, Acre has worked to establish itself economically with sustainable development projects and appreciation of the Amazon forest, one of its major assets.

The Secretary of Education in Acre, Maria Correa da Silva, has been in the secretariat since 1999 and says that education became a priority when she joined the new government team as director of basic education. In 1999, Acre ranked last in the country for education, there were no school improvement plans, school buildings were dilapidated, only 14 out of the 22 municipalities offered high school education, and only 27% of the teachers had a college education.

The education team started with teacher quality: working with teachers, they created a career plan and raised teacher salaries to a starting salary of BRL 1 200 per month (USD 680), which is 26% above the national minimum starting salary. They developed a teacher education programme with the federal university in Acre and provided training for teachers in the urban districts first and then the small cities and towns. FUNDEF funds were used to raise the level of teacher education for those without university education. Next they focused on infrastructure. They did not have the funds to renovate or rebuild all schools, but they defined standards for buildings and equipment for schools in urban, rural and indigenous areas so that they could develop cost estimates and create a budget for the work. Finally they guaranteed the opportunity for students in all municipalities to participate in high school education as well as youth and adult education. The illiteracy rate in Acre was nearly 25% in 2000; it is now under 14%.

In 2004, the team restructured the secretariat to be more responsive to schools, creating three functional areas: teaching and learning, resources, and management. The state decentralised supply budgets on a per-pupil basis and required school plans on how the funds would be spent. Some of the municipalities responsible for grades 1-5 decentralised funds at the same time, but the state could only mandate actions for the schools it runs, *i.e.* grades 6-9 and high school. It developed a partnership with the city of Rio Branco to focus on teacher education, with a non-governmental organisation providing training for teachers in both municipal and state schools. That took the improvement efforts a long way, since half of the students in the state are in Rio Branco. With teacher training underway, the state focused on quality of instruction in the classroom. It added co-ordinators for administration and pedagogy to the staffs of larger schools so the principal could lead the instructional team at the schools. Working with teachers, it developed a curriculum, "It's Time to Learn", for grades 1-5, and focused on literacy development for grades 1-2. One purpose of the new curriculum was to give students a strong start and reduce grade repetitions. This curriculum became part of the teacher training as well as the monitoring done by state supervisors. Since the secretariat worked with teachers from the beginning, there was little resistance. The results of external assessments, which showed that the students were learning more, provided the strongest argument for the changes.

Acre worked in partnership with the Roberto Marinho Foundation on two special programmes to accelerate the learning of students in grades 5-8 and high school who had experienced multiple grade repetitions. The PORANGA project provided curriculum and teaching materials focused on basic skills, work skills and citizenship skills. In addition, the state created the Book of Culture of Acre, which uses historical texts, poetry and photos of the inhabitants of that state to connect students to their culture. For students in isolated rural areas, it developed "Wings of the Forestinzenship" which provides relevant instructional materials for early childhood through high school.

Acre raised its IDEB index from 3.4 in 2005 to 4.3 in 2009 (for grade 4); from 3.5 in 2005 to 4.1 in 2009 (for grade 8); and from 3.2 in 2005 to 3.5 in 2009 (for grade 11). The secretary of education credits improvement to the continuity of policies since 1999, the close co-ordination with municipalities, and a consistent focus on classrooms, teachers and curriculum.

State of Ceará

Ceará is the 8th largest state in Brazil by population (8 million), although it is 17th by area. It is a poor state located on the northeast coast. The economy of Ceará was primarily cattle ranching, to provide plough animals for agriculture, and salt production from its northern beaches. By the 1980s, new investments enabled the state to start developing its 350 miles of Atlantic coast beaches and sand dunes as well as its mountains and valleys into one of Brazil's major eco-tourism attractions. Today over three-quarters of its population work in urban areas, with industry accounting for more than 35% of the jobs; and services, including tourism, for more than 55%. It also produces and exports leather products globally. While its economy is growing, the state still has few resources for development.

In terms of education, Ceará has been one of the lowest-performing states in the country. While it has been moving forward for the last 16 years in pursuit of a unified vision of what needed to be done, it was not achieving its goals until it received additional federal funding through FUNDEB in 2005. It is one of seven states whose resources were not sufficient prior to 2005 to bring per pupil funding to the federal minimum level. The education secretary for 1994-2002 became governor in 2003 and appointed his former deputy, Maria Izolda Cela de Arruda Coelho, as education secretary. Secretary of Education Coelho brought expertise in assessments and accountability as well as curriculum and professional development. She says that Ceará was one of the pioneering states working with the ministry of Education in 1993 to develop student assessment systems, but without integrating them into management reforms, they had little impact. Since 2005, she has used federal test results to guide management reforms by setting improvement goals for schools and providing required support services.

Coelho has established five axes for her work to support schools. Working with the federal university's centre for assessment and education development, she prepared and certified 100 professionals to work with teachers and principals in their improvement efforts. Coelho recognised that the problem with grade repetitions started in first grade, so she worked with municipalities to establish "Learning at the Right Age", an instructional programme to ensure students gained literacy and numeracy skills in grades 1 and 2. All municipalities signed on and worked with teachers to use curriculum, lesson plans and assessments structured for effective teaching in these grades. The state contracted an external assessment company to create a reading examination for every 2nd grader in the state, starting with benchmark testing in 2007 and repeated annually. In addition, 1st grade teachers received instruction in the use of formative assessments aligned to the grade 2 assessments. The state also established a matching funds programme for constructing early childhood centres. For every centre a municipality funded, the state funded one more. For poorer municipalities, the match required was much lower.

Following on from that experience, the state formed a partnership with the municipalities to expand the curriculum and training efforts. These included incentives to improve teacher salaries, a fair process for selecting principals based on expertise rather than political patronage, and support for more effective school organisation, including the use of multi-age classrooms in small schools. Coelho stressed that this was a partnership that did not encroach upon the autonomy of the municipalities in their grade 1-4 schools.

Coelho said that high schools have been historically low performing in Ceará, and they have been getting worse. Students arrive in 9th grade without the skills in Portuguese to read and interpret texts, so Coelho started an initiative to train 9th grade teachers in all subject areas to focus on reading comprehension and vocabulary development. While some teachers believe that students should not go to grade 9 until they have those skills, they recognise that the students will not make progress without them. For low-performing high schools, Coelho hired new principals and gave them a portfolio of data on the schools' past performance. The new principal then works with the instructional team at the school to develop a plan to submit to the secretary for approval. Superintendents from the secretariat monitor the plans on a bi-monthly basis.

Coelho established the Learning First initiative to address the high rates of dropout and repetition in the first year of high school. The secretariat worked with professors from the federal universities to develop interdisciplinary curriculum materials to close gaps in student background knowledge and improve reading and mathematics skills. These resources help students build the basic skills of reading comprehension, abstraction and problem solving. All high schools in Ceará received teachers' guides and student units for different disciplines, produced with funding from the ministry of Education.

Recognising that working conditions for teachers and students were problematic in many high schools, Coelho also used funds to focus on infrastructure, including establishing laboratories and sports areas where none had been available. She also ended centralised in-service teacher training in favour of offering it in the schools themselves so that it could more effectively meet the needs of individual schools.

Although high schools are still on double shifts, since 2008 Coelho has established 59 full-time (7:30 am to 5:00 pm) vocational schools across the state. They offer an integrated curriculum, both academic and technical, and students can choose which vocational fields to pursue. She plans to build an additional 52 of these as a way to motivate and prepare high-school aged students to stay in school. Students who get acceptable grades are also given computers as an incentive to stay in school. Coelho believes this is a way to close the technology gap for poor students and keep them motivated. The first participants graduate this year and will move into six-month internships in industry funded by the government at half the minimum wage. This gives employers a good opportunity to add to their staff at low cost and provide on-the-job training to future full-time employees. At the end of the internships, students will have the option to work full-time or to move onto higher education if they wish to do so.

To encourage improved performance, Coelho established an incentive programme for the 150 highest-performing schools in the state based on their IDEB scores. The high-performing schools get additional funds that can be used by the school for any purpose in the secretary's guidelines. The school submits a plan for how it will use the funds. In addition, the schools have to partner with a low-performing school and help it improve in order to get the last third of the incentive funds. She also created an assistance programme for the 150 lowest-performing schools. The low performing school also receives additional training, technical assistance and instructional resources from the state.

Many of the changes put in place in the last decade required legislative approval, but with the strong backing of the governor, there was little resistance. Coelho says that the teachers' union has not been active at the state level, and unions have not been a problem in the municipal areas either. Quality had not been at the centre of discussion before, but the education improvement measures changed that. She expanded assessments to cover all students in all grades in 2008, and the 2009 results at both the state and national levels have registered improvements. However, Secretary Coelho believes that with the resources they have in Brazil and Ceará, they should be in a better situation than they are. Their problems are still very much linked to management process and accountability. The state raised its IDEB index from 3.2 in 2005 to 4.4 in 2009 (for grade 4); from 3.2 in 2005 to 3.9 in 2009 (for grade 8); and from 3.3 in 2005 to 3.6 in 2009 (for grade 11). In fact, the state's national results have outpaced those in many states, moving Ceará out of the lowest performing group to rank 14th among Brazil's 27 states.

State of São Paulo

São Paulo is the most populous state in Brazil and one of the wealthiest. It moved from early coffee bean cultivation and export to industrialisation, and today it is the regional financial hub. São Paulo's capital is São Paulo, a city of 11 million inhabitants with a metropolitan area of almost 20 million, the largest in the Americas. Half of the state's population resides in the capital.

In education, the State of São Paulo has enjoyed continuity of vision for the last decade. The last three secretaries of education were either in the cabinet of the Brazilian minister of Education, Paulo Renato Souza or else Souza himself, who has been secretary since 2009. Secretary Souza was an economist by training who had been secretary in São Paulo in 1984-86 and was asked by the current governor, José Serra, to return for the rest of the governor's term. He says that although the office and its furnishings are the same, the opportunities are greatly expanded by public demand for better education and the federal actions in his term as minister of Education. He and his two predecessors in São Paulo shared a common vision for educational improvement that was forged in their eight years together at the ministry. Rather than sweep away what had been done by their predecessors, they each built upon each other's accomplishments.

The first order of business in 2003 was to provide opportunities for all students to enrol in school. Because attendance was mandatory through to grade 9 and the *Bolsa Família* added 15-17 year olds, there was suddenly a greater demand for high school education, but not enough schools to house them. Many students had to attend high school at night in one of the elementary schools until schools could be built – they became the third shift at the school. Over the last 15 years, São Paulo has been one of the few states that has created sufficient numbers of schools to accommodate all interested high school students.

The second priority was to take the IDEB concept one step further and to create a São Paulo system of assessment and indicators that provided a school-by-school target on a biennial basis based on PISA and international standards. While the national goal is to get to the PISA average performance by 2021, the targets in São Paulo are more rigorous in that they look at a school's performance by the percentage of students in each category: below basic, basic, adequate and advanced. This provides better information to parents and the public about the quality of school performance, but it also gives the districts and the state better information on where the school needs to improve. If the average looks great but there is a sizable group of student at the below basic level, the state knows how to customise its technical assistance to the school.

In 2007, Maria Helena Guimarães de Castro became secretary and initiated a number of reforms that built on the base already established. She was the President of INEP during the Cardoso Presidency. Governor Serra was very concerned about the quality of education, particularly because each school was creating its own curriculum without evaluating its impact on student achievement. That made it very difficult to scale better results across schools. De Castro's theory of action was based in part on the instructional management systems that have enabled other countries to move their education systems forward: curriculum standards, aligned instructional materials, teacher training on the system, and curriculum-based assessments that measure how well students are progressing. In addition, de Castro consulted the effective schools research done in the United States which found that the school should be the unit of improvement and that effective schools must have a principal who is an instructional leader.

De Castro worked with teachers and university professors to develop a clearly-defined common curriculum for every grade and subject to form the basis of student assessments; teachers were trained in its effective implementation. She hired 12 000 pedagogical assistant principals so that each school would have a coach to work with teachers on improving their practice. She revised the Evaluation System of Educational Achievement of São Paulo (SARESP) to reflect the curriculum so that teachers would know that the focus on curriculum would indeed prepare students for the exams. And through the São Paulo assessment and indicator system, she gave the schools the data on student achievement to enable them to gauge the impact of their efforts and to identify the areas of weakness that they needed to ameliorate. Training in analysing the data was a critical part of the programme.

De Castro also focused on school management. She knew schools had to be well-managed, which required principals selected for expertise rather than political affiliations. In addition, to keep families and the public informed so that they could knowledgeably participate in their children's education, schools produced report cards every two months on how students were doing.

Finally, believing that teachers needed to accept responsibility for their school's results, de Castro created a school-wide incentive system that rewarded everyone at the schools that met their improvement targets. The better a school's performance, the more autonomy it was provided. Schools that did not reach their targets were given additional technical assistance, infrastructure resources and teacher professional development. In 2007, she identified the 1 000 lowest-performing schools and provided them with technical assistance, targeted teacher development and additional learning resources. One year later, 95% of these schools had met their targets, and after two years, 98% had met them.

The curriculum project was not without its critics. The curriculum was not just a set of general statements about what should be taught and learned. Each school was given instructional resources: teacher guides that detailed the curriculum units, with specific strategies for teachers; notebooks of lesson plans for teachers for each week; and notebooks of activities for students. While the materials were recommended to teachers, their use was not mandated. However, the curriculum standards for what students should have learned by the end of grades 4, 8 and 11 were required. They were the basis for the SARESP assessments in Portuguese, geography, history, mathematics, and science for students. De Castro said that the Teachers' Union of Education of the State of São Paulo (*Sindicato dos Professores do Ensino Oficial do Estado de São Paulo*) opposed this, but the majority of teachers and staff, as well as civil society, supported the programme. However, the São Paulo Union president, Maria Izabel Azevedo Noronha, countered in an interview for this report that the lesson plans were so specific in both what to teach and how to teach it, that it removed teacher autonomy in pedagogic strategies. Noronha says that it devalued teachers as professionals. This is a classic battle in systems where management believes it has weak teachers who need structured assistance to perform adequately, while the union argues that scripted, "teacher-proof" materials devalue teachers and make teaching even less attractive. Certainly more effective teachers might not need or want such materials, but 40% of the teachers in São Paulo were on temporary licenses.

De Castro's second battle with the union was over teacher absenteeism. She was very concerned that on any given day, 12 000 out of 230 000 teachers were absent. Each teacher was allowed 40 absent days per 200-day year without prior permission or a medical reason. Despite being opposed by the union, de Castro was able to get the state legislature to reduce allowable absences to six days per year without a medical reason.

She increased teacher training, upgraded the qualifications and salaries of teachers, and provided school-wide incentives for schools meeting their targets with improved performance. Everyone at the school shared in the bonuses, which ranged from one to three months of salary. As with the federal system, the targets were set individually for each school so that schools were competing against their past record, not against other schools. However, the union believes the targets punish teachers for circumstances outside their control. De Castro disagrees, noting that low-performing schools received intensive support and interventions and therefore improved.

Secretaries de Castro and Souza, and Mrs Noronha, president of the union, all agree that the quality of teachers is too low. Their differences lie in terms of the solutions. Mrs Noronha points out that 40% of São Paulo's teachers are temporary and lack permanent contracts. Recent efforts by the ministry to improve the quality of new teachers by requiring them to pass an examination based on content and pedagogy produced 56 000 qualified teachers, but only 10 000 places were identified for them because of budget limitations. If all 100 000 positions currently filled by temporary teachers had been made available and 56 000 of them were filled by those teachers who did well in the exams, Mrs Noronha believes the state would have dramatically improved the quality of teaching.

Souza has continued to focus on teacher quality. He was concerned that the differential between starting salaries of BRL 1 830 per month (about USD 1 000 per month) and top salaries after 32 years of BRL 3 270 per month was much too low to attract and retain teachers. He therefore worked with the legislature to pass the Teacher Career Law which created a logical career ladder. To move up the career ladder teachers must earn specific grades on teacher assessments in content and pedagogy, as well as have better than average attendance and continuity of employment at a single school – at least three years. The ladder has five levels with 25% higher salaries at each step, resulting in a 100% increase in salaries for teachers at the top level. The plan allows teachers to apply annually for promotion to the next step, but each teacher can only be promoted once every three years. The examination grades required for promotion rise from 60% for level two to 90% for level five. This is intended to encourage teachers to improve their knowledge and skills in content areas as well as their pedagogic strategies.

When asked about the role of unions, Secretary Souza said they are a political force in São Paulo. He explained that he meets frequently with them to discuss issues, but when he presented the Teacher Career proposal to the union, it refused to support him. The union president, Mrs Noronha, explains that there is a ceiling limiting the number of teachers who pass the promotion threshold to no more than 44 000 per year (20% of the overall teaching force). This denies access to the other qualified teachers who deserve promotion. Souza realistically has no choice but to phase in the higher salaries.

The bottom line is that the state raised its IDEB index from 4.7 in 2005 to 5.5 in 2009 (for grade 4); from 4.2 in 2005 to 4.5 in 2009 (for grade 8); and from 3.6 in 2005 to 3.9 in 2009 (for grade 11). These significant improvements place São Paulo ahead of most other states.

LESSONS FROM BRAZIL

▪ Commitment to education and children

The federal government and some state governments have begun the journey towards quality education. Consistent vision throughout the last two presidencies and the increases in resources during this period have enabled under-resourced states to make great strides. However, the low quality of education is still preventing the country from moving to the next level of economic development. Minister Haddad recognises the connection between education and development and is working to align education policies and plans to produce a better educated workforce. The minister expects that in the next 10 years, investments in education will need to rise to 7% of GDP and focus on expanding full-time education to all schools.

▪ Cultural support for universal high achievement

Brazil has come a long way from the country that assumed that there was no need to educate the natives and imported slaves. Presidents Cardoso and Lula have focused on the need to educate everyone. But the low level of performance of students in both private and public schools demonstrates that high achievement is still problematic. It is clear that support for improving education must come from the top and both Cardoso and Lula have provided that. However a nation must guard against giving mixed messages to its population. Lula himself was only educated to 4th grade – he is a living example for the lower classes that anything is possible. On the other hand, he is also an example that education is not always necessary to succeed. This is reinforced when he reminds the well-educated elites of his ability to become president and run the country without their advanced levels of education. Still, Lula is a champion for education for all and has raised the federal contribution to FUNDEB during his presidency. His goal is for every child to gain a college degree or a vocational certificate. He understands that post-secondary education is key to Brazil's development, but the challenges are great: high school graduation stands at a little more than 30% of the age cohort.

▪ Benchmarking

Brazil demonstrates how low-performing countries can use both national and international benchmarking to focus their efforts and establish tools to improve their education systems. Using the US National Assessment of Educational Progress (NAEP) and PISA as models, Brazil has created IDEB, an internationally-benchmarked system that establishes goals for every school and measures their progress towards that goal. Brazil's focus on teacher quality, accountability and school management is consistent with the best practices of high-performing countries and can be a model for other countries starting on the path to improvement.

In both Acre and São Paulo, the secretaries of education placed a premium on the development of full instructional systems that took the federal standards and expanded them into curriculum, instructional materials, teacher training and assessments. Because the current level of performance is low, the standards, curriculum and assessments start from where students are and attempt to take them to higher levels of cognitive performance. States and provinces in other countries can use these strategies as models of how to move forward from general curriculum frameworks at the federal level to establishing what teachers need to change their practice and implement aligned instructional systems.

- ## System coherence and alignment

System coherence is far more difficult to accomplish in a federal system, especially one that has states with such different economic and social conditions. Yet a federal system can use the lessons from Brazil:

– Establish policies that foster a systemic approach to education and use funding to the states as incentives for implementing similar policies in their states.

– Create a synthetic index like the IDEB to establish standards for each school.

– Publicise scores that show performance levels in each state and school to create public pressure in states and schools that are not improving.

– Identify and publish promising practices that successful states have used and share them with state leaders as possible strategies for improvement.

– Hold meetings with state secretaries of education in low performing states and require improvement plans from their states.

- ## Teacher and principal quality

The most critical lesson from Brazil is the importance of the quality of the teaching force when improving education. Before the reforms, the standards for entering teacher education and becoming a teacher were very low. Teacher education institutions focused on philosophy of education rather than the knowledge and skills needed to be an effective teacher. The infrastructures to support in-service education were very weak. Until these problems are addressed, a country cannot make major strides in student achievement. Recent efforts by the ministry and the São Paulo Secretariat are models for where to start to improve the teaching force. The ministry is proposing an assessment system for new teachers that could establish standards for entry into the profession. Minister Haddad hopes that pre-service teacher exams may be a strategy to influence the teacher education programmes at the universities. In addition, the 1996 Law of Directives and Bases of National Education requires each state and municipality to establish career paths for teachers. Several states are creating career paths that link salary to expertise and some are developing incentive programmes. São Paulo's new career path system will include examinations.

Individual states are using different strategies to address teacher quality. Some are working with federal universities and NGOs to develop effective training for in-service teachers. Ceará and São Paulo have organised coaches to work with teachers in the classroom using the state's instructional materials to help them improve their practices. Acre raised its salaries to be competitive with other states, and it has been able to attract teachers to the state. Secretary da Silva believes that Acre is on the path to improved teacher performance.

- ## Accountability

Brazil provides good examples of how a federal system can establish accountability in its system. It has used the IDEB to establish accountability at the school, municipality and state levels. The ministry has used its public statements, planning documents, and public relations initiatives to create public interest in IDEB results as a measure of improvements in educational quality in local schools. The business and industrial constituencies support these efforts. Local communities want their school to score well in the ratings.

- ## Instructional practice

Surveys of instructional practices in Brazil indicate that the primary mode of instruction still involves the teacher at the front of the room and all students engaged in the same activities at the same time. It is not unusual to use this strategy when attempting to get all students to a basic level of literacy; many countries do. However, given the range of students in both ability and in age because of grade repetitions, this may not be the most effective strategy to recommend to others. The first challenge in any low-performing country is to improve teachers' content and basic pedagogical knowledge. Initiatives occurring in some Brazilian states show that improved instructional practices can be and are being addressed:

– Acre is focusing on primary curriculum with training provided by supervisors who monitor instruction.

– Ceará has a structured teaching programme for primary grades.

– São Paulo uses coaches to assist teachers in the implementation of the curriculum, lesson plans and instructional materials.

- ## Standards for teachers

Without high standards for professional practice, it is difficult for any country to move its education system forward. Brazil is attempting to change certain aspects of the current system rather than the whole system at one time. It will take time to see if this approach works or if Chile's approach of establishing the standards first and then aligning tools is more effective (The Framework for Good Teaching-*El Marco para la Buena Enseñanza*, see OECD, 2009a). Minister Haddad's proposal of an examination for teachers prior to entering the classroom is a first step towards a better-qualified teaching corps, as is the initiative for all states and municipalities to develop career plans that connect expertise with compensation. A nationally-available examination will help small states and municipalities that have not already developed examinations for entry level teachers. Secretary Souza's career plan for São Paulo, which involves assessments of teachers' knowledge of content and pedagogy, will set standards for those who wish to move up the career ladder. In addition, his use of an examination to qualify temporary teachers will raise the bar until qualified teachers are available for every post.

▪ Equity in the distribution of resources

As Brazil shows, money is not enough to improve education. The country spends 5.2% of its GDP on public education and almost 16% of the total government budget on public education. This is as much or more than most OECD countries, so insufficient funding is not the issue. The challenge is the efficiency and effectiveness of the education system. Part of this is the high cost of teacher pensions, taking up 30-50% of the states' spending on education. This reflects the pensions offered to other Brazilian civil servants, and is an issue common to many countries. Inequitable funding of different levels of education is another problem. Brazil funds its public universities at a much higher per student level than its basic education system. The 2010 OECD publication *Education at a Glance* notes that the spending per student on tertiary education (excluding R&D) is nearly six times higher than on primary education in Brazil, as compared to about 30% higher on average in OECD countries (OECD, 2010b). This results in first class public universities that few public school graduates are eligible to enter.

Although higher education is funded at a higher level than basic and secondary education, Brazil is a good example of how to use federal statutory authority to make the funding available for basic and secondary education more equitable. FUNDEF has identified a group of federal, state and municipal taxes and has dictated that a set percentage of these revenues must be dedicated to basic and secondary education. This establishes a firm base for educational expenditures, supplemented by federal "top-up" funds that ensure that every municipality would have at least minimum funding for education. To allocate these funds, FUNDEF moved from a formula based on population density – which was biased towards large cities – to a system based on minimum per-pupil allocations. This has provided states such as Acre and Ceará with the necessary resources to improve their education systems.

▪ Incentives for learning

To date Brazil is still experimenting with incentives. It has established incentives for student attendance through the *Bolsa Família*, which gives parents an incentive to keep their students in school and get regular health checkups. However *Bolsa Família* does not provide an incentive for students to work hard to achieve excellence. Acre and São Paulo have established incentives for schools that improve their performance levels, as have some other states and large cities. Here the school is the unit of improvement. The only incentive for students to take tough courses and work hard is the hope of entering a public university because they have excelled in the entrance exam. Because most students have not received the quality of education necessary to excel, that hope is beyond the realm of possibility for them. Intermediate incentives might encourage students to move to higher levels of performance.

WHERE IS BRAZIL ON THE EDUCATIONAL CONTINUUM?

Brazil's mixed economy is still heavily based on commodities and therefore still relies on unskilled labour in many sectors. However, in future the economy will increasingly be based on how much its labour force can add value to the raw materials it produces. Brazil knows it must produce much larger numbers of skilled workers than it is currently producing. It is this that is driving demand both for a greater quantity of educated workers and for improvements in the quality of education. On the quantity side, the challenge is to increase the length of the school day and the proportion of the cohort that completes high school. On the quality side, the challenge is to move towards the average national PISA scores. These are ambitious but appropriate goals for a country that until recently could be counted as among those well to the left on the economic development dimension line (Figure 1.1, Chapter 1).

In municipalities across Brazil, you find teachers at all points along the continuum as the country works to professionalise and educate its teacher corps. Most teachers are located just to the left of the middle of the continuum, especially if one includes the temporary teachers filling vacancies with the system. As a result, many states have developed curriculum materials that explicitly identify teaching strategies and student materials that allow students to learn independently.

As is normal for a country in the early phases of modern industrial development, Brazil is still struggling with basic literacy for the majority of its students. Grade repetitions increase the complexity of classrooms, with students of varied ages and backgrounds all in the same room with teachers who may not have the competence to deliver effective education in this environment. In public schools where the students come from more educated families, students and teachers are able to focus on more complex learning.

States are focusing on the management of schools as a key reform area. They understand the importance of professional principals who can lead staff in collaborative efforts of continuous improvement. School-based decision-making was part of the education law of 1996, but this is difficult to accomplish when teacher attrition and mobility are high and capacity is low. Indeed, this may be an arena in which the goal is well ahead of the capacity to achieve it.

FINAL OBSERVATIONS

Barbara Bruns, Lead Education Specialist for the Latin America region at the World Bank, notes that Brazil has transformed its education system over the last 15 years. Using a public administration framework, it has extended public basic education to over 95% of the population; it has established assessment systems using an internationally benchmarked index that characterises the progress of each school; it has created student-based funding formulas that distribute funds fairly within states; it has used conditional cash transfers to poor families to move the next generation out of poverty through education; and it has encouraged states and municipalities to take actions to improve education in individual schools. Brazil has enjoyed 15 years of economic and political stability that has enabled it to develop solid industries that export to the world. Consumption is up among its citizens and this continues to fuel its economy. Its challenge now is to raise the level of education of its citizens high enough to enable them to take commerce and industry to competitive levels in a global marketplace.

While all of the educators in the ministry and state secretariats agree that educational levels are still too low, they are working hard to use the best thinking on high performing schools to improve their systems. Their focus on instructional systems; improved teacher preparation, qualifications, salaries and training; the use of targets to identify best practices and to provide support for low performers are starting to make a difference. In each of the three states and in Brazil as a whole, performance has exceeded their targets, and they believe this is just the start of their journey to excellence. We close this chapter with the words of Minister Haddad: "We are more united than ever to achieve the objectives. The 20th century was a lost one for Brazil because the country did not address the issue of education reform. Maybe for the first time, I see the country mobilised; targets were established and everyone agreed to them. Nobody contests the national plan for education. I think we have a hard job ahead, but Brazil has a real chance to overcome its difficulties in this area."

■ Figure 8.2 ■
Brazil[1]: Profile data

Language(s)	Official: Portuguese
Population	191.9 million (2008)[2] 646 962 (2005)[3] (*Acre-North*) 8.1 million (2005)[4] (*Ceará-Northeast*) 10.9 m (2006)[5] (*Sao Paolo-Southeast*)
Youth population	26.4%[6] (OECD average 18.7%)
Elderly population	6.6%[7] (OECD average 14.4%)
Growth rate	1.04 (OECD 0.68%)[8]
Foreign-born population	0.04% immigrants[9] (2010)[10]
GDP per capita	USD 10 466 (2008) (OECD average 33 732)[11]
Economy-Origin of GDP	Services: 65.3%; Industry (including construction): 28%; Agriculture: 6.7% of GDP (2008)[12]
Unemployment	7.3%[13] (OECD average 6.1%)[14]
Youth unemployment	18%[15] (OECD average 13.8%)[16]
NEETs, 15-17 year-olds	10.7% (2007) (*North*) 10.3% (2007) (*Northeast*) 8.7% (2007) (*Southeast*) 9.6% (2007) (*Total*)[17]

Expenditure on education	5.2% of GDP; (OECD average 5.2%)
	    4.0% on primary, secondary and post-secondary non-tertiary
	    0.8% on tertiary[18] education[19] (OECD average 3.5%; 1.2% respectively)
	
	16.1% of total government expenditure (2007)[20] (OECD average 13.3%)
	    12.2% on primary, secondary and post-secondary non-tertiary
	    2.6 % on tertiary education[21] (OECD average 9%; 3.1% respectively)

Enrolment ratio, early childhood education	49.7% (2008)[22] (OECD average 71.5%)[23]
Enrolment ratio, primary education	95.6% (2008)[24] (OECD average 98.8%)[25]
Enrolment ratio, secondary education	76.4% (2008)[27] (OECD average 81.5%)[28]
Enrolment of 15-17 year-olds[26] in ISCED 2 and ISCED 3	M 39.1% ; F 36.2% (2007) (*North*) M 42.8%; F 34.5% (2007) (*Northeast*) M 23.5%; F 58.7% (2007) (*Southeast*) M 31.1%; F 47.9% (2007) (*Total*)
Enrolment ratio, tertiary education	21.1%[29] (OECD average 24.9%)[30]
Students in primary education, by type of institution or mode of enrolment[31]	Public: 88.4% (OECD average 89.6%) Government-dependent private: no data[32] (OECD average 8.1%) Independent, private: 11.6% (OECD average 2.9%)
Students in lower secondary education, by type of institution or mode of enrolment[33]	Public 90.3% (OECD average 83.2%) Government-dependent private: no data[34] (OECD average 10.9%) Independent, private : 9.7% (OECD average 3.5%)
Students in upper secondary education, by type of institution or mode of enrolment[35]	Public: 86% (OECD average 82%) Government-dependent private: no data[36] (OECD average 13.6%) Independent, private: 14% (OECD average 5.5%)

Students in tertiary education, by type of institution or mode of enrolment[37]	Tertiary type B education:
	Public: 16.9%
	    Government-dependent private: no data[38]
	    Independent-private: 83.1%
	    (OECD average Public: 61.8%
	    Government-dependent private : 19.2%
	    Independent-private: 16.6%)
	Tertiary type A education:
	    Public: 29.3%
	    Government-dependent private no data[39]
	    Independent-private:70.7%
	    (OECD average Public: 77.1%
	    Government-dependent private: 9.6%
	    Independent-private: 15%)

Teachers' salaries	Average annual starting salary in lower secondary education: missing data* (OECD average USD 30 750)[40] Ratio of salary in lower secondary education after 15 years of experience to GDP per capita: missing data (OECD average: 1.22)
Upper secondary graduation rates	63%[41] (OECD average 47%)[42]

*Data on Brazilian teachers' salaries missing from *Education at a Glance 2010* (OECD, 2010).
StatLink ᴬᴵˢᴸ http://dx.doi.org/10.1787/888932366750

Interview partners

Barbara Bruns, The World Bank, Washington, DC.

Maria Helena Guimarães de Castro, Former State Secretary of Education, São Paulo and Former President, Institute for Educational Studies and Research Anísio Teixeira (INEP), Brazil.

Reynaldo Fernandes, Former President of INEP, Brazil.

Maria Izolda Cela de Arruda Coelho, State Secretary of Education, Ceará, Brazil.

Fernando Haddad, Minister of Education, Brazil.

Sheyla Carvalho Lira, PISA Brazil, INEP, Brazil.

Joaquim José Soares Neto, President, INEP, Brazil.

Maria Izabel Azevedo Noronha, President, Teachers Union of Education of the State of São Paulo (Sindicato dos Professores do Ensino Oficial do Estado de São Paulo), Brazil.

Ogari Pacheco, CEO Cristalina Chemicals and Pharmaceuticals, Brazil.

José Henrique Paim, Executive Secretary, Ministry of Education, Brazil.

Maria do Pilar, Secretary of Basic Education, Ministry of Education, Brazil.

Simon Schwartzman, Political Scientist, Instituto de Estudos do Trabalho e Sociedade in Rio de Janeiro, Brazil.

Maria Corrêa da Silva, State Secretary of Education, Acre, Brazil.

Paulo Renato Souza, State Secretary of Education, São Paulo, Brazil.

Eunice Rios, Human Resources Department, Embraer – Empresa Brasileira de Aeronáutica S.A., Brazil.

References

Anderson, L.G., *et al.* (2006), "Competitiveness and Science and Math Education: Comparing Costa Rica, El Salvador and Brazil (Recife) to Sweden", *Hifab International* for IDB, Vol. I, June, Sweden.

Arboleda, R. (2006), "Latin America's Educational Challenge", paper presented to the *Democracy and Competitiveness in Latin America Task Force*, Center for Hemispheric Policy, University of Miami, September-December 2006.

The Brazil Institute (2007), "Basic Education in Brazil: What's Wrong and How to Fix It", *Thinking Brazil* No. 25, February, Woodrow Wilson International Center for Scholars, Washington, DC. *www.wilsoncenter.org/topics/pubs/ThinkingBrazil_25.pdf*.

Brooke, N. (2008), "Educational Accountability in Brazil", *Revista Iberoamericana de Evaluación Educativa*, Vol. 1, No. 1.

Cárdenas, M. and C. Henao (2010), *Latin America and the Caribbean's Economic Recovery*, The Brookings Institution, Washington, DC.

Castro, C. (2004) "Brazilian Technical Education: The Chronicle of a Turbulent Marriage", in C. Brock and S. Schwartzman (eds.), *The Challenges of Education in Brazil*, Symposium Books, Oxford.

De Castro, M. and S. Tiezzi (2004), "The Reform of Secondary Education and the Implementation of ENEM in Brazil", in C. Brock and S. Schwartzman (eds.), *The Challenges of Education in Brazil*, Symposium Books, Oxford.

De Castro, M. (2007), "Institutional Problems in Public Education" *Braudel Papers*, No. 41, Fernand Braudel Institute of World Economics, São Paulo, Brazil.

De Castro, M. (2010), *Estudo de Caso: Mudanças no Ensino Médio Paulista: Currículo, Avaliação e Gestão por Resultados* (Case Study: Changes in the São Paulo Schools: Curriculum, Assessment and Management for Results), Inter-American Development Bank, Washington, DC.

Council on Competitiveness (2007), *US-Brazil Innovation Summit – Delegation Background Resource*, Council on Competitiveness, Washington, DC.

The Economist (2010), "Brazil's Presidential Campaign: In Lula's Footsteps", *The Economist,* 1 July 2010, *www.economist.com/node/16486525.*

Erlick, J. C. (ed.) (2007), "Brazil: The Search for Equity", *ReVista: Harvard Review of Latin America,* (Spring), The David Rockefeller Center for Latin American Studies, Harvard University, Cambridge, MA.

Evans, L. (2002), *How Brazil Beat Hyperinflation,* Latin America Center, UCLA International Studies and Overseas Programs, Los Angeles, *www.econ.pucrio.br/gfranco/How%20Brazil%20Beat%20Hyperinflation.htm.*

Gall, N. (2007), "The Struggle for Better Schools, São Paulo and New York", *O Estado de S. Paulo,* 29 April, 2007, *www.estadao.com.br.*

Ganimian, A. (2008), *Despite Major Obstacles, São Paulo Aims High on Education,* Inter-American Dialogue, Washington, DC.

General Atlantic (2010), "Brazil: Opportunities in Latin America's Largest Economy", *Thought Leadership,* General Atlantic Global Growth Investors, São Paulo, *www.generalatlantic.com/en/news/article/1324.*

Hanushek, E. and **L. Woessmann** (2009), "Poor Student Learning Explains the Latin American Growth Puzzle", *Vox,* 14 August 2009, *www.voxeu.org/index.php?q=node/3869.*

Herrán, C. and **A. Rodríguez** (2000), "Secondary Education in Brazil: Time to Move Forward", *Inter American Development Bank Report* BR-014 and *World Bank Report* 19409- BR, Washington, DC.

Inter-American Development Bank (2006), "Competitiveness and Science and Math Education: Comparing Costa Rica, El Salvador and Brazil (Recife) to Sweden", *HiFab International,* Sweden, *http://idbdocs.iadb.org/wsdocs/getdocument.aspx?docnum=1028382.*

Inter-American Development Bank (2010), *Country Profile: Brazil,* IADB website, *www.iadb.org/research/LatinMacroWatch*

Lavy, V. (2010), "Do Differences in School's Instructional Time Explain International Achievement Gaps in Math, Science, and Reading Evidence from Developed and Developing Countries", *Working Paper,* No.16227, National Bureau of Economic Research, Cambridge, MA.

Martinez-Fritscher, A., A. Musacchio and **M. Viarengo** (2010), "The Great Leap Forward: The Political Economy of Education in Brazil, 1889-1930", *Harvard Business School Working Paper* No. 10-075, Harvard, Cambridge, MA.

Mello, G. de (2005), "Teachers for Quality in Education" in Reimers, *et al.* (eds.), *Teacher Involvement in Educational Change,* UNESCO Regional Bureau of Education for Latin America and the Caribbean, Santiago, pp. 25-37.

Menezes-Filho, N., R. Fernandes and **P. Picchetti** (2002), "Rising Human Capital but Constant Inequality: The Education Composition Effect in Brazil", *Revista Brasileira de Economia (RBE),* Vol. 60, No. 4, pp. 407-424, Rio de Janeiro, *www.scielo.br/scielo.php?pid=S0034-71402006000400005&script=sci_arttext.*

Ministry of Education (2007), *The Plan for the Development of Education: Reasons, Principles and Programs,* ministry of Education (MEC), Brasilia.

Murillo, J. (2005), "An Overview of the Teaching Profession in Latin America", in Reimers, *et al.* (eds.), *Teacher Involvement in Educational Change,* UNESCO Regional Bureau of Education for Latin America and the Caribbean, Santiago, pp. 52-59.

Myers, J.P. (2008), "Democratizing School Authority: Brazilian Teachers' Perceptions of the Election of Principals", *Teaching and Teacher Education* No. 24, pp.952–966, Elsevier Educational Research Programme, Maryland Heights, MO.

Neri, M. and **G. Buchmann** (2007), "Brazil Country Case Study", Country Profile commissioned for the EFA Global Monitoring Report 2008, *Education for All by 2015: Will we Make it?,* UNESCO, Paris.

OECD (2009a), *Evaluating and Rewarding the Quality of Teachers: International Practices,* OECD Publishing.

OECD (2009b), *OECD Economic Surveys: Brazil 2009,* OECD Publishing.

OECD (2010a), *PISA 2009 Results Volume I, What Students Know and Can Do: Student Performance in Reading, Mathematics and Science,* OECD Publishing.

OECD (2010b), *Education at a Glance: OECD Indicators,* OECD Publishing.

Oliveira, J. (2004), "Expansion and Inequality in Brazilian Education", in C. Brock and S. Schwartzman (eds.), *The Challenges of Education in Brazil,* Symposium Books, Oxford.

Palamadessi, M. and **M. Legarralde** (2006), *Teachers' Unions, Governments and Educational Reforms in Latin America and the Caribbean: Conditions for Dialogue,* Regional Policy Dialogue Inter-American Development Bank, Washington, DC.

Partlow, J. (2008), "Brazilian Companies Step in to Educate Future Workforce", *The Washington Post,* 9 December 2008, *www.washingtonpost.com/wp-dyn/content/article/2008/12/08/AR2008120803747.html.*

Puryear, J. and **T.O. Goodspeed** (2008), "Building Human Capital: Is Latin American Education Competititve", in J. Haar and J. Price (eds.), *Can Latin America Compete? Confronting the Challenges of Globalization,* Palgrave Macmillan, New York, pp. 45-62.

ReVista (2007), "Brazil: The Search for Equity", *ReVista*, David Rockefeller Center for Latin American Studies, Harvard University, Cambridge, MA., *www.drclas.harvard.edu/files/2007_Spring_-_ReVista_Brazil-The_Search_for_Equity.pdf*.

Rodrigues, P. (2009), "Brazil's Education Market", US Commercial Service, US Department of Commerce, Washington, DC, available at *www.focusbrazil.org.br/Events/Event-US-ExpoBelta2010_Report.pdf*.

Rodríguez, A. and **C. Herrán** (2000), *Secondary Education in Brazil: Time to Move Forward*, World Bank and Inter-American Development Bank, Washington, DC.

Reuters (2008), "Education Woes Haunt Brazil's Economic Revival", *ABC News* online 26 August 2008, *www.abc.net/news/stories/2008/08/26*.

Schwartzman, S. (2004), "The Challenges of Education in Brazil", in C. Brock and S. Schwartzman (eds.) *The Challenges of Education in Brazil*, Oxford Studies in Comparative Education, London.

Schwartzman, S. (2005), *Education-oriented Social Programs in Brazil: The Impact of Bolsa Escola*. Instituto de Estudos do Trabalho e Sociedade, Rio de Janeiro.

Schwartzman, S. (2010), "Benchmarking Secondary Education in Brazil", paper prepared for the *International Seminar on Best Practices of Secondary Education* (IDB/OCED/ministry of Education), Brasilia.

Soares, F. (2004). "Quality and Equity in Brazilian Basic Education", in C. Brock and S. Schwartzman (eds.), *The Challenges of Education in Brazil*, Symposium Books, Oxford.

Souza, P. and **M. de Castro** (2000), "Education in Brazil: Reforms, Advances and Perspectives", paper presented at the *IDB Brazil Seminar: Brazil 500 Years: Social Progress and Human Development,* Washington, DC, April.

Souza, P. (2010), "IDESP: São Paulo's Educational Development Index", presentation given at the *International Seminar on Grading Teachers of Basic Education*, Cesgranrio Foundation, São Paulo.

Stein, E., *et al.* (2006), *The Politics of Policies: Economic and Social Progress in Latin America,* David Rockefeller Center for Latin American Studies, Harvard University, Inter-American Development Bank, Washington, DC.

UNESCO (2000), *National Education for All Evaluation Report – EFA 2000*, UNESCO, Paris, *www.unesco.org/education/wef/countryreports/brazil/rapport_1.html*.

UNESCO (2009), *Youth and Adult Literacy in Brazil: Lessons from Practice*, UNESCO, Brasilia Office, *http://unesdoc.unesco.org/images/0016/001626/162640e.pdf*.

Uribe, C. (1999), "Colombia: Teacher and School Incentives", *David Rockefeller Center for Latin American Studies Newsletter*, Spring, Harvard University, Cambridge, MA.

US Diplomatic Mission to Brazil (2010), *Joint Communiqué of Brazilian Minister Haddad and the US Deputy Secretary Miller on Education*, Embassy of the United States, Brazilia, Brazil, *http://brazil.usembassy.gov/joint_education.html*.

Vaillant, D. (2005), "Education Reforms and the Role of the Teacher", in Reimers, *et al.* (eds.), *Teacher Involvement in Educational Change*, UNESCO Regional Bureau of Education for Latin America and the Caribbean, Santiago, pp. 39-51.

Vegas, E. and **J. Petrow** (2008), *Raising Student Learning in Latin America: The Challenge For the 21st Century,* World Bank, Washington, DC.

Vieira, F. H., J. Kovaleski, and **A. de Francisco** (2006), "Functional Literacy Numbers in Brazil – Potential Losses for Industries", paper presented at the *XII ICIEOM Conference*, Fortaleza, CE, Brazil, 9-11 October 2006, *www.pg.cefetpr.br/ppgep/Ebook/e-book2006/Artigos/38.pdf*.

Weinberg, M. (2008), "Interview: Maria Helena Guimarães de Castro: Reward for Merit", *Veja*, 13 February 2008, São Paulo, *http://veja.abril.com.br/130208/entrevista.shtml*.

Woodrow Wilson International Center for Scholars (2007), "Basic Education in Brazil: What's Wrong and How to Fix It", *Thinking Brazil*, Brazil Institute, Washington, DC, *www.wilsoncenter.org/topics/pubs/ThinkingBrazil_25.pdf*.

The World Bank (2008), *Looking Forward: The Challenge of Raising Education Quality in Brazil*, Brazil Country Management Unit, Human Development Unit, Latin America and the Caribbean Region, World Bank, Washington, DC.

The World Bank (2010), *Edstats: Country Profiles: Brazil*, World Bank, *http://web.worldbank.org*.

Worldfund (2010), *Education Gap: The Realities of Education in Latin America*, Worldfund, New York.

Notes

1. One group placed a three-year-old child in the lap of the Finance minister at a televised campaign stop so he could not speak against early childhood education.

2. OECD (2009), *Economic Survey of Brazil 2009*, OECD Publishing.

3. From the 2005 Brazilian census, Economist Intelligence Unit, 2008, Brazil Country Profile.

4. From the 2005 Brazilian census, Economist Intelligence Unit, 2008, Brazil Country Profile.

5. Estimate, Economist Intelligence Unit, 2008, Brazil Country Profile.

6. OECD (2010), *OECD Factbook 2010*, OECD Publishing. Ratio of population aged less than 15 to the total population (data from 2008).

7. OECD (2010), *OECD Factbook 2010*, OECD Publishing. Ratio of population aged 65 and older to the total population (data from 2008).

8. OECD (2010), *OECD Factbook 2010*, OECD Publishing. Annual population growth in percentage, OECD total (year of reference – 2007).

9. From the 2005 Brazilian census, Economist Intelligence Unit, 2008, Brazil Country Profile.

10. International Organisation for Migration, www.iom.int, The population breakdown is 54% of European origin, 39% Mixed race, 6% Black, and .5% indigenous Indians.

11. OECD (2010), *OECD Factbook 2010*, OECD Publishing. Current prices and PPPs (data from 2008).

12. OECD (2009), *Economic Survey of Brazil 2009*, OECD Publishing.

13. OECD (2010), *OECD Factbook 2010*, OECD Publishing. Total unemployment rates as percentage of total labour force (data from 2008).

14. OECD (2010), *OECD Factbook 2010*, OECD Publishing. Total unemployment rates as percentage of total labour force (data from 2008).

15. ILO Youth Unemployment Rate for selected urban areas. These data are drawn from official national statistical sources (labour force surveys) and are based on national definitions. http://laborsta.ilo.org

16. OECD (2010), *Employment Outlook*, OECD Publishing. Unemployed as a percentage of the labour force in the age group: youth aged 15-24.

17. Percentage of 15-17 year olds who are neither in employment nor education and training *Pesquisa Nacional por Amostra de Domicílios* 2007 (PNAD - National Household Survey).

18. The OECD follows standard international conventions in using the term "tertiary education" to refer to all post-secondary programmes at ISCED levels 5B, 5A and 6, regardless of the institutions in which they are offered. OECD (2008), *Tertiary Education for the Knowledge Society: Volume 1*, OECD Publishing.

19. OECD (2010), *Education at a Glance 2010*, OECD Publishing. Public expenditure presented in this table includes public subsidies to households for living costs (scholarships and grants to students/households and students loans), which are not spent on educational institutions (data from 2006). For Brazil, this figure is for public institutions only.

20. OECD (2010), *Education at a Glance*, OECD Publishing. Public Institutions only.

21. OECD (2010), *Education at a Glance 2010*, OECD Publishing. Public expenditure presented in this table includes public subsidies to households for living costs (scholarships and grants to students/households and students loans), which are not spent on educational institutions (data from 2006).

22. OECD (2010), *Education at a Glance* 2010, OECD Publishing. Net enrolment rates of ages 4 and under as a percentage of the population aged 3 to 4 (data from 2008). The rates "4 and under as a percentage of the population aged 3 to 4" are overestimated. A significant number of students are younger than 3 years old. The net rates between 3 and 5 are around 100%.

23. OECD (2010), *Education at a Glance 2010*, OECD Publishing. OECD average net enrolment rates of ages 4 and under as a percentage of the population aged 3 to 4 (year of reference – 2008).

24. OECD (2010), *Education at a Glance* 2010, OECD Publishing. Net enrolment rates of ages 5 to 14 as a percentage of the population aged 5 to 14 (data from 2008).

25. OECD (2010) *Education at a Glance 2010*, OECD Publishing. OECD average net enrolment rates of ages 5 to 14 as a percentage of the population aged 5 to 14(year of reference – 2008).

26. Enrolment ratio of 15-17 year olds, *Pesquisa Nacional por Amostra de Domicílios* 2007 (PNAD – National Household Survey).

27. OECD (2010), *Education at a Glance* 2010, OECD Publishing. Net enrolment rates of ages 15 to 19 as a percentage of the population aged 15 to 19 (data from 2008).

28. OECD (2010), *Education at a Glance 2010,* OECD Publishing. OECD average net enrolment rates of ages 15 to 19 as a percentage of the population aged 15 to 19 (year of reference – 2008).

29. OECD (2010), *Education at a Glance 2010,* OECD Publishing. Net enrolment rates of ages 20 to 29 as a percentage of the population aged 20 to 29 (data from 2007). This figure includes includes all 20-29 year olds, including those in employment, etc. The Gross Enrolment Ratio (GER), measured by the UN as the number of actual students enrolled / number of potential students enrolled, is generally higher. The GER for tertiary education in Brazil in 2008 is 34%, compared to the regional avg of 38% (UIS 2010).

30. OECD (2010), *Education at a Glance 2010,* OECD Publishing. OECD average net enrolment rates of ages 20 to 29 as a percentage of the population aged 20 to 29 (year of reference – 2008).

31. OECD (2010), *Education at a Glance 2010,* OECD Publishing. Data from 2008.

32. Data is not applicable because category does not apply.

33. OECD (2010), *Education at a Glance 2010,* OECD Publishing. Data from 2008.

34. Data is not applicable because category does not apply.

35. OECD (2010), *Education at a Glance 2010,* OECD Publishing. Data from 2008.

36. Data is not applicable because category does not apply.

37. OECD (2010), *Education at a Glance 2010,* OECD Publishing. Data from 2008.

38. Data is not applicable because category does not apply.

39. Data is not applicable because category does not apply.

40. OECD (2010), *Education at a Glance 2010,* OECD Publishing. Starting salary/minimum training in USD adjusted for PPP (data from 2008).

41. This figure only includes general programmes, not pre-vocational and vocational programmes.

42. OECD (2010), *Education at a Glance 2010*, OECD Publishing. Sum of upper secondary graduation rates – in general programmes – for a single year of age in 2007 (year of reference for OECD average – 2008).

9

Germany:
Once Weak International Standing Prompts Strong Nationwide Reforms for Rapid Improvement

For many years, the German public and policy makers assumed that Germany had one of the world's most effective, fair and efficient school systems. It was not until 2000 that they discovered this not to be the case at all, and that in fact Germany's schools ranked below the average when compared to the PISA-participating countries. Now, ten years into the 21st century, Germany has substantially improved its position in the PISA league tables. This chapter explains how Germany could have so misjudged the relative quality of its education system, how it could have fallen so far from where it had been generations before, what it did to reverse its unfavourable position, and what other nations might learn from this experience. It identifies the main factors behind Germany's strong recovery as being the changes it has made to the structure of its secondary schools; the high quality of its teachers; the value of its dual system, which helps develop workplace skills in children before they leave school; and its development of common standards and curricula and the assessment and research capacity to monitor them.

INTRODUCTION

The education systems of many of today's leading industrial nations were shaped a century or so ago. Though they took their ideas from many sources, one stood out: Germany. It was in Germany that they saw the first model of a nation determined to provide a free public basic education to all of its people. It was Germany that first developed the modern research university. In Germany, they found in the *Gymnasium* a model for secondary schools designed to prepare students for the modern research university. And it was Germany that provided in the *Realschule* – and, later in the dual system – two of the world's most compelling models for supplying a nation with highly trained workers in every field of endeavour.

It is hardly surprising in these circumstances that the German public and policy makers assumed that Germany had earned pride of place among the world's education systems for having one of the most effective, fair and efficient school systems. It was not until the close of the 20th century that they found out that that was not the case at all, and that Germany's schools ranked below the average for the PISA countries.

Now, 10 years into the 21st century, Germany has substantially improved its position in the PISA league tables. This chapter explains how Germany could have so misjudged the relative quality of its education system, how it could have fallen so far from where it had been generations before, what it did to reverse its unfavourable position, and what other nations might learn from this experience.

Table 9.1 **Germany's mean scores on reading, mathematics and science scales in PISA**

	PISA 2000	PISA 2003	PISA 2006	PISA 2009
	Mean score	Mean score	Mean score	Mean score
Reading	484	491	495	497
Mathematics		503	504	513
Science			516	520

Source: OECD (2010), *PISA 2009 Volume I, What Students Know and Can Do: Student Performance in Reading, Mathematics and Science*, OECD Publishing.
StatLink ⬛🖱⬛ http://dx.doi.org/10.1787/888932366769

A HISTORICAL PERSPECTIVE

German education takes shape in the 19th and early 20th centuries

Just as the modern Japanese education system emerged from the humiliation that followed the arrival of Admiral Peary and the Black Ships (Chapter 6), the beginning of the modern German education system is thought by some historians to have begun with the defeat of Prussia and the other German states by Napoleon at Jena in 1806. The Prussians were devastated in spirit as well as materially and emerged determined to rise once again to defeat Napoleon and reassert Prussia's key place in the European world order. Over the next seven years, Stein, Hardenberg and others set about reconstructing Prussia's military and its spirit. Up until then, the officer corps had been limited to a very narrow slice of the German nobility, who had grown lazy and corrupt. The new leaders concluded that they needed to draw on a much larger base of talent. To do that, they would have to educate a larger fraction of the nobility.

This proved to be a seminal moment for German education. The new leaders brought into their government the person with whom the genesis of the modern German education system is most closely identified, Wilhelm von Humboldt. Humboldt is widely regarded as the father of the modern German *Gymnasium*. He is also one of the key figures in the emergence of the modern research university.

Humboldt's ideas were framed by his association with the leaders of the second round of the German Enlightenment: Schiller, Goethe Fichte, Herder and others. They believed that the world is not a machine operating according to preset rules over which man has no dominion, but rather that the world is what we make it, good or bad, and that man's highest responsibility is moral. They believed that the duty of the school is to help the individual realise himself, and create a civilised state which would provide freedom to all. These are the tenets of German Idealism and the Romantic school of German philosophy. Built on the foundation of the German Enlightenment, this outlook emphasises a vision of education that could be said to be anti-instrumental, in the sense that its aim is to create the ideal human being. It is a moral and aesthetic vision, going way beyond the intellect. It is the antithesis of the idea that the purpose of education is to prepare the educated person to make a living.

Humboldt crystallised these concepts in the term "*Bildung*", an enlarged conception of education. In this conception, education, or *Bildung*, is a process of personal development that depends on an education in the humanities. It is centred on the individual and the organic, holistic formation of the individual from the inside. The study of history plays a special role in this development. Humboldt saw the study of history as a way for the individual to define himself in relation to the events and ideas of the past, in particular the classical past.

Humboldt's particular contribution was not philosophical but practical. In only one year in office, 1809-1810, he launched the process that would ultimately turn these ideas into a national system of education. The ideas just briefly described were moulded into a design for a new *Gymnasium*, a secondary school for the middle-upper classes which grounded students in the humanities and prepared them to take the state *Abitur* examination. This model of the *Gymnasium* was implemented in Prussia in 1812 and throughout Germany in 1871. In time, no-one could go to university in Prussia without passing the *Abitur* examinations; neither could one enter the civil service or enter learned professions, such as law, without having passed the *Abitur*.

The only institutions at which one could earn the *Abitur* were the rebuilt *Gymnasien* (plural in German for the singular *Gymnasium*). The curriculum was laid down in detail by the state. The only people who could teach in the *Gymnasien* were people who had themselves passed the *Abitur* and attended university. Indeed, the legislation provided that future *Gymnasium* teachers had to distinguish themselves in their studies of the core subjects in the university curriculum. The *Abitur* was established in this way as one of the world's most famous and most admired examinations.

The laws establishing this system made it quite clear that the purpose of education was a state purpose. The schools, including private and religious schools, were controlled in detail by the state and by detailed legislation.

The next key figure in the development of the German education system was the educator Georg Kerschensteiner, whose career spanned the last half of the 19th century and the first half of the 20th century. Born into genteel poverty and identifying all his life with the working class, Kerschensteiner focused his energies on the education of working people. A patriot, he believed that the best education prepared young people to contribute to the state through their work. The best way to prepare them for that work was to create an education system that would fuse schooling and apprenticeship in the workplace.

Earlier, in the 1870s, the German government had abolished regulations giving German craftspeople special status and protection in the German economy. Kerschensteiner played an important role in reversing that policy, re-establishing the special position of German craftspeople, and creating a new system of vocational education that would ultimately play a key – perhaps decisive – role in Germany's march to technological and manufacturing excellence. Germany is renowned the world over for its craftsmanship in manufacturing. It is not just the apprenticeship system that makes Germany an economic winner, but that the system emphasises first-class craftsmanship. This point is returned to later.

Among Kerschensteiner's voluminous writings, the following passage stands out:

> The value of our education, insofar as the greatest mass of the people will benefit from it, resides basically not so much in the development of an intellectual horizon, as in consistent instruction in conscientious, thorough, neat work, in the regular habits of absolute obedience and the faithful performance of duty. (Hahn, 1998, p. 3)

It is hard to imagine words that could contrast more vividly with Humboldt's elitist vision of schooling for the sons and daughters of the nobility.

German mass education in the 20th century

As the 19th century came to a close and the 20th was opening, Germany had uniform elementary schooling with compulsory elementary education for all children aged 6 through 10, providing four years of basic education. This demonstrated Germany's commitment to a state-run system of basic education. Following completion of elementary school, students were streamed into one of three types of school:

- *Volksschule* – The students thought to be of low ability (the majority), were streamed into the *Volksschule* (People's School, later call the Main School or *Hauptschule*) where they would get a few more years of education, and receive a qualification entitling them to apply for training leading to working-class jobs in Germany.

- *Realschule* – Students thought to be of higher ability were streamed into the *Realschule*, where they would prepare for a qualification entitling them to apply for more training that would lead to more prestigious jobs such as clerks, technicians and lower-level civil servants.

- *Gymnasium* – Those thought to be of the highest ability were streamed into the *Gymnasium*, where they would be given a broad preparation in the humanities and prepared to take examinations for the *Abitur*, which was the sole gateway to the professions, teaching and the upper levels of the civil service.

These school divisions corresponded rather neatly to the social divisions that characterised feudal Germany. The *Gymnasium* was for the sons and daughters of the nobility and the upper middle class – the class born during the first industrial revolution and composed of business people, high and middle state officials, artists and so on. The *Realschule* was for the sons and daughters of the lower middle class burghers. And the *Volksschule*, later the *Hauptschule*, was for the German working class – the people. In effect, beyond a few years of basic school for everyone, each social class had its own schools, though these secondary schools were not compulsory until 1918. Something similar happened in other northern European countries too, but, as we shall see, they subsequently abandoned this system, while Germany retained it.

Except under Hitler's Third Reich, the individual German states were responsible for the design and operation of their own education systems. Another system, managed though not run by the federal government, had developed to regulate the occupations and professions. Virtually all professions and occupations were subject to regulation by the state. Each had a set of entrance criteria to be satisfied by passing a written and practical exam. Those occupations could not, by law, be practised by people who had not met the criteria and passed the exams.

Up to 1918 the guilds, large industry employers' associations and chambers of commerce had managed and ran the system of in-company training, set up the rules and regulated the occupations on a legal basis. In the years following the First World War, the national government set the standards and regulated the occupations that had been drafted by the employers. The government introduced an obligatory day in school for apprentices. Unions were not involved, with some exceptions.

Since 1969, the criteria and standards for the occupations have been set by federal government in close co-operation with employers and trade unions, meeting together under the watchful eye of the national government, which ratify and publish them when agreement is reached. The place for negotiating standards between federal government, employers and unions is the federal institute for vocational education and training (BIBB), which also co-ordinates the curriculum for the school portion of the dual system with the federal states.

What Georg Kerschensteiner did was put these two quite separate systems – the schools on the one hand and the occupations on the other – together in an ingenious partnership. Later this came to be known as the "dual system" (Box 9.1). The idea was a simple extension of the ancient idea of the guild-based apprenticeship, in which students seeking jobs in the workplace would first apprentice themselves to masters of their chosen trades, work for them as apprentices at a reduced wage (sometimes just for room and board), in exchange for instruction in the trades. At the end of the training, there would be an examination and the young worker would be declared a "journeyman", with the right to work in that trade at prevailing wage levels. But the journeyman could not employ others without first becoming a master, which entailed passing another, much more demanding, exam.

Kerschensteiner updated the whole apprenticeship idea and married it to the highly evolved and very stratified German education system. Students who complete a secondary education in Germany are invited to become apprentices by firms, with their wages determined at a national level in a process managed by the government. The time spent on the job as an apprentice is augmented by time spent in a "continuation school", a special vocational school designed to provide the apprentice with the theory underlying the practical work, and, at the same time, continue his or her broader education, though at a level far below that provided by the *Gymnasium*.

The national legislation authorising and regulating this dual system of education does not require the student to have come into the system from any particular type of secondary school. But the student does not get into the dual system unless an employer who chooses to be part of the system offers that student an apprenticeship. Until quite recently, most employers looked to the *Hauptschule* as the primary source of their apprentices. Some employers, mainly those looking for white collar employees below the professional level, sourced their apprentices mainly from the *Realschule*. Very few came from the *Gymnasium*, whose *raison d'être* was to supply the universities with candidates.

Box 9.1 **Germany's "dual system"**

Germany's dual education system is called "dual" because it combines apprenticeships in a company and vocational education at a vocational school in one programme. In the company, the apprentice receives practical training which is supplemented by theoretical instruction in the vocational school. Around 60% of all young people learn a trade within the dual system of vocational education and training in Germany (UNESCO, 2010). There are around 350 state-recognised training occupations, such as carpentry, car mechanics and roofing. The period of training is usually two to three years and is concluded by a state examination. During this time, the apprentice is financially remunerated. Access to this training is not formally linked to a specific school certificate.

While the public education system is directed and operated by the *Länder*, the dual system is operated under the aegis of the federal government, working with the economic departments of the *Länder*, and the local chambers of commerce.

"For young people", according to Reinhold Weiss, "the dual system is attractive because it is an excellent entrance into the employment system. In Germany, without a formal qualification, your chances of entering a good paying job are low. While you are not guaranteed a career, you are guaranteed training in school and on the job. More short-term apprenticeships are now available that combine work experience with university degrees and financial support. Also, students who finish *Gymnasium* are going into an apprenticeship and then on to university."

German employers realise the value of the system and offer apprenticeships based on shrewd calculations of the economic benefits to be gained, not on outmoded cultural factors. For example, regular employees in Germany, as in many other countries, are hard to dismiss once they are formally employed. In the dual system, however, the employer has no obligation to hire the apprentice at the end of the apprenticeship. This gives the employer time to decide whether or not they will be suitable. And under German law, employers are allowed to pay their apprentices substantially less than the market rates for their labour. Analysts have found that the wage difference between apprentice wages and regular wages makes engaging apprentices a good economic deal for the employers. The value they get in work performed typically exceeds the cost of employing them as apprentices. These economic benefits to employers could be reproduced in other industrial countries relatively easily with the appropriate economic policies.

And it is not just the employers who benefit. For many students of all abilities, the approach to learning taken in most schools is dull and uninteresting. Learning only becomes engaging when put to use. In fact, learning becomes necessary in order to solve the problems these students find engaging. Problem-driven learning is the kind of learning most of us do when we leave school behind and enter the adult world. It is in this sense that the dual system is very much a part of the education system. Though students are accepting wages below the market level, they are gaining access to the possibility of employment with companies who might not otherwise be interested in looking at them. They are gaining important skills at the employer's expense. For students going to *Gymnasium* and hoping to go to university, doing a stint in the dual system first is a very important insurance policy in case their university application fails. Many employers are increasingly willing to send promising young people who come in through the dual system to university later at their own expense.

Germans are themselves divided on the value of the system. While many see it as a major source of Germany's industrial strength, some see it as an anachronism, a holdover from a bygone age that will eventually slow Germany's growth and leave it uncompetitive. This group points to the rapidly changing face of the job market and thinks that rather than training young Germans for specific jobs, they should be trained for a world in which jobs are constantly shifting and evolving as a function of new technology and new forms of work organisation. They see the swiftly rising corps of mostly immigrant students who do not succeed in getting into the dual system as a national tragedy that also threatens the viability of the German economy and undermines the legitimacy of the dual system.

Defenders of the dual system point out that whereas it used to take as much as 10 years to create a new occupation, the process of creating new occupations can now be accomplished in as little as 18 months. Of the 350 separate occupations, many are new occupations, reflecting the swiftly changing needs of business. They point to the greatly increased permeability of the system – the many pathways now available to students for moving in and out of the dual system from different kinds of secondary schools and into different kinds of employment and further education opportunities, including university. This reveals how the dual system is making the necessary adaptations to play as constructive a role in the future as it has in the past. And they point to the continued interest of employers in offering apprenticeships to students as further evidence that the system works. It is still the case that 60% of the age cohort go through the dual system.

Even so, in the decades immediately following the Second World War, it was not uncommon for the Chief Executive Officers and Board Chairman of global companies based in Germany to have come up from the *Hauptschule* and the dual system, rather than from the *Gymnasium* and university. Throughout the first half of the 20th century, the dual system was being continuously improved. Companies that had taken in smart, enterprising youth through the *Hauptschule* and dual system intake door had kept investing in them as they promoted them through the system. New technological universities had been created alongside the traditional universities and the system had been changed to create routes that would enable graduates of *Realschule* and even *Hauptschule* to attend them.

When interviewed for this report, Karl Ulrich Mayer, a sociology professor at Yale University, noted that a typical apprentice who successfully completed his training and became a master was the backbone of the German workforce and its competitive advantage. A former apprentice armed with this technical know-how and workplace experience, he said, could make a sales call, sell the equipment and repair it. There is just not the division between technical and sales staff that you find in other countries. In Germany, in contrast to France and Great Britain, the expansion of general education did not diminish the role of the apprenticeship at all.

These themes will appear again below in more detail, but the point here is that the twin impulses underlying the German education system, one driven by the Romantic, Idealist philosophers towards a very humanistic non-instrumental image of education, and the other just the opposite, a vision of education that put education for vocation and occupation at the centre, were both very much alive, each balancing the other.

The tripartite system of secondary schools was not unique to Germany at the opening of the 20th century. This system of separate secondary schools based on class and caste was widely used in Northern Europe. The system of dual education was used in some form in Denmark, Germany, Switzerland and Austria. But, in the first half of the 20th century, most of the other countries of Northern Europe abandoned the idea of separating 10-year olds into different kinds of secondary schools. They no longer thought it was a good idea to decide for such young children what class of job and place in society they would have for the rest of their lives. These other countries had also had feudal systems that allocated opportunity by clear divisions in the social class structure, but, as they developed as true political democracies and understood more clearly the demands of advanced industrial societies, they came to the view that they needed more of their population to have better education and skills than before.

The Germans might well have done the same, but for their reaction to the events leading up to the Second World War and their response to their loss in the war. There was great resistance to changes in the structure of the schools. And a governance structure that essentially required consensus reinforced the tendency to resist changes of this sort.

The tripartite system is transformed: The 1960s and 1970s

In the 1960s and 70s, when the German economy was booming, Germany developed major labour shortages. It solved its problem by inviting people from lower income countries to come and work in Germany, mainly in jobs that native Germans did not want. Many of these people came from Turkey and other countries with relatively low levels of education compared to Germany. At first, the presumption was that these "guest workers" would stay for a short time and then leave. But some came and recruited others. They settled in Germany and raised families there. Their children grew, married and raised children. Those children have now had children themselves. Their German was typically very poor.

At this time, demand was steadily increasing for workers with high skills, and decreasing for workers with low skills. That created increased demand for entry into the *Gymnasium*. It had always been true that students who went to the lower status secondary schools and then directly into the labour market through the dual system made more money initially than students to who went to *Gymnasium* and then to university. That fact was a prime attraction of the dual system.

As more students went to *Gymnasium*, and passed the *Abitur*, more decided to then enter the dual system and get a qualification, as a form of insurance against unemployment, before proceeding to university. More students who would formerly have gone to the *Hauptschule* put in the extra effort needed to get into the *Realschule*, which improved their chance of getting an apprenticeship from a good employer. But employers offering the best apprenticeships, who had earlier taken students only from *Realschule*, began to see a steady stream of *Gymnasium* students, some of whom already had an *Abitur*, knocking on their doors. Others who had formerly recruited only from the *Hauptschule*, found that they could get better candidates from the *Realschule*. Increasingly, the *Hauptschule* became a giant storage locker for the students who had no future, a road to nowhere for those students. As the public saw this happening, the children of the lower middle class and some in the working class abandoned the *Hauptschule* and headed for the *Realschule* and even the *Gymnasien* instead.

In this way the old tripartite system was quietly transformed. In the past, most of the graduates of the *Hauptschule* went on to apprenticeships and had a good shot at a decent job and a good career. When the transition was complete, the *Hauptschule* had become, in some schools and in some parts of the country, a dumping ground for students who would find it hard to get a qualification of any kind – these included immigrants and native Germans from lower class families alike.

Indeed the PISA data show that the most important predictor of failure to get a qualification was the socio-economic background of the student. The second most influential predictor was language. Regardless of whether you were an immigrant or a native German, if your German was poor when you were very young, you had little support from any institution to learn fluent German, and without fluent German, you were likely to flounder in school. The third most important predictor was immigrant status (though this generality masks large differences; for example, the majority of Greek immigrant children attend *Gymnasium*, but only a small minority of Turkish immigrant children do so).

When the German economy slowed, some native Germans who were short of work resented the competition from the immigrants for jobs. German elementary schools were ill equipped to deal with students who were not proficient German speakers. The immigrant population grew faster in the northern German cities and towns than in the south. Nationally, the immigrants grew to nearly 10% of the adult population and more than 25% of the population of the schools. But, in some northern German cities, the immigrant population accounted for half or more of the students in elementary schools.

The Germans had another chance to abandon their tripartite secondary school structure when the Berlin Wall dividing East and West Germany came down and reunification of the two previously divided parts of Germany began.

There was much wrong with the German Democratic Republic (GDR), but their education system was not one of them. When the GDR was created and became a satellite of the USSR, the GDR leaders abolished the distinctions among secondary schools and all secondary schools in the GDR became comprehensive secondary schools.

Most education experts now agree that the education system on the other side of the Berlin Wall dividing the two Germanys was a justifiable source of pride for the East Germans.[1] But when the wall came down in 1989, the former East Germans were eager to adopt everything Western and to abandon everything Eastern as soon as possible. And West German conservatives had no interest in adopting anything associated with the former Communist government.

According to Andreas Schleicher, Head of PISA Studies at the OECD, "The West German system was implemented in the East. Lost to East Germany was their more equitable, de-tracked education system along with their excellent early childhood system."

Former Head of the BIBB, Hermann Schmidt, was a member of one of the Reunification Commissions for education. He recalls arguing futilely with the education ministers of the former East German states that they should not abandon their upper secondary school programme which led to a combined qualification of *Abitur* and journeyman certificate. Only later did some of those education ministers tell Schmidt that they now realised they had made a terrible mistake. However, some states did collapse the tripartite system into two parts, one of them the familiar *Gymnasium* and the other a combination of the *Hauptschule* and the *Realschule*. Those former East German states that did maintain some of the former education structures outperformed most of the former West German states in the early years of the new millennium, according to the experts interviewed for this report (Hermann Schmidt and Rheinhold Weiss).

According to Schmidt, Germans on both sides of the Iron Curtain believed, as did the rest of the world, that West Germany had one of the world's best-performing educational systems. This was despite the fact that they had no way of knowing how well they were doing relative to other nations. The highest status parts of the system, the parts that spoke for the system as a whole, were the *Gymnasium* and the professional educators who staffed them, as well as the key education officials in the German states. All were still very much in accord with the vision of education defined in the term *Bildung* as first set forth by Humboldt. According to this vision, what is most important about education – the aesthetic ends, the search for freedom and truth, the ennobling exposure to history and so on – is simply not measurable. And so it was not measured. The national government had no legal authority to measure student achievement or progress, the teachers were opposed and the states had no interest in measuring these things.

THE GERMAN EDUCATION REFORMS

The first warning bell that all was not as it should be in German education came when Germany took part in the first TIMSS survey of mathematics and science in 1995 and scored poorly. However, according to a leading German journalist, Thomas Kerstan of *Die Zeit*, the German press took very little notice.

Nevertheless, some members of the federal government and the *Länder* had been worried for some time that German education might be less effective than widely thought. In 1997, the Standing Conference of the ministers of Education and Cultural Affairs of the Länder in the Federal Republic of Germany* – known henceforth in this volume as the Council of ministers – moved to make Germany an active participant in future international comparative studies of student achievement. They began to prepare the ground for the new PISA assessments.

The first PISA assessments, administered in 2000, focused on language literacy (Table 9.1). The results shocked the German nation. According to Kerstan, "No one expected that one quarter of German 15-year-olds could not read fluently. And worse yet, the PISA results showed that German at-risk students' performance was among the worst in the world." Germany came well below the average overall for all the countries tested. A substantial fraction of German students tested below Mexico. Germany did no better in mathematics and science than it did in language. And it turned out that student performance was more closely tied to the socio-economic background of the students than was the case for many other OECD countries.

Whilst the TIMSS results had hardly been reported, major newspapers ran four, five and six-page special sections on the PISA results. The news and discussions of the results were all over the radio and television. The news about Germany's poor results got far more coverage in Germany than the surprise news that Finland had topped the PISA league tables got in Finland.

Suddenly, educators could no longer make the case that what was most important about education could not be measured. If Germany was far behind in every important area of the curriculum, if Germany's education standards generally lagged those in the rest of the developed world and if Germans could no longer maintain, as they had for so long, that Germany had one of the most equitable education systems in the world, then, clearly, something had to be done.

The parties on the left of the political spectrum dusted off proposals they had been making to no avail for a long time. Edelgard Bulmahn, who was the German minister for Education at the time, had long thought that "the tripartite system of secondary schools was a mirror image of the feudal system, a system that only needed a small number with high qualification, a few with the middle range of education and the rest with only a basic education." In her view, "a modern knowledge-based economy would mostly need a work force with a very high level of education across the board."

She and others had been making this case for years. They had actually succeeded in getting a start on their agenda in a few German states in the 1970s. Among the items on their agenda were promoting better child care and more effective Kindergarten education. They wanted to abandon the time-honoured practice of sending their children home from school for lunch and ending the school day right there. And they wanted to end the tripartite division of the secondary schools and provide a more equal chance for students from poor and immigrant families. After unification, they had started to get some of the former East German states to combine at least two of the three secondary school types to create a fairer system, but they had not got very far.

Although they had made progress in some states on some parts of their agenda in the 1970s and 80s, there had been a conservative backlash. The progress on these and other elements of their agenda was undone and overall funding for the schools reduced substantially. Andreas Schleicher notes that in an export-driven economy where the demand from the rest of the world for German goods and services remained high, the system was not forced to change. German cars continued to be in high demand, and besides, if German business leaders could not find the skills they needed in Germany, they could find those skills elsewhere.

Now, however, that agenda was on the table as never before. The states had all the cards. The states had always played a strong role in Germany, but when the Allies took the reins after the war, they insisted on rewriting the German constitution so that a strong central government could never again take over education in Germany. Under the new constitution, there was even less room for a federal role in education than in the United States.

· ·

* The German translation for the English term Council of ministers is: Die Ständige Konferenz der Kultusminister der Länder in der Bundesrepublik Deutschland (Kurzform: Kultusministerkonferenz).

Fortunately, the *Länder*, acting through the Council of ministers, had already set the stage with their own first national report on education. This meant the reformers in the federal government and the *Länder* could join forces. Minister Buhlman proposed investing EUR 4 billion in an all day school programme. She also proposed developing national education standards, and creating a new national report on education. Agreement on this agenda did not come easily, but a compromise was reached on the all day school programme in 2003 and on national education standards in 2004. And the *Länder* agreed as well to a new national report on education.

Agreement on the overall reform agenda was possible because the politics were different this time. The PISA results had to be dealt with and could not be swept under the carpet. The left's agenda was for national standards, beefed up Kindergartens, more money for special language training for children and families that could not speak German fluently, a lot more money to pay for extending the school day well into the afternoon, more money for teacher training and fundamental reform of the old feudal structure of the schools. The right wanted to hold the educators accountable for their performance and they wanted the schools managed according to modern management theory, so that, in exchange for being more accountable for their performance, the school staff would be given more autonomy by the state bureaucrats. This part of the agenda, as it turned out, was also enthusiastically embraced by the left as well.

Each side had been effectively blocked by the other for years, producing gridlock on educational policy change. But the "PISA shock" changed all that. Now, for the first time in years real change was possible on a surprisingly large scale. The uproar in the press reflected a very strong reaction to the PISA results from the public. Politicians who ignored it risked their careers.

In the end, the states took the lead operating mainly through the Council of ministers, though the federal government took some initiatives in the limited domain available to it. The agendas of the right and left were fused together, something that could never have happened earlier, but which made it possible to forge a more-or-less common agenda through all the states, irrespective of political party. This led to a number of specific responses to the perceived problems behind Germany's poor performance, described below.

Changing the school structure to reduce the influence of socio-economic background on student achievement

Germany has a higher correlation between family socio-economic status and student achievement than any other OECD country. Many German education experts had been deeply concerned about this problem for decades and attributed it mainly to the tripartite structure of German secondary education.

As Schleicher points out, the data showed that even when students were matched on actual achievement, elementary school children whose parents had attended *Gymnasium* were three times as likely to be sent to a *Gymnasium* than children whose parents had graduated from a *Hauptschule*.

This undermines the assumption by German educators that the choice of secondary school is based solely on achievement in elementary school. The fact that this was not the case showed that the system is manifestly unfair. For a number of reasons, it systematically denies opportunity to those whose parents are from the lower classes. Another contributing factor is the fact that decisions to send students to a specific secondary school are made so early, for children aged only 10.

Different states have responded to these issues in different ways:

- A few states delayed the assignment of students to the tripartite system until they were 12 rather than 10 years old.
- More states chose to combine the *Realschule* and the *Hauptschule* into one school.
- Some states allowed students in any of the three types of lower secondary school to go to any type of upper secondary school. This greatly reduced, though did not entirely eliminate, the tracking system, because many secondary schools had their own streaming systems to differentiate students according to ability.
- Some states introduced or reintroduced comprehensive secondary schools which any child can attend and which offer the whole range of qualifications. However, this option is not offered throughout the country, and only in parallel with some or all of the options just listed. One obstacle to this was the bad reputation of these schools caused by their poor introduction in the 1970s.
- Some states decided to allow several of these options to coexist side by side.

By the end of the 2008/09 school year, there were 4 283 *Hauptschulen*, 2 625 *Realschulen*, 3 070 *Gymnasien* and 1 363 schools offering both *Hauptschule* and *Realschule* courses. There were also 705 comprehensive high schools (*Integrierte Gesamtschulen*) – see Figure 9.1. Some informed observers believe that within 10 years there will no longer be any separate *Realschule* and *Hauptschule*.

■ Figure 9.1 ■
Germany's education system organisation

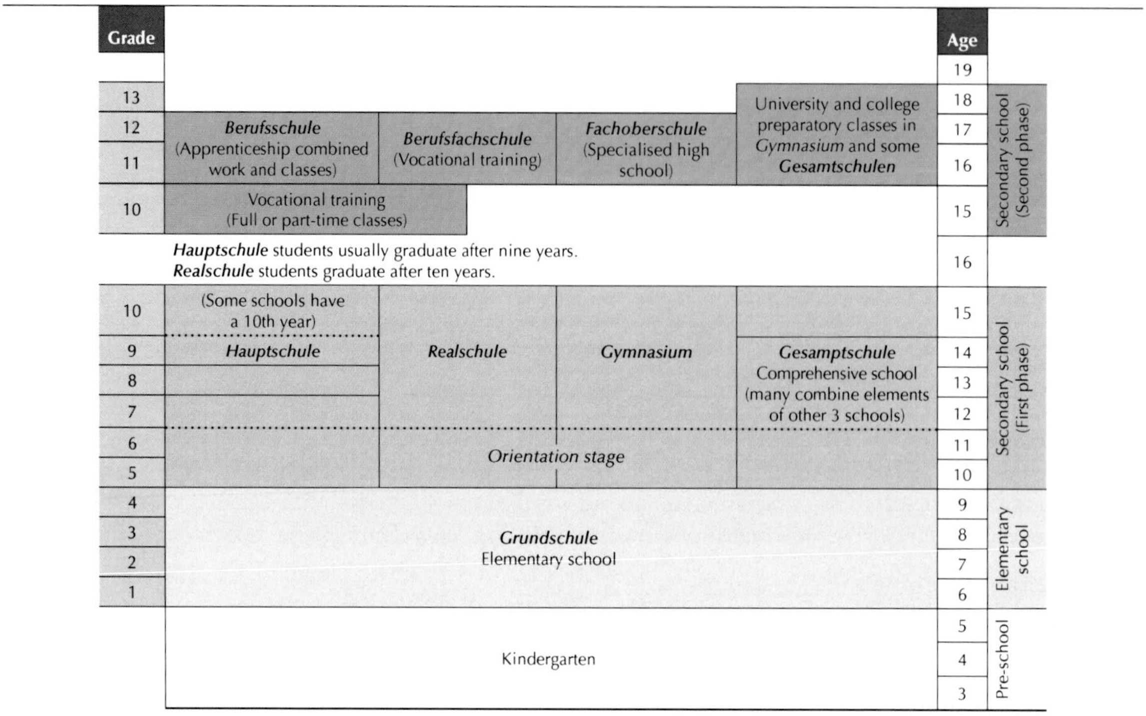

Grade					Age	
					19	Secondary school (Second phase)
13				University and college preparatory classes in *Gymnasium* and some *Gesamtschulen*	18	
12	*Berufsschule* (Apprenticeship combined work and classes)	*Berufsfachschule* (Vocational training)	*Fachoberschule* (Specialised high school)		17	
11					16	
10	Vocational training (Full or part-time classes)				15	
	Hauptschule students usually graduate after nine years. *Realschule* students graduate after ten years.				16	
10	(Some schools have a 10th year)				15	Secondary school (First phase)
9	*Hauptschule*	*Realschule*	*Gymnasium*	*Gesamptschule* Comprehensive school (many combine elements of other 3 schools)	14	
8					13	
7					12	
6		Orientation stage			11	
5					10	
4					9	Elementary school
3		*Grundschule* Elementary school			8	
2					7	
1					6	
		Kindergarten			5	Pre-school
					4	
					3	

Addressing the language problems

Data showed a very high correlation between children's command of German on entering elementary school and their subsequent performance (Werning, *et al.*, 2008). Because services for preschool children and Kindergarten are not part of the school system, the federal government is permitted by the German constitution to intervene in this arena. The federal government has introduced programmes, supervised by the states and run by municipalities or charities, to significantly increase the level of organised, high quality, affordable language training for children whose families do not speak Germany fluently at home. This language training is offered to Kindergarten-level students so that by the time they arrive in elementary school they are ideally as fluent as native Germans.

The data also showed that the children of poor, minority and immigrant parents were among the least likely to be in preschool, even though they needed these services more than the children who did attend. Preschool services were more likely to be offered as child care than as serious educational services and their child care workers were poorly trained. Because the mothers of poor, minority and immigrant children were more likely to be working out of the home than other mothers, the lack of access to affordable, quality child care and preschool services were contributing heavily to these children's lack of essential skills when they arrived at school at the age of six. Kindergarten is the traditional form of preschool in Germany. In a series of legislative actions, Germany created a right to a place in Kindergarten for every child from the age of three until they begin elementary school. Other legislation expanded the availability of preschool for children under the age of three. Further, the *Länder*, acting together, tried to beef up the educational content of the preschool programmes to include language, writing, communication, mathematics, natural sciences, information technology, fine arts and other subjects. However, these initiatives have not been extensively implemented.

Addressing the lack of transparency and accountability in the system

For many observers, the problem revealed by the "PISA shock" was first and foremost the lack of transparency and accountability in the German education system.

While standards were assumed to be high across Germany, the PISA data and analyses showed that standards were in fact low and highly variable. Though many people had called for uniform, high and transparent standards for years, they had always been successfully rebuffed. As pointed out above, Germans had a real aversion to formal measures of student achievement based exclusively on examination performance. Thus standards varied from qualification to qualification, school to school, teacher to teacher and state to state. And so did measures, if there were any at all. In many states, individual high schools set their own *Abitur* exams. Some higher education institutions and employers, for example, gave more credits to students who passed a Bavarian *Abitur* than they did to students whose *Abitur* came from other states.

The whole German education system also had a real aversion to the use of empirical evidence and rigorous analysis of data as the basis of educational decision-making. Policy was based on values, not on data. Several solutions have been proposed as part of the reform:

Common standards

In 2003 and 2004, the Council of ministers decided to develop national educational standards for Grade 4 in primary school in German and mathematics; and standards for German, mathematics, a first foreign language (English or French), and science (biology, chemistry and physics) for Grade 9/Grade 10 in lower secondary school.

In 2007, the Council of ministers announced additional standards at the end of upper secondary school in seven subjects: mathematics, German, French, English, biology, chemistry and physics.

These performance standards describe in some detail subject-specific competencies that students are expected to meet throughout Germany. There had never been national standards of this sort before in Germany. They are mandatory for all 16 German states, by common agreement among the states and are benchmarked against international standards. They emphasise the kind of skills and competencies measured by the PISA assessments where appropriate.

New assessments based on the standards

In 2006, the Council of ministers agreed to develop common assessments for comparing the performance of the 16 German states using common national scales, for 3rd graders in elementary school, 8th graders in certain secondary schools and 9th graders in others (Figure 9.1). These new assessments are based on a representative sample of students in each state, and do not have high stakes associated with them either for students or teachers.

In addition, each state undertook to develop state-wide testing systems set to the new standards. In many cases, states joined forces to develop these assessments. These assessments are conducted every spring and test entire student populations in grade 3 and, in some states, grade 6.

Participation in comparative international assessments

Germany also committed itself to participating in three major international programmes of comparative national student testing: PISA at the secondary school level, and TIMSS and PIRLS Progress in International Reading Literacy Study) at the elementary school level. It also announced it would publish the results of these assessments.

A new organisation to monitor the system

In order to implement these far-reaching changes in policy, the Germans created a new institution in 2004 – the Institute for Educational Progress based at the Humboldt University in Berlin – to provide the infrastructure and scientific capacity needed to support the development of the standards and assessments the new monitoring system would need, and to gather, analyse and disseminate the resulting information.

A new reporting framework

The federal government and the *Länder* agreed to publish an indicator-based system of reports, *Education in Germany*, to be based on a continuous, data-based, problem-centred examination of the German education system.

These reports are published every two years and present data based on a permanent core of indicators to guarantee consistent reporting. The first report, which focused on education and condition of migrants, came out in 2006. The second, produced in 2008, focused on transitions from early childhood education into and through the various stages of schooling and vocational education and from there into further education and work.[2]

Greater capacity for gathering and analysing performance data

As the Germans did not place a high value on the use of empirical data and its analysis in the education policy-making process, Germany had not invested much in educational research. While things had begun to improve from 1965, the PISA shock greatly accelerated the process. Now government is making systemic investments in the capacity of the educational research establishment to do the kind of research that is needed to base school policy on empirical data on system performance. For example, in 2007 the Federal ministry of Education announced a Framework Programme for the Promotion of Empirical Education Research. The framework lays out topics and methods for research that the government is particularly interested in pursuing. The ministry is collaborating with the *Länder* on the design of this research programme, thereby increasing the chance that the research will actually inform policy and practice.

Increasing school hours

The 2000 PISA results highlighted that German students spent much less time in school than students from other countries. Previously, students only attended school in the morning. Now, students in many schools do not leave school until 4:00 pm or later. However, schools do not have to participate in this scheme and schools that do participate are required to remain open in the afternoon for only three days a week.

Increasing autonomy for school heads

The German reformers were heavily influenced by the modern management model, which holds that competent management sets clear goals and clear measures of those goals, provides positive incentives to line mangers to accomplish those goals, and then gives them a lot of discretion over how to achieve those goals. But, traditionally in Germany, school heads had very little discretion. Following the PISA shock, however, the states generally found ways to give German school heads and faculties more authority over school budget, staffing decisions and programmes.

Ludger Woessmann, Economics Professor at the University of Munich, described the change as follows, "Until recently, schools in Germany had no autonomy. For example, schools were assigned teachers. In some states, schools can now choose their own teachers. Research shows that there is increased performance when you have central exams and strong school accountability. Let the schools figure out how to get to high performance on central exams."

Some of the changes described above were very expensive. However, even while the German schools budget increased, German education spending, at 4.5% of GDP, is still below the OECD average of 5.2%. Much of this increase can be explained by the enormous jump in the time students were required to spend in school. And more money was also needed, outside the education budget, on expanding early childhood education. Some of the increase in the education budget was offset by reducing by a year the time students were required to spend in *Gymnasium*.

Improving teacher quality

It is possible that Germany's teachers were a major source of the problems revealed by the PISA data. For example, Karl Ulrich Mayer suspects that, "one reason for the weakness of the education system after the eighties was a severe over-aging of the teacher population. Many were hired as a response to the baby boom in the sixties and early seventies and formed an age-homogeneous teaching staff who were burned out and unmotivated, and especially ill-equipped to deal with students from an immigrant background. I would not be surprised if some of the effects of the improvement in performance after PISA were due to the recent hiring of younger teachers."

One cannot become a teacher in Germany without an *Abitur*. Kaija Landsberg, Director of Teach First, the German version of Teach for America, explains further:

> After leaving *Gymnasium* with an *Abitur*, future teachers went to university, where they would have had to major in two subjects in which they had a special interest and study those subjects at the same level of challenge as other university students majoring in those subjects, thus producing an unusually high level of subject matter knowledge in these future teachers. Following their university education in the subjects they planned to teach

and in the pedagogy of those subjects, these candidate teachers still had to take another two-year programme of combined supervised teaching and related course work before they could enter the workforce, and, even then, had at least an additional year of mentoring and close supervision, as well as another examination, before they were allowed to assume the role of a full professional teacher. Thus we are looking at people selected in the first instance from the top third of the distribution who were then given a demanding education in the subjects they were going to teach followed literally by years of professional education in teaching, which included a multi-year apprenticeship.

When the PISA shock hit Germany, many people assumed that the teachers' unions would stonewall the reforms. Instead, the teachers' unions actually played an important role in supporting the reforms and paving the way for their passage. No doubt that role was made easier by the government's agreement that the new data on student performance would not be used in accountability systems with high stakes, or any stakes at all, for teachers. The teachers made sure that the new exams would use a sampling procedure that would by itself make it impossible to use student performance data to set teachers' compensation or affect the promotion of retention of individual teachers. But the teachers agreed to the extended school day without a comparable increase in pay. The result was a continued high standing for teachers among the German public and the right to an important place at the table as education policy is made.

One might ask why, if teacher quality was good before the shock and after the shock, what has changed? In other countries, when unexpectedly poor education results have been announced, the teachers are often the first to be blamed. The German teachers and their unions knew that and they knew how important it was for them to get out in front of the reform process if they were not to be steamrollered by it. And then there is the matter of professional pride. It would simply be human for capable people whose professional standing had been jeopardised by poor results to do their utmost to produce better results. That process would have been made easier by the reforms that devolved more authority to the schools than they had had before.

UNDERSTANDING THE IMPACT OF THE GERMAN EDUCATION REFORMS

There are several challenges involved in trying to link the reforms to the improvements in Germany's educational performance. For example:

- These policy changes were not made or implemented all at once, but were spread out over several years and were often implemented differently by different states. Some are only now being implemented at scale.

- There has not been enough time yet for the important improvements made to German preschool education and in the literacy of very young children from non-German speaking homes to show up in the performance of the 15-year-old students tested by PISA in 2009.

- Though the new standards have stimulated a great deal of discussion among German teachers, it is not clear that there has been enough time since their release in 2004 for them to have a strong impact on the performance of 15-year-old students. The results of the first national assessments of German students in grade 4 against the new national standards are only coming out in 2010, one year after the last PISA assessments were administered to German students.

- Though there has been some movement towards restructuring the famous German tripartite structure of secondary schooling in some states, the total number of restructured schools as a proportion of all German secondary schools is still fairly small, so one can not attribute a great deal of the gain in German students' performance on PISA to the school restructuring programme.

- It was not so easy in the past to measure performance. Germany's much improved research establishment should now be able to track implementation closely and soon more and higher quality data will be available to education practitioners and policy makers.

All these points can be interpreted as good news. There has been substantial improvement in performance since the PISA 2000 assessments, despite the fact that the reforms have been only partially implemented so far and have not yet had time to affect the performance of students who were 15 in 2009. We would therefore expect the performance of German students to continue to accelerate in the years to come, as a greater proportion of students are exposed to the reforms.

And because the PISA shock enabled Germany to combine the education agendas of both right and left, there should be more continuity in policy than is often found in most countries with a strong party system of politics.

According to Rheinhold Weiss, Director of Research at the BIBB, "It is not realistic to expect quick results. Germany is on the right track because there are increasing numbers of full-day schools, more support for early childhood education, and more data on the performance of the students and the system."

Most German observers are very tentative in making any judgements about which of the various policy initiatives are most responsible for the gains that have been made so far. Most suggest that it was the PISA shock itself that jolted German educators into action – that once teachers knew how poorly their students were performing, their sense of professionalism was enough to motivate them to improve the situation. Others think that the new standards give teachers a clear picture, for the first time, of what their students are supposed to accomplish. Others have suggested that the innate sense of competition among the *Länder*, combined with the strategy of producing publicly available data comparing the *Länder* on common measures, did the trick.

Below we list some of the factors that our research suggests are most likely to be important in this improved performance.

LESSONS FROM GERMANY

▪ Good quality teachers

Germany selects its teachers from the top third of its high school graduates. The preparation of most teachers in university is more extensive than it is for teachers in most other countries and for most other professions in Germany. All candidates for university degrees in teaching, including elementary school teachers, must undertake extensive work in the subjects they will teach. The recent reforms require the teacher education programmes to provide candidate teachers with skills enabling them to diagnose and address the specific problems faced by struggling students. All states require that teachers participate in an extended period of supervising and mentoring by master teachers before they can take up their duties and become regular full-time teachers. The high quality of Germany's teachers appears to have provided the reserve capacity Germany needed when PISA shock struck, enabling it to improve the achievement of Germany's students even before the new reforms had a chance to take effect.

▪ The value of the dual system

One cannot consider the effectiveness of the German education system without considering the workings of the dual system, which plays a very important function in Germany's education and training. All over the world, the demands of advanced industrial nations mean that to get ahead, school leavers need a new set of skills, such as the ability to set work goals, create a plan for achieving them and then working in a disciplined way to execute that plan; being an effective member or leader of a team; working independently; drawing on experience and theory to solve a wide variety of actual problems; and the ability to think analytically and creatively. Employees who cannot do these things are a serious problem, and a strong drag on competitiveness. The dual system is an efficient way of building these skills, as pointed out by a recent OECD vocational education and training (VET) policy review (Hoeckel and Schwartz, 2010).

Is the dual system applicable outside Germany? Many countries have dismissed it as irrelevant because they think it only suits cultural factors unique to Germany and perhaps a handful of other similar European countries. However, countries that do not have a dual system are now being forced to task their schools with developing these skills in their students, even though schools are not the best settings for developing these skills (Box 9.1). In the workplace, students quickly discover that their jobs are threatened if they do not show up on time or come prepared to put in a good day's work. The workplace teaches one how to be an effective team member and a good leader. It is the ideal place to figure out how to bring what one has learned in school to bear on the kinds of problems likely to be encountered at work, and elsewhere (Field, *et al.*, 2010). The strong involvement of social partners, a characteristic of dual systems, helps to ensure that VET systems are responsive to the needs of the labour market and teach relevant skills. This, in turn, helps young people to find employment.

Germany's flexible combination of formal schooling with the dual system represents a very powerful approach to providing students with skills, knowledge and motivation that could prove decisive on a national scale in international competition. It is possible that Germany's current resurgence on the global economic scene is due in some measure to this combination of formal schooling and apprenticeship.

▪ International benchmarking and accountability

In a way, the entire German story is a story about accountability. Prior to the PISA shock, Germany had no interest in what other countries were doing to bring their education systems up to world class status. But, after the PISA 2000 results, Germany became an avid, determined international benchmarker. Not only did Germany send teams all over the world to learn from other nations, but it quite deliberately built into its own national testing regimes participation in some of the international comparative testing regimes, so that it would never again be surprised by its own standing in relation to that of other countries and so that it could continue to benefit from the experience of other countries. The PISA shock also drove the ambitious reform programme, including whole new national systems of standards and tests. Germany chose not, however, to create a test-driven accountability system with high stakes for students or teachers. In part, this was the result of a desire to keep their teachers on board and enthusiastic about the whole reform package.

▪ Common standards and curricula

Germany thought it had strong standards and sound curriculum and discovered to its dismay that its standards differed wildly from school to school and state to state. It responded by developing common curriculum frameworks and common performance standards.

▪ The use of incentives, especially for students

German students work hard in school because they know that their opportunities in life are a function of the formal qualifications they earn, and the qualifications they earn are a function of how well they do in school. This is just as true of the bricklayer and auto mechanic in Germany as it is of the brain surgeon. The German case is one of the strongest examples of the use of qualifications systems to generate incentives for students to take tough courses and work hard in school.

However, the road ahead is full of challenges. Only last summer there were student and teacher strikes in Germany rooted in controversy over the reforms. *Gymnasium* students feel that there is much more pressure on them than formerly, as they find themselves forced to work against more demanding standards in many states, with far more requirements and one year less in school to meet those requirements than the students who went before them.

In Hamburg, in the summer of 2010, politicians from a Conservative-Green coalition asked whether the common elementary school should be extended to age 12 for students instead of the prevailing age 10. Both parties had agreed to this change, as had the school professionals. But, to the surprise of both political leaders and professional educators, the public, led by an aroused middle class, voted a resounding no.

WHERE IS GERMANY ON THE EDUCATIONAL CONTINUUM?

Germany is one of the world's great industrial powers, often referred to as Europe's economic engine. Wages and benefits in Germany are high relative to those in the rest of the world. Its economy is based not on the sale of commodities, but on the global sale of high-value-added manufactured products. Its success in this arena rests on the quality, creativity and skill of its workforce. By all these measures, one would have to say that Germany is at the far right end of the economic development dimension line described in the introduction to this report (Chapter 1).

With respect to the teacher quality dimension line, Germany made a very important decision when it decided many years ago to require that all teachers hold an *Abitur*. Other measures to assure high teacher quality followed. Most experts would place Germany at the right end of the teacher quality dimension line, though not all experts in Germany would agree. By some measures, other countries recruit from a more elite segment of their population.

When PISA shock descended on Germany, policy makers not only set national curriculum standards, but also required that they be benchmarked to international standards. That meant that they emphasised complex skills and the ability to apply high level skills to problems of the sort to be expected in high wage, heavily industrialised countries. The centuries-old German commitment to the arts and to literature, as well as to mathematics and science, assured that the new curriculum standards would not short change the development of students' creative abilities. However, some Germans continue to be concerned that standards will by their very nature endanger both creativity and the arts. Here, too, the Germans are clearly on the right end of the relevant dimension line.

Prior to the PISA shock, German schools had very little discretion. A great deal of control over the school was exercised by higher level authorities in the system. After PISA shock, the country moved towards awarding greater discretion to the school heads and faculty. But German schools still appear to have less discretion and control over the way they deliver services to students than is the case in other leading countries.

Again, prior to PISA shock, there was remarkably little accountability of any kind in the German education system. There are now two national tests, but neither is used to provide direct test-based accountability of the administrative kind that would place Germany on the left side of the accountability dimension line. Instead, Germany opted for professional and familial accountability, placing it on the right side of that dimension line.

Germany has progressed from the left side of the student inclusion dimension line to somewhere in the middle. It is breaking down the rigid distinctions between school types based on the class origins of its students, but it is not abandoning those distinctions.

Thus the picture is mixed, but generally tending strongly towards the right hand side of the developmental progression described in Figure 9.1.

■ Figure 9.2 ■
Germany: Profile data

Language(s)	German[3]
Population	82 772 160[4] (2008)
Youth population	13.8%[5] (OECD average 18.7%)
Elderly population	20.1%[6] (OECD average 14.4%)
Growth rate	-0.16% (OECD 0.68%)[7]
Foreign-born population	12.9%[8] (OECD average 12.9%)
GDP per capita	USD 35 432[9] (2008) (OECD average 33 732)[10]
Economy-Origin of GDP	Automobiles, machinery, metals and chemical goods. Services: 72%; Industry: 25%; Agriculture: 2%
Unemployment	7.3% (2008)[11] (OECD average 6.1%)[12]
Youth unemployment	10.4% (2008) (OECD average 13.8%)[13]

Expenditure on education	4.5% of GDP; (OECD average 5.2%)
	  2.9% on primary, secondary and post-secondary non-tertiary
	  1.1% on tertiary[14] education[15] (OECD average 3.5%; 1.2% respectively)
	
	10.3% of total government expenditure (OECD average 13.3%)
	  6.6% on primary, secondary and post-secondary non-tertiary
	  2.6% on tertiary education[16] (OECD average 9%; 3.1% respectively)

Enrolment ratio, early childhood education	101.5%[17] (OECD average 71.5%)[18]
Enrolment ratio, primary education	99.3%[19] (OECD average 98.8%)[20]
Enrolment ratio, secondary education	88.7%[21] (OECD average 81.5%)[22]
Enrolment ratio, tertiary education	28.4%[23] (OECD average 24.9%)[24]
Students in primary education, by type of institution or mode of enrolment[25]	Public: 96.4% (OECD average 89.6%) Government-dependent private: 3.6% (OECD average 8.1%) Independent, private (included in "government-dependent private" figure) (OECD average 2.9%)
Students in lower secondary education, by type of institution or mode of enrolment[26]	Public 91.5% (OECD average 83.2%) Government-dependent private: 8.5% (OECD average 10.9%) Independent, private (included in "government-dependent private" figure) (OECD average 3.5%)
Students in upper secondary education, by type of institution or mode of enrolment[27]	Public: 91.1% (OECD average 82%) Government-dependent private: 8.9% (OECD average 13.6%) Independent, private (included in "government-dependent private" figure) (OECD average 5.5%)

Students in tertiary education, by type of institution or mode of enrolment[28]	Tertiary type B education:
	  Public: 62.2%[29]
	  Government-dependent private: included in "public" figure
	  Independent-private: included in "public" figure
	  (OECD average Public: 61.8%
	  Government-dependent private : 19.2%
	  Independent-private: 16.6%)
	
	Tertiary type A education:
	  Public: 95%
	  Government-dependent private: missing data
	  Independent-private: missing data
	  (OECD average Public: 77.1%
	  Government-dependent private : 9.6%
	  Independent-private: 15%)

Teachers' salaries	Average annual starting salary in lower secondary education: USD 48 004 (OECD average USD 30 750)[30] Ratio of salary in lower secondary education after 15 years of experience to GDP per capita: 1.69 (OECD average: 1.22)
Upper secondary graduation rates	97% (OECD average 80%)[31]

StatLink 🔢 http://dx.doi.org/10.1787/888932366769

Interview partners

Edelgard Bulmahn, Former Minister, Federal Ministry of Education and Research, Germany.

Thomas Kerstan, Education Journalist, *Die Zeit,* Germany.

Kaija Landsberg, Founder, Teach First Deutschland, Germany.

Ulf Matyziak, Director of Training, Teach First Deutschland, Germany.

Karl Ulrich Mayer, Professor of Sociology, Yale University, USA and President, Leibniz Association.

Veronika Pahl, Former Director-General for Vocational Training and Education Reform, Federal Ministry of Education and Research, Germany.

Andreas Schleicher, Head of Indicators and Analysis Section, OECD Education Directorate.

Hermann Schmidt, Former Director, BIBB, Germany.

Bob Schwartz, Professor of Education, Harvard University, USA.

Reinhold Weiss, Deputy President and Head of Research, BIBB, Germany.

Ludger Woessmann, Professor of Economics, Head of Department of Human Capital and Innovation.

IFO Institute for Economic Research, University of Munich, Germany.

Answer received in writing:
Germany's PISA representatives:

Annemarie Klemm, Germany.

Elfriede Ohrnberger, Minister of Education, State of Bavaria, Germany.

Maximilian Müller-Härlin, Germany.

State Minister Spaenle, President of the Standing Conference of the Ministers of Education and Cultural Affairs of the *Länder* in the Federal Republic of Germany, Bavarian Ministry of Education, Germany.

References

Carey, D. (2008), "Improving Education Outcomes in Germany", *OECD Economics Department Working Papers*, No. 611, OECD Publishing.

CIA World Factbook (2010), *Germany: Country Background Information, www.cia.gov/library/publications/the-world-factbook/geos/gm.html.*

Conference of Heads of Government of the *Länder* (2008), *Getting Ahead Through Education: The Qualification Initiative for Germany*, Conference of Heads of Government of the *Länder*, Dresden.

Deutsche Welle (2003), *Germany Moves to All-Day Schools*, DW-World.de, retrieved from *www.dw-world.de/dw/article/0,,864144,00.html,* accessed 16 November 2010.

Dunham, L. (2008), "Why Zeros Should Not Be Permitted!", *Teaching the Slow Learner,* January/February 2008: 62, National Association of Elementary School Principals (NAESP), Alexandria, VA.

The Economist (2010), "Leave Them Kids Alone: A Setback for German Education Reformers", *The Economist*, 24 July 2010.

The Economist (2010), "Much to Learn: Germany's Education System is a Work in Progress", *The Economist Online*, 11 March 2010, *www.economist.com.*

Eurydice (2008), *Organisation of the Education System in Germany*, Education, Audiovisual and Cultural Executive Agency (EACEA), Brussels.

Eurydice (2009), *Germany*, National Summary Sheets on Education Systems in Europe and Ongoing Reforms, Education, Audiovisual and Cultural Executive Agency (EACEA), Brussels.

Eurydice (2009), *National Testing of Pupils in Europe: Objectives, Organisation and Use of Results*, Education, Audiovisual and Cultural Executive Agency (EACEA), Brussels.

Eurydice (2010), *Structures of Education and Training Systems in Europe: Germany*, Eurybase, Brussels.

Federal Ministry of Education and Research (2003), *Germany's Vocational Education at a Glance*, slide presentation published by the Federal Ministry of Education and Research (BMBF), Bonn.

Field, S., *et al.* (2010), *Learning for Jobs. Synthesis Report of the OECD Reviews of Vocational Education and Training*, OECD Publishing.

Grek, S. (2009), "Governing by Numbers: The Pisa 'Effect' in Europe", *Journal of Education Policy*, Vol. 24, No. 1.

Hahn, H. (1998), *Education and Society in Germany*, Berg, Oxford.

Halász, G., *et al.* (2004), *Attracting, Developing and Retaining Effective Teachers. Country Note: Germany*, OECD Publishing.

Hoeckel, K. and **R. Schwartz** (2010), *Learning for Jobs: OECD Reviews of Vocational Education and Training in Germany*, OECD Publishing.

Knowledge@Wharton (2009), "A Matter of Degrees: German Education Reform and its Consequences", *Knowledge@Wharton*, April 2009, Wharton School of the University of Pennsylvania, *http://knowledge.wharton.upenn.edu/article.cfm?articleid=2200*.

Klierne, E., *et al.* (2004), *The Development of National Educational Standards: An Expertise*, Federal Ministry of Education and Research (BMBF), Berlin.

Ladkin, P. (1997), "University Education in the US, UK and Germany: A Quick Comparison", *Rechnernetze und Verteilte Systeme*, Article RVS-J-97-12.

Mechan-Schmidt, F. (2010), "A Nation Groans Under the Weight of Reform", *Times Educational Supplement (TES)* 26 February, TSL Education Ltd., London.

OECD (2006), *Starting Strong II: Early Childhood Education and Care*, OECD Publishing.

OECD (2010), *PISA 2009 Results Volume I, What Students Know and Can Do: Student Performance in Reading, Mathematics and Science*, OECD Publishing.

Oelkers, J. and **K. Reusser** (2008), "Developing Quality – Safeguarding Standards – Handling Differentiation", *Education Research*, Vol. 27, BMBF, Berlin.

Phillips, D. (ed.) (1995), *Education in Germany: Tradition and Reform in Historical Context*, Routledge, London.

Powell, J., *et al.* (2009) "Comparing the Relationship between Vocational and Higher Education in Germany and France", *Discussion Paper* SP I 2009-506, Social Science Research Center, Berlin (WZB).

Reich, G. (2008), "The Development of Technology Education in Lower Saxony (Germany)", *Bulletin of Institute of Vocational and Technical Education*, Vol. 1, No. 5.

Reimann, A. (2010), "German Immigration Report Card: Integration Fairytale Fails to Spread from Football Field to Society", *Spiegel Online International*, 7 July, available at: *www.spiegel.de/international/germany/0,1518,705237,00.html*.

Rodgers, M. (2005), "Curriculum Reform and Development in Baden-Württemberg with Particular Reference to Teaching English as a Foreign Language", paper presented to the Sixth Israeli-German Symposium *"Teacher Education, School Reform and Development"*, Beit Berl College, Israel, October 2005.

Russell, J. (1899), *German Higher Schools: The History, Organization, and Methods of Secondary Education in Germany*, Longmans, Green and Company, London.

Schmidt, B., *et al.* (2009), *International Lessons About National Standards*, Thomas B. Fordham Institute, Washington, DC.

Tessaring, M. and **J. Wannan** (2004), *Vocational Education and Training – Key to the Future, Lisbon-Copenhagen-Maastricht: Mobilising for 2010: Synthesis of the Maastricht Study*, European Centre for the Development of Vocational Training (CEDEFOP), Luxembourg, *http://ec.europa.eu/education/lifelong-learning-policy/doc/policy/cedefop_en.pdf*.

Troltsch, K., G. Walden and **S. Zopf** (2009), "All Quiet on the Eastern Front?", *BIBB Report*, Vol. 3, No. 12, BIBB, Bonn.

UNESCO (2010), *TVETipedia, www.unevoc.unesco.org/tviki_front.php*, 16 November 2010.

Werning, R., J. Löser and **M. Urban** (2008), "Cultural and Social Diversity: An Analysis of Minority Groups in German Schools", *The Journal of Special Education*, Vol. 42, No 1, Hammill Institute on Disablities, Austin, TX.

Wößmann, L. (2007), "Fundamental Determinants of School Efficiency and Equity: German States as a Microcosm for OECD Countries", *IZA Discussion Paper* No 2880, Institute for the Study of Labour (IZA), Bonn.

Notes

1. A point made, for example, in interviews with Herman Schmidt and Reinhold Weiss.

2. These reports are called *Education in Germany 2006* and *Education in Germany 2008* and were prepared on behalf of the Standing Conference of the Ministers of Education and Cultural Affairs of the *Länder* in the Federal Republic of Germany and the Federal Minsitry of Education and Research (Bertelsman Verlag GmbH).

3. OECD (2010), *OECD Economic Surveys: Germany 2010*, OECD Publishing.

4. OECD.Stat, *http://stats.oecd.org* Germany's population is predicted to shrink to 65-70 million by 2060.

5. OECD (2010), *OECD Factbook 2010*, OECD Publishing. Ratio of population aged less than 15 to the total population (data from 2008).

6. OECD (2010), *OECD Factbook 2010*, OECD Publishing. Ratio of population aged 65 and older to the total population (data from 2008).

7. OECD (2010), *OECD Factbook 2010*, OECD Publishing. Annual population growth in percentage, OECD total (year of reference – 2007).

8. OECD (2010), *OECD Factbook 2010*, OECD Publishing. Foreign-born population as percent of the total population (data from 2007).

9. OECD.Stat, *http://stats.oecd.org*.

10. OECD (2010), *OECD Factbook 2010*, OECD Publishing. Current prices and PPPs (data from 2008).

11. OECD (2010), *OECD Factbook 2010*, OECD Publishing. Total unemployment rates as percentage of total labour force (data from 2008).

12. OECD (2010), *OECD Factbook 2010*, OECD Publishing. Total unemployment rates as percentage of total labour force (data from 2008).

13. OECD (2010), *Employment Outlook*, OECD Publishing. Unemployed as a percentage of the labour force in the age group: youth aged 15-24.

14. The OECD follows standard international conventions in using the term "tertiary education" to refer to all post-secondary programmes at ISCED levels 5B, 5A and 6, regardless of the institutions in which they are offered. OECD (2008), *Tertiary Education for the Knowledge Society: Volume 1*, OECD Publishing.

15. OECD (2010), *Education at a Glance 2010*, OECD Publishing. Public expenditure presented in this table includes public subsidies to households for living costs (scholarships and grants to students/households and students loans), which are not spent on educational institutions (data from 2006).

16. OECD (2010), *Education at a Glance 2010*, OECD Publishing. Public expenditure presented in this table includes public subsidies to households for living costs (scholarships and grants to students/households and students loans), which are not spent on educational institutions (data from 2006).

17. OECD (2010), *Education at a Glance 2010*, OECD Publishing. Net enrolment rates of ages 4 and under as a percentage of the population aged 3 to 4 (data from 2008). The rates "4 and under as a percentage of the population aged 3 to 4" are overestimated. A significant number of students are younger than 3 years old. The net rates between 3 and 5 are around 100%.

18. OECD (2010), *Education at a Glance 2010*, OECD Publishing. OECD average net enrolment rates of ages 4 and under as a percentage of the population aged 3 to 4 (year of reference – 2008).

19. Gross enrolment ratio, Data from 2007 *http://data.worldbank.org/country.*

20. OECD (2010), *Education at a Glance 2010*, OECD Publishing. OECD average net enrolment rates of ages 5 to 14 as a percentage of the population aged 5 to 14 (year of reference – 2008).

21. OECD (2010), *Education at a Glance 2010*, OECD Publishing. Net enrolment rates of ages 15 to 19 as a percentage of the population aged 15 to 19 (data from 2007).

22. OECD (2010), *Education at a Glance 2010*, OECD Publishing. OECD average net enrolment rates of ages 15 to 19 as a percentage of the population aged 15 to 19 (year of reference – 2008).

23. OECD (2010), *Education at a Glance 2010*, OECD Publishing. Net enrolment rates of ages 20 to 29 as a percentage of the population aged 20 to 29 (data from 2007). This figure includes includes all 20-29 year olds, including those in employment, etc. The Gross Enrolment Ratio (GER), measured by the UN as the number of actual students enrolled / number of potential students enrolled, is generally higher. The GER for tertiary education in Germany in 2002 is 46.3% (UNESCO) compared to the regional avg of 70% (UIS 2010).

24. OECD (2010), *Education at a Glance 2010*, OECD Publishing. OECD average net enrolment rates of ages 20 to 29 as a percentage of the population aged 20 to 29 (year of reference – 2008).

25. OECD (2010), *Education at a Glance 2010*, OECD Publishing. Data from 2008.

26. OECD (2010), *Education at a Glance 2010*, OECD Publishing. Data from 2008.

27. OECD (2010), *Education at a Glance 2010*, OECD Publishing. Data from 2008.

28. OECD (2010), *Education at a Glance 2010*, OECD Publishing. Data from 2008.

29. Excludes advanced research programmes.

30. OECD (2010), *Education at a Glance 2010*, OECD Publishing. Starting salary/minimum training in USD adjusted for PPP (data from 2008).

31. OECD (2010), *Education at a Glance 2010*, OECD Publishing. Sum of upper secondary graduation rates for a single year of age in 2007 (year of reference for OECD average – 2008).

10

Vignettes on Education Reforms: England, Poland and Sweden

This chapter provides brief vignettes describing some specific education reforms in three countries – England, Poland and Sweden:

- In England the government responded to a teacher shortage with a successful campaign to attract more potential teachers. The success of the English strategy rests on its two-pronged approach which combines a clever advertising campaign with a substantial package of financial relief. The government has now met its recruitment targets.

- Since 2000, reforms in Poland have made impressive gains in the quality of its secondary education. There were three elements to the reforms: *i)* increasing secondary and higher education qualifications in the population; *ii)* ensuring equal educational opportunities; and *iii)* improving the quality of education. Poland's PISA scores now show that the variance between schools in student performance in reading, mathematics, and science has been significantly reduced.

- Sweden has made a strong national commitment to Swedish language education for both immigrant adults and school children. It offers a comprehensive and extensive language programme, underpinned by financial incentives for schools to provide these services. As a consequence, the academic performance of Sweden's immigrant children is impressive.

This chapter provides brief case studies of specific reforms in three countries – tackling teacher shortages in England, reform of secondary education in Poland and educating immigrant children in Sweden.

■ ENGLAND: TACKLING TEACHER SHORTAGES

At the beginning of the decade, England's universities were finding it difficult to attract trainee teachers, and schools were consequently short-staffed. This case study describes how the government has responded with a successful campaign to attract more potential teachers.

Some background

The Training and Development Agency (TDA) – formerly known as the Teacher Training Agency (TTA) – falls under the English Department for Education. It is charged with improving the quality of teacher training and recruiting new teachers. The TDA had always been concerned with teacher recruitment, but in the early years the majority of its energy (and resources) was spent in driving up the quality of provision. In response to the teacher shortage crisis, the government gave the TDA greater responsibility for running national recruitment campaigns for new teachers to encourage university applications. The TDA took a very clear strategic approach to teacher recruitment, driven by its new Chief Executive appointed in 2000.

Working with the new CEO, the Secretary of State for Education at the time, David Blunkett, persuaded the Chancellor of the Exchequer, Gordon Brown, to announce an extra GBP 150 million of spending in his 2000 budget to support the TDA's new recruitment strategy.

The extra money was used in two key areas:

1) **A new national advertising campaign**. Leading international advertising and recruitment agencies were employed to undertake extensive market research on the motivations and barriers to becoming a teacher, and to develop award winning marketing strategies.

2) **Financial support for teacher trainees**, a new GBP 6 000 training bursary was offered to all trainees, as a one-off, tax-free payment to support them through their training. A "golden hello" was also introduced, of up to GBP 4 000. This amount was to be paid on employment, depending on which subject trainees were teaching. Teachers of subjects which were especially short of teachers, such as mathematics and physics, received the full amount.

The new support package of bursaries and golden hellos became a central pillar of the new advertising campaign. By focusing on the idea of teaching "making a difference", the new campaign aimed to improve the status of teaching as a profession. The campaign also encouraged people to pick up the telephone – for the first time the national information line number was included in the adverts. The message was easy to understand: "Don't just think about it – call us". This also allowed the TDA to collect data on people who were considering teaching, monitor the number of inquiries, and analyse the questions being asked, as well as sending out further information to targeted groups (for example, mathematics and physics students, where the supply shortage was most pronounced).

The final element of the new approach was to change the way the TDA talked about teaching, emphasising the flexibility and diversity of the skills teachers acquire and the variety of routes into teaching. The TDA also started to actively advocate teaching as "a first career" – something you could do for a few years before doing something else (Box 10.1). Some of these elements are outlined below in more detail.

A sophisticated recruitment campaign

One of the TDA's central aims was to understand its "customers" better. It divided the student population into three broad categories: 1) those planning on teaching; 2) those considering teaching; and 3) those not considering teaching.

Originally, the majority of the TDA's efforts went into recruiting teachers from the "might teach" category (2). They wanted to encourage people who were seriously considering teaching as an option, but were put off by various barriers – such as the financial burden of the training.

In order to refine its campaign further, the TDA then undertook more in-depth market research on potential teaching recruits. It divided the market into three main categories:

- **Undergraduates and recent graduates** – students looking for their first job on leaving university.

- **Career finders** – young people aged around 25-30 who had left university and not settled into a graduate career, but who were now looking for a career.

- **Career changers** – people who had embarked on a career, but were looking for a career which would bring them more job satisfaction.

During the last decade the proportion of career finders and changers amongst teacher training recruits has grown – today about 50% of teacher training recruits are over 25. This was reflected in the new advertising slogans – such as "Use your head: teach" – to appeal to people not making full use of their graduate skills in their current jobs. The latest campaign, "Turn your talent to teaching", is designed to appeal to all three categories of potential recruits.

After extensive profiling of potential recruits, the advertising agency also developed the profile of "self-interested idealists" to define potential teachers, and to shape the marketing campaigns. This acknowledged that potential teachers were motivated by making a difference and putting something back, but that they also wanted to enter a profession which would give them financial and personal satisfaction rewards.

Box 10.1 **Teach First**

TDA worked closely with Teach First, an independent educational charity set up in 2002 to address educational disadvantage by transforming exceptional graduates into effective, inspirational teachers and leaders in all fields. Teach First targets graduates who would not normally consider a career in teaching and places them in what it considers challenging schools across England. Based on America First's "Teach for America" model, these graduates are only required to teach for two years, but in poor performing schools. The attraction for graduates is that they are given a special form of teacher training and are also provided with a competitive graduate salary, mentoring by a blue-chip company or business, and a masters' degree.

Creating new ways of entering teaching

To broaden the potential pool of teaching applicants, the TDA developed a wide range of routes to becoming a qualified teacher. From 2006, there were as many as 32 ways of acquiring Qualified Teacher Status. The two most important include:

- An undergraduate or postgraduate course in Initial Teacher Training provided by a university or college. This is still the main source of teacher entry.

- The Graduate Teacher Programme (GTP). This programme was first established by the government in 1998, but remained small scale until it was developed substantially from 2005. It now recruits around 10% of new teachers. GTP is a programme of on-the-job training allowing graduates to qualify as a teacher while they are working. It is a particularly good choice for mature people who want to change to a teaching career but need to continue earning while they train. Under the scheme, new teachers are employed and paid as unqualified teachers during their year of training. The introduction of a training grant salary subsidy of GBP 13 000 in 2000 was a crucial element in ensuring the success of this programme. Despite the significant pay-cuts which many entrants had to accept, the new salary allowed those who had resisted a teaching career due to financial restraints to re-consider.

Encouraging more science and mathematics teachers

The lack of graduates with mathematics and physics degrees has proved one of the hardest nuts to crack. By offering up to six months' additional training to engineers, accountants, biologists etc., the TDA has added several hundred extra recruits to mathematics, physics and chemistry courses.

The TDA has moved rapidly to respond to the financial crisis – mounting special "bankers to teachers" campaigns, seeking to attract former financial market specialists to the teaching profession. The TDA also monitors carefully the value for money of the financial incentives it offers through frequent market research, and adjusts the levels of bursary offered accordingly.

The impact

Within three months of the launch of the advertising campaign, the number of people calling the national teaching recruitment helpline tripled. The teacher supply shortfall began to be reduced in 2000/2001. By 2003/2004 the vacancy-to-employment rate halved to less than 1% for all subjects. Mathematics and physics are the two subjects which had the greatest shortage of teachers. However, by 2003/2004 the TDA had made major gains in these subjects. The number of new recruits in mathematics almost doubled between 1999 and 2005. Recruitment to science subjects reached its target a year earlier, in 2002/2003. "Science" includes biology, popular among new teachers, as well as the priority shortage subjects of physics and chemistry.

Conclusion

The success of the TDA's strategy rests on its two-pronged approach. Combining a clever advertising campaign with a substantial package of financial relief proved to be very effective. Having now met the recruitment targets, the TDA can do more research into the barriers to recruiting the most able graduates. It has recently adjusted the focus of its advertising and marketing to appeal more to higher quality graduates.

Financial incentives tend to be a much greater incentive for teachers recruited as career changers, and in shortage areas, than among the general teaching population. The TDA's 2005 Review of Financial Incentives to enter teacher training and teaching makes this point strongly:

> The evidence – from focus groups and desk research – was overwhelming that the decision to consider teaching as a career was largely emotional rather than financial. For instance, the TTA McCann marketing survey revealed that the top factors were social value of the profession, working with children, long-term career, and love of subject. The PGCE bursary ranked only 13th out of 17.

> Financial incentives were, however, of greater importance to the key recruitment challenge groups – shortage subject trainees, men [for primary education] and career changers with shortage subject backgrounds […] This particularly applied to potential teachers of mathematics and science who were aware from media coverage of their shortage value – a finding confirmed particularly strongly by focus groups.

■ POLAND: SECONDARY EDUCATION REFORM

Since 2000, Poland has made significant gains in the quality of its secondary education. This case study tells the story, outlining the reforms the country has made that have improved its secondary education performance so impressively.

A highly tracked education system pre-1989

From the post-war period until 1989, education in Poland focused on preparing young people for jobs. In this communist state, vocational education was seen as the path to full, guaranteed, life-long employment, especially for the poor, less capable and disadvantaged. Students entered primary school at seven and stayed there until it was time to make career decisions at the age of 15. Options for secondary education were based on performance in stringent placement exams (*kuratoria*), with no retakes:

- The bottom half of the students were streamed into two-year basic vocational schools run by individual sector industries.

- About one-third of the students were sent to two-year technical secondary schools to prepare as technicians.

- The top 20% of students went into the three-year general secondary *lyceum*. Students at the *lyceum* took academic courses to prepare for the *Matura*, the university entrance exam.

By the early 1990s, Poland had one of the lowest participation rates in full secondary education and in higher education in the OECD (OECD, 2010).

Education reforms since 1989: The birth of the technical *lyceum*

With the demise of the communist government, the economy moved towards free market practices, and the industries that had run the secondary basic vocational schools backed away both from funding those schools and guaranteeing employment to their graduates. The ministry of Education stepped in to run basic vocational schools, but could not accommodate the large numbers of students who had previously attended such schools. In addition, parents, seeing more opportunities in the new society, wanted better options for their children. As a result, general secondary schools as well as technical secondary schools increased their enrolments. Some basic vocational schools became general secondary schools, but with lower entrance standards than the other *lyceum*s. This gave more students an opportunity to prepare for university, but not at a level that would enable them to gain admission to the national universities. Additional universities sprung up in smaller cities to accommodate these students.

In 1993, a new type of secondary vocational school, a four-year technical *lyceum*, was introduced. The technical *lyceum* provided students with a general secondary education, as well as training in electrical engineering, business and administration, various industries such as textiles, and communications and transport. Students also had the option of taking the *Matura* exam, as they would in the general secondary school.

Structural reforms of the late 1990s

In 1997, the latest government introduced a package of reforms, including to the education system. By January 1998, the minister of Education had set three major objectives for education reform:

- Increasing secondary and higher education qualifications in the population.

- Ensuring equal educational opportunities.

- Improving the quality of education.

To accomplish those objectives, the ministry implemented a number of structural reforms. Chief among them was a major change in the structure of the school system. Rather than an 8-3 or 8-2 structure, the country moved to a 6-3-3 structure. This meant that students would attend primary school from ages 7 to 12; lower secondary school – the *gymnasium* – between ages 13 and 15; and then one of the three upper secondary options: *lyceum*, technical *lyceum* or basic vocational school. Thus all students would study a common curriculum – including courses in reading, mathematics, and science – until they turned 15. This provided an extra year of academic studies for those students who otherwise would have spent that year in vocational training.

This new school structure provided an opportunity to make several other significant changes to the system, including:

- A new core curriculum for the *gymnasium*. This set high expectations to prevent teachers from teaching the same way they always had. This was especially important given the low expectations for students who were assumed to be going on to the basic vocational school.

- Curricular standards at the national level, but curriculum development decentralised to the local level. This would engage teachers in focusing on three dimensions of education: acquiring knowledge, developing skills and shaping attitudes. The hope was to change the teaching philosophy and culture of the schools.

- An accountability system to monitor results. The ministry created a system of external examinations to be implemented at the end of primary, the end of lower secondary, and the end of upper secondary schools, to ensure schools were moving in the right direction. The Matura exam was now taken by all secondary school students.

The results: A remarkable turnaround

PISA 2000 and PISA 2003 mark the divide between the old and new systems of Polish education.

In the 2000 PISA examination, Poland's students' average score was 479, well below the OECD average of 500 points (OECD, 2000). More troubling was the fact that over 21% of Poland's students only reached Level 1 or below. The PISA results also showed a real disparity between the educational competencies of students in the general education system and the basic vocational schools. Nearly 70% of the basic vocational school students tested at the lowest literacy level.

By 2003, Poland's students had made significant gains on PISA (OECD, 2003), with their average score increasing to 497. By 2003, the percentage of students who scored 400 points or less decreased to about 15% from 21.4% in 2000; 13.7% of students scored 600 or more points, as opposed to only 10.6% in 2000. A comparison of PISA 2000 and 2003 shows that the variance between schools in student performance in reading, mathematics, and science was significantly reduced. In fact, this was the most significant decrease for all European Union *and* OECD countries. The trend continued, and by 2006, the average scores of all students had risen another 37 points to 534. Furthermore, research done by the Polish Center for Social and Economic Research showed a remarkable 115 point improvement for students who previously would have been assigned to basic vocational schools but instead received an extra year of general secondary school curriculum under the new system (Wiśniewski, 2007).

The 15-year-olds tested in 2000 had already been streamed into their three distinct levels of schools. In 2003 and 2006, the 15 year olds tested on PISA were studying in the gymnasia. Not only did these students have a stronger foundation in academic areas, but the 2006 students had also participated in the revised primary curriculum as well as the new *gymnasium*. The reduced variance between schools may also be attributed to the fact that the 2003 and 2006 students attended gymnasia that were not streamed by academic ability, unlike the schools they would have attended under the old system.

■ SWEDEN: POSSIBLE EXPLANATIONS FOR THE PERFORMANCE OF IMMIGRANT STUDENTS

Sweden is far from homogeneous, with nearly 20% of elementary secondary school students speaking a language other than Swedish, and over 100 languages spoken nationwide. More than 13% of all residents were born abroad. To address this diversity, Sweden has made a strong national commitment to Swedish language education for both immigrant adults and school children. It offers a comprehensive and extensive language programme, underpinned by financial incentives for schools to provide these services. As a consequence, the academic performance of Sweden's immigrant children is impressive. This vignette explores government policy that may help explain such performance.

Steady immigration to Sweden started after the Second World War, when the country offered assistance to immigrants and refugees from Nordic, Baltic and other European nations. By the 1960s, many immigrants came to Sweden for economic reasons, often from within the Nordic countries. By the 1970s, however, immigrants began to arrive for political reasons. They came from Chile in the 1970s; Poland, Iraq and Iran in the 1980s; and the former Yugoslavia, Somalia and other parts of Africa in the 1990s (OECD, 2009). The proportion of immigrants from less developed countries increased from 13% to 36% from 1980 to 2000 (Taguma, 2010).

Sweden recognised the importance of language acquisition for immigrants early on. Since the 1970s, foreign-born adults with a residence permit have been entitled by law to 240 hours of free Swedish language training. Sweden also has a long history of equity in education and its legal framework entitles immigrant children to instruction in both Swedish and their mother tongue.

Language support for children

For immigrant children, Sweden has implemented an intensive immersion programme similar to that in other countries that have successfully narrowed the gap between immigrant and non-immigrant achievement, such as Australia, Canada, the Netherlands and Switzerland.

It is compulsory for newly-arrived school-age children to study Swedish at school as a second language (SSL) as part of a core programme of study. The goal is to provide students with the language skills necessary to understand and express complex ideas through speech and writing. SSL is an explicit curriculum, and the standards to be achieved for SSL are similar to those for non-immigrant Swedish students. In fact, SSL in secondary schools is equivalent to the regular Swedish language courses that allow students to be eligible for post-secondary education. Recent student immigrants remain in the SSL programmes on average between 6 and 12 months. They then transfer into the mainstream school programme, but through the "Study Guidance in Mother Tongue" programme they are provided with support teachers to help in the transition. These teachers often work with small groups of immigrant students within the mainstream classroom.

Not only are immigrant children entitled to classes in Swedish as a second language within the Swedish educational system; they are also entitled to instruction in their mother tongue from pre-school onwards. In compulsory education lasting through grade 9, immigrant children have the option of using "mother tongue tuition" to learn about the literature, history and culture of their country of origin. This emphasis on studying in one's mother tongue is thought to facilitate learning, literacy, and other skills that can then be transferred to the student's second language. Schools are required to provide these supplementary classes as long as there are at least five students at any school requesting them (OECD, 2009).

Schools in Sweden also have financial incentives to support these comprehensive language programmes for immigrants. A funding system put in place in the 1990s provides a grant to each student which follows them into whichever school they choose to attend. Municipalities receive top-up funds from the national government in order to equalise funding across municipalities. Municipalities have discretion over how they use their educational funds. They tend to provide lump sums directly to schools on a per pupil basis, topped up with an extra allotment for special student needs, including language instruction for non-native students. These extra funds provide an incentive for schools to serve students with these types of needs. They also encourage Swedish schools to provide high-quality language programmes to draw more parents and students from these demographics into their schools.

Language support for adults

Sweden does not just prioritise language education for immigrant school children, it is also important for their parents and other adults. As mentioned above, Sweden guarantees adults 240 hours of free language instruction through its Swedish for Immigrants (SFI) programme. This is focused on preparing immigrants for the workplace.

There have been recent efforts to strengthen SFI instruction through the Swedish for Immigrants initiative, whose slogan is "better quality and tougher requirements". This initiative provides clearer goals for the SFI curriculum, standard national final assessments and better support for SFI teachers, including a performance-based bonus. The new initiative has also created three varying syllabi for adults, since it was clear that some immigrants would need more intensive instruction to reach proficiency.

The impact on performance

The results of TIMSS 2007 show that both native and immigrant students in Sweden outperform their international counterparts in both mathematics and science (Taguma, 2009). Similarly, the 2006 PIRLS (Progress in International Reading Literacy Study) shows that second-generation immigrant students in Sweden performed better than second-generation immigrants in most other countries. In addition, they significantly closed the gap between their scores and those of native Swedes (Taguma, 2009). In the 2006 PISA study, while first-generation immigrants in Sweden performed near the middle, second generation immigrants in Sweden performed on par with the OECD average for science and mathematics and better than average in reading (OECD, 2007a). This suggests that spending more time in the Swedish school system may be beneficial to students with immigrant backgrounds.

Factors for success

The study *Language Policies and Practices for Helping Immigrants and Second-Generation Students Succeed* (Christensen and Stanat, 2007) has identified some possible ingredients for success of the Swedish programme:

- A systematic programme with explicit standards.

- Curricula that may be determined at the local level but that are based on centrally-developed key curriculum documents, including language development frameworks and progress benchmarks.

- High standards so students acquire language skills in the context of the mainstream curriculum and can integrate into the appropriate level of instruction.

- Time-intensive programmes.

- On-going support offered to students in both primary and lower secondary school.

- Specialist teachers for instructing second-language learners, trained either during their initial studies or through in-service training, or with postgraduate degrees in teaching the language of instruction as a second language.

- Good co-operation between teachers of second-language learners and class teachers to ensure they meet the needs of immigrant students.

References

Chatterjee, A. (2008), "The Swedish Model of Education", *CCS Working Paper,* No. 187, Summer Research Internship Programme 2007-08, Centre for Civil Society, New Delhi.

Christensen, G. and P. Stanat (2007), *Language Policies and Practices for Helping Immigrants and Second-Generation Students Succeed,* The Transatlantic Taskforce on Immigration and Integration, Migration Policy Institute (MPI) and Bertelsmann Stiftung.

Jakubowski, M., H.A. Patrinos, E.E. Porta and **J. Wiśniewski** (2010), "The Impact of the 1999 Education Reform in Poland", *OECD Education Working Papers,* No. 49, OECD Publishing.

Kerr, R. (2009), "A Swedish Model for Education?" *Education Forum,* No. 130, September 2009.

King, S., *et al.* (2004), *The Structure and Funding of the School System,* report to Victorian Department of Treasury and Finance, The Melbourne Institute of Applied Economic and Social Research.

Lemaître, G. (2007), "The Integration of Immigrants into the Labour Market: The Case of Sweden", *OECD Social Employment and Migration Working Papers,* No. 48, OECD (2000), *Knowledge and Skills for Life: First Results from PISA 2000,* OECD Publishing.

OECD (2003), *Learning for Tomorrow's World: First Results from PISA 2003,* OECD Publishing.

OECD (2007a), *PISA 2006: Science Competencies for Tomorrow's World,* OECD Publishing.

OECD (2007b), *OECD Factbook 2007: Immigration Population,* OECD Publishing.

OECD (2009), *OECD Thematic Review on Migrant Education: Country Background Report for Sweden,* OECD Publishing.

OECD (2010), *PISA 2009 Results Volume I, What Students Know and Can Do: Student Performance in Reading, Mathematics and Science,* OECD Publishing.

Patrinos, H.A. (2010), *Using PISA to Assess the Impact of Education Reforms,* World Bank, Washington, DC, available at *www.google.com/url?sa=t&source=web&cd=3&ved=0CCIQFjAC&url=http%3A%2F%2Fepdc.org%2Fpolicyanalysis%2Fstatic% 2FPatrinos_Session_4.ppt&ei=5EFsTIm_EYP98AbahsyqCw&usg=AFQjCNGVjWSs5DppXxiy9HXAYlEues10iQ.*

Swedish Ministry of Education and Research (2008), *Funding the Swedish School System,* Fact Sheet, Swedish Ministry of Education and Research, Stockholm.

Taguma, M., *et al.* (2010), *OECD Reviews of Migrant Education: Sweden,* OECD Publishing.

TIMMS (2007), *International Mathematics Report: Findings from IEA's Trends in International Mathematics and Science Study at the Fourth and Eighth Grades,* TIMMS & PIRLS International Study Center, Boston College, Chestnut Hill, MA.

US Library of Congress (2010), *Poland Country Report,* US Library of Congress, Washington, DC, available at *http://countrystudies. us/poland/42.htm.*

Wiśniewski, J. (2007), "Secondary Education in Poland: 18 years of changes", paper presented for the *Fourth ECA Education Conference,* Tirana, 24-26 October 2007, available at *http://siteresources.worldbank.org/EXTECAREGTOPEDUCATION/ Resources/444607-1192636551820/Secondary_education_in_Poland_jwi_4r.pdf.*

11

Lessons for
the United States

INTRODUCTION

United States President Barack Obama has launched one of the world's most ambitious education reform agendas. The federally-funded programme "Race to the Top", initiated in 2010, represents the cornerstone of this agenda and encourages states in the United States to change their aspirations and organisational culture by: adopting internationally benchmarked state-developed standards and assessments that prepare students for success in college and the workplace; recruiting, developing, rewarding, and retaining effective teachers and principals; building data systems that measure student success and inform teachers and principals how they can improve their practices; and turning around the country's lowest-performing schools.

Chapter 2 shows what the "top" looks like internationally, based on PISA and other comparative data from the OECD. Subsequent chapters then provide descriptions of some high-performing and rapidly improving education systems – illustrating not only major characteristics of top-ranked systems, but also showing how quickly some have been able to improve and even advance to the top, as measured by PISA.

In the time since May 2010 when the preparation of this volume began, one pillar of the reform, the development of internationally benchmarked educational standards by states, is well advanced for the fields of language and mathematics, and 40 states as well as the District of Columbia have signed up for their implementation. The OECD has been privileged to contribute to the review and validation of these standards, as part of the Validation Panel assembled by state organisations. The Obama administration continues to support the implementation of these standards by investing over a billion dollars in strengthening state and district instructional standards and delivery in literacy, science, technology, engineering and mathematics, and other subjects. The preceding chapters of this volume underscore the central role that such standards play in the education systems of many high-performing education systems, but they also suggest that setting a solid set of common standards is just the first step towards the delivery of world-class instruction in the classroom.

Virtually every country featured in this volume also mirrors Race to the Top's effort to support the recruitment, development, rewarding and retaining of effective teachers and principals. Indeed, such unwavering support for excellence in teaching and school leadership is perhaps the key element of the policies and practices that drive high-performing education systems, such as those in Canada, Finland, Japan, Shanghai-China and Singapore, that are portrayed in this volume.

Both the comparative analyses in Chapter 2 and the country reports in this volume also provide ample illustration of successful efforts to turn around low-performing schools and students at scale. Poland achieved this through a major restructuring of its school system – essentially removing a secondary school track designed for students with lower performance expectations. In doing so, Poland eliminated the possibility for teachers and schools to turn away students from disadvantaged social backgrounds; they now had to face head-on the challenges of offering high-quality learning opportunities to all students. Germany achieved similar improvements but through a concerted, system-wide effort that specifically targeted the learning opportunities of disadvantaged students. Shanghai-China transfers strong professionals to weak schools to improve their performance. These examples offer valuable lessons at a time when the Obama administration is placing strong emphasis on turning around the United States' lowest-performing schools to better serve its disadvantaged students.

The development of education data systems, the fourth pillar of Race to the Top, is not a focus of this volume, because data systems are an area in which the United States leads the field.

The following draws together the threads of earlier analyses in this volume to present some of the broader lessons that can be drawn from examining the successful policies and practices of education systems that have shown consistently high outcomes in PISA or seen rapid improvements in their outcomes over the past decade. National and state education systems are very complex. The way they function is highly dependent on their interaction with other systems that are no less complex, and with cultural, political, social, and economic factors that have a direct bearing on the goals and effectiveness of education systems. The chapter will focus on those factors that the preceding chapters suggest are related to the successes of national and state education systems. The way these factors are addressed in the comparison countries were described in the country reports.

The lessons drawn in this chapter are intended to show how countries have achieved high performance across systems and schools. But what is meant by "superior performance"? PISA defines countries as high performing if almost all of their students are in high school at the appropriate age, average performance is high and the top quarter of performers place among the countries whose top quarter are among the best performers in the world (with respect to their mastery of the kinds of complex knowledge and skills needed in advanced economies as well their ability to apply that knowledge and those skills to problems with which they are not familiar); student performance is only weakly related to their socio-economic background; and spending per pupil is not at the top of the league tables. Put another way, the volume defines superior performance as high participation, high quality, high equity and high efficiency.

As shown in Chapter 2, the performance of 15-year-olds in the United States places it around the middle of the OECD league tables in reading and science and below the average in mathematics. But as also shown, the distribution of student performance within the United States is large, with pockets of high performance but also a long tail of poorly performing students and schools. First of all, performance varies among states. On the PISA reading assessment, for example, public schools in the Northeast of the United States perform at 510 PISA score points – 17 score points above the OECD average (comparable with results from the Netherlands), followed by the Midwest with 500 score points (comparable with the performance of Poland), the West with 486 score points (comparable with the performance of Italy) and the South with 483 score points (comparable with the performance of Greece).

Performance varies even more between schools. Indeed, one reason why countries with acknowledged superior performance overall continue to send delegations to study education in the United States is that interesting, provocative, and possibly leading examples of education practice can always be found in the United States. Many observers report that some of the very best education institutions can be found in the United States, at every level from the elementary school to the research university.

There is another reason why people with a strong professional interest in education are often fascinated by the United States. There is a conviction among many top policy experts that the future belongs to the world's leaders in creativity and innovation – countries with environments able to create not just new businesses but completely new industries. Though the United States is challenged on this front by many nations, educators come to the United States from other countries to see how the United States educates for the high level of innovation demonstrated in the economy.

One might suppose that there is a single best way to organise a national or state education system to achieve world-class status. But the preceding chapters suggest otherwise. Furthermore, the introduction of this volume posits that nations tend to go through a progression of education development that loosely follows their trajectory of economic development. The education development progression is characterised by a movement from relatively low teacher quality to relatively high teacher quality; from a focus on low-level basic skills to a focus on complex high-level skills and creativity; from Tayloristic forms of work organisation to professional forms of work organisation; from primary accountability to superiors to primary accountability to one's professional colleagues, parents and the public; and from a belief that only some students can and need to achieve high learning standards to a conviction that all students need to meet such high standards. The objective of the preceding chapters is to provide a better understanding for how some countries have embraced this path more firmly and transformed more quickly.

Any exploration of the individual country trajectories towards high education performance must account for each country's unique history and economic evolution, recognising that countries hold different values, different assets and different liabilities in their education systems, and employ different strategies to gain world-class results. In more colloquial terms, "there is more than one way to skin a cat". These unique trajectories emerge through the case studies in this volume. But the processes of development and the ingredients of top performance are far from random. Common underlying principles of educational success are the focus of this chapter.

With respect to the United States, it is important to bear in mind that individual communities and states in the United States can be placed at many points along the development continuum, and the most effective system of education for one community or state may be very different from the one that is best suited to another, depending on where they are on that continuum. High-wage states, like high-wage countries, will need to reach and maintain high education performance as rapidly as possible to maintain and improve their standard of living in the long run. In the pages that follow, the focus is on comparing the United States to the best-performing countries, even if the United States may need to achieve high performance state by state and even if other countries may be more appropriately compared to individual states. For example, in size, population and demographics, a more appropriate comparison might be between Finland and Minnesota, Ontario and Massachusetts, or Poland and California rather than Finland and the United States or Poland and the United States.

Some contend that the value of educational comparisons for the United States is limited because the United States is unique among the family of nations. However, the analysis in Chapter 2 makes it clear that the United States is not unique, at least not demographically or socio-economically. In fact, the United States has many socio-economic advantages. As shown in Chapter 2, it is wealthier than any of the comparison countries and spends more money on education than any of them, its parents have a higher level of education than those in most countries, and the share of socio-economically disadvantaged students is around the OECD average. What the comparisons do show is that socio-economic disadvantage has a particularly strong impact on student performance in the United States: 17% of the variation in student performance in the United States is explained by students' socio-economic background. This contrasts with just 9% in Canada or Japan, two of the benchmark countries chosen for this study. In other words, in the United States two students from different socio-economic backgrounds vary much more in their learning outcomes than is typically the case in OECD countries: only Hungary, Belgium, Turkey, Luxembourg, Chile and Germany show a larger impact of socio-economic background on reading performance than the United States. The comparatively close dependency of the learning outcomes of students in the United States on socio-economic background is therefore *not* explained by a socio-economically more heterogeneous student population or society, but mainly because socio-economic disadvantage leads more directly to poor educational performance in the United States than is the case in many other countries. And yet, even if the relationship between socio-economic background and learning outcomes is strong, over 20% of American 15-year-olds enrolled in socio-economically disadvantaged schools reach the average performance standards of Finland, one of the best-performing education systems, and the same is true for some of the most disadvantaged American schools. This shows clearly that the challenges of disadvantage are not only successfully addressed in other countries but also by many individual students and schools in the United States.

Some educators in the United States have contended that other nations educate only their elites while they are responsible for educating everyone. That has not been true for decades. The PISA 2009 assessment shows 82% of 15-year-olds to be enrolled in the United States. Among the 34 OECD countries, that is the third lowest figure, after Mexico and Turkey. Similarly, some contend that the United States is unique in the proportion of minorities, immigrants and non-native language speakers in its student population. It is true that the proportion of such people is high but it is not true that the United States is alone in these respects. More important is that, as shown in Chapter 2, many countries with equal or higher proportions of immigrant students and non-native speakers of the local language are outperforming the United States and show a more moderate relationship between socio-economic background and learning outcomes.

Furthermore, most of the systems studied for this volume are the size of states in the United States. In larger federal systems, such as Canada, Germany and Brazil, the provinces and states have much the same degree of autonomy from the national government on education issues as do the individual states in the United States. In China, the municipalities of Shanghai and Hong Kong have significant autonomy. Thus all the jurisdictions that are the focus of this volume, with the exception of Germany and Japan, are the size of American states or are organised on the federal principle with states that have the same authority as American states. The lessons drawn from statistical comparisons and the in-depth country studies are those with which American states should be able to make improvements in student performance.

There is, of course, also the matter of culture. Some may dismiss the educational achievements of other countries on the grounds that the cultures of other countries are so different from that of the United States that the policies and practices of those countries could not possibly be adopted by the United States, or, if they were, would produce very different results. Indeed, culture can influence national student achievement results. Countries with cultures based on the Confucian tradition are recognised as placing a very high value on education and student achievement in school, and many observers believe that this cultural characteristic confers a large advantage on such countries. But the educational success of the countries with a Confucian tradition is relatively recent, and not all such countries show high levels of student performance. A Confucian heritage may be an asset but provides no guarantee of success. Furthermore, Finland and Canada also have cultures that place a very high value on education, showing that such shared beliefs are not unique to Confucian cultures. It is probably fair to say that, everything else being equal, countries that place a high value on education get better educational results than countries that do not. The extent to which educational aspirations of parents are the result of cultural values or determinants of these, and how such educational aspirations interact with educational policies and practices is an important subject that deserves further study.

So what is the lesson to be learned? If a country seeks better education performance, it is incumbent on the political and social leaders to persuade the citizens of that country to make the choices needed to show that it values education more than other areas of national interest. Culture is a matter of values, and some of the preceding chapters show how these values can change over time as a result of experience. If the United States does not place as high a value on education as those nations that get better education results, it is not likely to achieve the same level of education performance as those nations.

A century ago, when the United States was putting in place the education system that it has used ever since, it was eager to learn as much as possible from other nations as it designed its own system. It took the ideas of universal basic schooling and the modern research university from Germany. It borrowed the underpinnings of the world's best system of vocational and technical education from the Scots, who successfully developed the principles for Scotland's mechanics institutes, which were then among the world's high-technology leaders. And the design of America's leading private secondary schools was lifted whole from the model provided by England's leading "public" schools, such as Eaton and Harrow.

But this openness to borrowing ideas moderated afterwards. In the years following the Second World War, the United States alone had the resources to greatly expand its education system and soon topped all of the world's education league tables. Perhaps the United States assumed that once it was in the lead, it would always be in the lead. It was only over recent decades, when American educators began to hear that students in other countries outperformed the United States in many areas, that there has been renewed interest in internationally comparative analyses. Most recently,[1] Secretary Duncan devoted much of his address to OECD Education Ministers to the importance of international benchmarking and the collective benefits of global exchange and collaboration in the field of education.

LEARNING FROM HIGH-PERFORMING EDUCATION SYSTEMS

Developing a commitment to education and a conviction that all students can achieve at high levels

Many nations declare that they are committed to children and that education is important. The test comes when these commitments are weighed against others. How do they pay teachers compared to the way they pay others with the same level of education? How are education credentials weighed against other qualifications when people are being considered for jobs? Would you want your child to be a teacher? How much attention do the media pay to schools and schooling? When it comes down to it, which matters more, a community's standing in the sports leagues or its standing in the student academic achievement league tables? Are parents more likely to encourage their children to study longer and harder or to want them to spend more time with their friends or playing sports?

As shown in Chapter 2, in the countries with the highest performance, teachers are typically paid better relative to others, education credentials are valued more, and a higher share of educational spending is devoted to instructional services than is the case in the United States, where parents may not encourage their children to become school teachers if they think they have a chance of becoming attorneys, engineers, doctors or architects. The value placed on education is likely to influence the choices that students make about whether to study or head down to the ball field or hang out with their friends on the corner, and, later, whether the most capable students decide on school teaching, or something with higher social status, as a career. It has an effect on the willingness of the public to honour the views of professional educators or dismiss them.

Some will say that these are cultural matters and not amenable to change, but the preceding chapters suggest that in countries with little in the way of natural resources, such as Finland, Singapore and Japan, education appears to have a high status at least in part because the public at large has understood that the country must live by its wits and its wits depend on the quality of education. That is, the value that a country places on education depends in part on a country's view of how human capital fits into the way it makes its living. Placing a high value on education may be an underlying condition for building a world-class education system, and it may be that most countries that have not had to live by their wits in the past will not succeed unless their political leaders explain why, though they might not have had to live by their wits in the past, they must do so now.

But placing a high value on education will get a country only so far if the teachers, parents and citizens of that country believe that only some subset of the nation's children can or need to achieve high standards. This volume shows a distribution of attitudes on this point. Brazil inherited a situation in which the people who gained control of it when it was colonised assumed that the people they conquered and the people they enslaved had so little to offer they were not worth educating. Germany is a country in which it was widely assumed until recently that the children of working-class people would themselves get working-class jobs and would not profit from the curriculum offered by the *Gymnasium*. PISA shows these attitudes to be mirrored in the perception of students about their own educational future. While in Germany only a quarter of 15-year-olds in PISA said that they expect to go on to university, fewer than those who actually will, in Japan and Korea, 9 out of 10 students said they expected to do so. The results of these differences can also be seen in the distribution of student performance within each of these countries and in the impact that socio-economic background has on learning.

Furthermore, the writings of some educational psychologists in the United States, from Terman on, have fostered a widespread notion that student achievement is mainly a product of inherited intelligence, not hard work. This is also mirrored in results from the Third International Mathematics and Science Study, where a significant share of American students reported that they needed good luck rather than hard work to do well in mathematics or science, a characteristic that was consistently negatively related to performance.[2] Teachers may feel guilty pressing students who they perceive to be less capable to achieve at higher levels because they think it unfair to the student to do so. Their goal is then likely to enable each student to achieve up to the mean of students in their classrooms rather than, as in Finland, Singapore or Shanghai-China, to achieve high universal standards. A comparison between school marks and performance of American students in PISA also suggests that teachers often expect less of students from lower socio-economic backgrounds even if the students show similar levels of achievement. And those students and their parents may expect less, too. This is a heavy burden for the American education system to bear, and it is unlikely that the United States will achieve performance parity with the best-performing countries until it, too, believes, or behaves as if it believes, that, with enough effort and support, all children can achieve at very high levels.

In contrast, in Finland, Japan, Singapore, Shanghai-China and Hong Kong-China, parents, teachers and the public at large tend to share the belief that all students are capable of achieving high standards and need to do so. This volume provides a wealth of instructive examples for how public policy can support the achievement of universal high standards. One of the most interesting patterns observed among some of the highest-performing countries was the gradual move, in many of them, from a system in which students were streamed into different types of secondary schools, with curricula set to very different levels of cognitive demand, to a system in which all students now go to secondary schools with curricula set to much the same high level of cognitive demand. Those countries did not accomplish this transition by taking the average of the previous levels of cognitive demand and setting the new standards to that level. Instead, they "levelled up", requiring all students to meet the standards that they formerly expected only their elite students to meet. In these top-performing education systems, all students are now expected to perform at the levels formerly thought possible only for their elites.

Recognising that the road to dropping out of high schools starts early, Ontario created the "Student Success Initiative" in high schools. Rather than sending out a team from the ministry, they gave the districts money to hire a Student Success leader to co-ordinate efforts in their district. The ministry also gave money for the district leaders to meet and share strategies. Again, each high school was given support to hire a provincially-funded Student Success teacher and was required to create a Student Success team to track early indicators of academic struggles and design appropriate interventions.[3] The outcomes of this work have changed Ontario's system profoundly, and within a few years the high school graduation rate increased from 68% to 79%.

With a different institutional setup, Finland's special teachers fulfil a similar role of early diagnosis and support, working closely with classroom teachers to identify students in need of extra help, and then working individually or in small groups with struggling students to provide the extra help and support they need to keep up with their classmates. It is not left solely to the discretion of the regular classroom teacher to identify a problem and alert the special teacher; every comprehensive school has a "pupils' multi-professional care group" that meets at least twice a month for two hours, and which consists of the principal, the special teacher, the school nurse, the school psychologist, a social worker, and the teachers whose students are being discussed. The parents of any child being discussed are contacted prior to the meeting and are sometimes asked to be present.

Underpinning the entire Singaporean education system is the belief – for students of all ethnic backgrounds and all ranges of ability – that education is the route to advancement and that hard work and effort, not inherited intelligence, is the key to success in school. Singapore, too, had a system of streaming in its elementary schools that it later moderated as it raised its standards. And Singapore uses a wide range of strategies to make sure that student difficulties are diagnosed early and that students who are even just beginning to fall behind are immediately diagnosed properly and given whatever help is needed to get them back on track as quickly as possible. The success of the government's economic and educational policies has brought about immense social mobility that has created a shared sense of national mission and made cultural support for education a near-universal value.

In all these education systems, universal high expectations are not a mantra but a reality and students who start to fall behind are identified quickly, their problem is promptly and accurately diagnosed and the appropriate course of action is quickly taken. Inevitably, this means that some students get more resources than others because the needs of some students are greater; but it is the students with the greatest needs who get the most resources, for that reason.

It has taken most countries time to get from a belief that only a few students can achieve to the point where most educators embrace the proposition that all can do so. It takes a concerted, multifaceted programme of policy-making, capacity-building and the development of proof points to get to the point at which most educators believe it can be done. But no education system included in this study has managed to achieve sustained high performance without developing a system that is premised, in detail, on the proposition that it is possible for all students to achieve at high levels and necessary that they do so. The importance of recent developments in American federal education policy to set the clear expectation that all students should be taught to the same standards and held to the same expectations cannot be overestimated. The No Child Left Behind Act of 2001 required all schools to make progress towards a state-determined standard of "proficiency" for all students, and the Obama administration has supported the states in their efforts to put in place more rigorous state standards linked to college and career readiness, with an increased focus on the instructional systems and teacher support necessary to ensure that all students are held and taught to these same expectations. The challenge ahead will be to back those expectations up with the kinds of student, parent and school support systems that characterise today's most advanced education systems.

Establishing ambitious, focused and coherent education standards that are shared across the system and aligned with high-stakes gateways and instructional systems

Fifteen-year-olds in the United States often rate themselves comparatively highly in academic performance in PISA, even if they did not do well comparatively. In part, that may be due to culture, but one interpretation is also that students are being commended for work that would not be acceptable in high-performing education systems. The results from PISA suggest that, across OECD countries, schools and countries where students work in a climate characterised by high performance expectations and the readiness to invest effort, good teacher-student relations, and high teacher morale tend to achieve better results.

One trend across countries over recent years has been for countries to articulate the expectations that societies have in relation to learning outcomes and to translate these expectations into educational goals and standards. All of the high-performing countries profiled in this volume have developed world-class academic standards for their students and their existence tends to be a consistent predictor for the overall performance of education systems. The approaches to standard-setting in OECD countries range from defining broad educational goals up to formulating concise performance expectations in well-defined subject areas. Whatever the approach, such standards shape high-performing education systems by establishing rigorous, focused and coherent content at all grade levels; reducing overlap in curricula across grades; reducing variation in implemented curricula across classrooms; facilitating co-ordination of various policy drivers, ranging from curricula to teacher training; and reducing inequity in curricula across socio-economic groups.

The establishment, by states, of "common core standards" in the United States follows a similar line of reasoning, with the potential to address the current problem of widely discrepant state standards and assessment cut scores that have led to non-comparable results. These non-comparable standards often mean that a school's fate depends more than anything else on in what state the school is located. More important, students across the United States are left on an unequal footing as to how well they are prepared to compete in the United States labour market.

As shown in Chapter 2, most countries have incorporated their standards into systems of high-quality curricula and external examinations at the secondary school level that are used to construct clear gateways for students either into the workforce and good jobs or to the next stage of education or both.[4] The subjects included in these core instructional systems typically include the language of instruction, mathematics, physics, biology, chemistry, earth sciences, geography, world history, their own country's history, economics, art, music, foreign languages and, in the case of Finland, philosophy. The country report of Canada provides a good example of how such instructional systems can be established. While there is wide variation in the degree to which the curricula actually penetrate Canadian classroom practices, they do provide guidance as to what should be learned by which students at what ages.

It is noteworthy that every one of the high-performing education systems profiled in this volume is focused on the acquisition of complex, higher-order thinking skills and, in many, on the application of those skills to real-world problems. The re-organisation of traditional subjects into "learning domains", as described in the report for Shanghai-China, provides a more recent example of such efforts.

For that reason, examinations in most of the countries described in this volume rely little, if at all, on multiple-choice computer-scored tests, which educators in these countries believe cannot properly measure higher-order thinking skills. Instead, they mostly use essay-type responses on their timed examinations and also factor into the grade the pieces of work that could not possibly be produced in a timed examination. Many nations also use oral examinations. In contrast, state assessments in the United States still predominantly consist of multiple-choice questions with limited cognitive and meta-cognitive demands. Two consortia, comprising 44 states, are seeking to address this issue by designing a new generation of assessments with federal funding. This holds significant promise for assessing a broader range of student skills and knowledge, even if it will take both time and persistence for such assessments to reach classrooms and students at scale. This is an area where the United States can draw on rich experience accumulated in other countries.

In some countries, when the exams are over, newspapers publish many of the exam questions, mostly those that prompt students to write short essays, and the ministry publishes examples of answers that earned top grades. In this way, students, parents and teachers all learn what is considered to be high-quality student work, and students can compare their own work to a clear example of work that meets the standard. The standard in such systems consists of the narrative statements of what students should know and be able to do, the questions asked in the exams, and the responses of the students who earned good grades on the exams.

Often these examinations are linked to national qualifications systems. In countries with systems of this sort, one cannot go on to the next phase of one's education or begin a career in a particular field without a document showing that one is qualified to do so, according to a set of rules and standards laid down by the state. Everyone knows what is required to get a given qualification, in terms of both the content studied and the level of performance that has to be demonstrated to earn it. Countries using qualifications systems typically establish key gateways for students in their systems, one of the most important of which is a gateway that lies at the end of lower secondary education and the beginning of upper secondary education. In most of the countries studied, all students are expected to master a common curriculum by the age of 15 or 16. Then they pursue more individualised paths. Which opportunities are available to them is a function of the qualifications they have earned. Much the same thing happens at the end of upper secondary education, and in some countries the end-of-school examination determines access to university.

The idea of using examinations to create qualifications systems has often raised concerns in the United States, which takes pride in a system that offers second, third and fourth chances to students. Educators know that students are often not ready to make their mark when the system says they should be ready. Why should a student be forever denied an opportunity to succeed in such circumstances? If one is not a late-bloomer oneself, one certainly knows of someone who is. It seems both unfair and unwise to deny anyone such an opportunity. There is a finality about a qualifications system that seems threatening. Indeed, some qualifications systems are set up as screening and sorting systems, and those designed with that purpose can have exactly the effects identified above. However, even in the most exam-driven education systems in East Asia, there are considerable efforts underway to address these weaknesses while maintaining the strengths of the examination systems. As the chapter on Shanghai-China notes, public examinations are conceived as the baton that conducts the entire orchestra; and rather than discard the baton, the East Asian countries are trying to change it so that it conducts good music.

Perhaps more important, examination systems do not have to be set up that way. In Sweden, and a number of other northern European countries, the qualifications systems are established so that it is never too late to earn a given qualification. In such systems, it cannot be said that one has failed the exams, but only that one has not yet succeeded on them. Perhaps it is not a coincidence that Sweden is also the OECD country with the highest incidence and intensity of adult learning in both formal and non-formal education, and the country with the highest level of adult literacy and numeracy skills too. Contrast this with the American high school diploma. In most states, if one has not gotten one's high school diploma by the early 20's, one can never get it, and the best that one can do is to get a GED, which is widely regarded as inferior to a high school diploma. In Sweden and most of the northern European countries, one can get the equivalent of the American high school diploma in any adult education centre and, because the exam is exactly the same, everyone views the 45-year-old who just got her high school diploma as having met a standard every bit as high as the student who got one at the normal age just leaving Folkeschule.

In such systems, where it is never too late to get any qualification, the advantage of having a qualification system is that the examinations are always available and the standards are never lowered or waived. Students know that they have to take tough courses and study hard in order to get the qualification and so they do. One does not get to go on to the next stage simply because one has put in the requisite time. One gets to move on only if one has met the requisite performance standards. This is a system with very high stakes for the students. There are typically low or no stakes for the teachers in these systems. The result is a higher standard of education across the whole society than is the case in a society that is forever waiving the standards to give students second chances. It is true that high-stakes examination systems can lead to a focus on test preparation at the expense of real learning, the development of large private tutoring industries that tend to favour the wealthy, and incentives for cheating. These dangers are real and reflected in some of the country reports; but as most of the countries featured in this volume suggest, these dangers can be mitigated.

Because the examinations are typically externally graded, the teacher, student and parents feel that they are all on the same side, working towards the same end, and one does not see a situation where parents go to the school administration to change the student's grade, pitting the teacher, who wants to preserve some standard, against parents, who want the best possible future for their children. Parents and students know that neither the teacher nor the administration can change the grade, and therefore the only way to improve the outcome for the student is for the student to work harder and do better work. In many of those countries, training for teachers is focused on enabling them to teach those required courses to their students well.

In the countries that use these systems, the best minds in the country determine what topics will be taught in what sequence through the grades. In some of the countries profiled in this volume, the officials responsible for specifying the curriculum framework also play an important part in supervising the writing of textbooks. The result is a powerful, coherent system of instruction that is available to all students.

Again, the adoption of the Common Core Standards by the states and the work of the state consortia funded by Race to the Top open important opportunities for the United States to make real progress on this set of challenges. But to have a sustained impact on learning outcomes, further steps need to include developing world-class standards for all the subjects in the core curriculum; creating well-thought-out curriculum frameworks for those subjects that can guide the work of teachers and publishers of instructional materials; developing examinations focused on complex thinking skills, to assess whether students have met the standards across the core curriculum; and creating a system of gateways using the new examinations that constitute a well-developed qualifications system.

Developing more capacity at the point of delivery

The quality of an education system cannot exceed the quality of its teachers and principals. Corporations, professional partnerships, national militaries and national governments know that they have to pay attention to how the pool is established from which they recruit; how they recruit; how they select their staff; the kind of initial training their recruits get before they present themselves for employment; how they mentor new recruits and induct them into their service; what kind of continuing training they get; how their compensation is structured; how they reward their best performers and how they either improve the performance of those who are struggling or get rid of them; and how they provide opportunities for the best performers to acquire more status and responsibility.

Attracting high-quality teachers

With respect to the pool from which an industry or an organisation recruits its professionals, the aim generally is to do whatever is possible to generate a pool that comes from the highest-performing segment. Most firms and industries rely heavily on elementary, secondary and post-secondary institutions to do that sorting for them. That is what the top Japanese ministries are doing when they decide to recruit from the University of Tokyo and what the top Wall Street law firms are doing when they recruit mainly from among Harvard, Yale and Stanford graduates. They are more interested in these institutions because they believe they are good at getting the very best in terms of what the Japanese call "applied intelligence" than because of the specific knowledge and skills they are buying.

Because no industry can afford to source all of its professionals from the highest-performing segment, they structure their operations so that they can put the best of the best in key positions and use others who may not be quite as good in supporting positions. More often than not, they use pyramidal structures which both permit them to make the most of their best professionals and put those with lower performance in supporting positions.

So what determines the pool from which an entire industry can select its professionals? It varies, but the country reports suggest that it includes some combination of the social status associated with the occupation and work, the sense of personal contribution one can make, and the financial rewards one can expect. In some countries, the status of the teaching profession has changed significantly. Earlier chapters have shown how Finland raised the social status of its teachers to a level where there are few occupations that have higher social status than teaching. Finnish teachers have earned the trust of parents and the wider society by their demonstrated capacity to use professional discretion and judgement in the way they manage their classrooms and respond to the challenge of helping virtually all students become successful learners. In 2010, over 6 600 applicants competed for 660 available slots in primary school preparation programmes in the eight universities that educate teachers.[5] While teachers in Finland have always enjoyed respect in society, a combination of raising the bar for entry into the profession and granting teachers greater autonomy and control over their classrooms and working conditions than their peers enjoy elsewhere has helped to raise the status of the profession and make teaching one of the most desirable career choices among young Finns. Consequently, teaching is now a highly selective occupation in Finland, with highly-skilled, well-trained teachers spread throughout the country. Also, in the traditionally Confucian cultures, teachers have long had higher social status than is generally true in the West. In some of the East Asian countries, teachers' compensation is fixed by law to make sure that teachers are among the highest paid of all positions in the civil service.

By raising the bar to enter the teaching profession, these systems discourage young people with poor qualifications from entering teaching and attract people with high qualifications. Capable young people who could go into high-status occupations are not likely to enter an occupation that the society perceives as easy to get into and therefore likely to attract people who could not get into more demanding occupations.

The report on Shanghai-China shows the degree of change that is possible in that realm, as does the note about the English initiative to recruit teachers. As that note points out, the Blair administration faced one of the worst shortages of teachers in British history when it took office. Five years later, there were eight applicants for every opening. To some extent this had to do with raising compensation significantly, as well as with important changes in the work environment for teachers; but a sophisticated and powerful recruiting programme played a very important part in the turnaround. Singapore is notable for its own approach to improving the quality of the pool from which it selects candidates for training. Singapore carefully selects young people who the government is especially interested in attracting to teaching and offers them a monthly stipend while in training that is competitive with the monthly salary for fresh graduates in other fields. In exchange, these teachers-in-training must commit to teaching for at least three years. Singapore also keeps a close watch on occupational starting salaries and adjusts the salaries for new teachers. In effect, the country wants its most qualified candidates to regard teaching as just as attractive in compensation as other professions.

Generally, in the United States, teaching has been seen as a very attractive occupation for people whose parents had little education and may be the first members of their family to get a college education and leave the working class for the middle class. As more and more people in the United States have gone to college, however, the relative status of teachers seems to have declined, and schools of education are usually not regarded as highly as other professional schools. OECD data show that teachers' pay in the United States is fourth from the bottom among OECD countries, when teachers' compensation is compared to that for other occupations requiring the same amount of education.[6] Perhaps most important, when students who are deciding what careers to pursue look at teaching, they may see an occupation that looks more like a blue-collar occupation than a knowledge-based profession. All these things severely restrict the pool from which Americans select their teachers, relative to other countries.

Drawing on lessons from Britain's successful efforts to improve the occupational prestige of the teaching profession, the Obama administration has recently announced plans to attract high-calibre candidates into teaching and raise the prestige of the profession in the United States.

Preparing high-quality teachers

At the same time, the recruitment of top-performing graduates can only be one of several components of human resource management in education. The report of Ontario provides a compelling case for how a successful reform trajectory began not by waiting for a new generation of teachers, but by investing in the existing schools and teachers, wherever they stood, enlisting their commitment to reform and supporting their improvement. This involved extensive capacity-building in schools as well as in the system, and quarterly meetings between the system leaders and the major teachers' unions, superintendents' organisations, and principals' associations to discuss ongoing reform strategies.[7]

There is an instructive pattern here among the top-performing countries. Many of the countries studied in this volume have moved from a system in which teachers are recruited into a larger number of specialised, low-status colleges of teacher education, with relatively low entrance standards, into a relatively smaller number of university-based teacher-education colleges with relatively high entrance standards and relatively high status in the university. Finland is the archetypal case, but Singapore, Shanghai-China and Germany provide other examples. It would appear that countries interested in raising the quality of their teaching force understand that they cannot accomplish that goal without raising the standards for entrance into their schools of education, if only because the candidates they are trying to attract may not be interested in attending a professional school that has low status in the higher-education system and in society at large.

Apart from raising entrance standards to make them comparable to those of other professions, teacher-education programmes in the top-performing countries studied show some further common characteristics:

- Across the board, the best-performing countries are working to move their initial teacher-education programmes towards a model based less on preparing academics and more on preparing professionals in clinical settings, in which they get into schools earlier, spend more time there and get more and better support in the process. In Finland, this includes both extensive course work on how to teach – with a strong emphasis on using research based on state-of-the-art practice – and at least a full year of clinical experience in a school associated with the university. These model schools are intended to develop and pilot innovative practices, and foster research on learning and teaching.

- They put more emphasis on developing the capacity of teachers in training to diagnose student problems swiftly and accurately.

- They are working to develop the prospective teacher's capacity to draw from a wide repertoire of possible solutions those that are particularly appropriate to the diagnosis.

- They put more emphasis on the specific instructional techniques that are appropriate for the subjects that the prospective teacher will teach. Because teacher education in Finland is a shared responsibility between the teacher-education faculty and the academic-subject faculty, there is substantial attention to subject-specific pedagogy for prospective teachers.

- Some countries, notably Shanghai-China and Finland, provide teachers with the research skills needed to enable them to improve their practice in a highly disciplined way. In Finland, teachers are encouraged to contribute to the knowledge base on effective teaching practices throughout their career, with candidates not only expected to become familiar with the knowledge base in education and human development, but also required to write a research-based thesis as the final requirement for the Masters degree. The Chinese, too, emphasise giving prospective teachers the skills they will need for action research, and their method for improving their education system over time relies on research performed by teachers. China is also able to enlist teachers trained in this way as leaders of efforts organised by their ministries to systematically introduce and try out new ideas for improving their education systems.

- Part of the motivation for relocating teacher-education programmes to the university has been to make sure that the preparation of teachers in the subjects they will teach is comparable to that of people who will go on to be professionals in other arenas. In most of these countries, people who are going on to be elementary or primary school teachers are required to declare whether they will specialise in either mathematics and science or their native language and social studies, and they are required to attain a high level of substantive knowledge in the specialty they will teach.

These developments are hardly surprising. Given that these countries are pursuing a school structure in which all students are expected to perform at elite levels and teachers are expected to make sure that (literally) no students will be allowed to fall behind, it becomes essential that teachers identify students who are just beginning to fall behind, diagnose the problem, and have the skills and knowledge needed to create a large and constantly updated reservoir of solutions to the student performance problems they have diagnosed.

Development of teacher quality once teachers are in the work force
The country reports on Germany and Japan show how, once teachers have completed their pre-service training and begun their teaching, they enter with one or two years of heavily supervised teaching. During this period, the beginning teacher typically receives a reduced workload, strong mentoring by master teachers, and continued formal instruction.

Also, the top-performing countries in East Asia profiled in this volume have ways to make the most of their top-performing teachers that are instructive in the context of the United States. At the school level, the best teachers in these countries typically lead the process of lesson development. The master teachers are also called upon to coach beginning teachers and to play a key role in analysing the problems of students who are having difficulties with learning. The district and provincial offices of education often identify the best of the teachers who emerge from this process and relieve them of some or all of their teaching duties so that they can give lectures to their peers, provide demonstrations, and coach other teachers on a district, provincial and even national scale. Carefully picked schools are often asked to pilot new programmes or policies before they are scaled-up and the best teachers in those schools are enlisted as co-researchers to evaluate the effectiveness of the new practices. Because the initial preparation of teachers in those countries includes instruction in research skills, it is expected that teachers will use those skills to generate evidence to improve their practice in a disciplined way. Research is an integral part of what it means to be a professional teacher in those countries.

The policies and practices just described have implications for many aspects of system performance. But one important group of consequences has to do with the quality of the teacher workforce itself. The tradition of lesson study in East Asia means that Asian teachers are not alone. They work together in a disciplined way to improve the quality of the lessons they teach. That means that teachers whose practice lags behind that of the leaders can see what good practice is. Because their colleagues know whom the poor performers are and discuss it, the poor performers have both the incentive and the means to improve their performance. Because the structure of the East Asian teaching work force includes opportunities to become a master teacher and to move up a ladder of increasing prestige and responsibility, it also pays the good teacher to become even better.

There are other measures that top-performing countries use to maintain high quality in their teacher work force. In Shanghai-China, each teacher is expected to engage in 240 hours of professional development within five years. Singapore provides an entitlement of 100 hours of professional development per year to teachers to keep up with the rapid changes occurring in the world and to be able to improve their practice. And Singapore, like other countries, is improving its performance-appraisal system, making sure that each teacher is appraised by a whole group of people every year against 16 different competencies.[8] Teachers who do outstanding work receive a bonus from the school's bonus pool.

Teacher quality and teachers' unions

As PISA shows, in most OECD countries, once teachers are hired, it is very hard to remove them from professional service, irrespective of the quality of their work. The high quality of teachers in those countries appears to be a function of the policies that determine the pool from which teachers are initially drawn, their compensation, the status of teachers, the high standards of entering university-level teacher-preparation programmes, the quality of their initial preparation, and the attention given to the quality of their preparation following their initial induction.

Critics of American education are sometimes disapproving of the teachers' unions and of how they perceive these unions as interfering with promising school reform programmes by giving higher priority to the unions' "bread and butter" issues than to what the evidence suggests students need to succeed. But the fact is that many of the countries with the strongest student performance also have the strongest teachers' unions, beginning with Japan and Finland. There seems to be no relationship between the presence of unions, including and especially teachers' unions, and student performance. But there may be a relationship between the degree to which the work of teaching has been professionalised and student performance. Indeed, the higher a country is on the world's education league tables, the more likely that country is working constructively with its unions and treating its teachers as trusted professional partners. Witness the reports of Ontario in Canada or Finland.

The report on Canada, in particular, describes how issues of collective bargaining can be successfully separated from professional issues, where teachers and their organisations collaborate effectively with ministry staff in self-governing bodies to oversee issues of entry, discipline, and the professional development of teachers. Central to success in this area in Ontario was the signing of a four-year collective bargaining agreement with the four major teachers' unions. In reaching the accord, the ministry was able to negotiate items that were consistent with both its educational strategy and the unions' interests, thus providing a basis for pushing forward the education agenda while creating a sustained period of labour peace that allowed for continued focus on educational improvement. That was facilitated because union agreements could be reached at the provincial level, which may be more challenging in the context of the United States, with the more decentralised nature of union-management decision-making.

Unless the United States raises the professional status of its existing teaching force as Ontario has done, upgrades the pool from which it selects new teachers, is more selective in admitting candidates for initial teacher training and education, greatly improves the quality of, and includes much more clinical education in, that training, changes the amount and structure of teachers compensation, finds practical and effective ways of raising the status of teachers, greatly improves the process of initial induction and restructures the occupation to provide increased and appropriate responsibilities for the best teachers, and leverages more effective union-management relations at local and state levels, it is unlikely to match the performance of the best-performing countries.

Important beginnings in this direction are under way. For example, the United States has directed new federal funding for teacher preparation towards more clinical programmes such as teacher "residency" programmes, in which teacher candidates learn to teach in schools under the guidance of experienced teachers while taking classes outside of teaching hours. The Obama administration has also sought, through the Race to the Top programme and other efforts, to encourage states and districts to develop more rigorous systems of teacher evaluation that can inform new approaches to induction, compensation and career advancement decisions. These efforts are consistent with the approaches in the high-performing systems profiled in this volume.

Developing capable school leaders

In most countries researched for this volume, high schools are generally smaller than the typical school in the United States, and the people responsible for leading school faculties are head teachers who spend some of their time teaching, rather than full-time administrators, as is the common practice in the United States. Head teachers are often chosen for their instructional leadership rather than their administrative capacity. Such a leadership system appears to provide a supportive framework for professional accountability in which teachers feel more accountable to one another for their performance, unlike the United States form of administrative accountability, in which teachers are made accountable to the principal and others in supervisory positions.

Singapore's approach to leadership is exemplary in this respect and modelled on that found in large corporations, where the key is not just the training programme, but the whole approach to identifying and developing talent. This differs from the United States where, for example, a teacher can apply to train as a principal or school head, and then apply for a position in a school. In Singapore, young teachers are continuously assessed for their leadership potential and given opportunities to demonstrate and learn by, for example, serving on committees, then being promoted to head of department at a relatively young age. Some are transferred to the ministry for a period. After these experiences are monitored, potential principals are selected for interviews and go through situational leadership exercises. If they pass these, then they go to the National Institute for Education, the country's sole teacher-training institution, for six months of executive leadership training, with their salaries paid. The process is comprehensive and intensive and includes an international study trip and a project on school innovation.

More generally, countries are paying increasing attention to redefining school leadership roles to drive improvements in learning outcomes and to manage increased school autonomy and accountability. This comes at a time when greater decentralisation in many countries is being coupled with more school autonomy, more accountability for school and student results, better use of the knowledge base of education and pedagogical processes, and broader responsibility for supporting the schools' local communities, other schools and other public services. OECD's comparative review of school leadership roles[9] identified four groups of interrelated leadership responsibilities as central for improving schooling outcomes:

- First, a focus on supporting, evaluating and developing teacher quality as the core of effective leadership. Leadership responsibilities associated with improved teacher quality include recruiting high-quality teachers, providing a strong induction programme for new teachers, making sure the teachers have the skills and knowledge needed to teach the curriculum the school uses, organising the teachers to work together to improve the quality of teaching and instruction, monitoring and evaluating teacher practice, promoting teacher professional development, and supporting collaborative work cultures.

- Second, establishing learning objectives and implementing thoughtful assessments to help students reach high standards. Aligning instruction with central standards, setting school goals for student performance, measuring progress against those goals, and making adjustments in the school programme to improve individual and overall performance are the dynamic aspects of managing curricula and instruction. School leaders' purposeful use of data is essential to ensure that attention is being paid to the progress of every student.

- Third, the strategic use of resources and their alignment with pedagogical purposes to focus all operational activities within the school on the objective of improving teaching and learning.

- Fourth, leadership engagements beyond the school, in partnerships with other schools, communities, social agencies and universities to foster greater cohesion among all those concerned with the achievement and well-being of every child.

Providing a work organisation in which teachers can use their potential: Management, accountability and knowledge management

Earlier in this chapter, a distinction was made between the Tayloristic management paradigm and the kinds of paradigms more suited to managing professionals or "knowledge workers". In the former, one typically sees bureaucratic "command and control" systems, leaving little discretion to the workers and supervisors at the factory floor or service-delivery level of the organisation. In the latter, the people responsible for actually making the product or delivering the services have much more control of the way resources are used, people are deployed, the work is organised and the way in which the work gets done.

Many of the best-performing countries have had education systems far more centralised, bureaucratic and controlling than the United States has ever had, but most of those countries have rebalanced their systems to provide more discretion to school heads and school faculties, a factor that Chapter 2 shows, when combined with accountability systems, to be closely related to school performance. In many cases, these countries concluded that top-down initiatives were insufficient to achieve deep and lasting changes in practice, because reforms were focused on things that were too distant from the instructional core of teaching and learning; because reforms assumed that teachers would know how to do things they actually didn't know how to do; because too many conflicting reforms asked teachers to do too many things simultaneously; or because teachers and schools did not buy in to the reform strategy. The chapters on Finland and Ontario provide examples of how formerly centralised systems have shifted emphasis towards improving the act of teaching; giving careful and detailed attention to implementation, along with opportunities for teachers to practice new ideas and learn from their colleagues; developing an integrated strategy and set of expectations for both teachers and students; and securing support from teachers for the reforms. This is also the direction towards which Japan and other Asian countries are moving. In some countries, great discretion is given to the faculty, as a whole, and its individual members. In others, more discretion is given to schools that are doing well and less to those that might be struggling. In some countries, the school head is little more than the lead teacher. In others, the authorities continue to look to the school head to set the direction and manage the faculty. But the common element is the degree to which they are all creating forms of work organisation that are moving from Tayloristic, bureaucratic management to the kinds of professional forms of work organisation more likely to be found in professional partnerships than in mass-production industrial operations.

The Finnish system of accountability is entirely built from the bottom up. Teacher candidates are selected in part based on their capacity to convey their belief in the core mission of public education in Finland, which is deeply humanistic as well as civic and economic. The preparation they receive is designed to build a powerful sense of individual responsibility for the learning and well-being of all the students in their care. The next level of accountability rests with the school. Again, the level of trust that the larger community extends to its schools seems to engender a strong sense of collective responsibility for the success of every student. While every comprehensive school in Finland reports to a municipal authority, authorities vary widely in the quality and degree of oversight that they provide. They are responsible for hiring the principal, typically on a six- or seven-year contract, but the day-to-day responsibility for managing the schools is left to the professionals, as is the responsibility for assuring student progress.

One might assume that schools in the United States, with its tradition of local control, have more autonomy than schools in other countries. But that is not the case, because American schools, at least in the cities and most suburbs, get much more direction from the local district central office than is typically the case in other countries. In that sense, the United States may have traded one form of centralised bureaucracy for another. It is also true that the more recent unionisation of American education, given the American style of union-management relations and the pressure to have contracts mirror neighbouring localities, may produce a more rule-bound environment than will be found in systems embracing more professional forms of work organisation.

So here, as elsewhere, the devil is in the details. The United States may appear to have a more devolved management system than those typically found in many high-performing countries, but, because of the way school-district management typically works, especially in middle-sized and larger districts, it will have to make major changes in that system to match the flexibility of those used by the highest-performing countries. What is important here is that a truly professional staff has both the responsibility and the authority to design, manage, budget for and organise the school's programme in its entirety, within the framework provided by the goals, curricula, examinations and qualifications systems put in place by the state.

To some extent, the "charter" public school model in the United States, which has grown into wide use over the past 20 years, offers a model to address some of these issues and, in particular, for school heads and faculty to take on greater autonomy from the district over decisions around the school's instructional programme. However, these schools may have to accept greater accountability for improved student achievement outcomes. What is striking about the high-performing countries portrayed in this volume is that they provide not just some of their schools, but all of their schools, with the scope for school-based decision-making that is characteristic of charter schools in the United States. These schools are considered to be regular public schools and they are expected to implement the state curriculum, administer the state tests, produce the same public data on their performance, have the same budget resources, be accountable to the public and their own community, and take in all students just like any other schools are expected to do. In this sense, in many of these countries, all public schools are charter schools and all charter schools are public schools.

Many charter schools in the United States have significantly outperformed traditional public schools, especially among disadvantaged students, but the performance of many charter schools is similar to or worse than that of traditional public schools. The Obama administration has encouraged states to allow for such autonomous school models matched with stronger accountability for performance, and has provided additional funding targeted at high-performing public charter schools.

Institutionalising improved instructional practice

The country reports made the point that, in many Asian countries, classes are much larger than in the United States and teachers typically use whole-group instruction through the entire class period. They also pointed out that, in these countries, one sees little lecturing by the teacher. Instead, the teacher gives real-world problems to the whole class and, having observed the students attempting to solve those problems, asks several to come to the blackboard to talk about their approaches to the problem, knowing that some of those students have made errors in the strategy they have selected for solving the problem. As described in the country reports for Japan and Shanghai-China, the teacher uses these differences in strategy to develop a class discussion that focuses on the underlying concepts involved in problem-solving, and thereby promotes a deep understanding of the topic under discussion among both the quickest and the slowest students in the class. Nothing could so vividly demonstrate the point that instructional practice matters.

In this way, Japanese teachers maximise their contact time with each student in the class. Students are not whiling away their time when the teacher is dealing with a small group in the classroom. Students who misunderstand some important point in mathematics will find that they can identify with a student who is at the blackboard and has made a similar mistake and can, in effect, get individual attention without monopolising the teacher's time. Asian teachers often complain about class sizes getting too small to find a useful range of student solutions to a problem in order to conduct a good class, instead of complaining that the class is too large to teach effectively, as in the United States.

The Finnish education system pursues very similar goals but with different strategies. It applies a learner-centred approach that places considerable emphasis on student self-assessment, in which students are expected to take an active role in designing their own learning activities and work collaboratively in teams on projects that cut across traditional subject or disciplinary areas. By the time students enrol in upper secondary school (grades 10-12), they are expected to be able to take sufficient charge of their own learning to be able to design their own individual programme where, without a grade structure, each student proceeds at his or her own pace within the modular design of the system.

Similarly, the inquiry-based curriculum component in Shanghai-China asks students, with support and guidance from teachers, to identify research topics based on their experiences, seeking to develop the capacity of students to learn to learn, think creatively and critically, participate in social life, and promote social welfare. In fact, one very significant change implemented in Shanghai-China through the slogan "return class time to students" was the increase in student activities in classes relative to teachers' lecturing. This has caused a fundamental change in the perception of a good class, which was once typified by good teaching, with well-designed presentations by the teachers. Videos of model teaching used to concentrate on teachers' activities. Now, model classes are filmed with two cameras, one of which records student activities. Teachers' performances are now also evaluated by the time given to student participation and how well student activities are organised.

These are all matters of instructional practice. In the United States, educators often consider these to be entirely in the purview of the individual teacher in the sanctuary of his or her classroom. This volume shows that, in countries as different as Finland, Japan or Shanghai-China, the practice of individual teachers is open to inspection by the other teachers in the school, and the quality of teachers' practice is seen as a matter for all the teachers in the school to be concerned about.

Teachers work together to produce lessons that are superior in their power to engage students in the work and convey the knowledge and skills specified in the syllabus. Because teachers work together on this, no teacher's classroom is private. It is not uncommon in Asian classrooms for teachers to occupy the last rows in a classroom as they observe the practice of a teacher they particularly admire. As was noted above in another context, in this kind of setting, there is no mystery about which teachers are most capable. Those who are less capable are under considerable pressure from their colleagues to improve their practice, and they have plenty of opportunities to do so, simply by observing their most capable colleagues and participating in the critiques of their practice, especially on the new lessons they are creating.

Finland has incorporated a similar approach in its teacher-development programmes. Student teachers regularly participate in problem-solving groups, a common feature in Finnish schools. The problem-solving groups engage in a cycle of planning, action and reflection/evaluation that is reinforced throughout the teacher-education programme and is, in fact, a model for what teachers will plan for their own students, who are expected to use similar kinds of research and inquiry in their own studies. In a way, the entire Finnish system is intended to improve through continual reflection, evaluation and problem-solving, at the level of the classroom, school, municipality and nation.

Some may contend that teaching is not a true profession because the craft of teaching is an individual matter, and there are no shared standards of practice, a hallmark of true professions. But the countries profiled in this volume generally consider teaching a profession where teachers work together to frame what they believe good practice to be, conduct field-based research to confirm or disprove the approaches they develop, and then judge their colleagues by the degree to which they use practices proven effective in their classrooms. This amounts to the collective search for ever more effective practices of the sort seen in Canada, Finland, Japan, Shanghai-China and Singapore. In this way, standards of practice can emerge and the effectiveness of practice can be steadily improved over time. This may be how a profession of teaching emerges. As pointed out above, in the East Asian countries studied here, as well as in Canada and Finland's teacher-training schools, those teachers who exhibit the very best practice are released, full-time or part-time, from their regular classroom duties to mentor new teachers, provide demonstrations to teachers in their own schools and other schools, and lecture to education audiences in their province or even nationally. They conduct their own research and university researchers examine their practice. In this way, classroom teachers codify and continually advance the standards for acceptable teaching practice.

In most of the countries studied in this volume, the way teachers work may be compared with the way physicians think about the practice of medicine. Doctors would not think of developing their own drugs; nor would they think of themselves as professionals if they did not carefully study the most effective procedures yet developed to deal with the presenting symptoms. Indeed, their sense of themselves as professionals comes in large measure from their deep knowledge of a wide range of presenting symptoms, their capacity to successfully diagnose a patient with those symptoms, and their capacity to identify and execute the most effective procedures available for the treatment of the diagnosed problem. It is much the same with the teachers in the schools of the countries with the most effective education systems. It is their capacity to diagnose individual students to identify the difficulties they are having, their encyclopaedic repertoire of effective solutions to the problems in student learning they encounter, their capacity to execute a lesson with such panache and skill that the students find it enthralling and totally engaging, and their devotion to the improvement of their craft that makes them professionals.

One must remember that all of this is going on in countries in which the standards for what students are meant to know and be able to do are much clearer than is typically the case in the United States. While teachers often tend to think of themselves as professionals to the extent that they have the freedom to choose what they will teach, as well as how they teach it, in the highest-performing countries, teachers have a great deal of freedom with respect to how they teach, but less with respect to what students are expected to know and be able to do. In the United States, the initiative to establish common standards among the states will offer an opportunity to establish greater clarity about what teachers should teach, while continuing to allow them flexibility in how to design and deliver instruction in the classroom. But institutionalising high-quality instructional practice of the sort observed in high-performing systems, consistently and at scale, will remain a formidable challenge.

Aligning incentive structures and engaging stakeholders

To understand why people do the things they do, ask yourself what sort of incentives they have to act that way. Examining whether the incentives that operate on students, parents, teachers and others in those countries are more likely to produce higher performance than the incentives that operate on those actors in other countries can provide important insights into why some countries rank higher on the education league tables than others.

In countries with high-stakes examination systems, that is, systems in which students cannot go on to the next stage of their life – be it work or further education – unless they show that they are qualified to do so, students know what they have to do to realise their dream and they put in the work that is needed to do it.

As pointed out above, in the United States, high school students may be led to believe that the outcome is the same whether they take easy courses and get Ds in them or take tough courses and get As. Either way, they might think, they can get into the local community college and get on with their lives. Contrast this with a student of the same age in Toyota City, Japan, who wants to work on the line at a Toyota plant. That student knows that she must get good grades in tough subjects and earn the recommendation of her principal, so she takes those tough courses and works hard in school. The same is true of the student in Germany who wants to work for Daimler Benz in their machine shop or the student in Singapore who wants to go to work in the factory automation shop a few blocks from his home. The reason examination systems matter is that they provide strong incentives for students to take tough courses and study hard. One of the most striking features of the American education system, in contrast with the education systems of the most successful countries, is its failure to provide strong incentives to the average student to work hard in school. If the reader does not, for whatever reason, like the idea of examination systems, then the lesson learned here should be that some other means, no less effective, should be found to motivate students to work as hard in school as students in other countries do.

Similarly, if teachers do not work as hard at their job as teachers in other countries do, they are not likely to get the same results. The question is what incentives are most likely to produce that result. In Tayloristic work environments, the answer is that management should measure output carefully and then provide rewards to those whose measured output exceeds expectations. In those environments, workers are competing with one another, and most workers, resenting the worker who outperforms them, create social norms in which the outstanding performer is an outcast in the group. But in professional work environments, such as professional partnerships, the success of the whole group depends on maximising the output of each worker, so workers tend to collaborate to increase output, workers support getting rid of workers who pull the performance of the group down, and they approve of paying more to those who, by their effort or skill, increase the rewards coming to the group as a whole.

The learning environment is also shaped by parents in important ways. Parents who are interested in their children's education are more likely to support their school's efforts and participate in school activities, thus adding to available resources. As discussed in Chapter 2, PISA shows that school principals' perceptions of parents' constant pressure to adopt high academic standards and to raise student achievement tends to be positively related to higher school performance in 19 OECD countries, although that relationship is not apparent in the United States. PISA also shows that the socio-economic background of students and schools and key features of the learning environment are closely interrelated, and that both link to performance in important ways. This may be because students from socio-economically advantaged backgrounds bring with them a higher level of discipline and more positive perceptions of school values, or because parental expectations of good classroom discipline and strong teacher commitment are higher in schools with advantaged socio-economic intake. Conversely, disadvantaged schools may experience less parental pressure to reinforce effective disciplinary practices or ensure that absent or unmotivated teachers are replaced. In summary, students perform better in schools with a stronger school climate, partly because such schools tend to have more students from advantaged backgrounds who generally perform well, partly because the favourable socio-economic characteristics of students reinforce the favourable climate, and partly for reasons unrelated to socio-economic variables.[10]

There are significant differences in the way education systems involve parents in different countries. As pointed out above, in many countries in both Europe and Asia, certain teachers are designated as either homeroom teachers or classroom teachers. These teachers follow the student through a number of grades. They assume a certain holistic responsibility for the students in their class and form a close relationship not only with the student but with that student's parents. In both Asia and Europe, it is typical in such cases that a notebook is passed back and forth between the teacher and the parents, in which each party shares information about the student with the other party. These relationships lead to a kind of parent involvement in the education of their children that is rare in the United States, as well as to a spirit of collaboration between teacher and parents that is also unusual.

The idea of the "classroom teacher" has often been described as a cultural artefact that could not be imported into the United States at scale because there is no cultural history that would support it. But, in fact, it is a notion that has been adopted in countries with cultures as diverse as those in Asia and Europe. This particular policy has indeed been adopted by individual schools and some districts in a limited way in the United States, but not as a matter of state policy.

It is not just a way to involve parents but, perhaps even more important, it is a way to provide strong accountability to parents in a form that seems appropriate to teachers. Parents in systems that have adopted the idea of classroom teachers as universal policy tend to feel a strong bond with their children's classroom teachers. In a series of focus groups conducted in Denmark by the National Center on Education and the Economy, parents were asked what happens when their children gets a less competent classroom teacher and has to put up with that teacher for years. Was that not a problem? But parents said that the advantages of the system far outweighed any disadvantages that might come in the way suggested and reported that the classroom teacher system was one of the most important and most successful educational policies in their country.

There is another, rather subtle, advantage of this system. A teacher who teaches a given student for only one year typically feels that, while they will do the best they can with the students they get, there is little they can to do in one year to correct the problems they have inherited from the poor practice of teachers who had that student in the lower grades, and little they can do to protect the student from the less competent teachers who might come in the succeeding grades. But, in the classroom-teacher system, the teacher in the earlier grade is the teacher in question, and so is the teacher who comes later. In this system, there is no way for the classroom teacher to evade personal responsibility for what happens to the student. As a matter of professional pride, and as a result of being close to the student for years and developing a sense of personal responsibility for the student, it is natural for the teacher to reach out to the parents, co-ordinate the education of her students with those students' specialist teachers, and counsel and guide her students as they grow up.

Complementing accountability to agents outside schools with accountability professional colleagues and parents

Every high-performing country studied in this volume appears to have an effective accountability system. The experience of Germany is an object lesson in that respect. Having believed itself to be among the world's best performers without any means to validate this, it was shocked into action when the data from PISA showed that it was not. But the form that accountability takes differs from country to country and that form of accountability appears to matter.

Some accountability systems publish data on the performance of students and schools to inform the public and the system managers about their performance. In systems that permit parents and students to choose among schools, this data can also influence those choices and thus to hold schools accountable with market forces based on performance data supplied by the schools among which they are choosing (for details, see Chapter 2). In some of the systems this volume has studied, these data are also used by school administrators to allocate resources of various kinds, often to provide additional resources to schools that are struggling.

Beyond that, accountability systems in the best-performing countries can be divided into those that employ administrative (or vertical) accountability and those that employ professional (or lateral) accountability systems.

Administrative accountability refers to systems in which student-achievement test data are used by administrators to reward good teachers, good schools and good districts and to punish teachers, schools and districts that consistently produce poor results. Among the features of administrative accountability are often test-based accountability systems that use data on student performance to make decisions about which teachers and school principals to hire, promote and retain, and for making decisions about the compensation of individual teachers.

Professional accountability refers to systems in which teachers feel themselves accountable not so much to external agents as to their fellow teachers and school principals, as professionals in most fields feel themselves accountable for their performance to other professionals in the same field. In the case of education, professional accountability includes the kind of personal responsibility that teachers feel to the parents of their students in countries that have homeroom teachers or classroom teachers of the sort described in the country chapters.

Jurisdictions such as Ontario in Canada, Japan and Finland that place greater emphasis on the more professional forms of work organisation tend to pursue collegial forms of teacher and school-leader accountability, seeking to ensure that reform becomes a two-way street, rather than something imposed from above. This is because people who expect to be treated as professionals and think of themselves that way are more likely to respond to professional and familial modes of accountability, and to view negatively the use of administrative forms of accountability of the sort that they identify with Tayloristic work environments. The example of Ontario shows how, rather than relying on methods of informed prescription advocating particular uses, the emphasis was placed on creating partnerships with teachers and schools in the field to identify good practices, consolidating these and bringing them to scale. Rather than mandating reform, seed money was put into the field to encourage local experimentation and innovation, sending a strong signal that teacher-generated solutions to weaknesses in reading and mathematics performance were likely to be more successful than solutions imposed from above. The dramatic reduction in the number of low-performing schools was not achieved by threatening to close them but by flooding them with technical assistance and support, on the premise that teachers are professionals who are trying to do the right thing, and that performance problems are much more likely to stem from a lack of knowledge than a lack of motivation. At the same time, the Ontario government made no attempt to dismantle or weaken the assessment regime put in place by the previous government, and consistently communicated the message to the field and the public that results matter, as defined by performance on provincial assessments.

Singapore provides an example where both administrative and professional accountability are combined in an approach centred around performance management, with a wide range of indicators and with involvement of a wide range of professionals in making judgements about the performance of adults in the system. Teachers, principals, ministry and other staff, as well as students, all have incentives to work hard. For maintaining the performance of teachers and principals, serious attention is paid to setting annual goals, garnering the needed support to meet them, and assessing whether they have been met. Data on student performance are included, but so, too, are a range of other measures, such as contributions to school and community, and judgements by a number of senior practitioners. Reward and recognition systems include honours and salary bonuses. Individual appraisals take place within the context of school-excellence plans.

Perhaps the greatest challenge to reform has to do with trust. Trust cannot be legislated. Some may argue that this lesson may be less relevant to others wanting to learn from Finland, especially if one views trust as a precondition for the kinds of deep institutional reforms embodied in the development of the comprehensive school. But in the case of the relationship between teachers and the larger society, one can argue that trust is at least as much a consequence of policy decisions as it is a pre-existing condition. Given the respect that teachers have historically enjoyed in Finland, there was a solid base on which to build reforms. But the combination alluded to in the country report for Finland – much more rigorous preparation, coupled with the devolution of much greater decision-making authority over things like curriculum and assessment – enabled teachers to exercise the kind of autonomy other professionals enjoy. This granting of trust from the government, coupled with their new-found status as university graduates from highly selective programmes, empowered teachers to practise their profession in ways that deepened the trust accorded them by parents and others in the community.

However, it is important that an emphasis on professional accountability at the frontline is not in conflict with the establishment of centralised standards and assessments; rather, these go hand-in-hand.

These are very important issues in the United States right now. Through the previous several administrations, both major political parties have strongly favoured administrative forms of accountability over professional or familial forms of accountability. This may be appropriate because, as noted above, it makes sense to introduce professional forms of accountability only if a nation can rely on appropriate capacity in schools. But if the United States aspires to world-class education performance, it will need to staff its schools with world-class classroom teachers and, when that happens, if the experience of the best-performing countries is any guide, it will need to shift the balance in accountability at some stage more towards professional accountability systems. For the reasons discussed above, it may prove difficult to attract enough high performers into the teaching service otherwise, because teachers will expect to be treated the way other professionals are treated. The Obama Administration has made a start by encouraging states and districts to move in this direction by using evaluation and support systems to provide teachers with the information and feedback they need to take greater responsibility for the progress of their students, and to create a professional culture in schools focused on collaboration and peer learning.

Investing resources where they can make the most difference

The most obvious point to be made about financing the American education system is its gross inequities, a point that has been the subject of more or less continuous litigation for many years. This issue is discussed in Chapter 2 and is dealt with at some length below. The relationship between the total amount spent, without respect to how it is distributed, and the results obtained for what is spent, may be the single most important factor for the United States.

The PISA data show no strong correlation between the overall amount of money spent on education and student achievement, whether what is spent is calculated on a per capita basis or as a proportion of GDP. Indeed, the United States is a prime example, inasmuch as the United States has long been one of the world's biggest spenders on elementary and secondary education with only average results compared with those in OECD countries.

If the United States is to move from the middle ranks in performance to the top ranks, either it will have to radically improve the efficiency with which its education funds are spent, or it will have to greatly increase the amount spent. But every level of government in the United States faces severe financial constraints, and that situation is likely to remain unchanged for many years to come. So money to finance a great expansion in education spending is not likely available. The challenge is thus to get much more for every dollar spent. The question is how that might be done. The country reports offer several possible approaches.

The first is to keep the general design of the American education system in place, but to make substantial changes in the allocation of funds within that system. The country report on Japan provides a telling example. As pointed out above, Japan puts a greater share of its resources into core instructional services by spending much less on extravagant school buildings, school services (cafeterias and janitorial services), glossy textbooks, elaborate local school-administrative services and expensive sports programmes (the United States spends 11.6% of its resources for schools on capital outlays, a figure that is higher only in the Netherlands, Norway, Luxembourg and Greece, while the OECD average is 7.6%[11]). Some of what is saved is used to increase teachers' pay substantially relative to American teachers' pay. The rest is returned to taxpayers (public and private spending on schools in Japan only amounts to 2.8% of GDP, as opposed to 3.6% on average across OECD countries and 4% in the United States). Some of these changes would entail major challenges to current American preferences. But that raises the point made above about values and, in particular, the value that Americans place on their children and their children's education vis-a-vis other priorities. The question is: if Americans knew that other countries have produced decidedly better results than the United States by making different spending choices, would they choose to make similar tradeoffs? The United States may benefit from lessons learned in other countries to galvanise around commonly accepted spending choices.

The second possible approach to getting much better results without spending more money to do it is to make basic changes in the way the whole system of education works in the United States. Here again, the country report on Japan provides a telling illustration. Until recently, the teacher/pupil ratio in the United States and Japan were almost identical. But the Japanese chose much larger class sizes than are seen in the United States, up to twice the size of United States classes. That enabled the Japanese to give teachers much more preparation time, lesson-development time, time to confer with other teachers about students facing particular difficulties, and time to tutor students who are behind in class. Same cost, very different approaches.

The example just given shows how both countries had similar ratios of students to teachers. Japanese teachers traded larger class size for more time to plan and work with small groups of students, while American teachers opted for smaller classes and less time to plan and work with small groups of students. As Chapter 2 has shown, other tradeoffs are possible. In the United States, teachers may often be recruited from the lower-performing segment of high school graduates in relatively low status teacher-education institutions, but a substantial share of the teachers who enter the system are gone after five years, and many higher priced specialists are needed to assist the average classroom teacher. In other countries, more is paid to classroom teachers, but that allows those countries to recruit more competitively and train candidates in higher-status teacher-preparation institutions. Those teachers stay in teaching longer, need to be replaced less frequently and require much less specialised assistance in the classroom. That means that fewer teacher-education institutions are needed and more money can be spent on those that remain on a per-teacher-trained basis. The apparently low-cost solution (hiring lower-quality teachers and training them in lower-cost institutions) can turn thus into a higher-cost solution, when all costs are taken into account. Or consider the costs of operating a Tayloristic management system as opposed to one based on the principles involved in managing professionals. As was just noted, employing lower-cost teachers means that more specialists from central office are needed in schools and more managers are needed in the central office to manage and co-ordinate those specialists. In the top-performing countries, though teachers are paid more relative to classroom teachers, fewer administrators are needed and fewer specialists are required, making it possible to employ higher-quality teachers overall, while still enjoying lower net costs. These are what are called system effects, the result of thinking about the design of the system, as a whole, and the net costs of those systems, rather than thinking only about programmes and programme costs.

The third approach is to allocate resources where the challenges are greatest and those resources can have the largest impact. As shown in Chapter 2, the United States is one of only three OECD countries in which socio-economically disadvantaged schools have to cope with less favourable student-teacher ratios than advantaged schools, which implies that most disadvantaged students may end up with the least resources and the students who come to school with the greatest advantages get the most resources. This also implies considerably lower spending per student for students in disadvantaged schools than what the figures on average spending in Chapter 2 suggest. This problem is discussed below.

It is well established that one of the most important factors affecting a student's performance is the socio-economic background of the other students in the class. The implication is that one of the most important resources to be allocated to schools and classrooms is the students themselves. This volume has shown that Germany's failure to join the northern European nations in moving away from a tripartite secondary school organisation based on social class in the years leading up to and just following the Second World War has made it difficult for that country to provide the quality of education to its lower-income, and especially non-German-speaking, students that they need to have a decent chance to get a qualification and become productive members of German society.

However, this volume has also shown how Germany's dual system gets its intake from every segment of its secondary education system and, in doing so, provides opportunities for all but the lowest stream of German students to advance to the higher, if not the highest, rungs of German society.

The move in Germany to reduce the system from three to two divisions may have also contributed to the impressive improvement in student achievement in recent years. Along the same lines, Poland produced a substantial improvement in overall performance by converting a secondary school system that was organised according to the social class of its 15-year-olds to one in which comprehensive schools enrol all social classes.

And Japan's decision during the Meiji Restoration to break with the kind of school and social structure on which Germany's school structure is still based made it possible for Japan to create schools in which all Japanese children have a very good chance of achieving world-class outcomes, in schools that are heterogeneously organised all over the country. This decision by the Meiji government clearly contributed to that country's ability to produce high overall performance with high equity of results over the past century.

The American reader might wonder how any of this could be relevant in a country whose secondary schools have been organised as comprehensive schools for a long time, and whose elementary schools are open to all. However, there is a considerable amount of tracking and streaming occurring within schools in the United States, in ways that are much less amenable to system-wide policies and practices than is the case in systems where such tracking occurs by design. It tends to be done as a matter of practice and custom, rather than as a matter of formal policy. Students in elementary schools are typically separated into ability groups within the classroom, with each group getting instruction at different challenge levels and, at the high school level, students are often separated into groups that follow different curricula reflecting different levels of cognitive challenge, based on estimates of their ability. In addition, the United States is now virtually alone among the OECD countries in having a system in which its citizens can organise school taxing districts that set their own tax rates and in which, as pointed out before, it is the more advantaged students who tend to enjoy a higher proportion of better-qualified teachers and who tend to get the best of other resources as well.

By contrast, all OECD countries except the United States, Israel and Turkey now devote equal if not more resources to schools facing greater socio-economic challenges.[12] Singapore sends its best teachers to work with the students who are having the greatest difficulty reaching Singapore's high standards. Sweden calculates the Krona that it sends to each school on a formula intended to make sure that every school has what it takes to implement Sweden's demanding curriculum, with the result that isolated communities above the Arctic Circle get more for the education of their students per capita than students in Stockholm do. This is because there will be fewer students in rural high schools to take physics than in the city, so class sizes will be smaller, but students in both places are entitled to physics teachers because physics is a required course in the curriculum. Along the same lines, Swedish schools with a greater share of immigrants receive more resources than schools with fewer immigrants. In Japan, officials in the prefectural offices will transfer good teachers to schools with weak faculties to make sure that all students have equally capable faculties.

Similarly, the most impressive result of Shanghai-China's performance on PISA is not just its high average score, but the very low variability in school performance that is achieved despite considerable social and economic inequalities in the population of the province. This has not come about by chance but, as described in the country report, should be seen in the context of determined efforts to improve the school system by converting "weaker schools" to stronger schools. These efforts include:

- systematically upgrading the infrastructure of all schools to similar levels;
- establishing a system of financial transfer payments to schools serving disadvantaged students and transferring high-performing teachers from advantaged to disadvantaged schools, either temporarily[13] or permanently;
- pairing high-performing districts and schools with low-performing districts and schools, where the authorities in each exchange and discuss their educational development plans with each other and work together to deal with problems such as teachers' development, and where institutes for teachers' professional development affiliated with both authorities share their curricula, teaching materials and good practices;
- implementing arrangements under which the government commissions "strong" public schools to take over the administration of "weak" ones, by having the "strong" school appoint its experienced leader, such as the deputy principal, to be the principal of the "weak" school and sending a team of experienced teachers to lead in teaching, in the expectation that the ethos, management style and teaching methods of the high-performing school can be transferred to the poorer-performing school.

Contrast this with a system of school finance in the United States that allows wealthy people to form a school taxing district with other wealthy people who, collectively, are able to pay very low tax rates and produce very large tax revenues, enabling these wealthy people to hire the best teachers in the state for their children and to surround their children with other children from other wealthy families, thereby creating overwhelming educational advantages for their children. At the other end of the spectrum, poor families, who cannot afford the homes that are available in the communities that are home to wealthy people, end up paying very high tax rates but raising very little revenue. While the best-resourced school districts get buildings that are richly equipped with advanced science laboratories, sophisticated equipment, elaborate theatres, Olympic-sized swimming pools and advanced computer-based graphics labs, as well as teachers who majored in the subjects they teach at some of the most elite colleges in the country, the schools serving the poor must content themselves with old and worn school buildings and some of the least competent teachers in the state. In between are many gradations of educational opportunity, each calibrated to a different socio-economic segment of the population.

What Germany accomplished indirectly by having different secondary schools for students from different social classes, the United States achieved directly though its system of local control of school finance. The effect of that system is exactly the same as the effect of having different schools for different socio-economic segments of the population in other countries. There are schools for the rich, schools for the middle classes, schools for the working classes and schools for the poor. The difference is that in those few industrialised countries that still practice this sort of streaming, it is practiced only at the secondary level, while the United States continues to practice this sort of social class segregation at the elementary or primary school level, as well as the secondary level.

In the introduction to this volume, the point was made that, in the early stages of a country's economic development, the demand for highly educated people is limited and so are the resources for developing such people. One way to meet that need in those circumstances is to put what money there is into the children who are, by virtue of the education and income of their parents, the most advantaged students in the whole society. That is why segregating schools by social class was a very efficient strategy providing education when the United States was in the heyday of mass-production. But now, when far larger proportions of highly educated people are demanded in the world's high-wage economies, it is not only socially unjust but highly inefficient to organise an education system this way. Until the 1960s, most northern European countries organised their education systems in ways that were very similar to Germany's current tripartite system, but, for all the reasons just stated, they have since abandoned that approach.

Some years ago, when the immigration of low-literacy guest workers was rapidly increasing in Europe, the Netherlands chose to accommodate them in large housing blocks specially constructed for their use in the cities. The Flemish Community of Belgium, whose schools are run on policies very similar to those in the Netherlands, chose to give vouchers to guest workers to supplement the amount that they would otherwise have to spend on housing. They could use these vouchers wherever they wished. The result was that there were fewer Flemish schools composed entirely of the sons and daughters of guest workers. Years later, the Netherlands faced an enormous challenge to educate students from the public housing projects, whom they have not been able to successfully integrate into their education system and whose achievement remains very low. But in the Flemish Community of Belgium, the students from families indistinguishable from the immigrant families in the Netherlands are doing far better. Housing segregation led to school segregation in this case. In other cases reviewed in this volume, there was school segregation without housing segregation. In the United States, there is both housing segregation and school segregation caused by income disparities and by local control of school finance. The results are the same as can be seen in the other countries studied where one or the other of these two kinds of segregation are practiced.

It is noteworthy that Canada had a similar system of school financing to that in the United States, but it has been abandoning that system in recent years by shifting funding entirely or almost entirely to the province level. Provinces now provide block grants based on numbers of students; categorical grants used either to fund particular programmatic needs (*e.g.* special education) or to help districts meet specific challenges in providing basic services (*e.g.* more remote districts need more funds for transportation); and equalisation funding, which is used in the districts that retain some local funding to equalise the poorer districts.

For the United States, following the lead of its neighbour to the north and gradually changing the system of school finance and organisation to abandon local financing of education would be, of course, a very complex matter involving tax, education and housing policy, housing values, race relations, local control vs. state control and much more. No one should, and few would, underestimate the difficulties involved. But is hard to see how the United States can succeed in matching the performance of the world's highest-performing countries unless it levels the playing field for its students in the way that almost all of its competitors have already done.

Very recently, the United States announced the formation of an "Equity and Excellence Commission" that will examine and make recommendations around addressing the inequities in the United States system of school finance and K-12 education. The above lessons from other countries may be informative in addressing these issues.

Any serious effort to redress the inequities in school finance in the United States would, of course, have to take into account the effects on children of the growing inequalities in income in the United States. There is perhaps no better example for how this can be addressed than Finland's full-service schools described earlier. These provide a daily hot meal for every student, as well as health and dental services, which also offer guidance and psychological counselling, and access to a broader array of mental health and other services for students and families in need. None of these services is means-tested. Their availability to all reflects a deep societal commitment to the well-being of all children. But because spending choices are made differently, at the end of the day, Finland spends considerably less on its schools than does the United States.

Balancing local responsibility with a capable centre with authority and legitimacy to act

Many countries have pursued a shift in public and governmental concern away from mere control over the resources and content of education towards a focus on outcomes. This becomes apparent when changes in the distribution of decision-making responsibilities in education are reviewed across successive PISA assessments. Coupled with this have been efforts to devolve responsibility to the frontline, encouraging responsiveness to local needs. As noted before, PISA shows a clear relationship between the relative autonomy of schools and schooling outcomes across systems – when autonomy is coupled with accountability.

The data presented in Chapter 2 shows that, once the state has set clear expectations for students, school autonomy in defining the details of the curriculum and assessments relates positively to the system's overall performance. For example, school systems that provide schools with greater discretion in making decisions regarding student assessment, the courses offered, the course content and the textbooks used, tend to be school systems that perform at higher levels on PISA. Data from PISA also show that in school systems where schools do not post achievement data publicly, a student who attends a school with greater autonomy in resource management than the average OECD school tends to perform worse than a student attending a school with an average level of autonomy. In contrast, in school systems where schools do post achievement data publicly, a student who attends a school with above-average autonomy scores higher in reading than a student attending a school with an average level of autonomy.

Of course, the United States is a decentralised education system too, but while many systems have decentralised decisions concerning the delivery of educational services while keeping tight control over the definition of outcomes, the design of curricula, standards and testing, the United States is different in that it has decentralised both inputs and control over outcomes. That has only just begun to change with the recent introduction and progressive adoption of common core educational standards by states. Moreover, as discussed in the above section on work organisation, management and accountability, while the United States has devolved responsibilities to local authorities or districts with decentralised union-management agreements, their schools often have less discretion in decision-making than is the case in many OECD countries. In this sense, the question for the United States is how to build the capacity for all schools to exercise responsible autonomy, as happens in most of the systems discussed in this volume. All in all, the United States has allocated authority for governing education more diffusely than any other nation studied in this volume.

Contrast this with the case of Ontario. Here the role of the ministry is to set clear expectations and targets, provide funding, create a working collective-bargaining agreement that supports improved teaching and learning, provide external expertise, and provide support for struggling schools. The role of the district is to align its personnel and hiring policies with the overall strategy, and support the schools as they go through continuous processes of learning. Much of the real action happens in the schools, where teachers work in communities to think about practical problems and learn from one another. While the mission and pressure comes from the top, there is clear recognition that it is at the school level where change has to be implemented, and that the role of other actors in the system is to support the learning and change occurring in schools. An important, yet often underestimated, barrier to achieving system coherence is often the lack of a shared understanding among stakeholders about how key government leaders see the problems of the system and what lies behind the policies and programmes they have designed in response. The tireless efforts of the Ontario government to build a sense of shared understanding and common purpose among stakeholder groups provides an example of how this can be achieved.

Singapore's "thinking schools – learning nation" reform pursued similar goals, organising schools with greater autonomy into geographic clusters that were given more autonomy, with successful principals appointed as cluster Superintendents, to mentor others and promote innovation. Along with greater autonomy came new forms of accountability. The old inspection system was abolished and replaced with a school-excellence model, under which each school sets its own goals and annually assesses its progress towards them against nine functional areas: five "enablers" and four results areas in academic performance.[14] As described in the country report, greater autonomy for schools also led to a laser-like focus on identifying and developing highly effective school leaders who can lead school transformation, backed up by an external review every six years.

Importantly, all of the high-performing systems studied in this volume have some level of authority in their system of education governance at which the buck stops, some agency or group of agencies that can be said to be responsible for the effectiveness and efficiency of the whole education system. This is typically the national or state ministry of education. As preceding chapters show, these agencies are held responsible by everyone concerned for the effectiveness and efficiency of education in their state or nation. They tend to attract capable people. Employment in these agencies is widely thought to be a worthy goal for leading educators in these countries. Their wishes are taken seriously, even if not mandated by law, because of the respect in which their staff is held. Because they are held accountable for the quality and efficiency of education in their country, they assume responsibility for long-range planning for their education systems. They commission research to assist them in making those decisions. They make deliberate use of that research in their decision-making.

All of this has consequences. The various parts of the education systems in these countries appear to have been designed to work harmoniously with each other. These systems can make effective plans and can mobilise the capacity to make sure those plans are carried out. They have the capacity to do the necessary analyses, deliver effective support to the field, monitor the degree to which their plans are being implemented, judge the results and change course if needed. If a country or a state or group of states in a federal system lacks this capacity, it may not be able to make comprehensive, coherent plans; and if it has the capacity to plan, it may not matter very much what its policies are if the nation or state lacks the staff needed to carry them out well.

All this may sound obvious, but it is important to note that no unit of government at any level of the American education system seems to have the authority of a ministry of education in most of the countries portrayed here – not at the national level, not at the state level and not at the local level. Furthermore, the National Center for Education and the Economy has found that the average state department of education has less than half the staff it had 15 years ago,[15] when they all had many fewer responsibilities than they do now. Indeed, in recent years, the federal government has turned to state departments of education to produce very detailed, complex plans for improving education in their state, monitoring student progress, administering complex accountability programmes, developing curricula, and creating new state-wide assessment programmes, even as their staffs were cut by state legislatures running short of tax receipts. The experience of the best-performing countries suggests that high performance relies on the willingness to invest in the capacity to do the planning and management necessary to produce high performance at scale.

The experience of countries with federal oversight for education provides useful insights on how states can collaborate to establish national policies in areas where coherence is important. Canada's Council of Ministers of Education provides a forum through which provincial Ministers of Education meet frequently for co-ordination purposes. While the formal powers of this body are limited, as it can make decisions only by consensus, it fulfils an important information-sharing function and enables good ideas and practices to spread across provincial lines. The power of ideas and the possibilities of diffusion have generated good practice and encouraged jurisdictions to learn from and blend in with each other. In the case of Germany, the federal government is prohibited by the constitution from doing much more than supporting research; but the states, operating through a council of state ministers, have created a strong set of national standards and a reporting system to match.

The importance of workplace training to facilitate school-to-work transitions

Thus far, this volume has focused on school education. This section, however, turns to a closely allied arena of public policy that is often forgotten but which emerges from the research done for this study as highly important to countries that see their education system as a powerful tool for producing a globally competitive workforce. There seems broad agreement all over the world that education should be about much more than preparation for work. But there is also agreement that preparation for work is a very important goal of education. The evidence strongly suggests that effective preparation for work entails success in academic courses, the acquisition of strong generic work skills – everything from showing up on time and putting in a good day's work to being an effective team member and working to meet deadlines – and technical competence in the job-specific skills needed to do the entry-level work in careers that pay well. Countries vary widely in the degree to which they provide each of these bundles of skills and knowledge. In countries that do well on all three, youth unemployment tends to be lower, it takes less time for young people to get and keep good jobs, and economic competitiveness is higher, so there are strong reasons for a country to pay attention not just to the development of young people's academic skills and knowledge but to make sure it has a strong school-to-work transition system.

Germany and Japan present two different examples of countries with strong systems of that sort. Germany's dual system, in which the two-thirds of students who enrol in the vocational tracks alternate between a few days in school and a few days at the workplace, is famous for its success in enabling young people from widely varying social backgrounds to integrate the learning of academic skills with the mastery of job-specific skills, so that students understand the theory behind the practice as they practice their generic work skills. For many, perhaps most, employers, the generic work skills – motivation, persistence, effort, discipline and interpersonal skills – are essential. And for many students, this practice-based, highly applied learning system is a far more effective way to learn than sitting in school studying material with no obvious application to anything they know or care about. In addition, OECD research suggests that workplace training facilitates recruitment of employees because potential employers and employees get the chance to get to know each other and apprentices make productive contributions such that employers benefit directly from the training.

The Japanese system is very different. There, as discussed in the chapter on Japan, students do not work until they leave school and enter the full-time workforce. But most firms in Japan invest heavily in the further formal and informal education of their young workers. Indeed, a good deal of the new employee's initial time in the workplace is devoted to a continuation of the educational process begun in school, and there is a heavy dose of mentorship for new employees. Though the system is very different from that in Germany, the results are surprisingly similar.

At first glance, neither of these systems is readily transferable to the United States, because both appear to depend on industrial systems that are very different from those that prevail in the United States, and for other reasons, including what appears to be a cultural disposition on the part of employers, including prestigious, high-paying employers, to invest heavily in the education and training of young people. But the point was made in the chapter on the German system that German employers do not do offer apprenticeships out of the goodness of their hearts, but because it makes good business sense to do so.

There is no reason, in principle, why the United States could not extend its apprenticeship programmes by providing incentives to American employers to offer apprenticeships to more young people. As in Germany, those incentives could involve relaxing minimum-wage standards, and could also include providing certain tax breaks, including payroll-tax breaks. A combination of appropriate incentives and regulations could establish relationships among community colleges and other postsecondary institutions, regional technical schools and employers that could bring to the United States many of the benefits of the German dual system help extend workplace training more generally, including in the form of internships and shorter work placements as an alternative to full apprenticeships requiring multi-year apprenticeship contracts.

The point here is not to make a particular policy proposal but rather to point out that a careful study of the incentive structures that underlie some of the most effective school-to-work systems in the world could be adapted to the American context in ways that could produce major gains for American education, American business and American youth.

Ensuring coherence of policies and practices, aligning policies across all aspects of the system, establishing coherence of policies over sustained periods of time and securing consistency of implementation

As described throughout this volume, the most successful education systems are setting goals for the curriculum and for student achievement that emphasise the attainment of complex, higher-order thinking skills and the ability to apply those skills to problems they have never seen before, rather than the mastery of the kinds of basic skills they formerly settled for as a minimum standard. They are shifting the structure of their systems from ones that track students from different social backgrounds into different schools and programmes, intended to supply the economy with workers suited for elite jobs, middle-class jobs, working-class jobs and lower-class jobs towards systems designed increasingly to provide almost all workers with the skills needed for jobs previously thought to be held only by elite workers. Many countries on this trajectory are working to improve the quality of the pool from which they recruit their teachers, and they are finding that, in order to recruit and retain these young people, they need to abandon bureaucratic and administrative control for systems in which accountability to other professionals and to parents produces a constant pressure for improved performance. They find that they have to finance their education systems so that all students have access to the educational resources they need to meet high standards.

These are not independently conceived and executed changes. They are, and were, pieces of a whole. In high-performing education systems, policies and practices tend to be aligned across all aspects of the system, they tend to be coherent over sustained periods of time, and they tend to be consistently implemented without excessive administrative control. That is not to say that the process of reform is smooth. The preceding chapters show that the path is often confusing, fraught with political controversy and sometimes clouded. Quite apart from the inevitable political economy issues, moving away from administrative and bureaucratic control towards professional norms of control can be counterproductive if a nation does not yet have teachers and schools with the capacity to implement these policies and practices. Pushing authority down to lower levels can be as problematic if there is not agreement on what the students need to know and should be able to do, and if the standards are not high enough. Recruiting high-quality teachers is not of much use if those who are recruited are so frustrated by what they perceive to be an inadequate system of initial teacher education that they will not participate in it and turn to another profession. Or if they become school teachers, but are so turned off by the bureaucratic forms of work organisation they find there that they leave teaching for some other occupation.

Thus a county's success in making these transitions depends greatly on the degree to which it is successful in creating and executing plans that, at any given time, produce the maximum coherence in the system. No country does this perfectly, though Finland, Japan, Ontario in Canada, Singapore, Hong Kong-China and Shanghai-China seem to have had success in this respect over the years. Singapore demonstrates perhaps the most consistent alignment between policies and their implementation, in which the Ministry of Education, the National Institute for Education and schools share responsibility and accountability. No policy is announced without a plan for building the capacity to implement it. One of the most striking things about visiting Singapore is that the visitor hears the same clear focus on the same bold outcomes, careful attention to implementation and evaluation, and orientation towards the future wherever he or she goes – whether in the ministries of manpower, national development, community development, or in the universities, technical institutes, or schools. "Milestone" courses bring together top officials from all the ministries to create a shared understanding of national goals. And a focus on effective implementation runs throughout the government. "Dream, Design and Deliver" is an apt characterisation of Singapore's approach to public administration. Because of the value placed on human resource development and the understanding of its critical relationship to economic development, Singapore's government provides a very clear vision of what is needed in education. This means that the Ministry of Education can then design the policies and implement the practices that will meet this vision. Whenever a policy is developed or changed, there is enormous attention to the details of implementation – from the Ministry of Education, to the National Institute of Education, cluster superintendents, principals and teachers. The result is a remarkable uniformity of implementation and relatively little variation across schools.

While different mechanisms would be needed in the much larger and more multi-layered and decentralised system of the United States, finding ways to make all the parts work together is essential for producing the best results. The lesson for the United States is that, no matter where a country or state is on the development spectrum, coherence – the degree to which the parts and pieces fit well together and reinforce each other – is an important feature of system effectiveness. This is particularly important for the United States precisely because its education system is inherently less coherent than that of almost every other industrialised country. This is because, as noted above, there is no government body, at either the state or national level, that has responsibility for co-ordinating the different parts of the system. It is not because the United States has a federal system in which the states have some authority, especially in education. That is just as true in Canada, whose results are decidedly superior. In Canada, however, the provincial offices of education also have the legitimacy and capacity to do the job that needs to be done at the centre to bring all the parts and pieces together.

The United States risks lagging behind the most advanced education systems unless it can find a way to ensure that: the tests it uses are evaluating what students should be taught; the instructional materials that are available match the content that teachers are supposed to be teaching; schools of education are preparing teachers to teach what the state expects students to learn; there is a pool of potential teachers who are up to the task; the standards for admission to the institutions that prepare teachers are high enough to attract the kinds of people who will be needed; the programmes of those institutions are designed to attract young people who could choose to be doctors and architects and engineers; the incentives that influence young people include those to take tough courses and work hard in school; the credentials that young people learn in school match the needs and expectations of employers and colleges; and so on. This is a partial list, but the point should be clear: the parts and pieces have to fit together, and there will be a lot of them in a successful plan.

The United States has a variety of initiatives under way to address many of these challenges in areas including assessment quality, instructional materials and supports, recruitment of high-calibre teaching candidates, alignment of teacher preparation with classroom needs, and the alignment of standards for student learning with the expectations of employers and colleges. As these initiatives continue and develop, the United States needs to pay close attention to the coherence of these initiatives and to support effective implementation at the state and local levels.

Ensuring an outwards orientation of the system to keep the system evolving, and to recognise challenges and potential future threats to current success

Looking at five of the world's highest performers examined in this volume – Finland, Canada, Japan, Shanghai-China, Singapore – the reader will see five of the world's most determined international benchmarkers. In his interview for this volume, Premier McGuinty in Ontario made a point of saying that his own views about the right strategy for Ontario to pursue were shaped by the visits he made to other countries with high education performance to see how they did it. Finland was benchmarking the performance and practices of the world's best performers in the run-up to its dramatic emergence as one of the world's top performers. Japan launched its long-running career as one of the world's leading performers when the government that it installed during the Meiji Restoration visited the capitals of the industrialising West and decided that it would bring back to Japan the best the rest of the world had to offer in education policy and practice. It has been doing so ever since. When Deng Xiaoping took the helm in China and launched its rise on the world's industrial stage, he directed China's education institutions to form partnerships with the best educational institutions in the world and to bring back to China the best of their policies and practices. In the latter half of the 20th century, Singapore did exactly what Japan had done a century earlier, but with even greater focus and discipline. Singapore's Economic Development Board, the nerve centre of the Singaporean government, is staffed with many engineers who view the government and administration of Singapore as a set of design challenges. Whether Singapore is interested in designing a better sewer system, retirement system or school system, it sends key people in the relevant sector to visit those countries that are the world's best performers in those areas with instructions to find out how they do it, and to put together a design for Singapore that is superior to anything that they have seen anywhere. Whenever Singapore seeks to create a new institution, it routinely benchmarks its planning to the best in the world. If Singapore is not in a position to create a world-class institution in a particular field, it will try to import the expertise. All Singapore educational institutions – from the National University of Singapore ("A global university centred in Asia") to individual schools – are being encouraged to create global connections in order to develop "future-ready Singaporeans". They have never stopped learning from other countries as systematically as possible. A strong and consistent effort both to do disciplined international benchmarking and to incorporate the results of that benchmarking into policy and practice is a common characteristic of the highest-performing countries.

AMERICA'S ASSETS

The United States brings many assets to the table to catch up with the world's most advanced education systems. The challenge is to leverage these assets in the same ways that today's high performers have leveraged their economic and cultural assets to create superior educational outcomes. Germany has made the most of its heritage of Romantic Idealist philosophy and effective apprenticeship. Finland has made the most of its age-old veneration of teachers and its capacity to engage its people in its great efforts of survival in perilous times. Canada has turned what might have been a weakness in its federal system into a national asset. Japan has made the most of its meritocratic values. These countries, while similar on many of the general principles involved in making first-rate national education systems, have recognised that there are tradeoffs among the goals they all share, and they have chosen different priorities among those goals and employed different strategies to realise them. Each country has faced different obstacles in implementing its designs and has developed different ways to surmount those obstacles.

One of the American assets is the amount of money American citizens are willing to invest in public education – more per student than any other country save one. This means that there is a lot of room to get better performance by reprogramming what is currently being spent.

The second great asset of the United States is its history of reform, in education and in general. While many Americans may worry that their politics are gridlocked and little in education is really changing, the history of the United States tells a story of endless fundamental change. The whole system of public education in its current form was established in the first two decades of the 20th century in one great wave of reform. The schools of the United States were racially desegregated in a comparable period of time. Common standards were instituted with national agreement to create matching assessments. These are massive changes. In each one of these cases, what was instituted was widely considered practically impossible before it actually happened. The impact that Race to the Top has already had in its first year on shaping the discourse on education in the United States, on state legislation and on the behaviour of key stakeholders shows what can be achieved if the direction is clear and the incentive structures are working.

The third great asset of the United States education system is its status as an engine of innovation. Examples of fresh, exciting and practical education ideas can always be found somewhere in the United States. As was noted earlier, that is why the United States is a mandatory destination for people from all over the world interested in new and useful ideas in education. American education is nothing if not inventive, and that is a great asset in age in which the future depends on doing things differently.

The United States is also the locus of the largest concentration of education researchers and analysts in the world, even if that remains true only in absolute and no longer in relative terms. This is a great scientific asset that can be enlisted in a disciplined search for better ways of doing things. Consider the possibilities if the Singaporean zest for international benchmarking research was married to the technical capacities of the American educational research establishment.

It is time to return to the analytical framework with which this volume began. It started with the observation that, as countries move from low-income, low-valued-added economic systems in which countries compete on price to high-income, high-value-added economic systems in which they compete on quality and innovation, they tend to move from one end of this dimension line to another as their economies change and they accumulate the resources needed to enable them to take the next step in the development of their education system.

One can see how this process is working in Brazil, as it tries to overcome a history of ignoring the educational needs of its native population, and in Poland, as it moves towards a more inclusive stance in its education policy. The linkage between education and economic development has been particular close in Singapore, driven from the top of government. As Singapore evolved from an economy based on port and warehousing activities, through a low-wage, labour-intensive manufacturing economy, then to a more capital- and skill-intensive industry and finally to its current focus on knowledge-intensive industrial clusters, the education system ramped up the quality of its work force to make Singapore globally competitive. None of these countries has moved all the way towards the right hand side of the economic development spectrum, but they are well on the way.

The lesson for the United States might be that different states, even some regions within states, or regions across several states, might be at different points on the economic development spectrum. Some states might be in a situation not far from that of Brazil, where the priorities are setting up effective systems for tracking student and school performance, establishing standards for student achievement, making sure that teachers meet minimum qualification standards, producing more equity in school finance, developing a cadre of experienced professionals who can help out struggling schools, and so on. These states are likely to find, just like Brazil and other nations at a similar stage of their development have found, that the most effective management systems are those in which there is a lot of detailed direction from the top, administrative accountability works best, and the curriculum needs to be specified in some detail.

Other states might be at a very different point on the development curve. They might have the management, financial resources and institutional infrastructure needed to match the performance and adopt the systems developed by the world's most educationally advanced countries. Where their education systems do not yet match the best-performing systems, they might directly adapt the methods used by Finland, Canada and the East Asian countries. They will be in a position to recruit a substantial proportion of their teachers from among the best university students in the country and offer them a lot of discretion in the way they do their jobs. They will be looking for ways to build the capacity of their systems and support their teachers. Their accountability systems will tend to the professional model, not the administrative model. Rather than regulating and directing what goes on in the school, they will focus on devising incentives and support systems that will align the interests of the school faculty with the public interest.

Most states will be somewhere in between, and the challenge will be to develop policies that encourage states to move forwards on this trajectory. There is no one best system. But as this volume demonstrates, there are clear pathways from any starting point on the trajectory to wider participation, raising the quality of educational outcomes, improving equity in the distribution of educational opportunities and producing greater value for money.

The international achievement gap is imposing on the United States economy an invisible yet recurring economic loss that is greater than the output shortfall in what has been called the worst economic crisis since the Great Depression. As noted in Chapter 2, the gains from improved learning outcomes, put in terms of current GDP, exceed today's value of the short-run business-cycle management by far. This is not to say that efforts should not be directed at ways to mitigate the effects of the economic recession, but it is to say that long-term issues cannot be neglected.

The world is indifferent to tradition and past reputations, unforgiving of frailty and ignorant of custom or practice. Success will go to those individuals and countries that are swift to adapt, slow to complain and open to change and continuous learning from the best in the world. The task of governments will be to ensure that countries rise to this challenge.

The OECD will continue to help countries support these efforts through facilitating peer-learning and collaboration among countries. Competitiveness in education is not a zero-sum game, in which one nation's gain is necessarily another country's loss. Instead, enhancing educational achievement – at home and abroad – is a win-win for the world.

Notes

1. The address was presented at the meeting of the OECD Education Committee at Ministerial level on 4 November 2010 in Paris.

2. The Third International Mathematics and Science Study (TIMSS) shows that the national percentage of students who report that to do well in mathematics or science they needed good luck was negatively related to student performance in these subjects, both within and across countries. For details, see Earling E. Boe (2002), *Predictors of National Differences in Mathematics and Science*, Research Report No. 2002-TIMSS2, University of Pennsylvania.

3. As described in the country report for Canada, an important element in the development of the Student Success strategy was the creation of a new programme in high schools called the High Skills Major. This aimed to take high school students who were not engaged by the traditional academic curriculum and give them a different menu of courses. While earlier approaches in this vein have justifiably been accused of tracking working-class students away from higher end jobs, by working with prospective employers, the High Skill Major programme created more hands-on courses to give students practical skills and lead to employment opportunities.

4. Among OECD countries, in the Czech Republic, Denmark, Estonia, Finland, France, Hungary, Iceland, Ireland, Israel, Italy, Japan, Korea, Luxembourg, the Netherlands, New Zealand, Norway, Poland, the Slovak Republic, Slovenia, Turkey and the United Kingdom, standards-based external examinations exist throughout the secondary education system. In Australia, they cover 81% of secondary students, in Canada 51% and in Germany 35%. In Austria, Belgium, Chile, Greece, Mexico, Portugal, Spain, Sweden, Switzerland and the United States, such examinations do not exist or only exist in minor parts of the system (Table IV.3.11 in *PISA 2009 Results Volume IV*). Across OECD countries, students in school systems that require standards-based external examinations perform, on average, over 16 points higher than those in school systems that do not use such examinations (Figure IV.2.6a in *PISA 2009 Results*).

5. As described in the country report for Finland, the admission process occurs in two stages. The initial paper screen is based on the applicant's Matriculation Exam score, upper secondary school record, and out-of-school accomplishments. Those who pass that screening must then take a written exam; be observed in a teaching-like activity in which their interaction and communication skills can be assessed; and finally be interviewed to assess, among other things, the strength of their motivation to teach.

6. OECD (2010), *Education at a Glance 2010*, Table D3.1, OECD Publishing.

7. The ministry also created the Ontario Education Partnership Table where a wider range of stakeholders could meet with ministry officials two to four times a year.

8. As described in the country report, included in this Enhanced Performance Management System is their contribution to the academic and character development of the students in their charge, their collaboration with parents and community groups, and their contribution to their colleagues and the school as a whole.

9. OECD (2008), *Improving School Leadership*, OECD Publishing.

10. The effect of parental pressure is particularly closely related to socio-economic background, with little independent effect, whereas factors related to the climate within the school such as discipline and student-teacher relationships are also related to performance independently of socio-economic and demographic effects in many countries.

11. OECD (2010), *Education at a Glance 2010*, Table B6.2, OECD Publishing.

12. For example, Chapter 2 shows that in around half of OECD countries, the student-teacher ratio relates positively to the socio-economic background of schools, in other words, disadvantaged schools tend to have more teachers per student.

13. Teachers transferred temporarily from rural to urban schools are expected to return to the rural schools to enrich them with their new urban experiences.

14. The five enablers are leadership, staff management, strategic planning, resources and student-focused processes. The four result areas are outcomes of holistic development of students, which includes academic results, staff well-being results, administrative and operational results, and results of engagement with partners and community.

15. Tucker, Marc and Tom Toch (May 2004), "Hire Ed", in *The Washington Monthly*, Washington, DC.

ORGANISATION FOR ECONOMIC CO-OPERATION AND DEVELOPMENT

The OECD is a unique forum where governments work together to address the economic, social and environmental challenges of globalisation. The OECD is also at the forefront of efforts to understand and to help governments respond to new developments and concerns, such as corporate governance, the information economy and the challenges of an ageing population. The Organisation provides a setting where governments can compare policy experiences, seek answers to common problems, identify good practice and work to co-ordinate domestic and international policies.

The OECD member countries are: Australia, Austria, Belgium, Canada, Chile, the Czech Republic, Denmark, Finland, France, Germany, Greece, Hungary, Iceland, Ireland, Israel, Italy, Japan, Korea, Luxembourg, Mexico, the Netherlands, New Zealand, Norway, Poland, Portugal, the Slovak Republic, Slovenia, Spain, Sweden, Switzerland, Turkey, the United Kingdom and the United States. The European Commission takes part in the work of the OECD.

OECD Publishing disseminates widely the results of the Organisation's statistics gathering and research on economic, social and environmental issues, as well as the conventions, guidelines and standards agreed by its members.

OECD PUBLISHING, 2, rue André-Pascal, 75775 PARIS CEDEX 16
(98 2011 01 1 P) ISBN 978-92-64-09665-3 – No. 57795 2010